Zoogenesis

Pavement Books
London, UK
www.pavementbooks.com

First published 2014 © Richard Iveson

British Library Cataloguing in Publication Data.
A catalogue record for this book is available from the British Library.

ISBN: 978-0-9571470-4-1

Zoogenesis

Thinking Encounter with Animals

Richard Iveson

PAVEMENTBOOKS

This book is dedicated, in every sense, to its vulpine progenitors, and to the memory of Y.

Contents

Acknowledgments

I am very grateful to all those who have helped with the writing and the publishing of this book, among them Jennifer Bajorek, John Hutnyk, Joanna Hodge, Joanna Zylinska, Sophie Fuggle, Lynn Turner, Mark Fisher, Bhaskar Mukhopadhyay, Andrew Benjamin, Vasile Stanescu, and Linda Leatherbar-row; as well as to all my companion animals: Poppy, Little Bear, Tuna, Maoki, and Miu. Thanks too, of course, to Jo. And finally, thanks to Makiko, for everything.

Parts of this book originally appeared in the following journals, which have graciously allowed them to be reprinted here:

An earlier version of Chapter Two appeared as 'Animals in Looking-Glass World: Fables of Überhumanism and Posthumanism in Heidegger and Nietzsche' in *Humanimalia* I:2 (Spring) 2010, 46-85.
A version of Chapter Five first appeared as 'Domestic Scenes and Species Trouble: On Judith Butler and Other Animals' in *Journal for Critical Animal Studies* 10:4 (Winter 2012), 20-40.
Part of Chapter Six was originally published as 'Deeply Ecological Deleuze and Guattari: Humanism's Becoming Animal' in *Humanimalia* 4:2 (Spring 2013), 20-40.

Introduction:
Thinking Encounter with Animals

> For everything which arises is worthy of perishing
> – Goethe, *Faust*

How might we understand this oddly phrased heading, *thinking encounter with animals*? A number of readings quickly present themselves, a brief consideration of which, along with the various stresses such readings demand, will help to introduce the purpose and scope of the present volume which, while primarily philosophical, nonetheless transgresses traditional disciplinary boundaries in order to enter arenas at once both ethical and political.

It is, to begin, a question of *thinking*, of who *can* think, and of thinking about how one animal engages with another. It is also to ask what we mean by 'encounter', and thus how such encounters might be circumscribed. Is it even possible to think *about* encounters with other animals, and more, are these 'other animals' always necessarily nonhuman? Does the 'with' then paradoxically bear the mark of an insuperable division, one which in fact denies every encounter?

Perhaps this demands a different question, a different stress. Rather than a direct encounter with another animal, perhaps we need to ask if an encounter might not be *shared with* other animals, that is, whether a human and a nonhuman animal might not experience an encounter *together*? Or indeed, is it perhaps a case of 'permitting' nonhuman animals to partake of such encounters, even among themselves?

To think encounter with animals equally raises questions as to how – as scholars, as activists, as readers, but also as animals – we should, both inside and outside of the university, conduct ourselves towards other animals, both nonhuman and human. How might we think differently with animals about 'animals'? With what gestures or concepts or phrasings might new encounters be forged? What remains when humans can no longer relate to other animals as inferior beings, as instruments or pets, mute or dumb, as irrational machines of meat or flesh? Is there an ethics not only of *thinking with* and of *living with* other animals, but also of *thinking about* other animals? And what are the ways of such meetings, what *politics* might such encounters demand?

Further readings jostle to be heard, as they always do, but hopefully this is enough for the reader to gain at least some idea of the complex issues addressed in this book. Such issues will be familiar to some, whilst completely new to others. Indeed, while the so-called 'question of the animal' has garnered ever greater critical attention over the past two decades, 'animal studies' itself remains very much a loose and emerging interdisciplinary domain.

As such, animal studies is caught between two opposing yet complimentary manoeuvres – and needs to remain so as far as possible. Indeed, this imperative of remaining *between* two forms of delimitation is central to the entire project outlined here. On the one side, animal studies risks an always too hasty circumscription of its subject area, such attempts at delineation being indissociable from acts of mastery and authority. We see this risk to its emergent status in the current struggle over the act of *naming*, with a number of groups – and not always with the requisite academic generosity – each seeking to carve out a proper domain by denying legitimacy to its rivals. On the other side, it is all to easy to forget that thinking with animals outside of the natural sciences remains largely a marginalized pursuit, and that to most 'animal studies' refers only to the very different subdisciplines within the biological and agricultural sciences. The French philosopher and psychologist Vinciane Despret, for example, has noted that even as recently as 2006 her work would have been automatically sidelined by way of a gender-based accusation of sentimentality – the very same accusation which, far from coincidentally, served for so long to bar women from access to the sciences.[1] The double threat to the superbly uncertain field of animal studies thus comes from two opposing forces: circumscription, consolidation and centralization on the one hand, marginalization, inefficacy and dismissal on the other. How then, to trace its contours without erecting barriers?

In the first place, animal studies calls to anyone who feels unable *not* to 'bring up' animals, anyone for whom the right of putting to death sticks in their throat, who cannot *not* see industrialized murder. At its theoretical core is a concern over the 'admittance' of nonhuman animals, an admittance which involves not merely an extension but rather a *transformation* of the

---

[1] As recounted by Florence Burgat in her preface to Vinciane Despret, *Penser comme un rat*, Versailles: Éditions Quæ, 2009, 4 (my translation).

philosophical. At the heart of its praxis, meanwhile, two fundamental yet inseparable positions undergird the vast diversity of its materializations. On the one hand, the attempt to dismantle the machinery of power by which 'other' humans are 'animalized,' a movement that constitutes the *sine qua non* of the various nationalisms founded upon boundaries of blood, soil or language. On the other, and of equal importance, is the determination to put a halt to the exploitation, torture, and extermination of nonhuman animals by their human kin.

Given the inextricability of these two positions, it quickly becomes clear that the 'animal question' is simultaneously a question of and to the *human*. This is by no means to claim for animal studies an anthropocentric or even humanist perspective. Far from it. Rather, by this I mean that it is imperative that animal studies put *humanness* itself into question. Only then does it become possible to understand how speciesism – marked fundamentally by the *killing*, rather than the *murder*, of nonhuman animals – forms the excluded support of myriad other structural exclusions, namely those which exclude, extort, and distort others on the basis of race, gender, class, sexuality, and so on. Only once we grasp this salient fact will the importance of animal studies be understood by all those who dismiss animal concerns as perhaps laudable but nonetheless most definitely secondary, maybe even self-indulgent or sentimental.

One cannot, in short, discharge oneself of the responsibility of thinking with animals simply by laying claim to a 'more important' concern with *human* oppression. No one would suggest that one must unfortunately support racism, at least until the exclusion and abjection of women is undone, or that one is free to sexually abuse women, at least until racism has been eradicated. When it comes to speciesism, however, such opinions are not only generally tolerated, but are often explicitly celebrated. By contrast, it is only by tracing the interrelations and interarticulations of oppression that an effective political response become possible. One cannot, for example, put into question the privileged sexuality afforded to the ideal of whiteness without an understanding of the speciesist machinery that devalorizes people of color by way of a displacement which shifts nonwhite sexuality towards 'animality.'

We thus begin to understand how the exclusion of 'the animal' is inseparable not only from an abstract determination of 'the human,' but also from questions both of autonomy and sovereignty, and of the subject and subjection. The exclusion of the animal, put simply, functions to inscribe 'properly' human ends, one result being the privative determination of 'animality' which, variously and fabulously clothed, pads mutely throughout Western philosophy.

Indeed, the list of what animals are alleged to lack is both finite yet endless, depending as it does upon the ever-shifting requirements of what it means to be 'properly' human.[2] Given that any exhaustive documention inevitably risks falling into the trap of repetition with which feminism in particular has had to contend, I offer in its stead a short and brutal summary: throughout Western philosophy, albeit with some notable exceptions, 'the animal' is constituted as an unfeeling object under the technical mastery of man and definable only by negativity. One cannot murder such an animal, only kill her over and over again and, moreover, one can do so with impunity. It is this all too human construction of 'the animal' therefore, which holds open the space for what philosopher Jacques Derrida describes as a 'noncriminal putting to death,' be it the site of war, of capital punishment, or of the unprecedented subjection and subjugation of human and nonhuman beings all around us today.

Exploring the machinations of power that legitimize the slaughter of human animals is thus, alongside and entangled with the exclusion and murder of nonhuman animals, a major preoccupation of this book. Such legitimation consists in the prior 'animalization' of a specifically targeted human or human grouping, a reconfiguration that strips its target of a fully human status and, in so doing, constitutes a non-subject that can be killed with impunity. One thinks here of the Nazi demonization of Jews as *Saujuden* ('Jewish swine'), or again of Lynndie England parading around Abu Ghraib with an Iraqi prisoner on a dog leash. Indeed, the reduction of a singular, nonsubstitutable living being to an essential identity which is in turn reconfigured as 'animal' is nothing less than the *economy of genocide*. Excluded from itself through a murderous theatrics of displacement, a nonhuman animal or an animalized human is in this way effectively rendered speechless, a subjugated body which may be slaughtered but never murdered.

The interruption of this murderous economy is therefore of the utmost importance, not only for other animals, but also for those millions of 'other' humans excluded from a properly human status by way of various reg-

---

[2] For two excellent intellectual histories of 'the animal' in Western philosophy, one crafted in meticulous detail and the other brief yet highly illuminating, see Elisabeth de Fontenay, *Le silence des bêtes: La philosophie à l'épreuve de l'animalité* (Paris: Fayard, 1998) and Gilbert Simondon, *Deux leçons sur l'animal et l'homme* (Paris: Ellipses, 2004). It is both interesting and puzzling that at the time of writing neither text has yet been translated into English, despite their quality and influence.

ulatory norms including those of gender, sexuality, race, and class. We are thus faced with an extremely urgent question: are there perhaps, in contrast to reductive metaphors and anthropomorphisms of 'proper' identity, tropes that rather *function in the opposite direction* to the tropological displacement of animalization, that instead make it unthinkable that living beings can be 'legitimately' put to death? It is this question that I explore throughout this book, a question that demands the inclusion of other animals within the domains of philosophy, ethics, and politics and which, by way of its core notion *zoogenesis*, opens up the possibility of a 'new' – and originally supplemental – politics of animal liberation.

Clearly, this approach is radically different, indeed antagonistic, to those founded upon a theory of animal *rights*. Nevertheless, it inevitably incurs a debt to work done in this area, as well as to other, more contemporary approaches to related questions – feminism and posthumanism in particular. By briefly considering these debts, I hope to further clarify both the focus of my enquiry and the differences such an approach will make.

The wrongs of animal rights

One might perhaps be forgiven for thinking that the proponents of rights for animals are the only ones left who have not yet heard about the challenges posed to the liberal subject of right from all sides. While this is not strictly true, neither is it particularly false.

A large part of the problem centers upon the fact that the so-called 'fathers' of contemporary animal rights theory absolutely refuse any truck with possible alternatives, dismissing them out of hand as irrelevant. As a result, a great many activists today – having inevitably turned to animal rights discourse in the first instance due to its privileged media position – believe that rights theory is not so much the *best* as rather the *only* position from which to address animal concerns. This is part of a retrograde and, at times, extremely bitter defensive battle concerned only with preserving that privileged position. While this is of course an all too human reaction, it is, however, just such anthropocentric conservatism that must be done away with.

Instead, the discourse of 'animal rights' must be contested from both sides, that is, as regards both *animal* and *right*. Ironically perhaps, this can best be illustrated by way of its two greatest proponents, Peter Singer and Tom Regan, whose books, *Animal Liberation* (1975) and

The Case for Animal Rights (1983) respectively, are generally considered the founding texts of contemporary animal rights theory.

According to Singer's utilitarian position, insofar as nonhuman animals are *sentient* they are therefore entitled to have their interests taken into account in any utilitarian calculation. In this, however, Singer is *not* – as he himself makes clear – making a case for animal *rights*, but only for the necessity of including sentient animals in the determination of morality by utilitarian calculation in order to avoid falling into contradiction. Singer's basic position, in other words, remains inevitably inscribed within the calculus of ends, a human mastery which thus views the animal only according to its enclosure within an ordered technological schema. A schema, moreover, within which any oppression of a minority for the sake of that judged – by the 'human' standards of the patriarchal West – as the 'common good' can all too easily be justified.

While Singer is not strictly proposing a theory of animal *rights*, Tom Regan meanwhile is not proposing a case for *animal* rights. Rather, Regan seeks only to demonstrate that certain privileged nonhuman animals are the 'same' as humans insofar as they too are 'subjects-of-a-life,' that is, that they, in common with humans, possess interests and desires regarding their own individual existences. In other words, Regan's neo-Kantian liberal approach determines the place of the nonhuman animal only according to an essential human morality, and in so doing inscribes human subjectivity as the ground of the animal. As philosopher Matthew Calarco notes, 'Regan's work is not a case for animal rights but for rights for *subjects*, the classical example of which is human beings.'[3]

In both cases then, it is *man* who must both determine and delimit the animal, thus redrawing again and again the same unthought lines of exclusion. In short, for both Singer and Regan it is only ever *sentient* animals who count, that is, only the most *human* animals who matter. Similarly, the bourgeois liberalism upon which rights theory rests is clearly evident in the shared privileging of the individual – of individual consciousness (Regan) and of an individual capacity for suffering (Singer) – at the expense of wider considerations. It is thus not only the anthropomorphising of the animal that renders rights theory hugely problematic, but also the liberalism inhering within the notion of 'right' itself. As Derrida insists, insofar as rights theory remains structurally incapable of dissociating itself from the Cartesian *cogito*, it finds itself helpless but to reiterate an interpretation of the masculine

[3] Matthew Calarco, *Zoographies: The Question of the Animal from Heidegger to Derrida* (New York: Columbia University Press, 2008), 8.

human subject which itself 'will have been the very lever of the worst violence carried out against nonhuman living beings.'[4]

This inevitable contamination of the notion of 'right,' as well as the refusal of its principal theorists to consider other possible avenues, has resulted in the alienation of several potentially sympathetic groups from thinking with other animals, feminists chief among them.

Finally, this chasm is further broadened in that, insofar as the Western human male constitutes the measure of everything, rights theory fondly imagines that the inferior status of nonhuman beings can be fundamentally challenged by way of the legal and political institutions of that same Western human male. As a result, as Calarco again points out, animal rights activism is left with no other choice than to adopt the language and strategies of identity politics, a move which further isolates animal liberation from other arenas of political activism – ecofeminism, for example – that are similarly seeking to challenge structures of oppression.[5]

Animals and women

The relation between feminism and nonhuman animals has always been complex. Nonetheless, feminist writers Josephine Donovan and Carol Adams have identified three basic positions or stages: *liberal feminism, autonomous feminism,* and *ecofeminism.*[6] Liberal feminism, exemplified by Simone de Beauvoir, refuses any relation whatsoever, affirming instead rationality and the rights of women. The adherents of autonomous feminism, meanwhile, argue that feminism simply has nothing to do with nonhuman animals, who serve only to detract from its 'proper' concerns. Lastly, ecofeminism, in direct contrast to the other two positions, explicitly embraces the woman-nature connection, arguing that oppressive patriarchy founds itself upon both the denial of the animal body and an understanding of 'nature' as a passive (i.e., 'feminine') receptacle.

---

[4] Jacques Derrida and Elisabeth Roudinesco, *For What Tomorrow ... A Dialogue,* trans. Jeff Fort (Stanford: Stanford University Press, 2004), 65.

[5] It would seem that, forming a group dedicated to exposing connections between sexism and speciesism, ecofeminists Carol Adams and the late Marti Kheel sought perhaps to 'queer' the associations of rights theory by naming the group *Feminists for Animal Rights* (FAR). This, however, only confuses the issue, which is that of removing the focus on 'rights' entirely.

[6] See the 'Introduction' to *Animals and Women: Feminist Theoretical Explorations,* 1-8.

My own approach owes a significant debt to the ongoing labor of ecofeminism, which Adams describes as being founded upon an understanding of structures of oppression as both interlinked and mutually supporting. As ecofeminists have shown, traditional dualisms such as culture/nature, rationality/emotion, and subject/object come together in order to constitute a rigid masculinist hierarchy. The application of the subject-object schema to both nature and women, for example, demonstrates all too clearly the indissociability of anthropocentrism and androcentrism.[7] Seeking to interrupt this program of universalizing principles, ecofeminists propose in its place a resolutely local praxis-based ethics.

As with animal studies, however, it is impossible to neatly delineate the domain of 'ecofeminism,' and in particular to separate it from a *feminist ethics of care*, which constitutes a second major contribution of feminism to a thinking encounter with animals. Based originally upon Carol Gilligan's care theory, an ethics of care similarly refuses abstract, universalizing programs that valorize reason in favor of forming contextually-specific *dialogical* relations with other animals that privilege the so-called 'emotional' social relations such as empathy, compassion, and sympathy. We must, writes Donovan, *listen*. This, she argues, means paying attention to what human ideological constructions elide by reaching out 'emotionally as well as intellectually to what is different from oneself rather than reshaping (in the case of animals) that difference to conform to one's own human-based preconceptions' ('Feminism and the Treatment of Animals,' 48).

What I retain here from feminist care ethics is the important notion of ethics as a contextually-specific praxis that recognizes 'the qualitative heterogeneity of life-forms' (48), as well as a focus upon *relation* that does not therefore give up on the *individual*. Grace Clement, for example, suggests that the ethic of care is both individualistic and holistic insofar as 'relationships, rather than individuals' characteristics, define the moral realm, but the particularities of individuals dictate the appropriate moral response' ('The Ethic of Care and the Problem of Wild Animals,' 448).

Such a concern with relation that does not lose sight of individuals must be contrasted positively with the focus upon the *species body* at the cost of individual entities characteristic of Deep Ecology. In dealing with *other* animals simply as homogeneous, circumscribable species, practitioners such as Arne Naess, George Sessions, and Bill Devall are left with little choice but some form or other of utilitarianism. Indeed, insofar as the separation be-

---

[7] On this, see for example, Carol J. Adams, *Neither Man Nor Beast*, 89-90; and the appendix to Barbara Noske, *Beyond Boundaries*.

tween humanity and nature is absolute in the world of Deep Ecology, the stumbling block is inscribed right at the start. As we will see in chapter six, such a separation inevitably results in a severely limited concept of ethics that can only ever reiterate contemporary structures of oppression.

In this context, we can also understand the importance of cognitive ethology which, in contrast to Deep Ecology, continues to open up rich new veins of thought for animal studies. First appearing in its current form in the late 1970s, cognitive ethology sought to challenge the widespread behaviorist dogma that the inner life of animals is unknowable, and thus of no consequence.[8] In so doing, ethologists moved away from the collection of standardized quantifiable data, focusing instead – and here we see the overlap with feminist animal concerns – on the complexity of social life within specific contexts. In similarly focusing upon contextual relations yet without giving up on individuals, ethologists and primatologists have subsequently revealed, and continue to reveal, the existence of a whole slew of complex concepts among other animals that were previously thought the preserve of human animals alone, further putting into the question the notion of human exceptionalism.

This shift of focus can also be found at work in contemporary feminist science studies. In her studies centering on the various meanings attributed to the cloned sheep Dolly, for example, anthropologist and feminist Sarah Franklin writes that she found it necessary to replace the traditional quantitative frame with 'a qualitative, interpretive, and comparative approach' (*Dolly Mixtures*, 8). Only in this way, she continues, does it become possible to analyze the ways in which Dolly functions as a nexus that extends and transforms a series of diverse practices, the relations between which had not been previously acknowledged. This too marks an extremely important move as regards thinking with animals.

Returning to feminist care ethics, however, the emphasis on *listening* constitutes a fundamental obstacle, insofar as it ultimately ensures that such an ethics remains essentially within an anthropocentric hierarchy. Donovan, for example, insists that we must 'learn the languages' of other animals, which is all well and good, except that she then goes on to qualify this by suggesting that 'we' do so by *extrapolating* from our own experience ('Feminism and the Treatment of Animals,' 50). A simple example highlights the problem here: 'we (humans)' experience pain as a result of being wounded and, *therefore*,

---

[8] This unthinking dogma is, however, still with us, as I discovered in attempting to discuss the event of animal love with a group made up of supporters of Alain Badiou's philosophy.

so does a dog – but not necessarily, *therefore*, does an ant or a fish (or not, at least, in any simple extrapolative fashion). In short, this founding relation of empathy and *thus* sympathy can be extended only as far as those other animals *perceived by humans* as capable of dialogue.

As a result, feminist care ethics ultimately constitutes yet one more form of liberal contract theory, excluding thus all those 'others' considered by those *instigating* the dialogue as incapable of properly reciprocating it. Thus, Donovan asks herself, 'who is to be included in the caring circle? … who is to be granted moral status?' To which she answers, 'that status should be granted to living creatures with whom one can communicate cognitively and emotionally as to their needs and wishes' (49). Hence, rather than a thinking *encounter with* animals, care ethics proposes only a 'conversation of two subjects' (Rosemary Radford Ruether, cit. Donovan 52), a proposition which places it uncomfortably close to Regan's liberal circumscription of ethics as concerning only the *rights of the subject*.

In place of this traditional (and, as Derrida and others have argued, *masculinist*) emphasis on the *voice*, and thus on *presence*, I argue instead that emphasis must rather be placed upon a notion of language understood as a *writing* that is fundamental to the production and reproduction of *every* living being, however alien it may be to a human animal. In this way, an inclusive ethics of *emergence* replaces an exclusive ethics of *reciprocity*, while simultaneously subjecting the signal points of liberal ethics such as subject, object, relation, mutuality, and respect to a critique.

Animals and posthumanism

Lastly in this section, it is necessary to acknowledge the importance of posthumanism, both in general and for this project in particular. Prior to this, however, it is crucial that posthumanist thinking be differentiated from the liberal notion of 'the posthuman,' for which the term '*trans*human' is the more accurate.

While this distinction will be explored in detail in the final chapter, it is sufficient for the moment to note three defining characteristics of transhumanist discourse. First, the prefix 'trans-' (or 'post-') signifies an *historical* succession during which the human comes to be transformed by technological developments. Second, an explicit or implicit support of an individualist ideology founded upon an unquestioned notion of the liberal subject. And, third, a simplistic decontextualization which, in bracketing out everyone but the tiny fraction that is the wealthy of the global North from its concerns, carries with it a particularly repugnant form of capitalist ideology.

By contrast, post*humanism* refers both to the interruption that necessarily takes place before and beyond every conception of 'the human,' and to our historical situatedness as subsequent to the deconstruction of the liberal human subject. Posthumanism, in other words, is that which doubly marks us as 'coming after' the interruption of the human, and as such demands a thinking which takes place beyond any humanist metaphysics. In this, it refuses the destructive yet empty concept of 'the human' which, as we shall see over the course of this book, serves only to prop up the tottering relics of reductive division in what is a profoundly conservative movement that functions to severely constrain what animals – human and nonhuman alike – might become. In short, *posthumanism* as it is understood here marks *an open relation to potential becoming.*

This is not, however, to identify posthumanism with animal studies, but rather only to locate an extensive overlap. For me, two philosophers in particular typify the immense scope and range of current debates, N. Katherine Hayles and Donna Haraway.

In *How We Became Posthuman* (1999), Hayles examines the history of informatics in order to disclose the movement by which information lost the sense of its body, that is, of its *material substrate*, subsequently producing the myth that information's supposedly 'bodiless fluid' can flow from substrate to substrate without any loss of meaning or form. This is best illustrated by Hans Moravec's well-known claim that in the future humans will be able to download their individual consciousnesses into a computer, thereby achieving immortality of a sort. With this example it is easy to discern the underlying assumption of an autonomous liberal subject.

By contrast, the restoration of the lost body of informatics, as Hayles clearly demonstrates, has a number of important and wide-ranging consequences. Not least of which for this book is the fact that emergence thereafter replaces teleology, distributed cognition replaces autonomous will, and dynamic partnerships replace 'the liberal humanist subject's manifest destiny to dominate and control nature' (288). Subjectivity, in other words, is not a quantitative given, but rather an emergent quality infinitely exceeding its containment in 'consciousness' as it both emerges from, and integrates into, a chaotic common world where '"thinking" is done by both human and nonhuman actors' (290). Only from such an understanding, Hayles concludes quite rightly, can we craft versions of the posthuman 'that will be conducive to the long-range survival of humans and of the other life-forms, biological and artificial, with whom we share the planet and ourselves' (291). It is just such a notion of the posthuman, as being-in-a-relation-of-openness, which I further explore here.

Extremely important too is the concept of the post-gender *cyborg* proposed by Haraway. Again, the breaking down of boundaries is crucial. The cyborg, explains Haraway, is a being between nature and culture, between the animal and the machine, and between the material and the nonmaterial, with the result that 'the one can no longer be the resource for appropriation or incorporation by the other' ('Cyborg Manifesto,' 9). Here, my own project clearly shows its allegiance.

Equally significant, however, is Haraway's assertion that the cyborg is inextricably *double*, that is, that a cyborg world is about both 'the final imposition of a grid of control' and 'lived social and bodily realities' that take place in 'joint kinship with animals and machines' (13). Moreover, continues Haraway, a politics, if it is to be effective, requires that one 'see from both perspectives at once' (13). It is this attention to the 'double cyborg' that underlies my own argument that the creative spirit is indissociably doubled by its parodic ghost, just as the posthuman too finds its double in the transhuman. Hence, I share with Haraway the position that improper couplings are indeed 'the illegitimate offspring of militarism and patriarchal capitalism,' but that such illegitimate offspring are nonetheless 'often exceedingly unfaithful to their origins' (10).

From this all too brief acknowledgment of just some of the major intellectual debts accrued by this book, it should nonetheless be clear that 'animal studies' is both a part of, and different from, all these other domains. Moreover, the very impossibility of neat circumscription is essential. Whatever 'animal studies' may be said to mean, it is its very *in*discipline that is its greatest strength. Any attempt at delineation, insofar as it consists of a disciplinary action demanding lines of exclusion, denotes a complete failure to recognize its potential. Animal studies must not become simply another university discipline. Rather, the place of animal studies, both within and outside of the university, must itself put into question any notion of circumscription in general, as well as those of the so-called 'humanities' in particular.

The ends of humanity: *telos* and *eskhaton*

As we have seen, the exclusion of the animal functions throughout Western philosophy to inscribe human ends. To begin, it is necessary that we concern ourselves with this invariant, as only by way of a rigorous engagement with philosophy might we come to understand finitude and history as the condition for every animal encounter, and thus counter the traditional operation that excludes nonhuman animals by dissolving their singular beings within the perfect identity of immortal, changeless species. Moreover, by distinguishing between two very different conceptions signified by the phrase 'the end of man,' we discover that the proper end of man in fact ultimately resides in the rupturing of humanism itself.

Readers familiar with philosophy will have doubtlessly recognized the above reference to Jacques Derrida's famous lecture 'The Ends of Man,' first presented in 1968, wherein Derrida draws attention to the disjunction between the teleological and eschatological 'ends' of man, that is, between *telos* and *eskhaton*.

Put simply, within the metaphysical tradition *telos* marks the end in the sense of the *completion* of man, of man's end as his highest and most proper accomplishment in a transcendence of finitude that indissociably links metaphysics with humanism. In this way, what awaits humanity is humanity itself, that is, a fully human humanity. At the same time, however, the end of man in the *eschatological* sense of the *destruction* or *overcoming* of the human cannot be divorced from the thinking of the truth of man within this same tradition.

This problematic doubling of ends, suggests Derrida, can be seen most clearly at work in the philosophy of Immanuel Kant. For Kant, the end of man as *telos* cannot come about by way of finite human knowledge, but only by way of the unmixed concepts of pure *a priori* reason. The end of man, in short, can only take place *after* the end of man, that is, only when every specifically human experience has been removed. Conversely, however, Kant *simultaneously* insists that this end is possible only because man is in essence a rational being, that is, because only man *as* man thinks the end, and in so doing raises himself above and beyond the absence of reason claimed to characterize every other animal. Hence, it is only the *specificity* of the human that opens up the possibility of the end as *telos*.

Here, Kant is confronted with an antimony or aporia that must be dealt with: the *telos* of a fully human humanity demands both the specificity of the human *and* the eschatological elimination of that specificity. It is an aporia, moreover, which constitutes a rupture within every humanism insofar as every humanism is metaphysical.

Kant attempts to control this aporia with the notion of *universal history*. He argues that Reason organizes the regular, teleological progress of human-

ity only at the level of the *species*, guided in advance by nature and indifferent to the free will of individuals. However, individual free will nonetheless
serves to ensure the ongoing trial and ordeal of Reason's *telos*, and thus the
development of man's original capacities. By contrast, nonhuman animals
pursue their 'natural,' i.e., irrational, teleology purely by instinct, meaning
that the 'law-governed history' of every other species can be identified by a
simple 'internal or external' examination of any given animal, each of whom
is identified with the species as a whole.[9]

Here we see how 'the animal' functions as the constitutive outside of the
properly human. On the one hand, humans cannot proceed by instinct, as
this would reduce them to 'mere' animals. Hence, man must have free will.
On the other, the idea that man acts without an innate, divinely-instilled *telos*
is simply unbearable for Kant, not least because this would reduce humans to
something *less* than 'mere' animals. This is Kant's first antimony: the simultaneous free will *and* machinic programming of humanity. Hence, man's free
will must be subordinated to the guiding hand of *history*. Only then might
man be free while simultaneously assuming his God-given superiority above
the mechanical ordering of animal existence.

For this reason, it is humans alone who are *finite*. Given the empirical
specificity of every freely willing human individual, she or he cannot therefore be identical to the species, as Kant claims to be the case for all other
animals. Instead, death is necessary to ensure that the germs of reason 'im-
planted by nature in our species' not be squandered by foolish individuals
but rather be passed along the 'incalculable series of generations,' guaranteeing the progress of universal history ('Idea for a Universal History,' 43).
Nonhuman animals, however, have no need of finitude, and no death in any
real sense. Rather an animal *is* only the species, each example being identical
to every other of the same species. Hence, if a particular animal ceases to live,
nothing has been lost. *An* animal, in short, cannot die. Only humanity, while
immortal as a species, consists of mortal individuals.

This conflict between selfish mortality and selfless immortality, Kant continues, is the motor constituting society, which is thus only ever human –
other animals being ontologically incapable of a separation of individual and
group interests. While Kant goes on to argue that bourgeois capitalist society in fact constitutes the divine vehicle to realize the *telos* of humanity, this
should not distract us from our initial problematic, that of the *telos-eskhaton*
aporia that this idea of universal history hopes to circumvent.

---

[9] 'Idea for a Universal History with a Cosmopolitan Purpose' (1784), 42.

As we have seen, the movement of history *in general*, that is, universal history at the level of the species, must once again bracket out every *specific* human experience. At the same time, however, universal history is for Kant necessarily *human* history, depending upon the gradual transformation of an incalculable series of *specific* individual moments. In other words, the divinely-ordained completion of humanity demands the transcendence of human finitude, a transcendence which at the same time requires human finitude as its very condition of possibility. Here, the same telos-eskhaton aporia quickly reestablishes itself, this time at the heart of historicity itself.[10]

The positing of the *telos* of a fully human humanity, the continuous but gradual perfection of the species, requires *as its condition* that every individual human being *dies*, destroyed in an *eschatological* moment of transformative limit. Returning to our specific focus, what does this discussion of the ends of the human offer for an encounter with animals?

Put simply, it offers a specific example of how traditional philosophy must exclude other animals in order to inscribe 'properly' human ends, that is, to circumvent the intolerability of purposelessness and godlessness. At base, the exclusion of other animals throughout Western philosophy enables the fragile human ego to deal with the anxiety of cosmological insignificance, producing instead reassuring myths of universal importance. With Kant's particular ideology, moreover, we also begin to better understand the importance of finitude and historicity for any thinking encounter with animals.

Finitude, as we have seen, is the condition for history and for the fulfilment of humanity as reasoning being. It thus comes as no surprise to find that, throughout Western philosophy, other animals are somehow *reduced* to immortality as a result. Our first task therefore is to consider how this paradoxical *reduction to divine status* is accomplished, as this is intimately connected to the economy which opens the space for a noncriminal putting to death. This economy, which I have no hesitation in calling *genocidal*, depends not simply upon the exclusion of 'the animal' from 'the human,' but simultaneously upon the *finite* bodies of nonhuman animals being paradoxically constructed as *undying* (be that as untouched by the Fall into self-awareness or as genetically-determined automata). By this I mean that 'the animal,' functioning as both homogeneous category and constitutive outside of 'the human,' is *necessarily* defined as lacking the possibility of death and thus (for reasons that will become clear) as sharing a transparent pathic communication.

---

[10] The distinguishing within 'history' of historicity and historiology was first proposed by Heidegger in *Being and Time*. At its most basic, *historicity* refers to the *movement* of time, whereas *historiology* refers to the *discursive construction* of History as a discipline.

The choice of the term 'ideology' above is not fortuitous: the claim that non-human animals lack individual deaths is indeed an ideology, one which, as Carol Adams notes, 'ontologizes animals as usable' (*Neither Man Nor Beast*, 15). The kettle logic undergirding Martin Heidegger's hugely influential philosophy, as will be examined in depth in the second chapter, is essential to grasping this process. For the moment, however, it is sufficient to note that, with 'the animal' thus constituted as both undying and transparently pathic, the murder of a *given* nonhuman animal becomes ontologically impossible, even as corpses pile up in exponentially increasing numbers. Our initial question is thus clear: do nonhuman animals 'have' finitude? And, if it is indeed undeniable that all animals do in fact *die*, what does this mean as regards thinking encounter with animals?

Infamously, in *The Gay Science* Friedrich Nietzsche declares the death of God, previously imagined to be immortal. While this death undoubtedly occurs in time – with Kant on one side of the fire break, Darwin and Nietzsche on the other – this is not an event that can simply be consigned to history. Rather, it is one to which we must forever continue to attend. For us here, it concerns the very future of Kant: what becomes of the ends of mankind following the demise of the divine?

With the death of God, philosophy is forced from the pale pre-dawn of Kantianism: humanity must leave behind its hubristic myths of transcendence, jolted from its childish dreams of a divinely ordained end (*telos*). No longer concealed behind the linear teleology of universal history, evolution reveals itself as an infinitely diverse multiplicity of trajectories and transformations. With Nietzsche, the end ceases to be that of a fully human humanity and becomes instead immanent to the creativity of existence itself. Such is the moment of delirious destruction (*eskhaton*), a moment requiring neither divine *telos* nor human privilege. As such, the death of God thus irredeemably explodes the illusory boundary dividing culture from nature. Ultimately, humanism – from the theological to the secular – necessitates its own demise.

Things do not end here, however. Rather, it still remains necessary to consider the further critique of humanism proposed by structuralism. This critique, as Derrida notes, consists neither in *restoring* meaning to the metaphysical system as ordered by *telos*, nor in simply *destroying* meaning and thereby leaving only that dismal reign of chance so unbearable for Kant. Instead, writes Derrida, 'it is a question of determining the possibility of *meaning* on the basis of a "formal" organization which in itself has no meaning' ('The Ends of Man,' 134). The structuralist critique, in other words, centres on *transformations* in the conditions that *produce* meaning, and it is both within and outside this anti-humanist space of the structure, at the very limit of sense or meaning, that the eschatolgical encounter takes place. Not, however, as restoration or destruction, but as *invention* and *revaluation*.

Thinking such encounters, however, must first and foremost come to terms with a danger inherent in *language*, with 'language' broadly construed here as a species-specific *way of being*. Insofar as it must 'ceaselessly reinstate the new terrain on the oldest ground,' language can never free itself from the risk of repeating precisely that which it aims to critique (Derrida, 'The Ends of Man,' 135). Language, in other words, is at once the condition of transformative critique *and* that which necessarily entraps us, forcing us in a certain way to remain always on the same terrain, to always move along the same path. Here, we discover the return of our original aporia, *eskhaton* once again constrained by *telos*, only now all delusions of anthropocentric grandeur have been excised.

In direct contrast to the movement of exclusion characterising the genocidal economy, the route taken throughout the first half of this book is, following both Nietzsche and Derrida, an attempt to think creatively *with* animals from within this originary aporia of *shared* existence. Along the way, the *eskhaton-telos* pairing will take on the fleshless Nietzschean bodies – albeit, and this is extremely important, with all their hubristic anthropocentric delusions again cut away – of the overman (*Übermensch*) and the higher man (*höhere Mensch*). Taken together in their uncanny similarity and ultimate complicity, they figure the *inventive encounter* and the *parodic shadow* that is its identical twin.

As Derrida writes, the overman 'burns its text and erases the traces of its steps' in a burst of laughter ('The Ends of Man,' 136, trans. modified). Despite this, the overman can never escape the parody constituted by the higher man in a 'last movement of pity,' one that simultaneously mourns the revolutionary encounter as already lost. This return without end, scarred by the death throes of revolutionary encounters, *is* historicity, *is* the creation of the infinitely diverse ways of being alive. To wit, Derrida's conclusion becomes ever more important: 'we are between these two eves, which are also two ends of man. But who, we?' (136).

To think this return without end, this revolutionary encounter that at the same time offers only a parody of itself, it is thus necessary to *give death* to other living beings. Only the giving of *a* death has the potential to interrupt the brutal economy of genocide. While it perhaps sounds simple, to include other animals within the realm of the finite has explosive consequences, not least for *all* those animals, human and nonhuman, currently being exploited to death all over the globe. Indeed, to *give* death means never having the authority to *put* life *to* death.

On thinking originary technicity: philosophy and politics

This book thus has a double focus: the notion of *giving death to other animals* on the one hand and, on the other, *the possibility of tropes that function in the opposite direction to that economy of genocide* I call 'animalization'. In turn, this results in a new conception of the political as the necessary supplement of an ethical demand – a movement, denoted by the term *zoogenesis*, which offers new possibilities both for encountering and thinking with animals, and for the praxis of animal liberation. It is thus aimed at both theorists *and* activists, even as it thoroughly blurs the lines between them.

At its heart is an understanding of the *originary technicity of being*, which is examined in detail in the first part. Originary technicity is, in short, the condition of being alive, with one consequence being that the divisions between 'Nature' and 'Culture' and between the 'natural' and the 'artificial' break down utterly – indeed, it remains of the utmost importance that these oppositions be thoroughly deconstructed. Even the traditional opposition between the living and the dead can no longer be rigorously maintained. Rather, every living being is a living-dead machine, a dead body buried in material institutions and yet resuscitated each time anew by 'a breath of living reading'.[11] 'Living beings,' in other words, are bodyings or materialities which, while already technical, need be neither organisms nor even 'organic' in any traditional sense. As such, the term 'living' is used as a kind of shorthand which, if not for its awkwardness, should really be ensnared within scare quotes throughout.

An understanding of originary technicity and its consequences are therefore crucial. First of all, both vitalism and biological continuism find themselves *a priori* excluded, just as every judgment of absolute truth and value is necessarily derailed. Secondly, the murderous ideology of the undying animal is irredeemably ruptured, thus undoing along the way every hierarchy of proximity and every narcissistic notion of identity politics.

Moreover, once we comprehend that being alive is to be already riven by originary technicity, it soon becomes clear that every living being is necessar-

---

[11] This phrase is taken from the second volume of Derrida's *The Beast and the Sovereign*, 131.

ily dispossessed, irredeemably foreign to the 'there' of its being. Consequently, it will be argued, every living being demands hospitality and yet, insofar as hospitality requires an autonomous sovereign decision, every living being is similarly incapable of offering it. It is this shared incapacity that marks the reciprocity demanded by liberal contract theory as impossible, and thus its exclusion of nonhuman animals from ethical concern both unjust and unjustifiable. By contrast, it is in fact only by attending with all rigor to the demand of this impossible hospitality shared by every living being that 'crimes against the *human* status' become impossible. Only then might that the brutalizing machineries of animalization be rendered unworking and the global torture-slaughter of other animals finally brought to a halt.

In opposition to the liberal delusion – whether naïve or cynical – of imaginary consensus, originary technicity, as we will see, demands instead the affirmation of an encounter with another whose language 'I' do not recognize and with whom consensus remains impossible. At the same time, 'language' – in a narrow sense of human verbal language – ceases to be the privileged site from which one can sovereignly attribute to another only a mute bestiality. This is by no means, however, to subsume 'the human' beneath 'the animal,' which would be simply to reiterate an uncritical biological continuism. Rather, the difference of originary technicity necessarily structures infinitely diverse ways of being and, moreover, structures them differently. In this sense, just as 'the human' as a secure conceptual category can no longer be maintained, neither does 'the animal' escape unscathed. Indeed, it is not only the habitual concept of 'the animal' that turns out to be absolutely empty, but so too does the entire imaginary bestiary of autonomous 'species' denoted by notional practices of science.

Finally, originary technicity ensures that every living being *a priori* retains the potential to undergo a rupture in its specific way of being that is the moment of *invention*. Hence, it will become clear that, while differences subsist, a humanist hierarchy does not. Furthermore, it is here that we discover an ethical opening that is indeed an *imperative*, but not, however, a moral *ought*. Rather, the ethical opening *is* in potentia: a *can* rather than a *should*. In this creative event of the breach, a given existence with its structural ordering of potentialities, matter, and time is disrupted, opening up differential temporalities of materialities and potentialities. Finally, it is only as a result of the technicity of *life in general* that previously unthinkable entities come into being – such are the monstrous creations that mark the irruption of the most undeniably *real* and which, we will discover, function in the opposite direction to the genocidal economy of animalization.

Hospitality as methodology: an ethic of discussion

We can gain a preliminary sense of such an ethic from the discussion above concerning 'animal studies' and its struggle between circumscription and marginalization. Such a 'being in-between' of circumscription and marginalization shares an intimate relation with hospitality, insofar as both mark the opening of *ethical* space. Always both shared and incomplete, a caesura between past and future ossifications, the ethical opening is a space of *undetermined inclusion and infinite affirmation*. This, however, in no way implies either a refusal of critique or an embrace of moral relativism. In fact, just the opposite is the case.

This newly hospitable ethics is, in the words of Jean-Luc Nancy, 'a generosity of *ethos* more than an ethic of generosity.'[12] This generosity, as we shall see, constitutes both a responsibility and an ethic of *reading* that grounds every singular encounter between beings. Nonetheless, this generosity is such that it cannot blind itself to the violence at work in the structure of language itself. Instead, this violence must, each time anew, be accounted for *as far as possible*. The question of naming, of setting limits, necessarily haunts every encounter, academic or otherwise. We must not, in short, be too hasty, albeit with the understanding that we always will be.

Ethical responsibility thus resides both in a rigorous contextualization and in the recognition that the reconstitution of a given context, in that it remains necessarily partial, can never be nonviolent or apolitical. Hospitality, at the very least, requires the faithful acknowledgment of accrued debts. And yet, if it is to be hospitable, such fidelity at the same time must insist upon its own *in*fidelity. By this I mean that genuine hospitality demands not repetition but *transformation*, a transformation that nonetheless retains an intimate relation with that which is transformed. This is what it means to take place in a living community of beings – beings inorganic as much as organic, natural as much as artificial, immaterial as much as material. It is of the utmost importance to the emergence of animal studies that its practitioners both employ and instill an ethic of discussion, otherwise it forever risks falling into unproductive factional disputes while animals of all kinds continue to die senselessly (this 'senselessly' is meant literally, that is, in the sense of not leaving a trace).

Hospitality and the magic of names

This book is not therefore concerned with 'correction,' but rather with making perceptible and moving beyond the unseen limits that remain as a barrier to thinking encounter with animals. This has important consequences for my

---

[12] Nancy, *The Experience of Freedom*, cit. Derrida *On Touching*, 146.

selection of texts – as much for those I do *not* choose as those I do. Firstly, the exposing of previously concealed limits requires a rearticulation of texts which, at first sight at least, seem little concerned with other animals. On closer examination, however, we discover that this apparent lack of concern in fact disguises a ferocious violence that is all the more violent for being largely unmarked.

Secondly, every episteme finds its shorthand and its limit in the magic of names, itself a violence of decontextualization through which diverse bodies of work are at first determined, and then replaced, by a name that renders these bodies unified and internally consistent. Today, in the West, the ways in which humans encounter other animals owes a great deal to this enchantment. Again, we bump up against the name as the imposition of a limit and as a problem that always remains to be negotiated.

It is with this sense of negotiation that, in setting up the terms of reference for discussion in this work, I privilege the magical names of four dead, white, male philosophers: Plato, Friedrich Nietzsche, Martin Heidegger, and Maurice Blanchot. With the exception of Nietzsche, this privilege is strategic: these four distinct 'moments' being taken to re-present, with all the violence that entails, the movement of 'the animal' *through* philosophy. Historical chronology, however, is not our chronology. Here, Nietzsche *comes after* – in every sense – not only Plato, but Heidegger and Blanchot as well. My aim here is threefold: firstly, to render explicit the functioning of the 'undying' animal in the reproduction of Western patriarchy as founded upon the illusion of a freely willing human subject. Secondly, to show how the repeated constitution of 'the animal' as an unfeeling object under the technical mastery of man stems from a fear of exclusion that is at once the terror of emasculation. And, finally, in order to dispel a certain 'magic' whilst at the same time honoring my debt to that which here founds – but not grounds – a new engagement with animals. Hence, while this initial selection of texts may appear problematic as much in terms of androcentrism and ethnocentrism as of anthropocentrism, I argue instead that such an engagement is initially required precisely in order to counter the exclusion of women, people of color *and* nonhuman animals by making clear the concealed interests that belie the magic of these names.

As we shall see in the first part, the influence of Platonic thought, insofar as it excludes all other animals as beings lacking memory, reason and death, remains profound. Pre-figuring two millennia of Christianized thought, this allows a line to be drawn, by way of the Judeo-Christian tradition culminating with Hegel, to the double negation of the Blanchovian animal. It is in order to mark this continuance which, in part, informs my choice of Blanchot, whose name is certainly less well-known than the others. There is, however, a further – and more important – reason behind this decision: the radical decentering of the subject performed by Blanchot sets the stage for much of poststructuralism to follow, and hence for this text also. In particular, this book owes a great deal to his concept of the 'neutral' or 'neuter,' as explained in more detail in chapter three. Nonetheless, the fact that Blanchot's thought remains wedded to the maintenance of such rusty old machines as metaphysics and humanism demonstrates, in addition to the general homogeneity of the philosophical treatment of 'the animal,' that the decentering of the liberal subject is insufficient *on its own* once consideration is extended to include other animals, as indeed it must be. Last but not least, Blanchot's exemplary position here resides with his exposition of the simultaneous differentiation and imbrication of *being* mortal and *becoming* mortal, an analysis that is essential to understanding the relation between a *taking* place that has already *taken* place that is central to this book.

Moreover, this exegesis and excess of mortality conducts us almost inevitably towards Heidegger who, as is well-known, denies the possibility of death to every nonhuman animal. Nevertheless, the importance of Heidegger's existential analytic both to contemporary philosophy and, somewhat paradoxically, to the emergence of animal studies cannot be overstated, and this in itself constitutes sufficient reason for engaging with the Heideggerian animal. A further reason, however, compels its place in this text: that of Heidegger's singular account of *anthropo*genesis, an account which forms the basis of my own enlarged notion of *zoo*genesis.

Finally then, it is *with* Nietzsche that I attempt to move beyond the limit of the human. Platonic thought, I suggest, only essentially comes into question with Nietzsche. We have already seen something of the importance of what Derrida describes as 'Nietzsche's procedure' in the discussion concerning the twin ends of man above. It is a procedure, moreover, which is possible 'only if one takes the risk of a continuity between the metaphor and the concept, as between animal and man, instinct and knowledge' (Derrida, 'White Mythology,' 262). This risk consists in a *new articulation*, that is, a new folding or placing together that interrupts the oppositions between these three interrelated dualities. In his own terms, Nietzsche's texts both call for and provoke a *revaluation of all values*. In ours, they are the motor behind an epistemic shift that largely remains still to come – indeed, Nietzsche undoubtedly also comes after us.

It is neither in the spirit nor the word of Nietzsche, however, to mobilize his texts so as to assemble a program of action to be followed. The reader will find neither universal truths nor categorical imperatives. Instead, following Nietzsche, one learns of the compulsion to draw upon the reserves of language understood as originary force and resource of creation itself. It is with the name 'Nietzsche' that, in folding together 'Plato,' 'Blanchot' and 'Heidegger,' a new articulation can be seen to be taking place. And indeed, beyond a certain magic of names, we discover that it has already *taken* place.

Other names, other places

For this reason, the first part of this book, entitled *formations*, focuses exclusively upon philosophical texts. In the remainder, however, this focus is broadened to include imaginary bestiaries from a variety of other genres, including literature, cultural studies, political theory, and science studies. Of course, and irrespective of how insecure their boundaries may be, specific genres demand specific protocols of readings. However, insofar as I am attempting to articulate a certain ethic of reading *in general*, that is, of reading *hospitably*, there is inevitably something of a tension between these apparently conflicting demands. While different, the stakes are not, however, incompatible. Put simply, hospitable encounters demand the very act of folding together improperly at the same time as they demand fidelity to context – precisely in order to make manifest its *in*fidelity.

The various texts examined here were selected – or imposed themselves – on the basis that, in their different ways, they all, positively or negatively, knowingly or otherwise, attempt to articulate, to map or, indeed, to block, the epistemic shift that concerns us here. It thus becomes possible to track various 'animal encounters' across disciplinary boundaries: stumbling across their traces in a short story by Franz Kafka, in the bathroom of Jacques Derrida, in a politically galvanising slogan, in the brutal murder of a transgender prostitute, in the deaths of centipedes both actual and fictional, in the newfound plasticity of the gene, and in the sharing of an inhuman knowledge that saves novelist William S. Burroughs from a life of deadly ignorance. Together, these diverse texts inform a new infolding – a new articulation – of the pairings metaphor-concept, animal-human, and instinct-knowledge. Put simply, and in common with animal studies as a whole, I put forward here an articulation that remains resolutely *between* disciplines, an *in*discipline that seeks neither the delimitation nor the marginalization of this or that genre.

The taking place has already taken place: language and the conceptual terrain

Having only briefly indicated the major terms to be explored throughout this book, some further introductory clarification is perhaps required in some cases. One in particular stands out, that of the philosophical enlargement of the term 'language' to designate a *species-specific way of being and at once originary force and resource of creation*. Further elucidation is necessary, however, only because 'language' inevitably carries its burdensome anthropocentric history before it, a burden that, unwittingly or otherwise, elides the *sense* of nonhuman beings.

The importance of righting this wrong cannot be overstated, and the work of Jacques Derrida is essential in this regard. From beginning to end of his *oeuvre*, Derrida repeatedly attempts to rectify the misunderstandings of readers blinded by the very anthropocentrism that his own notion of language seeks to contest. Hence, in the final seminar before his death, we find him again insisting that language must be understood rather as *the constructed community of the world*, simulated by 'codes of traces being designed, *among all living beings*, to construct a unity of the world that is … nowhere and never given in nature.'[13] Language, in short, marks the community of all living beings.

The 'crude and primitive, not to say stupid [*bêtise*]'[14] reduction of language to that of a uniquely human production similarly continues to dog philosopher Judith Butler's notion of *performativity*, with the result that the latter is all too often dismissed as some sort of linguistic constructionism which therefore ignores all 'natural' material and biological strata. This same crude reductionism, moreover, leads invariably to the alienation of animal activists from poststructuralist and deconstructive political strategies insofar as they mistakenly imagine that such strategies have nothing to do with nonhuman animals, who they imagine are left behind in the non-linguistic darkness of pure biology. Given that the opposite is in fact the case, this is an extremely serious mistake that must be overcome, as demonstrated throughout this book. (This is not to say, however, that some of the founding gestures of Butler's theory of performativity do not need to be challenged, and precisely in regard to the place of nonhuman animals, as will be explored in chapter five.)

That said, I would like to offer my own preliminary definition of language as referring broadly to the varied machineries of *making* sense. Or, to put it in more philosophical terms, language designates *the originary relation of being as such as that in which the transfer of sense can take place*. Hence, language concerns not only the *tongue* [*lingua*], but rather every forming and performing that is *to body*. While this will be explored in detail throughout the first part, an initial clarification of this notion of *making* sense, that is, of a body's production or reproduction *of* sense, rather than its passive receptivity *to* sense, will perhaps be helpful.

---

[13] *Beast II*, 8-9; emphasis added.

[14] Ibid., 222.

Making sense presupposes, first of all, the *taking place* of language. However, in order for sense to be *made*, that is, for the sense of something to be recognized, language must have already *taken place*. That is, a body can make sense of something only in reference to prior and potential manifestations, an operation that habitually elides that which is singular in any given encounter. Put simply, in order for any relation to make sense, and thus to have *taken* place, it must simultaneously obscure the singular event of its relating, that is, it must render inaccessible the immediacy of its *taking* place. Language, in short, ensures the *a priori* withdrawal of immediate cognition in favor of mediated *recognition*. A grasp of this nondialectical relation, which will be considered in detail, is essential to an understanding of the relation between *chance* and *necessity*, and thus of the potential for future change.

Zoogenesis and the economy of genocide

As I have already stated, the reader will find here no program to follow and no moral righteousness to adopt. Nonetheless, this is a work of philosophy that translates, via the opening of the ethical event, into a politics of liberation. Such, it will be argued, is the event and the movement I call *zoogenesis*. To accept its premises is to accept that humans do not have the right to do whatever they like with other animals. It is to accept that our given state of affairs is unacceptable and must be radically transformed. Put simply, it is to no longer accept the economy of genocide into which we have all been thrown.

The economy of genocide, I have suggested, consists of a founding and conserving operation of power that, through the movement of 'animalization,' constitutes singular living beings as nonsubjects who can be thereafter killed with impunity. In ancient Greek, *zōe* refers to the simple or 'mere' fact of being alive in terms of subsisting, in contrast to *bios*, which is generally taken to refer to the 'higher' form of human life alone (hence 'biology' is distinguished from 'zoology'). Hence, the movement of animalization can be more accurately described as the economy of *zoo-genocide*, insofar as the target of its slaughter is *always* a 'mere' animal.

Zoo-genesis, by contrast, names the emergence of a new living being. Such is the demand of a thinking encounter that interrupts the reductive calculation of zoogenocide. Responding to its imperative, moreover, requires an excessive hospitality from which nonhuman beings cannot be excluded. *Zoogenesis*, in short, is a local movement or emergence in response to an ethical

25

demand, one which interrupts instrumentalization and exploitation and puts in its place a responsive praxis that rests upon a giving finitude.

While the economy of zoogenocide and the rupture of its resistance requires a detailed step by step analysis, as a point of reference I offer here a skeletal definition of the three-stage movement of *zoogenesis* – stages that will become fully fleshed over the course of this book:

(1) the *animal encounter* as an address that manifests itself *as* meaning without content and *as* sensibility without meaning, one which –

(2) calls forth a new transductive being improperly dressed in the prosthetic *phrasing* of a *placeholding metonymy*, a manifestation which –

(3) marks the emergence of a liberatory politics of resistance, albeit only insofar as it remains *between* sense.

Itinerary

There are of course many possible ways of approaching this book. In one sense, insofar as it begins with Plato and the inauguration of metaphysical humanism and concludes with a consideration of Bernard Stiegler's recent reinstitution of the human-animal dichotomy by other means, this book constitutes a somewhat unorthodox journey through a greatly contracted history of the philosophical animal. It is also an account of the deconstructive implications of originary technicity, beginning with the singular encounter before moving in ever widening circles to consider the political, the ethical, the communal, and finally the global. More importantly, it is also an attempt to supply the necessary theoretical grounding for a new – and considerably more effective – politics of animal liberation.

In this, I begin with a reading of the Greek myth of Persephone through which is disclosed an otherwise obscured accord that stretches across history from Plato to Blanchot and beyond. This accord, however, as explored in chapter two, undergoes a radical rupture in the form of Nietzsche's early text 'On Truth and Lie in the Extra-Moral Sense' (1873). Here, with the help of Derrida's key notion of *iterability*, I show how a stammering *translation* opens the space for a far more radical understanding of 'being-with' [*Mit-sein*] than that generally allowed by philosophical tradition.

In the second part, I explore in detail the notion of an 'animal encounter.' At the limit of language, I argue that such an encounter exceeds every determinable form, thus demanding a necessarily *monstrous* placeholder that holds the place of invention itself. After tracing the consequences of one such encounter in a short story by Kafka, I consider how the inventive encounter relates to the two figures of nihilism proposed by Nietzsche. Thereafter, by contrasting what Karl Marx calls 'the spirit of revolution' with the 'walking ghost' of parody, I show that the animal encounter necessarily gives rise to the revolutionary spirit of a monstrous zoogenetic *phrasing* only insofar as it both *no longer* and *not yet* makes sense. Only in this way, I argue, can a hitherto imperceptible relation make legible its prior exclusion from the dominant culture of recognized value, a legibility that then allows sense to be made of its prior exclusion by making perceptible various concealed interests. This is further illustrated by way of a critical examination of the exemplary political performative 'We are all German Jews' in chapter four.

In part three, I focus on the ethics of the inventive encounter, arguing with and against Judith Butler that it has as its condition an excessive hospitality from which nonhuman animals cannot be excluded, and without which racist, sexist, classist and speciesist norms are inevitably reinforced. Furthermore, it is shown that, in preserving itself through a supplemental political phrasing, the ethical demand, in conflicting dangerously with the hegemonic identifications of a given social state of affairs of whatever species, inevitably brings with it the risk of being judged socially non-viable. Indeed, it is to risk being reduced to silence by the very machinery of animalization it otherwise disrupts. An ethics of hospitality, in short, necessarily runs the risk of becoming a foreigner at home. While the risks – isolation, mockery, even madness and death – are great, it is only thinking unthinkable, unheard-of encounters that offers an emergent trajectory of escape. This need for a dangerous politics rooted in an excessive hospitality is then further explored through readings of several 'post-encounter' texts of William S. Burroughs.

The centre piece of this book remains with Burroughs, focusing on the 'queer centipede' as an exemplary figure of political monstrosity. Such a figure, I argue, in being welcomed within the shared space of the domestic, shifts the Burroughsian posthuman beyond the limits of its imperialist logic and opens up the possibility of a 'hospitable community'.

The fourth part then examines how the notion of 'community' traditionally relates both to hospitality and sharing. Here, by way of a consideration of the suicidal fascist state, it is shown that not only does nationalism employ the very same economy as humanism, but also that the 'fully realized' body of humanism is ultimately indistinguishable from that of the undying animal against which it seeks to found its essential difference. Against this, a new definition of community is proposed, that of *the shared condition of not-be-ing-able to share*. It is within such a community that I locate the Nietzschean posthuman animal who, as a lone wanderer ever seeking community and commonality, paradoxically constitutes a new figure of vigilance, responsibility, and loyalty.

In the last part I explore the relation of the posthumanist animal to the neoliberal promise of the 'transhuman,' beginning in chapter 10 with an examination of developments within capitalist production processes in general, and in biotechnology in particular. Here, a Foucauldian analysis enables us to understand the apparent conflict or conflation of orders which today both organizes and produces nonhuman bodies – bodies such as Dolly, a sheep whose very being promises both eternal life for the few and accelerated death for the many. Engaging directly with Bernard Stiegler's ongoing attempt to reinstall a secure human-animal distinction in chapter 11, I then rework his core concept of 'epiphylogenesis' to resituate the posthumanist promise within the wider concerns of *excessive mutability* and, in so doing, draw together the various threads of this book. Ultimately, I argue, it is only in the ever-renewing *promise* of zoogenesis that we find a curative to the poison of a certain neoliberal politics of the transhuman, replacing its reductive calculation with an ethics of emergence.

Part One. Formations

1. Persephone Calls

Power and the Inability to Die in Plato and Blanchot

> We must not expose the scientific investigation of any subject to a
> comparison with the blind – or with the deaf, for that matter.
> – Plato, *Phaedrus*

Introduction: Calling Persephone

Let us begin, as is only fitting in considering the domination of the human-animal dichotomy throughout the Western tradition, with an ancient myth.

One fine day, while collecting Spring flowers, Persephone is spied by Hades who, inflamed with love and desire, kidnaps her and carries her off to his underworld kingdom. Demeter, Persephone's mother and mother to the earth, is inconsolable, searching the earth and heavens for her daughter. Eventually, she encounters a river nymph who, for fear of Hades, suggests only that Persephone has been taken inside the earth itself. Enraged, Demeter inflicts a devastating infertility upon the land. A second nymph, however, tells Demeter not to punish the earth, for she has seen Persephone with Hades in the Underworld. Deeply shocked, Demeter begs Zeus to arrange the return of her daughter to the upper world. Zeus agrees, with but a single condition: her daughter must have eaten nothing whilst in the Underworld. Persephone, however, has already partaken of a single suck of pomegranate pulp, and so a compromise is offered: Persephone must spend half of every year in the Underworld until Spring arrives and restores her to her mother for the remaining months. Somewhat pacified, Demeter thereafter returns fertility to the earth.

So goes the myth of Persephone, an allegory of rebirth, of the eternal movement of the seasons, and of the casting of the seed inside the earth. It is a myth too, both of feminized Nature as reproduction, subject to the desires of men, and of the promise of resurrection, Persephone's fate offering consolation to anyone anxious about the afterlife. Put simply, it tells tales of transcendental return. It is in this sense, as we shall see, that Socrates, in dialogue with Meno, evokes the name of Persephone in support of his claim that the soul of man is immortal.

The tale of Persephone's return, however, is also marked by a prior detour through the earth, shifting briefly from the eternal concerns of gods to the finite world of men. Exhausted from her search, a disguised Demeter is forced to rest upon a stone for nine days and nights. On the tenth day, an old man happens by and offers Demeter compassion and hospitality. Upon reaching his home, however, Demeter discovers the man's son Triptolemus is desperately ill, and thus proceeds to heal him. When she places the boy in the fire, however, his mother snatches him away, unwittingly preventing his transformation into an immortal. As a consolation, a newly-revealed Demeter promises instead to teach the boy the hitherto unknown art of agriculture, a knowledge which he in turn will impart across the earth. For this act of original pedagogy, Triptolemus later founds the worship of Demeter, erecting a temple in the city of Eleusis on the site of the stone upon which she sat, and staging there the famous purification rituals known as the Eleusinian Mysteries.

This is a less well-known part of the myth of Persephone, telling of the singular gift of the art or technique of agriculture. Here, rather than a Socratic *recollection* as the proof of transcendental reason and thus of the immortal soul, we find instead an *original* act of learning. An act, moreover, directly linked to the Mysteries, the very same rites which Meno is unable to attend, and which Socrates evokes in the *Meno* in order to suggest an analogous relation between the revelatory initiation into divine secrets such as those experienced by Triptolemus and during the Mysteries, and the equally revelatory initiation into philosophical truths offered by Socrates himself. It is this, however, which is impossible, insofar as it is the former which puts the latter into question.

For Plato, as we shall see, the name of Persephone authorizes the *transport* of transcendental return, and yet, as the price of divine consolation, she thus becomes a figure of all too human disavowal. While the revelatory initiation into divine secrets undoes the Socratic return of immortal truths, this is not, however, to suggest that the rites practiced at Eleusis might somehow partake of the divine. Rather, I will argue, these rites are the obverse of this human disavowal insofar as they too, in their own way, seek to purify the human of its animal baseness. Whether Meno chooses to be initiated into the teachings of Socrates or into the Mysteries of Eleusis, either way his initiation will come at the expense of other animals.

Here, I will argue, philosopher Maurice Blanchot too calls on the name of Persephone, not with Socrates on behalf of transcendental reason, but rather in articulating his own variant of the initiation rituals of the Mysteries. For Blanchot as for the Eleusinian initiates, the animal is ritually sacrificed twice over, firstly *as* the human, and then again *in the name of* man. More precisely, the myth of Persephone figures the anthropogenetic movement of double death we find in Blanchot: a redoubled death first of the external animal which marks the becoming man of man, and then of a second, exclusively human death that is the act of mastery that condemns all other animals to the hecatomb.

It is with these twinned offerings, these Persephone calls, that Plato's inaugural disavowal of the nonhuman animal is drawn out across millennia of Christianized humanism in a line which, ever renewed, ties the Platonic dialogues to the 'posthumanist' discourse of Blanchot. With these two purifications, the natural and the supernatural, the empirical and the transcendental, I aim to render explicit the *constitution* of those exclusively human properties – soul, reason and language – which have, since the 'beginning' of philosophy, served to exclude other animals as beings without memory, without trace, and without death. Along the way, I will introduce Derrida's 'quasi-concept' of iterability which, in deconstructing exactly these apparently exclusive human properties, is of central importance to this book.

I. First movement

Before Plato, the idea of an essential immortal soul existing independently of its corporeal incarnation was not generally a part of Greek thought.[1] Facing a variant of the 'trick argument' in the *Meno* (80e), however, Socrates finds himself obliged, in order to save philosophy from sophistry, to have recourse to just such an idea if he is to prove that adequate knowledge can indeed be achieved. Meno's 'trick argument', as summarized by Socrates, runs as fol-

---

[1] The reading of the *Meno* which follows is indebted to Bernard Stiegler who, in a lecture at Goldsmiths in February 2009, spoke briefly about the *Meno* and the *Phaedrus*. See also Stiegler, *Technics and Time, 1: The Fault of Epimetheus*, 97-100.

lows: man can never discover what he knows because either, (a) he already knows and thus has no need to discover it, or else (b) he does not already know and hence cannot even know what to look for or, indeed, if he has found it.

Before he can stage his reasoned defense of philosophical knowledge, however, and immediately prior to the famous geometrical demonstration of transcendental reason, Socrates is compelled to set the scene by calling upon two *non*philosophical substantiating sources. First of all, he recalls the discourse of 'priests and priestesses', and then, by way of Pindar's 'divine inspiration', invokes the goddess Persephone to his cause (81b-c). Both, suggests Socrates, say that the soul of man is immortal, forever reborn within new corporeal incarnations.

One quickly understands the need for such a theological authorization, insofar as it immediately transpires that for Socrates it can only be on the basis of corporeal reincarnation that knowledge and truth can be recollected, that is, recovered or *reborn*. At this point, however, the soul or spirit has not yet left the body: 'the soul, since it is immortal and has been born many times, and has seen all things both here and in the other world, has learned everything that is' (81c). As a result, Socrates argues, a man can indeed *re*cover, rather than *dis*cover, full knowledge insofar as, once he 'has recalled a single piece of knowledge – *learned* it, in ordinary language – there is no reason why he should not find out all the rest' (81d). It is this which Socrates sets out to prove by engaging a slave boy in a discussion of geometry. Here, knowledge available for recollection has been learned through prior experience over a great extension of time and number of incarnations, and it is not the case that the soul always already possesses full knowledge.

The problem then arises that, if future knowledge is necessarily the re-collection of previous experience, how will one have *first* learned that of which knowledge is necessarily a recollection? The demonstration of the slave boy's recollected knowledge only serves to highlight this aporia: the boy can recollect geometry only because he has already learned it, so how will one have *first* come to learn that geometry that all men can subsequently recall? At this point, Socrates *appears* to hesitate. It is a hesitancy, an uncertainty, that finds its fore-echo when earlier he talks of reincarnation only as a clerical and mythical 'they-say' (81a-b).[2] Indeed, throughout this earlier part of the dialogue, and in contrast with the certain movement of the later demonstra-

---

[2] This position is taken up again and explored more fully by Plato in the *Phaedo*, beginning with the Argument from Opposites and its less than convincing 'leap' to its conclusion (70b–72e).

tion, there is no *knowledge*, but only an uncertain reiteration of hearsay and opinion. At times, it even seems to take on the ironic tone characteristic of the Socratic style in which a thesis is apparently affirmed only then to be taken apart, stingray fashion. However, the leading of the witness to confess the collapse of common opinion, of the 'they say', never materializes. Rather, as we shall see, there is only an absent question, a passing over in silence. Despite this, following the slave-boy's performance this *uncertain* hypothesis, that of a redoubled knowledge learned both here *and* there over multiple incarnations, becomes instead a certainty which, in so doing, departs from the body to become a supernatural apparition, evoked from out of this world.

Having drawn a number of transcendent geometrical truths from the mouth of the slave boy, Socrates then presses Meno:

> Either then [the boy] has at some time acquired the knowledge which he now has, or he has always possessed it. If he always possessed it, he must always have known; if on the other hand he acquired it at some previous time, it cannot have been in this life ... if he did not acquire them in this life, isn't it immediately clear that he possessed and had learned them during some other period? (85d-86a).

There is, in this suspension, an obscurity hidden within its clarity – 'isn't it *immediately clear* that he possessed *and* had learned them?' –, the moment which marks in silence the shift from knowledge as empirically learned to knowledge as essential possession. When Meno concedes that the slave-boy must indeed have 'possessed *and* learned' the recollected knowledge during another period, Socrates then insists, 'When he was not in human shape?' to which Meno simply replies 'Yes' (86). Whereas earlier, calling upon Persephone and the priests, Socrates suggests that knowledge is acquired '*both* here and in the other world', he thus now insists upon such a possession as *only* being inhuman and supernatural. There is, however, no explanation as to *why* the slave-boy could *not* have learned geometry throughout his having been born many times and thus having seen all things. Meno, as is so often the case with Socrates' interlocutors, merely affirms this without question.

This disavowal of the corporeal, of the material, in seeking to efface the problem of the recollection of *learned* knowledge, concerns, as we have seen, the problem of the Origin and of *hypomnēsis*. It concerns, in other words, the *first* learning which makes possible the revelation (*alētheia*) that is recollection (*anamnēsis*), that is, which makes a discontinuous past available for return in the future. At this point, and still attempting to extricate philosophy from the Sophist aporia, Socrates can thus *only* side with knowledge as an essential possession proper to man. That is, he is compelled to do so if he is to avoid becoming ensnared in a second aporia – that of an originary site and citing of knowledge. Hence, Socrates continues to press Meno:

> If then there are going to exist in him, both while he is and while he is not a man, true opinions which can be aroused by questioning and turned into knowledge, may we say that his soul has been forever in a state of knowledge? (86a).

Knowledge, in a move that Nietzsche much later terms nihilistic, is thus shifted beyond and before the sensible, constituted as an essence that always *precedes* corporeal being, and opposed therefore to being encoded in the language of its institution (i.e., *hypomnēmata*).

Here though, Persephone eternally returns to haunt Socrates, in that the myth not only offers the consolation of supernatural rebirth, but also recounts the pedagogy of Demeter, who imparts to man a knowledge of nature and its cultivation that is at once original *and* empirical. Where these two aspects cross, however, is with the notion of an infinite *natural* reproduction, that is to say, in the 'immortality' of its cycles.

Absolute animals

As we have seen, in order to avoid becoming ensnared within twin aporia, Socrates is compelled to remove knowledge from the sensible world. Knowledge, the mark of an immortal human soul, cannot henceforth be *learned* (and thus taught), but is rather an essential property of the ensouled that is always available for reactivation. What is of particular interest here, is that in this calculated and arbitrary staging it is *non*human animals – indeed, all *other* living beings – who find themselves sacrificed *to* knowledge in this unquestioned elision of the corporeal and empirical. That nonhuman beings might employ reason does not, according to Socrates, mark the possession of a soul and thus knowledge but rather, as a result of this decision on behalf of philosophy, only the paradox of a learned *non*knowledge. Animal 'reasoning,' in other words, comes to mark instead an unknowing, that of an automatic response. Indeed, by the time of the *Phaedrus*, it even becomes its fabulous figure.

Thus, in his speech to Phaedrus on Love, Socrates insists that a man who surrenders to the sensible and the corporeal is 'like a four-footed beast' and thus 'unnatural' (250e-251a). At the same time, the essential state of the soul in knowledge is no longer a hesitant hypothesis, but has been transformed into simple dogma: 'It is impossible for a soul that has never seen the truth to enter into our human shape; it takes a man to understand by the use of universals, and to collect out of the multiplicity of sense-impressions a unity arrived at by a process of reason' (249b-c). Truth, therefore, is the *a priori* condition for the soul which, *in order to become*, must first see Truth *and then* enter a *human* body. No soul, Socrates says earlier, can be born into a wild animal in its first incarnation (248d). As subsequent to Ideas but prior to corporeal existence, the soul thus functions as the intermediary *between* essence and existence, *between* Ideas and their recollection in being.

In this, the soul functions much as the *khōra* in Plato's *Timaeus*, that is, as the *non*place which is the condition of place or, rather, the *taking place* of place which must withdraw in its having *taken* place, and therefore in the appearance of being through which the truth is *empirically* regained, and thus of temporality and historicity. With the Platonic 'soul,' therefore, appears a first version of the 'taking place that has already taken place' as discussed in the Introduction. Along the way, the distinction between the sensible (*aisthēton*) and the intelligible (*noēton*), which subsequently grounds the sacrifice of the animal to reason, has replaced the tragic composition of *anamnēsis* as *hypomnēsis*.

Put simply, insofar as the soul's archiving of truth is the taking place of man proved via transcendental reason, it necessarily follows that truth, soul, space and time are denied to all other animals. The soul, for Plato, can only be *born* into a man, although man can subsequently be reincarnated in animal form,[3] because it is *only* man and *all* men, from slave-boy to philosopher-patriarch, who can recollect knowledge. By contrast, nonhuman animals are, as Elisabeth de Fontenay writes, both 'absolute animals' and 'dead souls' (*Le silence*, 71). Moreover, in this patriarchal gendering of knowledge, women are thus, in the same movement, implicitly aligned with the soulless irrationality of animals.[4]

Every other living being, every single nonhuman animal of whatever stripe – and, perhaps, every woman, a 'perhaps' which marks the opening movement of the machinery of animalization –, thus finds herself *a priori*

---

[3] It should be noted that the possibility of the ensouled human being reincarnated as an animal would seem, in a variant of the incest prohibition, to thus prohibit the eating of other animals. This question of consuming 'animals-with-souls' remains a problem until, with the specific aim of allaying fears of postmortem vengeance, Saint Augustine disavows its possibility absolutely.

[4] While for the moment at least the male slave stands within the enclosure of man, he is nevertheless – in that a soul can be reincarnated, but never originate, in the form of an animal – held out to a future in reserve and reverse, so to speak. One in which the slave, as a soulless animal reincarnated in human form, finds himself (or herself) penned outside with the animals.

excluded from transcendental knowledge. Consequently, she is also denied access to its two correlates: *virtue* and *memory* (*Meno*, 87b).[5] 'The animal,' this putatively homogeneous category of everything that is not man, thus lacks not only a soul, but also the taking place of place – that of 'being' itself. She can be neither virtuous nor noble, nor can she recall anything, and thus her being-in-the-world lacks even the trace of existence.

One can better understand this nonrelation of virtue and nonhuman animals when, in the *Meno*, Socrates employs the bee as an example of essential being (*ousia*) in order to clarify the distinction between the essential being of virtue and its various worldly modalities (72a). This analogical ontological-ontical structure suggests that the *ousia* of 'the bee' as *eidos* shares a common structural discontinuity from the manifold ways of being-bee as that of Virtue from virtues. However, only *man* has the capacity to recollect the *eidos* of the bee (or the dog, or the monkey, etc.) whereas a bee (or a dog or a monkey or, indeed, even an anthropomorphized virtue) cannot recall its own essential form against which *finite* existence is measured. Hence when, in introducing the myth of the charioteer with two horses in the *Phaedrus*, Socrates speaks of how 'we must try to tell how it is that we speak of both mortal and immortal living beings' (246b), he is referring not to soulless animals and ensouled humans, but rather to finite human bodies in possession of an infinite soul. As the trace of existence, the soul is necessarily the condition of finitude. Ultimately then, nonhuman beings are neither mortal nor immortal, being unable, in truth, to *die*.

Hence, from the *Meno* to the *Phaedrus*, Plato sets upon the stage of tragedy, first through the myth of Persephone and then through the charioteer allegory, a new foundation which, in placing both reason and soul superior and anterior to being, sacrifices nonhuman animals to the certainty of a metaphysics saved from sophistry. The soul, before and beyond its manifest withdrawal in and as a finite body, 'is' infinite wisdom, that is, full knowledge without boundaries. This limitless knowledge, however, remains forever beyond the grasp of every finite incarnation. In his mortal incarnation therefore, man in his turn constitutes an imperfect copy of an incorporeal, immortal, and infinite wisdom. In this, with a call to Persephone and with the help of the *polis* priests, Plato thus pre-figures two millennia of Christianized thought that will only essentially come into question with Nietzsche. Indeed, it is not by chance that Nietzsche's critique takes aim at both the Platonic and

---

[5] Throughout this text I follow the example of Carol Adams and use 'she' to refer to any animal, alive or dead, whose sex is unknown. I will, however, retain 'it' both when citing or paraphrasing another if appropriate (marked by *sic* where necessary) and when referring to a generic concept rather than to specific human or nonhuman animals.

the Christian at once. Nor is it a surprise that, with explicit disregard for the Socratic advice which serves as an epigraph to this chapter, it is Nietzsche, as we shall see, who exposes the scientific investigation of *any* subject to a comparison with the blind and the deaf.

Iterability and the phantasm of Return

Despite, and indeed because of, having condemned 'the animal' to an irrational, mute and deathless nonexistence, Socrates' difficulties with the Sophists are far from over. The ground now shifts again, this time with regard to *anamnēsis*. Whereas knowledge was initially re-collected by accessing the *temporal* storehouse of reincarnated reason (the *hypomnēmata*), now *anamnēsis* refers instead to the revelation (*alētheia*) of prior *atemporal* knowledge. As a result, the transcendental Idea – the essence or truth of the thing – must necessarily be always superior and anterior to its manifold appearance in existence, which in turn can only ever be 'like' or 'as,' but never identical with, its origin. Socratic recollection then, *anamnēsia* as *alētheia* (and seeking to evade *hypomnēsia*), is thus structured as a trope, that is, as a vehicle seeking to faithfully re-present the anterior tenor. Indeed, this is not simply *a* trope, but in fact *the* trope of metaphysics: the metaphor of transcendental Return, as figured by the goddess Persephone. *As* a metaphor, however, this notion of Return is deeply problematic, as Jacques Derrida demonstrates in 'White Mythology' (1971).

Insofar as metaphor 'organizes its divisions within syntax,' writes Derrida, it necessarily 'gets carried away with itself, [it] cannot be what it is except in erasing itself, indefinitely constructing its destruction' (268). This self-destruction, moreover, follows one of two courses which, while different, nevertheless mime one another relentlessly.

The first is the metaphorical movement of the Socratic vehicle, one that claims to fully penetrate the tenor and thus, as Derrida writes, 'finish by rediscovering the origin of its truth ... without loss of meaning, without irreversible expenditure' (268). This is, in short, constitutes 'the metaphysical *relève* of metaphor in the proper meaning of Being' (268) – a specular circularity of philosophical discourse, of loss without loss, which describes, as Derrida writes with reference to Hegel, 'a metaphor which is displaced and reabsorbed between two suns' (268). Things are not so simple, however, insofar as the spreading of the metaphorical in syntax inevitably 'carries within itself an irreducible loss of meaning' (268). Indeed, to rely on an imitation to 'reveal' the plenitude of its origin is necessarily paradoxical. Given the temporal discontinuity – its abyss of puckish irony – between the two realms, the revealed 'original meaning' can only ever be an *effect* solely of the copy. In other words, instead of revealing its origin, the trope of transcendental Return only ever produces an endless dissemination. To be otherwise requires that the *mimeme* exist in two temporal realms simultaneously: both completely inside (plenitude of origin, sunrise) and completely outside (imitation, sunset).

Against and within this first *aufhebung* of Return, the second self-obliterative recourse is to that of senseless metaphorical suicide. While similar in appearance to the metaphysical metaphor, the suicidal trope instead disrupts the philosophical hierarchy, wresting away its 'borders of propriety' that subordinate the syntactic to the semantic and unfolding in its place a notion that, in its dissemination, is explicitly without limit (268). In its passage through the 'supplement of syntactic resistance,' the 'reassuring relationship' of the metaphoric and the (return of the) proper thus explodes, resulting in the suicide of unisemic sense.

The metaphor therefore always carries its own death. Moreover, the 'difference' between its two deaths, the apparent choice between 'good' and 'bad,' between transparency and undecidability, is in fact no choice at all. By definition, metaphor already *supplements* an anoriginal absence, and is thus always syntactic and already carried away. Rewriting this in the terms of our discussion, in its withdrawal in and as the appearing of the mortal being, the immortal Socratic soul thus marks a lack to be supplemented *in addition* to its absolute plenitude. Put another way, both to be an essence *and* to be represented, an essence must be able to properly repeat itself, and yet in repetition an essence necessarily ceases to be proper. As Derrida says elsewhere, 'the presence of what is gets lost, disperses itself, multiplies itself through mimemes, icons, phantasms, simulacra, etc.' ('Plato's Pharmacy,' 166). No return without loss, the sun, infinitely exposed, shatters upon the sea.

The translative movement in and as language in its broadest sense – i.e., that of *making sense*, as will become clear in the next chapter – is necessarily governed by the temporal structure of the act of interpretation, and thus discontinuous with truth. In summary, the tropological structure which organizes the Platonic Idea must already bring into play, through the similarity of recollection, the paradoxical play of *mimēsis*. That is, the doubling of the recollection must be faithful and true (i.e., identical), and yet, in that its duplication within existence manifests a necessarily inferior copy, it therefore already divides its indivisible essence. In short, the existential recollection of the essential Idea is already interrupted by what Derrida calls *iterability*, with the result that the proposed cure for *hypomnēsis* turns out to be the poison of *hypomnēsis*.

Inscribed as the structural characteristic of every mark, every grapheme, it is iterability which determines that language can never be meaning*ful*, insofar as a given word or phrase can always be detached from its anterior temporal position and reiterated in another context, a reiteration whose sense inevitably differs from its previous articulation. Repetition, in short, *alters*. At the same time, however, it is this same possibility of repetition, as the necessary condition for any mark to function ritualistically *as* language, which constrains language to always return and yet always begin anew. Alteration, in short, *identifies*. While this will be explained in more detail in the next chapter, for the moment it is sufficient to note that iterability marks the similarity of recollection as necessarily *fantastic*. Indeed, according to Plato the fantastic refers precisely to a trope which pretends to simulate faithfully, and thus deceives with a simulacrum – a (false) copy of the (true) copy – that is, with a *phantasm*.[6] Put simply, the fantastic or phantasmic trope is a deceptive transport by which one is persuaded to mistake interpretation for truth – what Maurice Blanchot describes as mistaking the *labor* of truth for truth itself.

The deadly labor of truth

This dangerous fantasticity from which a truly faithful copy can never save us is nothing less than the existence of every so-called 'living being.' It is, in other words, the translative movement of be-ing. While, as noted above, this remains to be explored in more detail, the point here is to signal the originary interrelation of two apparently unrelated concerns. At its advent, the valorizing of essence and intelligibility (*noēton*) over and against existence and sensibility (*aisthēton*) thus articulates a founding disavowal of other animals together with an attempt to efface the monstrous phantasm of the fantastic. With this, we already get a sense of the potential political dynamite that is 'Nietzsche's procedure,' a procedure that explodes the machinery of exclusion by way of a risky 'articulating together' of animal and man, metaphor and concept, and instinct and knowledge – the very dualities that found Platonic thought.

---

[6] Plato, *The Sophist*, 234b-235a. See also Derrida 'Plato's Pharmacy,' 286-288, note 14.

I began by arguing that 'man' can exist 'properly' only by externalizing and excluding the improper animal upon which it depends, and here, in this same moment and movement, we thus discover that *mimēsis* too, can *properly* be only by externalizing and excluding the impropriety upon which it depends. These twinned movements, the closure of the circle of Return (the organizing trope of metaphysics) and the exclusion of the animal in and as the constitution of this closure (the proper delimitation of the human), are indissociable.[7] Moreover, beyond our three Platonic binaries, we discover a further duality that sets the entire machinery in motion: that of the *proper* and the *improper*.

The inextricability of these twin exclusions ultimately returns us to Persephone. On the one hand, her consoling return figures not only the transcendence of the human, but also of the eternal return of the sun and thus of a fruitful earth forever offering itself for man's harvest. On the other, however, this myth simultaneously names the phantasm of an all too human disavowal, insofar as the name of Persephone is called upon – and not only by Socrates – to authorize an access to the essential that is restricted to man alone.

Meno, we are informed, must unfortunately leave Athens prior to the celebration of the rites of the Eleusinian Mysteries dedicated to Persephone's mother Demeter – rites which seek a divine revelation that Socrates, in a seemingly curious move, compares to the revelation of philosophical truths (*Meno*, 76e). Here, Meno's future absence marks the dialogue, an absence that is at once the removal from knowledge. In Ancient Greece, those initiated into the Mysteries perform the following ritual: first, initiates undergo a ceremonial purification in the sea while holding in their submerged arms a sacrificial piglet. They then walk in silence to Eleusis whereupon they fast and, still in silence, sacrifice their domestic animals in their own stead. Finally, after a ritual handling of objects, a dramatic performance is staged, very possibly the myth of Persephone itself.

In this ritual based on the return of Persephone to the sun, the animal is thus doubly sacrificed. First, a piglet – in one sense *property* but nevertheless not yet fully domesticated, not yet *proper* – is sacrificed in order to purify man, to rid man of his own untamed bestiality. Second, as dispensable representatives and imperfect copies of man, any number of domesticated – that is, completely dominated – animals are sacrificed in order for man to live on,

---

[7] On this, see Andrew Benjamin, 'Indefinite Play and 'The Name of Man''' (*Derrida Today*, 1:1 (2008), 1-18). Benjamin too refers to the Socratic bee in the context of virtue (4).

to survive beyond the constraints of finitude and existential appearance. In short, the animal within is first of all externalized, after which it must then take on the death of man in order that man can live forever. Here then, we can understand better why Socrates affirms an analogical relation between divine revelation of the Mysteries and the revelation of 'proper' knowledge: any number of imperfect, improper animal copies are sacrificed in order to install in man alone an immortal soul which accedes to the essential.

What remains as doubly foreclosed, therefore, is the impropriety of the animal, a foreclosure that seeks to guard against the potential interruption of an improper animal *relation* which is nonetheless ontologically prior to the exclusion upon which the delimitation of the human depends. Here then, a preliminary hypothesis irresistibly suggests itself: *given that the proper appearance of 'the human' depends upon the exclusion of both 'the animal' and 'the improper,' a potential disruption of humanist metaphysics would therefore seem to reside within an animal encounter marked by an improper relation.* It requires, in short, that animal and man, metaphor and concept, and instinct and knowledge be folded together in a risky new articulation.

II. Double movement

The metaphysical metaphor of closure and return has enjoyed a long and various career, as we shall see in turning now to consider the function of 'the animal' within the 'posthumanist' philosophy of Maurice Blanchot. Here, I will argue, the myth of Persephone, with its relation to both finitude and nonhuman being as well as the ritual double death enacted in Eleusis, calls to the notions of essential solitude and inessential existence as articulated by Blanchot in his struggle to move beyond Hegel. Indeed, that Hegel should appear at this point is far from incidental, insofar as it is with Hegel, at the beginning of the nineteenth century, that the movement of transcendental Return receives its most compelling example. In the East, he writes, 'rises the outward physical [i.e. sensory] Sun, and in the West it sinks down: here consentaneously rises the Sun of self-consciousness, which diffuses a nobler brilliance.'[8] It is the repressive, irrepressible romantic yearning to master dissemination that is here taken up again by the *tēlos* of Hegel's Spirit, understood as that which reveals as it regains and retains the plenum (the essence of man) *at last* illuminated by the 'true light' of the Western sun.

---

[8] Hegel, *Lectures on the Philosophy of History*, cit. Derrida 'White Mythology,' 269n84.

While Socrates places man above the nonhuman animal by virtue of the capacity to transcend the sensible in the unity of useful universals, Blanchot follows Hegel in arguing instead that it is the articulation of death, that is, the act of *making mortal,* which founds 'the human' and at once marks out 'the animal.' Indeed, Blanchot more than once cites Hegel in this context: 'the life of the mind begins with death.'

The importance of the reiterated reference to Hegel becomes evident once we understand of what this founding act consists. In an important yet complex passage in *The Space of Literature* (1955), Blanchot writes:

> Can I die? Have I the power to die? This question has no force except when all the escape routes have been rejected. It is when he concentrates exclusively upon himself in the certainty of his mortal condition that man's concern is to make death possible. It does not suffice for him that he is mortal; he understands that he has to become mortal, that he must be mortal twice over: sovereignly, extremely mortal. That is his human vocation. Death, in the human perspective, is not a given, it must be achieved. It is a task, one which we take up actively, one which becomes the source of our activity and mastery. Man dies, that is nothing. But man *is,* starting from his death. He ties himself tight to his death with a tie of which he is the judge. He makes his death; he makes himself mortal and in this way gives himself the power of a maker and gives to what he makes its meaning and its truth. The decision to be without being is possibility itself: the possibility of death (96).

While the density of this passage may appear daunting at first, things will nonetheless become clear so long as we take it slowly. Firstly, Blanchot suggests that to be human requires that one not only *be* mortal, but also that one *become* mortal. Whereas all other animals, insofar as they are blind to even a simple sense of their mortality, merely 'perish,' the vocation that gives to humanity its unique perspective is this doubling of mortality. Here then, the human is distinguished from the animal by virtue of a founding reciprocity: whereas every living being perishes (which, as we shall see all too clearly, 'is nothing'), only a human animal, insofar as she perceives her own mortality, must thus simultaneously *become* mortal and, in so doing, become *human.*

Man thus achieves death, and at once himself (that is, the human perspective), through the doubled articulation of mortality: being-mortal and becoming-mortal. How might we understand these two movements? Being-mortal is, firstly, the *meaningful* articulation of mortality *as* the possibility of our future not-being-in-the-world. Moreover, only now can the *possibility of dying* be comprehended, insofar as such an understanding could not exist prior to the 'as' of the originary articulation of mortality by which the human alone gives itself and the world meaning. The human, first and foremost, is the being who experiences itself *as* mortal, a cognition that necessarily takes place *of* and *in* language. The act that founds the human is thus at once the first human act: the taking place of language as the originary experience of being-mortal as mortal. Hence, that I can still die is, as Blanchot writes in *The Infinite Conversation*, 'our *sign as man*' (42).

For Blanchot, being human as being-mortal is thus to be thrown into the *inessential* world of language, inessentiality being the very condition of possibility of language, as we shall see. Meanwhile language, for its part, is both a *re*cognition and a *re*presentation of mortality, insofar as 'death alone … exists in words as the only way that they can have meaning' (Blanchot 'Literature,' 324).

Ignoring for the moment Blanchot's reduction of language to words alone, in this founding *of* and *as* the human, we necessarily discover in this difference of itself from itself the mark of an iteration which corrupts any unity of origin. To be able not to be is at once to be able to be born: we die, and at the same time are born, *in and as language*. Put simply, as the moment in which a body conceives of its possible nonbeing, and thus possibility *in general,* the human comes into being and at the same time is thrown from the realm of essential being and into the inessential world of language. Here, we find our first point of contact between Blanchot and Plato: excluded by definition from this movement of anthropogenesis, nonhuman animals are thus once more excluded from the taking place of place, and thus from language and the 'there' of being.

Moreover, insofar as other animals are excluded from the ability not to be, and thus from possibility in general, not only can they never *become* mortal, in fact they can never *be* mortal and nor, in truth, can they be born. Every nonhuman being, in other words, is denied the possibility of having her own singular death, is refused the possibility of ever dying *this* death. And yet, as we shall see in considering the complementary movement of *becoming*-mortal in the next part, for Blanchot the exceptional positing power of the human nevertheless depends upon the singular violent death of a nonhuman animal who, somewhat paradoxically, essentially cannot die.

The memory of death

Having made a preliminary comparison with the Platonic exclusion of the animal, we can now, by way of a detour through Hegel, begin to approach Blanchot's own peculiar version of the Eleusinian Mysteries. Having constituted itself in its capacity *not* to be, it is through this originary power to *negate* that the human thereafter avails itself of the power of the negative. Man, we recall, must be mortal *twice over*, must both *be* and *become* mortal, just as death must both *be* and *be achieved*. Hence, writes Blanchot, it is necessary that death be '*seized again as a power*, as the beginning of the mind' ('Literature,' 324, my emphasis). This, he continues, 'is at the centre of the universe where truth is the labor of truth' (ibid.). Becoming-mortal, in other words, is the *appropriation* of negation that gives to man the power of a maker and is the source of his activity and mastery. Death, in short, is the condition of possibility itself. The question thus arises as to how, exactly, this appropriation of death's power might take place.

As we have seen, the moment must concern the *seizing again* of death that is the emergence of negation as possibility, and which is at once the taking place of language as that which, at the founding of the human, grounds the emergence of meaning and truth. If we are to understand this strange movement from a being who is able not to be (being-mortal) to that of a maker laboring in the inessential world of truths (becoming-mortal), we need to heed Blanchot's repeated enjoinders in this context to 'remember the earliest Hegel' and, more specifically, the Hegel of the Jena System of 1803-4. Hardly fortuitously, Hegel argues therein that it is the seizing of an animal's death in a movement of negation that, in its appropriation as the *word*, reserves and preserves not only the animal's absence, but also the possibility of truth itself.

According to Hegel, the extended vowel of pain that marks the dying of an animal is at once the founding act of the human. This *vowel of sensuous animality*, he suggests, transcends its singular violent death in its universal expression: 'Every animal finds its voice in violent death; it expresses itself as a removed [*aufgehobnes*] self. ... In the voice, meaning turns back into itself; it is negative self, desire. It is lack, absence of substance in itself.'[9] In this, Hegel argues, is given the pure sound of the voice, a pure sounding interrupted by the silence of death, the latter constituting a mute consonant that is 'the true and proper arrestation of mere resonation' through which 'every sound has a meaning for itself.'[10] It is as a result of this 'fact,' claims Hegel, that language becomes the voice of consciousness. In other words, the 'mere' vowel of animal noise is *pure syntax* that is negated not by the breath, but by the death of the animal. In the dialectical negation of the negation, this death is thereafter preserved as it is raised up (*aufhebung*) into a universal expression that finds its meaning only with the founding of man.

---

[9] *Jenenser Realphilosophie I*; reproduced in Agamben, *Language and Death*, 45.
[10] Ibid.

The *non*human animal, however, as *prior* to the advent of this death-word is thus excluded from the possibility of both consciousness and meaning. In his fine reading, Giorgio Agamben summarizes this movement:

> 'Voice (and memory) of *death*' means: the voice is death, which preserves and recalls the living as dead, and it is, at the same time, an immediate trace and memory of death, pure negativity. Only because the animal voice is not truly 'empty'..., but contains the death of the animal, can human language, articulating and arresting the pure sound of this voice (the vowel) – that is to say, articulating and retaining the *voice of death* – become the *voice of consciousness*, meaningful language (*Language and Death*, 45).

In other words, it is because, in *dying*, a nonhuman animal expresses her absence (death arresting the vowel of pain) that language thus takes on the *power* of death. Returning to Blanchot, it is in the precise moment when an animal voices her absence in death – an articulation that is *no longer* animal 'noise' but *not yet* verbal language – that the originary being-mortal of man is expressed in the *taking place* of language. Before this can be fully understood, however, it is necessary that the human *become*-mortal, as we shall see now.

First of all, it is clear that there can be such a thing *as* world for the human only insofar as the existence of the animal is suspended through negativity. There is world, Blanchot writes simply, only 'because we can destroy things and suspend their existence' ('Literature,' 336). The human, in other words, is that being who, insofar as it arrives only through the taking place of language, comes to itself as *already* thrown into a world of meaning and truth. Only with the *word* is death is seized once again, and thus only with the word does man *become* mortal. In this doubling of death, the animal is negated twice over: its particularity is negated first in universal expression, and then again in the word or name which rather marks 'the absence of that being, its nothingness, what is left of it when it has lost being – the very fact that it does not exist' (322).

From this, it becomes possible to pinpoint the very moment of anthropogenesis, as related by Hegel and repeated by Blanchot, in which the power of death is seized again *as* language and thus becomes the source of activity and mastery: 'Adam's first act, which made him master of the animals, was to give them names, that is, he denied them as independent beings and he transformed them into ideals.'[11] Here, in this 'second' movement, language has

---

[11] The German original reads: '*Der erste Akt, wodurch Adam Seine herrschaft über die Tiere kinstituiert hat, ist, das ser ihnen Namen gab, d.h. sie als Seiende vernichtete und sie zu für sich Ideellen machte*' (Hegel, *Jenenser Realphilosophie*, repr. in Agamben, *Language and Death*, 43). Blanchot cites this passage in 'Literature and the Right to Death,'

already *taken* place. The human *is*, in other words, only on the condition of first negating the particularity of animal death (the *taking* place of language) and then by annihilating her independent existence (language having *taken* place). The human, in short, is the exceptional animal that twice over denies being to every other animal.

According to Blanchot therefore, the seizing-again or *re*-cognition of mortality is both *a human production and the production of the human*. Without this recognition, existence remains dissolved in its 'original depths,' and yet *with* this recognition existence is simultaneously *negated*: The 'existent,' writes Blanchot, 'was called out of its existence by the word, and it became being.' However, in thus summoning forth the 'dark, cadaverous reality from its primordial depths,' the word gave it in exchange 'only the life of the mind' ('Literature,' 326). Beyond and before the word, existence consists in 'the intimacy of the unrevealed,' an intimacy that is necessarily lost once beings are recognized *as* beings: Thus, Blanchot continues, '[t]he torment of language is what it lacks because of the necessity that it be the lack of precisely this. It cannot even name it' (326-7). This 'lack' is what Derrida describes as 'the wound without a name: that of having *been given a name*' (*Animal*, 19).

The work of death

Lastly, before we can fully disclose the 'place' and the function of nonhuman animals within this schema, as well as how their double disavowal reiterates the practice of Eleusinian sacrifice offered up to Demeter, it remains for us only to consider the labor of the negative as it informs Blanchot's notion of *essential solitude*.

To begin with, insofar as it is the event of both anthropogenesis and worlding, the appearance of the word in the seizing-again of death has thus already taken place. As such, it is necessarily 'an unsituated, unsituatable event which, lest we become mute in very speech, we entrust to the work of the concept (negativity)' (Blanchot, *The Writing of the Disaster*, 67). Here, we must understand that the negating word or name through which death works is already in the strict sense a *concept*, that is, it *conceives* of an existent. Indeed, it is precisely this *conceptual power* which simultaneously constitutes the human and withdraws it from unmediated existence. Hence, the articula-

---

the last phrase of which Charlotte Mandell, in order to remain faithful to Blanchot's text, translates as 'he annihilated them in their existence (as existing creatures) [*dans leur existence (en tant qu'existants)*]' (cit. 323).

tion of the concept, its work of negativity, is the decisive event – decisive, that is, as regards the anthropogenetic and the anthropological – that plunges all of creation into a total sea, the event Blanchot calls the 'immense hecatomb.'[12]

Things don't end here, however, as a further twist of negativity awaits the concept. In being posited as an *ideal*, that is, as having exchanged primordial reality for 'the life of the mind,' this *non*existence that is the word- or name-concept is thereafter taken to be the *essence* of the thing. This metaleptic reversal marks, in Blanchot's terms, the 'forgetting of forgetting' through which *value* is created. The thing, in other words, is forgotten first of all in being *exchanged* for an empty concept, and thereafter this forgetting is itself forgotten in the subsequent taking of this empty concept for an ideal value. As such, in the culmination of the 'life-giving' negation of language, the image becomes the object's 'aftermath' in which the object itself is withdrawn from understanding in such a way as to allow 'us to have the object at our command when there is nothing left of it' (*Space of Literature*, 260).

Language can now be understood as the work of death in the world, that which drives –

> the inhuman, indeterminate side of things back into nothingness .... But at the same time, after having denied things in their existence, it preserves them in their being; it causes things to have meaning, and the negation which is death at work is also the advent of meaning, the activity of comprehension ('Literature,' 338).

We are now in a position to summarize the movement of anthropogenesis in Blanchot's philosophy. First of all, the death of the animal constitutes the human as a mortal *being*, that is, as having the possibility *not* to be. Simultaneously, this singular nonhuman death realizes the power of negativity which, in being seized again as activity and mastery, marks the *becoming*-mortal of the human. This latter inheres in the act of naming which constitutes the power of a maker, giving to what she or he makes its meaning and its truth.

The animal, in short, ends where the human begins: in *language*. Indeed, in its double appropriation of death the human 'is' the unsituated and unsituatable event of language itself, of its *taking place* that has already *taken place*. Hence, for Blanchot the articulating and preserving of the voice of death as *both* memory *and* absence, that is, as the *trace of withdrawal*, constitutes the *taking* place *of* language. At the same time, this taking of place is the opening of the space of recognition and thus of the name, that is, of language having

---

[12] The use of the word 'hecatomb' is interesting in this context, referring as it does to the ritual sacrifice of one hundred 'cattle.'

taken place. On the one hand then, death, doubled and divided, simultaneously constitutes, in addition to the human, both the world and its representation. On the other, being-mortal and becoming-mortal are nothing but tropes, anthropomorphized figures of language itself.

How then, might we define the exceptional beast that is the human? According to Blanchot, quite simply as the non-animal for whom, insofar as he or she takes place *of* and *in* language, the essential is *a priori* withdrawn and replaced by empty ideals. At best, the immediacy of existence may be approached in a work of art, but even then its hovering appearance has necessarily escaped. Admittedly, this doesn't sound like much – presumably existing intimately within the real, animals, we might think, are the lucky ones. However, if philosophy teaches us anything, it is that we should reserve judgment on this for the moment. Existence 'is,' in short, 'the side of the day that day has rejected in order to become light' ('Literature,' 328). Only in the obliterating clarity of a meaningful humanity, in other words, can the work of death be found. *Im*mediate existence, by contrast, is necessarily deathless, wordless, meaningless, and inhuman – the primordial realm, in Blanchot's words, of 'essential solitude.' Condemned to exist only as an undifferentiated part of this underworld machinery with neither beginning nor end – 'death as the impossibility of dying' (328) – other living beings, it seems, are not so lucky after all.

An initiation into the new Eleusinian Mysteries

Clearly, it is only the human who, coming to be upon the death of a deathless animal, can give meaning to nonhuman existence. Only 'man' stands in the light of the negative, only the human animal is enlightened. This, I will argue, turns us back across millennia to the myth of Persephone's return to the light and, in particular, to Demeter's place of rest and worship in Eleusis. As we have seen, to be initiated into the Eleusinian Mysteries an appellant must first sacrifice a piglet, followed by any number of domestic animals. We have seen too, how this relates to the Platonic exclusion of 'the animal' from 'the human,' and how, having first being externalized, the animal is thereafter forced to bear the death of man in order that man might live forever. With Blanchot, however, we now discover the *mirror-image* of this all too human movement. In place of the 'birth' of an immortal human soul, we find instead the annihilating genesis of the human at the origin of the world. In place of the double sacrifice that installs in man alone an access to the essential, we find the double sacrifice that installs in man alone an access to the *in*essential.

In Ancient Greece, we recall, the initial sacrifice involving the death of a single nonhuman animal served to purify the human of its bestiality. In other words, by way of this first death the human ceases to be an animal. It is in this same moment therefore, that the human equips itself with the capacity to master nature, to dominate, domesticate and exploit other 'merely' living beings. Such mastery, however, requires a second sacrifice, a second death. Indeed, the fact of being domesticated alone condemns the other animals to annihilation, to a hecatomb that serves only to vouchsafe the mastery of the human. This, as should be clear, equally describes the double sacrifice that underpins Blanchot's own metaphysical anthropocentrism: 'the animal' is ritually sacrificed twice over, firstly as the human, and then again *in the name of* the human.

Doubly deceased: the mute deposition of nonhuman animals

The question now arises, as to how might the *taking place*, or otherwise, of nonhuman animals arrive to potentially interrupt these sacrificial schemas imposed upon them from without for millennia. As suggested earlier, this potential disruption would seem to reside in an animal encounter marked by an improper relation. To this we can now add that such an encounter appears equally to require the reinscription of death within *non*human ways of being. Indeed, by further considering the placeless place of the animal in Blanchot's philosophy in these final sections, as well as its proximity or otherwise to the Heideggerian animal, we begin to open the space for just such an animal encounter to come.

Blanchot's animal is, as we have seen, doubly deceased, that is, doubly depositioned and decomposed. Nevertheless, nonhuman animals continue to keep getting in the way, an uncanny obtrusion which brings into the open the implicit humanism of Blanchot's discourse.[13] As being-in-the-world and yet deprived of the deluge of language that 'is' death and vice versa, an animal 'is' therefore mortal without recognizing it (and thus not, in truth, mortal). Moreover, as that which does not have her (own) death, she 'is' necessarily senseless and meaningless being. In other words, insofar as she is excluded from the 'unsituated, unsituatable event' that is language's having already

---

[13] While Blanchot indirectly addresses 'actual' nonhuman animals in relation to Rilke (*Space of Literature*, 135), their position nonetheless remains obscure.

taken place, and thus from finitude that is its condition, the nonhuman animal necessarily exists *before* the annihilation of Adam's positing power. At the same time, however, she nonetheless remains, indeed co-exists, *after* the world thus posited – a world, therefore, of cohabitation. At the very least then, she exists in some strange sense that 'is' at once both before and after the Fall.

Without language, and therefore *prior* to being *as* such, nonhuman animals are thus allotted only some uncanny kind of *not yet-world world*, that is, a 'world' with neither possibility nor resemblance. At the same time, however, there can *be* nothing beyond or before being *as such* either, that is, beyond or before what Blanchot terms *essential solitude*. This paradoxical equation of being as such with essential solitude, however, requires further clarification, serving as it does to ultimately exclude nonhuman living beings even from the primordial realm of the *real*. Essential solitude is, for Blanchot, simply *im*mediate existence that is withdrawn in and as the taking place of the human. As such, essential solitude can only ever 'take place' as that which remarks the hiddenness of existence by the disappearance, the *hecatomb*, of everything that is. Hence, put simply, essential solitude *marks* the originary withdrawal of being, a withdrawal that becomes meaningful in being marked *as such*. Indeed, it is only insofar as essential solitude constitutes the originary *taking place* of meaning in this way that a work of art may thus *approach* its unsituated, unsituatable event but, in having necessarily *taken* place, can never actually reach it.

While the synonymity of being as such and originary taking place will be further elucidated in the reading of Heidegger in the next chapter, it is already possible to perceive the paradox under which the Blanchovian animal labors. As we have seen, there can be no hiddenness of existence – no essential solitude and no primordial reality – for nonhuman animals, which thus leaves only the nonbeing that 'is' inessential being-in-the-world. However, insofar as there can be no nonhuman 'as,' and thus no articulation or image, neither can animals exist within the inessential 'world' that would be the mark of this nonbeing. In short, nonhuman animals neither *are* nor *are not*, neither being nor nonbeing, but something absolutely other. They 'are,' in other words, both *within and outside* the world at the same time as they are *neither within nor outside* the world: animal spirits or ghosts of nonhumanity.

Specters of Heidegger

This spectrality of the philosophical animal points to an initial point of both proximity and distance between Blanchot and Martin Heidegger. In Heidegger's *Being and Time* (1927), the animal is similarly (non)placed in negativity: neither present-at-hand [*Vorhandensein*], nor ready-at-hand [*Zuhandensein*], nor the Dasein who, as something other and more than a living being, is abysmally distanced from the nonhuman animal who 'merely' has life and can only ever 'perish' [*verenden*]. Indeed, Blanchot employs a very similar vocabulary in order to get his own metaphysics up on its rear legs and running. Men and only men, he writes, 'are infinitely mortal, a little more than mortal. Everything is perishable, but we [humans] are the most perishable' (*Space of Literature*, 140). As with Heidegger then, the exceptional *supra*-mortality of the human-Dasein, in refusing death to other animals, simply leaves them to 'perish' in the manner of used-up or useless objects, like worn-out tires or unused condoms. As 'a power that humanizes nature, raises existence to being, and … is within each one of us as our most human quality' (Blanchot, 'Literature,' 337), death now becomes the exclusive property of man, appearing –

> between me, *as I speak* [emphasis added], and the being I address: it is there between us as the distance that separates us, but this distance is also what prevents us from being separated, because it contains the condition for all understanding. … Without death, everything would sink into absurdity and nothingness (324).

By contrast, in being essentially deprived of death's power that makes of man a mortal being, nonhuman animals therefore exist as *absurdity and nothingness*. Existence, in other words, that *is not* being (and thus nothingness) and is not nonbeing (and thus an absurdity). At the same time, in being excluded from meaning, that is, from becoming mortal, the hugely divergent ways of being animal are reduced to an *un*differentiated existence which at once lacks that which *prevents* absolute separation from one another.[14] Here, with the further discovery of a dizzying proximal distancing that posits nonhuman animals as those who are cast off but who cannot be separated, who are excluded but cannot be excluded, the inconsistencies surrounding Blanchot's fundamental exclusion of 'the animal' are clearly proliferating beyond all

---

[14] And all this, it should be noted, without either communication or community, both of which, according to Blanchot, have death as their condition. On this, see Andrew Benjamin 'Another Naming, a Living Animal: Blanchot's Community,' *SubStance* #117, 37:3 (2008), 207-227.

control. Indeed, such a proliferation inevitably infects every attempt to erect a secure humanist foundation.

Given that the human founds its being on the negation of the negation, that is, on the negation of the animal as absolute lack (of death, of being, of meaning, of separation, of community and of communication), Blanchot ultimately elaborates what is a very traditional humanist dialectical teleology. Put simply, it is the concept of 'the animal' that prevents Blanchot from breaking free of Hegel.[15] Moreover, this specter of Hegel marks a further, profound difference that separates Blanchot's formulation from that of Plato. For the latter, insofar as the animal plays no part in the *genesis* of the human, humans and animals are, in a strict sense, *incomparable*. For Blanchot, however, the genesis of the human is predicated on the death or nonexistence of the animal in what is a specifically *Christianized* form of the human-animal relation. As we will see in the next chapter, these dominant Christianized forms in fact depend upon what I call the *humanist paralogism*, that is, the fallacious inference that nonhuman animals are in fact incomplete *humans*.

In concluding this prefatory sketch of the mirroring of ancient and modern philosophical constructions of the undying animal, it is nonetheless the case that, in spite of this important difference, Blanchot's modern initiation offers only yet another Mystery: that of the uncanny placeless place of 'the animal' that calls again upon Persephone and the myth of undying Nature – that is, upon a theology and a teleology – in order to preserve for 'the human' alone both privilege and mastery within an otherwise soulless world. However, in moving beyond this untenable conservation in the next chapter, we shall discover instead that the movement of *anthropo*genesis necessarily gives way to a far more radical movement of originary *zoo*genesis.

---

[15] Along with the animal, 'primitive' man, for whom 'the name has not emerged from the thing' ('Literature,' 322), also finds himself uneasily (non)placed according to this dialectical movement. In this context, see Gayatri Spivak's reading of Hegel and the native informant in *A Critique of Postcolonial Reason*, 37-67.

2. Animals in Looking-Glass World

Fables of Überhumanism and Posthumanism in Heidegger and Nietzsche

'—then you don't like all insects?' the Gnat went on, as quietly as if nothing had happened.
'I like them when they can talk,' Alice said. 'None of them ever talk, where I come from.'
'What sort of insects do you rejoice in, where you come from?' the Gnat inquired.
Lewis Carroll, *Through the Looking-Glass*

Introduction

In Heidegger's *Being and Time*, as we have seen, animals are located more or less by default in the realm of pure negativity. This spectral figure of the animal, however, obviously remains to haunt Heidegger and, just two years later in a seminar entitled *The Fundamental Concepts of Metaphysics: World, Finitude, Solitude* (1929/1930), he devotes almost one-hundred-and-forty pages to a questioning of the 'essence of animality' – a questioning, it should be noted, which presupposes an essential identity common to every nonhuman living being, from chimpanzee to centipede to influenza virus. Along the way, he reiterates the unbridgeable distance between the human-Dasein and the animal in much the same terms as before, asserting that, despite their physical proximity, 'being-with [*Mitsein*] [animals] is not an *existing-with* [*Mitexistieren*], because a dog does not exist but merely lives.'[1]

Such a way as Heidegger embarks upon is thus, as he makes explicit, most certainly not 'an animal kind of way,' but is rather 'a going along with … and yet not' (210). Another way to say this would be that for Heidegger, as we will

---

[1] Martin Heidegger, *The Fundamental Concepts of Metaphysics: World, Finitude, Solitude*, 210; my emphasis. Henceforth cited as FCM.

discover, it is the very proximity of the nonhuman animal that paradoxical-ly functions to instaurate a human (or at least human-Dasein) exceptional-ism. Given the importance of the 'way [*Weg*]' for Heidegger's thinking, such a way of going which explicitly involves *not* going *with* calls for a detailed analysis of its own, but in the present context it is enough to wonder about this uncanny crossing of proximity and distance that makes of every nonhu-man animal irreducibly other. Is this not another crossing which is perhaps a haunting, perhaps even a possession, in that the Dasein would seem to share without sharing its 'there' with a living being who does not exist?

Unusual too is that in *The Fundamental Concepts* Heidegger sets out on the way of a comparative analysis centered upon three guiding theses: the stone is worldless [*weltlos*], the animal is poor-in-world [*weltarm*], the hu-man is world-forming [*weltbildend*].[2] Here, in exploring how this analysis reveals various differences and similarities between Heidegger's existential analytic and traditional metaphysics, I aim to demonstrate how the her-meneutic circle functions within Heidegger's commitment to a 'humanism beyond humanism' as outlined in his 1947 paper, 'Letter on Humanism.' In this, I argue that Heidegger's thinking does indeed break with the traditional metaphysical configurations of the human-animal relation. However, insofar as nonhuman animals are unthinkingly reinscribed as essentially undying, his philosophy nonetheless remains ultimately enclosed within a 'metaphysi-cal anthropocentrism' which, alongside traditional metaphysics, continues to underwrite the industrialized holocaust of animals.

Despite this, I argue in the second half of this chapter that Heidegger's attempt to 'go along' with animals nonetheless better enables us, in turning back, to scent the multiple paths of animals in Friedrich Nietzsche's early essay 'On Truth and Lie in the Extra-Moral Sense' (1873). This short text, I suggest, offers a way for us to think about being with others who do not share our language and who are not mere reflections of ourselves, while at the same time rejecting as illusory the liberal myths of consensus and disclosure. In this, I set off – albeit blindly, as we shall see – along a way to a thinking of inhuman genealogies that speak rather of a primordial, machinic being-with in which invention can only ever be a nonhuman monstrosity.

---

[2] In *Of Spirit: On Heidegger and the Question* (1987), Derrida acutely contends that the median character of Heidegger's animal threatens the order, implementation, and conceptual apparatus of the entire existential analytic. Here, however, I am pursuing a different reading of its ordering dialectic.

I. Fables of origin: Animals in the Mirror

Via the work of biologist Hans Driesch and ethologist Jakob von Uexküll, Heidegger argues in the second part of *The Fundamental Concepts* that non-human animals are excluded from the *worlding* of world as a necessary result of their 'captivation' [*Benommenheit*], which confines them instead within an environment (FCM, 239). In other words, as far as Heidegger's animal is concerned, there can be neither anything *beyond*, nor any differentiation *within*, the 'disinhibiting ring' which marks the absolute limit of her environmental capture. As a result of this essential undifferentiated absorption [*Eingenommenheit*], an animal can therefore never 'have' her own captivation, that is, she can never apprehend her own capture within a set. Because of this, concludes Heidegger, she is thus 'poor-in-world [*weltarm*].'

More importantly for Heidegger, however, is that this conclusion concerning the way of animals serves as the scenery against which the essence of the *human* can thenceforth be disclosed: 'In the end our ... analysis of captivation as the essence of animality provides as it were a suitable background against which the essence of humanity can now be set off' (282). It would seem then, that the analysis of animal environments is undertaken solely in order that the proper essence of 'the human' can be subsequently disclosed through the negation of its negation, that is, through the dialectical disclosing of the essence of *world*. Such a methodology thus presupposes a categorical and teleological human-animal distinction.

Setting off from the animal then, Heidegger contends that the condition of possibility of worlding is the 'having' of captivation as such. Hidden in this apparently simple gesture, however, is the award of *ontological difference* to human animals alone – a gesture with devastating consequences. Put simply, the human differs from the animal insofar as the former can perceive the difference between Being (as existence), and beings (as discrete entities). For Heidegger, this founding distinction consists in the having of 'the 'as'-structure [*die 'als'-Struktur*]' as that which gives to the human alone the ability to apprehend beings as beings and thus, in contrast to the absorbed captivation of the ringed animal, to perceive itself as *an* individuated being. The worlding of world is, quite simply, the wonder that beings *are*. For other animals, however, there can be no discretization but only dissolution. A chimpanzee, for example, can never perceive another chimpanzee *as* another chimpanzee (or *as* a non-chimpanzee), nor can she cognize water *as* water, *as* a liquid that quenches thirst, nor recognize her mother *as* her mother. Moreover, the apprehension of ontological difference is at once the apprehension of *fini-*

tude, that is to say, of the possibility of *not being*. Hence, the having of 'the "as"-structure' is fundamental to the possibility of authentic existence insofar as, for Heidegger, this consists of the existential projection of the Dasein's ownmost being-toward-death [*eigenst Sein zum Tode*].

We can thus see how, in negating the 'poor' ringed animal as essentially lacking the revelation that beings are, Heidegger is thus free to posit the Dasein, whom we can now positively identify as the human, as that which 'is' closest to Being, and thus reserve for it alone the possibility of authentic existence. It is here then, with the capacity to apprehend something *as* something, that Heidegger draws the line between the human-Dasein and the nonhuman animal, a line that permits neither the possibility of a human animal nor that of a nonhuman Dasein. For as long as such a divide remains unquestioned, Heidegger's discourse remains safely within the metaphysical enclosure that is humanism.

However, the poverty [*Armut*] attributed by Heidegger to nonhuman animals raises an immediate problem. Given the *essential* withholding from the animal of the apprehension that beings *are*, it is clear that this apparent 'poverty' can be a 'deprivation' [*Entbehrung*] only when viewed from the perspective of the human, and is thus, in truth, neither poverty nor privation. This, as Heidegger himself points out, would appear to disallow the positing of the tripartite thesis (the stone is worldless, the animal is poor-in-world, the human is world-forming) from the first, insofar as such an essential characterization is in fact conceived only in comparison with man and 'not drawn from animality itself and maintained within the limits of animality' (270).

Curiously, Heidegger does not object to this charge: to imagine otherwise, he says, is perhaps the privilege only of poets (271). Is Heidegger thus staking a claim to philosophical poetry in opposition to the dialectic? Rather than objecting to the objection, Heidegger sets out instead to '*weaken*' [abschwächen] it, to set about removing its force [seine *Entkräftung*] (270). Somewhat paradoxically, he achieves this by *affirming* it. While the perhaps unassailable charge remains, he argues, it nevertheless '*surely suffices*' that his admittedly problematic thesis has nonetheless 'led us to our destination in a *practical* fashion' (272, emphasis added). Let us defer our objection, he suggests, because '*[i]n spite of everything* it has brought us closer ...' (272, emphasis added). We have found our way, in other words, because the essence of animality as captivated and thus poor-in-world – a thesis 'which follows only if the animal is regarded in comparison with humanity' (271) – serves us in a pragmatic fashion as the 'negative' by which our own 'positive ... proper essence has constantly emerged in contrast' (272).

Here, however, there is no talk of dialectical sublation, no labor of the negative in what is only – as Heidegger repeatedly makes explicit – a *comparative* examination. It is rather the case, I will argue, that the animal in Heidegger's discourse is less a negative to be negated than a mirror which reflects only the essence of being-human which being-human itself renders invisible. Within such a mirror 'we humans' will always find ourselves, but without ever disclosing – if indeed such a disclosure is possible – the essence of animality.[3]

Building frames and booking passage

As is well known, Heidegger explicitly seeks to position his own discourse on the far side of the closure of metaphysics, and thus, as he makes clear in the 'Letter on Humanism' (1947), outside of any traditional humanist expropriation:

> Are we really on the right track toward the essence of man as long as we set *him off* as one living creature among others in contrast to plants, beasts, and God? ... [W]e must be clear on this point, that when we do this we abandon man to the essential realm of *animalitas* even if we do not equate him with beasts but attribute a specific difference to him. ... Such positing is the manner of metaphysics. But then the essence of man is too little heeded and *not thought in its origin*, the essential provenance that is always the essential future for historical mankind. Metaphysics thinks of man on the basis of *animalitas* and does not think in the direction of his *humanitas* (227, my emphasis).

In order to understand the distance from metaphysics claimed by Heidegger, we must first recognize the two dominant metaphysical configurations that, since the beginnings of the Christian era in the West, have shaped the conception of the human-animal relation, and which continue to do so today.[4] Together, these twinned configurations make up what in the previous chapter I termed the *humanist paralogism*.[5] In the first configuration (exemplified previously by Blanchot), the genesis of the human is predicated upon the

---

[3] Such captivity is both echoed and complicated by French psychoanalyst Jacques Lacan's capture of animals in the mirror (stage). See for example 'The mirror stage as formative of the function of the I' in Lacan, *Écrits: A Selection*, trans. Alan Sheridan (London: Routledge, 1995), 1-7.

[4] In *Of Jews and Animals* (113-118), philosopher Andrew Benjamin provides an excellent analysis of these two importantly different determinations, an analysis which in large measure helped to clarify my own understanding of the humanist paralogism.

[5] Following Immanuel Kant, the term *paralogism* refers here to a fallacious inference as regards the form of a syllogism. On this, see Kant, *Critique of Pure Reason*, A341/B399.

death or nonexistence of the animal, thus marking an absolute break between human and nonhuman being; whereas, in the second, the human remains in a constant struggle with his or her own animality, an animality that must be repeatedly overcome in being-human. As a result, and regardless of whether the break is absolute or iterated, in every instance 'the human' is thus defined in *contrast* to other animals and at once as ontologically *incomparable* – a fine example of what Freud calls kettle logic. Moreover, insofar as both configurations define the nonhuman animal by what he or she lacks within a teleological dialectic, every nonhuman animal is paradoxically determined *only* as that which the human transcends, that is, as incomplete and thus *sub*human, while nonetheless absolutely, incomparably other. Such is the contradictory position that, thickly sandwiched between Olympian metamorphoses and Nietzschean becomings, the metaphysical tradition has forced nonhuman animals to occupy, and which Heidegger sets out to escape.

Given what I have argued above, however, it would seem at first glance that Heidegger has failed in this escape attempt insofar as he has indeed set off man in contrast to 'beasts' – precisely the argument levelled at Heidegger by philosopher Giorgio Agamben, as we shall see. But this is *not* to say, however, that Heidegger has therefore 'abandoned' man to the essential realm of *animalitas*, that is, to the realm of 'merely' living creatures. The opposite is in fact the case: Heidegger essentially abandons *animalitas* in order to think the essence of man. We ourselves, as Heidegger says, 'have also been in view all the time' (FCM, 272).

At this point it is helpful to return to Heidegger's comment which serves as a coda to his analysis of the animal: 'In the end [*Am Ende*],' he states, 'our earlier analysis of captivation as the essence of animality provides as it were [*gleichsam*] a suitable [*geeignete*] background against which the essence of humanity can now be set off [*abheben*]' (282). Any reading of the Heideggerian animal is forced to negotiate around these words, occurring as they do just prior to the formal interpretation of the 'as'-structure. Knowing now that, 'in the end,' there can be no sublation, no laboring negative, we thus find here only a hesitant aestheticism regarding the suitability or fittingness [*geeignete*] of the background which is – albeit prefaced by the so to speak 'innocent' qualification 'as it were' [*gleichsam*] – *provided* by the animal.

Against the background of the animal then, the setting off of the human is thus doubled. In the first place, the human 'stands out,' set off [*abheben*] from a background animality that serves to focus attention whilst harmonizing with its object, like a setting that displays a jewel to best effect. In the second, the animal provides the point of departure from which the Dasein might set off along the way that is proper to the human. It is, in other words, to take off [*abheben*] from the animal and, in so doing, withdraw her value [*abheben*] in constituting the proper economy of man. Heidegger is thus drawing a very different kind of line, that of an organizational frame which, like that enclosing a painting, negotiates with both sides in order to establish and delineate its focus. Moreover, as we shall see, this frame is at once a boundary wall, the determined limit of which is rendered invisible by its mirrored surface and which, while appearing to open up the space of 'the animal,' in fact serves to enclose 'the human' within an infinitely regressive image of itself.

Hence, we can begin to understand Heidegger's insistence that the correctness or otherwise of his claim for an essential poverty on the part of nonhuman animals must paradoxically await the disclosure of the essence of human worlding. Only then, writes Heidegger, might one finally 'understand the animal's not-having of world as a *deprivation after all*' (272).

Heidegger is thus booking a return passage, a circling back to the animal such as is available *only from within* the human world, and he does so in order legitimate in retrospect the posited essence of animality which 'founded' that world. For this reason we humans have been in view all the time, 'whether we wanted to be or not, although not in the form of some arbitrary and contingent self-observation or in the form of some traditional definition of man' (272). In a gesture familiar from *Being and Time*, Heidegger thus sites his discourse outside both the human sciences (represented by Driesch and von Uexküll) and traditional metaphysics. In this, he claims for himself an absolute distance from discourses which, on the one hand, 'abandon' the human to animal physiology and, on the other, from those which posit the human as dependent upon the dialectical negation of the animal. Heidegger is thus claiming, despite the familiar, all too human attribution of ontological privation common to the existential and the metaphysical, to have set off along a different way. Whether this in fact brings us any closer to a thinking encounter with animals, however, still remains to be thought.

Turning circles with Saint Paul

As readers of Heidegger will no doubt have recognized, this other way of thinking is through the turning of the hermeneutic circle that is the existential analytic itself. In *Being and Time*, Heidegger claims that this circle of understanding is not, however, that through which any random kind of knowledge operates. Rather, the hermeneutic circle is 'the expression of the existential *fore-structure* of Dasein itself' within which is hidden 'a positive possibility of the most primordial kind of knowing' (195). It is this privileged position within the circle, Heidegger continues, which determines that, of all the beings-in-the-world, only the Dasein has the '*possibility* of existence,' thus awarding it 'ontological priority over every other entity' (62).

Hence, according to Heidegger, what both metaphysics and the human sciences miss is that for the Dasein, as the sole entity for whom being-in-the-world belongs essentially, an understanding of Being necessarily 'pertains with equal primordiality both to an understanding of something like a "world," and to the understanding of the Being of those entities [such as other animals] which become accessible within the world' (33). With this statement, we can understand why, in his subsequent lecture course, Heidegger passes through 'the essence of animality' in order to disclose 'something like a "world",' and why contemporary biology provides the requisite point of departure. As we know, for Heidegger the movement of the hermeneutic circle, irrespective of what knowledge operates within it, always expresses the fore-structure of the Dasein as the sole entity with a relation to Being. Thus, he insists further, even if 'an ontology takes for its theme entities whose character of Being is other than that of Dasein,' it nonetheless always has its 'foundation and motivation in Dasein's own ontical structure, in which a pre-ontological understanding of Being is comprised as a definite characteristic' (33). The real question of other beings, in other words, is always the Dasein.

To summarize, it is the Dasein's privileged relation to Being that retrospectively legitimates the essential poverty of animality against which the understanding of the Dasein emerges. By contrast, the notion of 'the animal' as it is constituted within the discipline of biology for example, is rather a superficial 'empty form,' insofar as its founding and motivating sources have being detached from it. In short, the animal of biology is simply 'a free-floating thesis' that remains to be secured by 'the proper method' that is its turn through the hermeneutic circle (61). Again, Heidegger insists that such a turn is indifferent to its apparent object ('the animal,' in this case), remaining instead always within the orbit of the human-Dasein. Philosophy, he writes, 'takes its departure from the hermeneutic of Dasein, which, as an analytic of *existence*, has made fast the guiding-line for all philosophical inquiry at the point where it *arises* and to which it *returns*' (62). The animals of biology and ethology are thus merely 'everyday' points of departure, set forms from which, and in comparison with, Heidegger's existential analysis can 'set off' in search of the authentic human-Dasein to which it will always return.

The way that takes us through the 'essence of animality' such as proposed by Heidegger in *The Fundamental Concepts of Metaphysics*, must thus be understood solely in terms of an ontical departure point that sets the stage for an ontological understanding of the human-Dasein. While indeed *going along with* nonhuman beings, such a passage or way, it should by now be clear, never in fact encounters any other animals whatsoever.

The most immediate problem here concerns this apparent 'fact' that nonhuman animals are without the 'as'-structure, which is simply *assumed* by Heidegger from the very beginning of *Being and Time* – an assumption that is inevitable, given the indissociability of language, Being, and human privilege that is fundamental to his thinking during this period.[6] However, there is little or no evidence for assuming that other animals do not relate to other beings *as* beings. Indeed, nonhuman animals give every demonstration imaginable of doing just that. Put simply, Heidegger's thinking is stymied by the very metaphysical tradition he claims to escape. That is, it is the unthought fixity inhering in the concept of *language* that prevents Heidegger from breaking new ground insofar as he is unable, despite having posited the inseparability of language and Being (and thus liberating the former from its constricting identity with the *word*), to think language apart from the human. It is, however, only once we commit to actually thinking the formative conjunction of language and being – an articulation in which the identity of the language user is also in process of transformation – that we gain access to the encounter understood as the truth of what arrives.

Ultimately, Heidegger grounds his reiteration of human exceptionalism on perhaps the most traditional and 'common sense' metaphysical definition of all: that nonhuman animals are without language and thus essentially condemned to the capture of 'instinctual drivenness' (FCM, 237). Moreover, he in fact extends this traditional definition in denying even a *world* to nonhuman animals. Indeed, that Heidegger chooses to illustrate this not with a poet, but with Saint Paul, should certainly give pause to all poor creatures deprived of voice along the way. It is difficult too, not to hear in this silencing Heidegger's infamous attribution just five years later of an exclusive linguistic privilege, and thus a privileged relation to Being, to those who inhabit the *German* language alone.[7] Here too, 'others' are rendered dumb in a further restriction of access to both world and destiny.

---

[6] On this, see Heidegger's recapitulation in *On the Way to Language*, 30.

[7] See Heidegger's *An Introduction to Metaphysics*, first published in Germany in 1935.

Anthropos as jewel and fable

Despite this, Heidegger's notion of worlding, once stripped of its anthropo-centric constraints, nonetheless offers a way beyond the humanist enclosure. In order to understand this, it is helpful to begin with the reading of the Heideggerian animal offered by Giorgio Agamben in *The Open: Man and Animal* (2002), a reading that will provide both a counterpoint and our own point of departure.

Seeking to problematize Heidegger's claim to have moved beyond 'the manner of metaphysics', Agamben's reading rests upon the claim that what Heidegger terms *profound boredom* – the event, as we shall see, in which the Dasein experiences the wonder that beings *are* – is in fact 'the metaphysical operator in which the passage from poverty-in-world to world, from ani-mal environment to human world, is realized' (*The Open,* 68). This in turn has important consequences for Agamben's reading. While we will consider the experience of boredom as Heidegger understands it in detail shortly, we can nonetheless already understand Agamben's argument that, if profound boredom does indeed mark the evolutional and teleological *passage* from the animal to the Dasein, then it can only be that the 'jewel set at the center of the human world and its *Lichtung* [clearing] is nothing but animal captivation' (68). In other words, according to Agamben, the wonder that beings *are* is simply the grasping of 'the "essential disruption" that occurs in the living be-ing from its being exposed in a nonrevelation' (68). Hence, he continues, the 'irresolvable struggle … between disconcealment and concealment, which defines the human world, is the internal struggle between man and animal' (69). As a result, concludes Agamben, insofar as humanity comes into being only through 'a suspension of animality', one which moreover must 'keep itself open to the closedness of animality', Heidegger necessarily fails in his attempt to 'escape the metaphysical primacy of *animalitas*' in grasping the essence of man (73).

In reaching this conclusion, however, there occurs an unremarked shift-ing of terms that takes place precisely at the moment Agamben introduces the notion of *passage*. Immediately following the description of profound boredom as 'the metaphysical operator' through which the passage from an-imal environment to human world is realized, Agamben asserts that 'at issue here is nothing less than anthropogenesis, the becoming Da-sein of living man' (68). Here, as we shall see, Agamben's reading is only partially correct. While it is indeed the case that, by way of the event of profound boredom, the 'having' of captivation as such is 'nothing less than anthropogenesis, the becoming Da-sein, this is *not*, and nor can it ever be, the *becoming* 'of living man' in the sense of the founding passage from the 'merely' living to the properly human-Dasein – a passage which thus passes in silence over the nonlocalisable moment between the still-animal and the already-Dasein, and between the no-longer animal and the not-yet human.

In order to appreciate the stakes of Agamben's reading, it is necessary to recall the two dominant metaphysical configurations of the human-animal relation. As we know, in the first the genesis of the human depends upon the death or nonexistence of the animal, whereas in the second the human comes into being only by repeatedly overcoming his or her own animality. Here, I will argue, Heidegger's signal attempt to think *humanitas* outside of just this metaphysical tradition is taken by Agamben and erroneously placed back within the second configuration. This should perhaps not surprise us too much, however, in that this same configuration of constant struggle is common not only to what Agamben terms the modern anthropological machine, but also to Agamben's own notion of a sacred community prior to the positing of identity.[8]

As I have argued, becoming-Dasein, that is, the Dasein 'thought in its origin,' remains for Heidegger a thinking solely in the direction of *humanitas*, insofar as the background from which he 'sets off' is not that which is preserved and annihilated in the animal's being raised up to the human, nor is it that which grounds the Dasein like its shadowy sub-form. In fact, such a setting-off marks out Heidegger's discourse on anthropogenesis rather as a speculative thesis, one which offers itself as a fantastic hypothesis or, better, 'as [if] it were' a *fable*. It is a fable, moreover, which, true to the form, has already sacrificed the animal to its very taking place.

We recall that, according to Heidegger, insofar as nonhuman animals are captivated [*benommen*] within an environment, the possibility of apprehending something *as* something is therefore withheld [*genommen*]. This possibility, however, is not merely withheld in the historically contingent here and now, but is for Heidegger 'withheld in the sense that such a possibility is "not given at all"' (FCM 247). The possibility of having the 'as'-structure is,

---

[8] The modern anthropological machine clearly depends upon this second configuration insofar as it produces 'bare life' by 'excluding as not (yet) human an already human being from itself, that is, by animalising the human, by isolating the nonhuman within the human … the animal separated within the human body itself' (Agamben, *The Open*, 37). Agamben's utopian community prior to identity, meanwhile, in simply inverting the dystopian machinic production of bare life, necessarily remains caught within the same economy. On this, see also Andrew Benjamin, *Of Jews and Animals*, 113-129.

in short, *a priori* withheld from the animal. As a result, what is most proper to the nonhuman animal is her inability to disclose the undisconcealed *as* undisconcealed, and at once therefore, neither can she ever apprehend concealedness which, insofar as it presupposes its opposite, remains just as essentially unavailable. Consequently, an animal can never *become* the Dasein, there being *a priori* no possible passage between animal and human.

Hence, whereas for Agamben animality abruptly comes to *signify* concealment, making of the struggle between disconcealment and concealment the struggle between human and animal, in fact the latter can be positioned at neither pole. As essentially without relation, there can be no dialectical teleology, no possible negation of the negation of the animal. Instead, there is only an abyss that marks *out* 'the animal' at the limit of thinking, of thinking the Dasein, and of thinking finitude. Thus, while Agamben seeks to criticize Heidegger for unwittingly reformulating the moment of anthropogenesis as the bridge between animal and human, in fact there can be no crossing, no passage, and no irresolvable struggle. There is, in short, no *between* of the animal and the human for Heidegger.

As a result, nonhuman animals remain for Heidegger absolutely other, beyond that which gives itself as food for thought and, as such, just as essentially excluded from concealment and disconcealment as they are from propriety and authenticity. Instead, the reiterated yet irresolvable conflict between concealment and disconcealment is nothing other than the struggle between the impropriety of the 'everyday' being-Dasein and the propriety of authentic *becoming*-Dasein, as initially proposed by Heidegger in *Being and Time*.

In other words, at one pole we find being-Dasein understood in the sense of a uniquely human *captivation*. Such is the habitual absorption in the idle chatter and facile opinions of 'the They' [*das Man*] that, concealing the world behind sham untruths, serve only to bring 'tranquillized self-assurance' into the inauthentic everydayness [*Alltäglichkeit*] of the human-Dasein (*Being and Time*, 233). Such, writes Heidegger, is being-there [*Dasein*] as facticity [*Faktizität*] and falling [*Verfallen*]. At the other pole, becoming-Dasein is rather the 'truth' of existential projection, the taking place of the *possibility* of authentic Being-toward-death, the taking-place of the 'having' of the 'as' which Heidegger in *The Fundamental Concepts* identifies with the genesis of Man in a moment of profound boredom. In this moment, beings as a whole disclose themselves *as* withdrawn, *as* concealed, in what is a truly shattering experience insofar as the Dasein ultimately finds itself '*face to face* with the "nothing" of the possible impossibility of its existence' (*Being and Time*,

310). Shocked thus from its captivation in the everyday, the angst-ridden human-Dasein thereafter finds itself 'face to face with the possibility of being itself' (311).

In an important move, however, Heidegger argues that both the proper and the improper modes of the Dasein are 'equiprimordial', that is, the three modes – existence, facticity, and falling – are ontologically co-constitutive of the Dasein. Indeed, Heidegger rightly goes further, arguing that the proper is thus only ever a modification of impropriety, the truth always a modification of untruth, disconcealment always a modification of concealment. In this way, the constitutive distinction between concealment and disconcealment is taken up and affirmed by Heidegger from within, overcoming its opposition and rendering it transformative.

Becoming and bodying

Despite this crucial transformation of the proper-improper binary, non-human animals, it is clear, *essentially* have no place in this struggle. Rather than a conflict between *humanitas* and *animalitas*, Heidegger puts forward a thesis which can only ever concern an entirely human struggle. The question thus remains: where does this leave the animal? Before we can answer this, we must first consider how, exactly, the human-Dasein arrives to take its unique place in the world.

Whereas Agamben, in mistakenly identifying the animal with the blindness of the everyday, wishes to 'restore to the closed, to the earth, and to *lēthē* their proper name of "animal" and "simply living being"' (*The Open*, 73), in fact the apprehension of the closed is rather *the sense of that which exceeds sense*. This is hugely important. What gives the Dasein to apprehend that beings *are* is their appearing *as* closed or *as* concealed in the obdurate materiality of their withdrawal. In other words, the withdrawal into undisclosed materiality constitutes the taking place of beings *as* such, a withdrawal producing *only* the sense of something *as* concealed, that is, producing the *sense* that some being is *without sense*. For Heidegger, it is here, and nowhere else, that the essence of man is finally 'thought in its origin'. Only here, in a moment of profound boredom, does the Dasein arrive in a world of beings that simply *are* in the obdurate materiality of their withdrawal.

Given that such a genesis depends upon a moment of 'affective manifestness' [*Offenbarkeit*] during which beings are sensed *as* concealed, the human-Dasein thus finds itself already 'in' language at its origin. This is because, when beings are apprehended as beings, the sense of that which withdraws has necessarily already *taken* place, that is, the withdrawal of meaning has already become meaningful in its being apprehended, and in the subsequent wonder of the fact that beings *are* we are thus already anxiously constituted within infinitely entangled structures of meaning. The apprehension that beings *are* is, in other words, necessarily a singular, historically situated event. The Dasein, in short, is *thrown* into a world that precedes it.

We get some sense of this in Heidegger's notions of 'mood' [*die Stimmung*] and 'attunement' [*die Gestimmtheit*] which, in the decade following *Being and Time*, acquire a robust materiality that goes far beyond any limited conception of the organism. Every feeling, argues Heidegger in the first of his lectures on Nietzsche in 1936, 'is an embodiment attuned in this or that way, a mood that embodies in this or that way' (Nietzsche, I:100). Every attunement, moreover,

> always just as essentially has a feeling for beings as a whole, every bodily state involves some way in which the things around us and the people with us lay a claim on us or do not do so. … Mood is precisely the basic way in which we are *outside* ourselves. But that is the way we are essentially and constantly (99).

In the third of the Nietzsche lectures two years later, Heidegger further clarifies this notion by way of a move from *embodiment* [*das Leiben*] to *bodying* [*das Leibende*]. This grammatical shift serves to highlight the fact that 'the body' [*der Leib*] refers not to its apparent 'encapsulation' within the physical mass of the organism, but rather to 'a stream of life' understood as transmission and passage simultaneously (Nietzsche, III:79). As a result, it becomes possible to re-read the above indented citation thus: every laying claim of *sense*, every wash and tunnel, every drift and detain that is at once passage and transmission in both directions, is a bodying in this way or in that way, a being-outside that singularly bodies. While I will return to this notion of bodying later, for the moment it suffices simply to note that attunement never refers to a self-same being that subsequently exposes itself, but rather names a co-constitutive relation that depends *a priori* upon being-exposed.

Returning to our question, the genesis of the human-Dasein thus has as its condition a co-constitutive exposing of being. Rather than giving to apprehension the closedness of animality, as Agamben claims, the jewel of authentic becoming is to be found in the unexpected arrival of a truly original com-position; an event the unpredictability and originality of which is marked by the withdrawal of sense *as such*. It is this shattering moment of genesis, and this alone, which *a priori* remains to interrupt the Dasein's habitual absorption within the inauthenticity of the everyday.

Heidegger's anthropo-magical mirror

Despite all apparent evidence to the contrary therefore, in *The Fundamental Concepts* just as in *Being and Time*, Heidegger does not in fact think *animals* at all. Ultimately, he proposes only an extended *fable*, a fabulous sacrificial myth that focuses upon the origins of humanity to the exclusion of all else. While it is indeed inevitable, writes Heidegger, that in our questioning we 'end up talking *as if* [emphasis added] that which the animal relates to and the manner in which it [*sic*] does so were some being,' in truth some such being can only ever be a *human* being (FCM, 255). In *The Fundamental Concepts*, that is to say, Heidegger is, in the end, always talking about nonhuman animals *as if* they were human animals. He *anthropomorphizes* them, in short, forcing their infinitely diverse ways of being into the petrified form of a fable with a violence that exceeds even that of Procrustes.

Traditionally dealing with origins, the generic fable is, by definition, a pedagogic mirror within which 'we' humans, reflected in an exemplary animal caricature, are expected to recognize our own 'proper' mode of being. Heidegger's speculative thesis can thus be understood as the staging of a fabulous drama, one which enacts, *as if* in a mirror, the rigorously anthropocentric struggle between *being* the Dasein with its everyday *demise* [*ableben*] and *becoming* the Dasein which has *dying* for its way of Being (*Being and Time*, 291).

It remains to ask, however, 'who' or 'what' precedes the coming into being of the human-Dasein? Clearly, it can be neither a nonhuman animal nor a worldless object, and as such there can *be* no possible site corresponding to the phylogenetic origin of the human-Dasein. In this sense, Heidegger's fable is also an anti-fable, insofar as tales regarding the 'origin of the species' are rendered *a priori* untenable. Rather, argues Heidegger, being, language, and the human-Dasein are 'equiprimordial,' that is, ontologically conterminous. 'The human,' in other words, comes to be, and at once receives its privileged relation to Being, only through being already 'in' language.

Here, we are at last in a position to answer our original question concerning the place and function of 'the animal' within Heidegger's existential analytic, as well as what, if anything, of the nonhuman escapes its fabulous capture. Initially at least, the spectral Heideggerian animal appears as close kin to Blanchot's given that, lacking even the possibility of impossibility, it too finds itself uncannily (non)placed both before and after the world.

Things, however, are slightly more unsettling. Given the animal's sense-less absorption in an undifferentiated environment, what then, asks Heidegger, of the apparent fact that the 'animal's *way of being*, which we call "*life*," is *not without access* [*nicht zugangslos*] to what is around it and about it' (FCM, 198)? The answer, Heidegger assures us, is that appearances are deceptive. Whatever 'not without access' might mean, what it most certainly does *not* mean is access to being as such – the proper preserve of the human-Dasein. So where does that leave the animal? According to Heidegger, nowhere at all. Such a 'not without access' is, he argues, rather only a '*seeming* to have access', a 'not-having-in-the-mode-of-having.' It remains essentially the case, in other words, that the animal only '*appears* as a living being [*als seiendes Lebewesen* vorkommt]' (198, emphasis added), and it is this mere 'seeming *like*' or 'appearing *as*' which gives rise to the mistaken claim that nonhuman animals too 'have' the 'as'. With this move, Heidegger thus writes off every single piece of evidence, now and forever, which might even *suggest* that other animals exist as beings-in-the-world. Indeed, his reference to an animal appearing *as* a living being simultaneously illustrates this point: for Heidegger, both the appearing and the mistaken claim are pure anthropo-morphisms, a necessarily human 'talking as if' which transforms all other animals into anthropo-magical mirrors that only ever reflect an image of the human-Dasein.

Put simply, insofar as they are unable to differentiate beings *as* beings, nonhuman animals thus only *appear* as living beings as a *consequence* of one exceptional animal's 'having' of the 'as'-structure, an exclusive property that subsequently reduces every other being, whether poor elephant or worldless stone, to a dependence upon the existence of the human. It is the human who constitutes other animals as beings, and in this sense the animal must always *come after* the human. Hence, one can now better understand Heidegger's deferral of the disclosure of the essense of animality as something available *only* from within the *human* world. Other than as a ghosted out-line therefore, a phantom individuation through the looking glass that is the human-Dasein, all other beings come into being merely as a frame for the human jewel and to reflect its uncanny brilliance.

Humanism beyond humanism

With this revelation, it now becomes clear how Heidegger's 'decentred exceptionalism' both relates to, and differentiates itself from, the tradition of metaphysical humanism.

On one side, the radical antihumanism of the decentred subject is indeed, and contrary to Agamben's argument, other to the traditional metaphysical definitions of the human. However, its decentring of an exclusively *human* subject serves at the same time to institute the higher, *über*humanism which, in the 'Letter on Humanism,' Heidegger claims is to be found only within the existential analytic, the 'sole implication' of which –

> is that the highest determinations of the essence of man in humanism still do not realize the proper dignity of man. To that extent the thinking in *Being and Time* is against humanism. ... [But] Humanism is opposed because it does not set the *humanitas* of man high enough (233-4).

Heidegger, in other words, does indeed break with the traditional configurations of humanist metaphysics which, insofar as 'the human' depends upon the dialectical exclusion of its 'animalistic ground,' thus mark down every nonhuman animal as incomplete and subhuman. However, insofar as *being* arrives *as such* only with the arriving of the human, thereby excluding the possibility of a founding sublation of animal negativity, the *constitution* of nonhuman animals thereafter finds itself entirely dependent upon the human. It thus becomes clear that Heidegger's existential analytic, while enacting a radical reversal of the movement of dependence-exclusion characteristic of metaphysical humanism, nonetheless remains caught within its economy, as if in a mirror. Entrapped by the conceptual fixity of a tradition that unthinkingly restricts language to the spoken word, Heidegger's fabulous tale thus unwittingly reflects that everyday tradition by reproducing nonhuman animals as 'merely' spectral beings-for-man.[9]

In 'going along with' the metaphysical tradition in denying death to nonhuman beings, Heidegger's überhumanist *a priori* refusal of thinking animals – in every sense – has far-reaching and murderous consequences. For Heidegger, as for both Blanchot and Hegel and in common with Christian and Enlightenment traditions, *nonhuman animals have no death, no possi-*

---

[9] It is not insignificant that Aristotle in the *Politics* infers the new Western concept of 'just war' from the condition that nonhuman animals are solely 'beings-for-man.' In the same context, for Stoics such as Chrysippus all nonhuman animals are also only beings-for-man, from the mice who ensure humans put their things away, to the pigs whose souls serve only to keep them fresh to eat.

bility, and no meaning. They are, in other words, written out in what is an all too familiar, all too human fashion as soulless mechanisms functioning only until they run – or are ran – down. In short, by reiterating the undying figure central to the two dominant configurations of metaphysics, Heidegger reiterates too the hubris of a human exceptionalism which, based upon the surety of absolute superiority, sanctions our doing whatever 'we' like to other animals.[10]

Hence, in its restaging of the eternal animal predicated upon the lack of language, Heidegger's existential analytic in fact reproduces a *symbolic* economy serving the ends of capitalist instrumentalization. It ensures, in other words, that the singular deaths of nonhuman animals, that is, *this* death of *this* (farm, laboratory, or feral) animal, are considered at best epiphenomenal – rendered both symbolically and actually as a fortuitous by-product – and, at worst, a simple impossibility, that is, that such deaths are without meaning and thus literally unthinkable. In this, the otherwise divergent 'posthumanist' philosophies of Blanchot and Heidgger join forces in further underwriting the current, resolutely material global practice of systematic violence and mass murder on a truly unthinkable scale.

In summary then, the figuring of 'the animal' as undying, as found throughout the history of Western philosophy, functions in the last instance to mimetically reproduce as 'natural' the instrumentalization of nonhuman animals, thus constituting the ideological support of Capital's waging of a massively unequal war on other animals.

On the far side of the looking-glass

This, however, is not necessarily the end of Heidegger's 'just so' story. Insofar as nonhuman animals are for the Dasein only ever reflections of itself, animals 'in themselves' necessarily remain, in the strongest sense, beyond the grasping of human cognition. The human-Dasein, in other words, inevitably yet mistakenly projects its own way of being onto other animals in such a way as to *essentially* blind itself to their differing ways of life. This, suggests Heidegger, 'compels us to the thesis [*nötigt zu der These*] that the *essence of life is accessible only through a destructive observation* [*Wesen des Lebens nur im Sinne einer abbauenden Betrachtung zugänglich ist*]' (FCM, 255). Nonethe-

---

[10] The fact that Heidegger, as we will see in a subsequent chapter, will later suggest that during the Shoah Jews were treated just as nonhuman animals are treated by modern industrial agriculture thus raises a number of deeply unsettling questions regarding Heidegger's own relation to National Socialism.

less, adds Heidegger in what is an extremely important coda, this 'does not mean that life is something inferior or that it is at a lower level in comparison with human Dasein. On the contrary, life is a domain that possesses a wealth of being-open [*Offenseins*] of which the human world may know nothing at all' (255, trans. modified).

Even Heidegger, in other words, is compelled to acknowledge that, on the far side of the rupture dividing man from animal, life dwells in an openness whose wealth is perhaps entirely unknown from within a world inhabited by the human alone. It is this openness that, in the infinite ways of being-with other animals, remains to be differently thought. In the second half of this chapter, I aim to do precisely that by way of the inextricability of sense and *memory* in Nietzsche's philosophy. Along the way, Heidegger's crucial notion of anthropogenesis will be stripped of its anthropocentric and metaphysical constraints, and forced thereafter to cede both place and privilege to the transformative encounter of zoo-genesis.

II. Fables without Origin: Animals in the World

Turning to Nietzsche, a turning that retains the senses of both circle and dialogue throughout, enables us to gain a glimpse of what it might mean to think the infinite ways of being animal and the destructive observation *together*, rather than as mutually exclusive conditions.[11] Fundamental to this thinking together is a refusal to efface the deaths of nonhuman animals, a refusal that necessarily engages us in thinking encounters shared between any number of animals thrown in the world *in and of language.*

This is not to suggest, however, a (slightly or greatly) more inclusive, yet nonetheless homogeneous, category of beings. Any such delimitation would necessarily remain dependent upon that which it excludes, and would thus already be undone by the nonlocalisable moment of its fracture or fault-line. In fact, the opposite is the case. Just as it is not possible to efface the threshold of nonhuman-human difference by placing (and thus excluding) animals

---

[11] The huge nonhuman animal population of Nietzsche's texts, all those gnats, spiders and worms, the entire bestiary that attends Zarathustra's under-going, the birds that soar above and the blond beast that stalks throughout, has inspired an equally huge variety of interpretations. Notable examples include Heidegger's 'Zarathustra's Animals' in the second volume of *Nietzsche*; Margot Norris, *Beasts of the Modern Imagination: Darwin, Nietzsche, Kafka, Ernst, and Lawrence* (1985); Vanessa Lemm, *Nietzsche's Animal Philosophy* (2009); and Christa D. Acampora & Ralph Acampora, eds. *A Nietzschean Bestiary: Becoming Animal Beyond Docile and Brutal* (2004).

as 'before' the taking place of language according to some kind of genetic, evolutionary timescale, neither is it possible, any more than it is advisable, to evade or to efface differences *between* animals, be they human and/or non-human, in the sharing of that very taking place in and of language.

A body, as Heidegger argues, is never a pre-existing substance that subsequently encounters the world. Rather, in its attunedness that is the essential and constant laying claim of sense, a body 'is' always a being-outside that singularly *bodies*. In this, I will argue, *every* so-called body, irrespective of whether it is commonly called 'animal' or commonly called 'human,' is abysmally situated in relation. To body, in other words, is to be exposed together across sense, meaning, and world. Furthermore, creation in its true sense, as we shall see, can only ever take place by way of the essential indiscernability – the 'systematic madness' – of one bodying to an other.

Curative blinding

Working through Nietzsche's well-known but vertiginously productive 1873 essay, 'On Truth and Lie in the Extra-Moral Sense [*Über Wahrheit und Lüge im aussermoralischen Sinne*],'[12] we discover that, like Blanchot, Nietzsche calls 'image' that originary forgetting which marks the having taken-place of language. Nietzsche's 'image,' however, is explicitly *non*anthropocentric, insofar as 'language' refers here to the production of *sense* in general. In other words, Nietzsche enlarges the notion of language to include the *tropological* functioning of perception and affection. Hence, he argues, the experience of sensation is a *translation* [*übertragung*] within a *non*necessary, and thus creative or aesthetic, relationship.

'To begin with,' writes Nietzsche, 'a nerve stimulus is transferred [or translated, *übertragen*] into an image [*Bild*]' (82). Here then, and right at the beginning, Nietzsche thus makes clear that 'image' refers neither solely to *human* perception nor solely to *visual* perception. Rather, any and all perception and affection, any filtering of information whatsoever, is already a produced image, that is, always a translation.[13] Such is the image that 'is' the touch of the sun's warmth, that 'is' the smell of honey, or that 'is' the sound of thunder, and so on. Moreover, given that every translation necessitates an

---

[12] Henceforth cited in the text as TL.

[13] In this context, see also Jakob von Uexküll, *A Foray into the Worlds of Animals and Humans with A Theory of Meaning*, trans. Joseph D. O'Neil (Minneapolis & London: University of Minnesota Press, 2010), 147ff.

overleaping [*überspringen*] from one sphere into a second, absolutely heterogeneous sphere, every image is therefore a 'perceptual *metaphor*' [*die anschaulichen* Metaphern]. The image, put simply, is the *vehicle* to the stimuli's *tenor*.

More than this, however, the inescapability of this discontinuity of domains necessarily makes every perceptual metaphor inadequate, 'a *stammering* translation into a completely foreign tongue' (86). The metaphoric sense-image, in other words, is a deciphering and at once a ciphering which cannot help but truncate, mutilate, and make monstrous. Nothing less than a material laying claim *in* and *as* which a body comes into being, the sense-image is thus a vehicle ever lost to an errant transmission, to *dissemination*.

All sensitive beings can thus be said to possess only discontinuous metaphors *of* physical responses, responses which themselves mark the taking place of founding material *encounters*. Hence, insofar as a body comes into being only in and as a metaphorical vehicle marking the *originary being-with* of an encounter that necessarily escapes it, it thus follows that the Kantian 'thing in itself', which Nietzsche describes as 'what the pure truth, apart from any of its consequences, would be' (82), is necessarily an illusion.[14] Furthermore, given that the originary encounter by definition can neither be perceived nor represented, every image, every sense by which (a) being is outside itself, is thus not only a metaphor, but also already an *abuse* of metaphor, insofar as its analogy remains necessarily incomplete. For Nietzsche then, language in its broadest sense is the operation of *catachresis*.[15]

Never in a relation to or of truth therefore, the sense-image is, 'at most', 'an *aesthetic* relation or disposition' [*ein ästhetisches Verhalten*] (86). As well as deconstructing the Platonic distinction between the sensible [*aisthēton*] and the intelligible [*noēton*], this 'aesthetic disposition' can never, given the impossibility of independently existing entities, be that of a subject-object relation. Similarly, it follows that that which appears to us simply as 'our' body, that is, the sense *of* a body, as well as the sense *of* the self, of self-aware-

---

[14] See also *On the Genealogy of Morals*, 1:13.

[15] On metaphor in Nietzsche, important texts include Sarah Kofman's now canonical *Nietzsche and Metaphor* (1972); Philippe Lacoue-Labarthe, *The Subject of Philosophy* (1979); and Andrzej Warminski's 'Prefatory Postscript: Interpretation and Reading' in *Readings in Interpretation: Hölderlin, Hegel, Heidegger* (1987). For texts which take 'On Truth and Lie' as their focus, see also Paul de Man 'Rhetoric of Tropes (Nietzsche)' in *Allegories of Reading: Figural Language in Rousseau, Nietzsche, Rilke, and Proust* (1979) and 'Anthropomorphism and Trope in the Lyric' in *The Rhetoric of Romanticism* (1984); Andrzej Warminski 'Towards a Fabulous Reading: Nietzsche's "On Truth and Lie in the Extra-Moral Sense"' (1991); and Jean-Luc Nancy '"Our Probity" On Truth in the Moral Sense in Nietzsche' (1983).

ness, is necessarily founded upon *a priori* infoldings of the outside which already interrupt any such delimitation. Every passion, in other words, being a moment and movement of translation, is thus at once an act of interpretation, just as every action is at once dependent upon a passive infolding of externality. The ek-static production of sense therefore exceeds the modern Cartesian notion of egological 'consciousness,' as well as divesting itself of both anthropocentric and organismic restrictions. Every nonhuman animal too comes into being outside itself and thus, as Nietzsche insists, comes to his or her senses only in and as metaphoric perceptions marking our originary being-with.

Lastly, by illuminating the necessary *tropology* of sense, and thus bringing to the fore an originary *technicity* of life that stands in stark contrast to both biologism and vitalism, Nietzsche irredeemably fractures any secure distinction between the 'natural' and the 'artificial.' In so doing, he discloses the dark machinations of power that blind us to even the most transparent perception. Hence, when describing the movement of translation in *The Birth of Tragedy* (1872), Nietzsche writes of a kind of inverse blinding in which 'the bright image projections' are 'luminous spots to cure eyes damaged by the gruesome night' (67). In this way, Nietzsche, *avant la lettre*, forces us to recognize *ourselves* in the sightlessness of Heidegger's captivated animal, essentially blind when faced with beings we can never apprehend as such. Moreover, by closely following the traces of 'On Truth and Lie,' it soon becomes clear that *any* attempt to draw such a bold (Aristotelian, Cartesian and Heideggerian) dividing line separating animal reaction from human response is ultimately untenable.

This blinding, deafening, benumbing production of perceptual metaphors necessarily places *all* sensitive bodies, that is, bodyings constituted in the translation of originary encounters, always already '*in*' language. We *are*, in and as the transfer – and thus in and as existence – already in and as trope, inhabiting and being-inhabited by machines for generating meaning. Obviously, however, the various praxes of sense-production are not reducible to language understood in the narrow sense of the written and spoken word. Nor is it the case, as we will see, that the 'image' represents a primitive intermediate stage between nerve stimulus and intelligible word-concept. It is *not* the case, in other words, that the image is *not yet* 'language proper,' lacking its teleological fulfillment.[16] As a result, and without erasing difference(s),

---

[16] Hence it is in no way an attempt to attribute degrees of *human* language to *nonhuman* animals, which would be to reiterate precisely the kind of calculated hierarchical thinking in which, given that the criteria is 'which animals are the most human?', the human will always come out on top, followed by a descending scale of (human) value.

Nietzsche neither places 'the animal' in a median position between non-life (understood as such beings that do not translate stimuli into imagery) and being-human (or being-Dasein), nor does he mark out animals for ontological exclusion predicated upon their death or overcoming in the manner of metaphysics.

Eccum sic, absolutely

What then, is at stake in the disposition of the metaphoric image? As we know, the sense-image is a stammering translation of a nerve stimulus, a stimulus that requires as its condition an originary *relation* or encounter. At this point, however, Nietzsche introduces what he calls the *first* image, described as a 'unique and entirely individual original experience' which, insofar as it is 'without equals,' is therefore 'able to elude all classification' (TL, 83, 84-5). This raises an immediate problem, in that the notion of originary technicity would seem to preclude *a priori* the very possibility of an 'original experience' or a 'first' image. Nonetheless, as we shall see now, this elusive experience that Nietzsche calls the 'first' image can only be the perception, that is, the translation, of a *singularity*.

First of all, this original and primary sense-image can never be the perception of a thing-in-itself. In contrast to Kant who argues that there can only be no *access* to things-in-themselves, for Nietzsche, as we know, there *are* no things-in-themselves, but rather only beings constituted through differential relations of force. That said, the 'first' image must therefore be the *im*mediate sense of a given, uniquely situated relation in and as which a body comes into being. In other words, its 'entirely individual original experience' is the perception-translation of being *as such*, that is, of being *such* that it is only *as* it is. Given the excessive and discontinuous transport of metaphor that defines the 'as'-structure for Nietzsche, however, how could such a primary, immediate perception even be possible?

In order to answer this question, it is necessary to cognize the singular event of being *as such* as a taking place of and in *language*. In *The Coming Community* (1990), Giorgio Agamben offers a very fine description of this event:

> I am never *this* or *that* [substance], but always *such, thus. Eccum sic*: absolutely. Not possession but limit, not presupposition but exposure. ... Whereas real predicates express relationships within language, exposure is pure relationship with language itself, with its taking-place. It is what happens to something (or

more precisely, to the taking-place of something) by the very fact of being in relation to language, the fact of being-called [into language]. ... Existence as exposure is the being-*as* of a *such*. ... The *such* does not presuppose the *as*; it exposes
it, it is its taking-place. ... The *as* does not suppose the *such*; it is its exposure, its
being pure exteriority (97-8).

The primary, immediate perception of the as such that is Nietzsche's 'first'
image thus refers to *a uniquely situated sense-experience of the taking place
of language*. A taking place which, as we saw with the apprehension of the
closed or the earth in Heidegger, consists of the singular laying claim of obdurate materiality that withdraws in the relation that 'is' being as such.

Despite Nietzsche's apparent claim to the contrary, however, this immediate *relation* can never manifest itself in experience, that is, it can never be
the translative production of an image, insofar as it is precisely this relation
which must escape in its translation into the discontinuous domain of its interpretation, its *sense*. Indeed, Nietzsche insists on this: the X of the original
'acquaintance,' he writes, remains always 'inaccessible and undefinable for us'
(TL, 83). The image, in other words, can only ever mark the *escape* of originary relation, of being *as such*, in its being-sensed; the moment and movement of translation having always already taken place *of* and *in* language.[17]

Put more simply, the originary relation of being as such is that in which
the transfer of *sense* can *take place*. This *taking* place of sense, however, necessarily escapes in its translation, that is, in the *experience* of sense, which has
thus always already *taken* place. Unlike 'language,' with is weight of anthropocentric appropriation, the term 'sense' is useful in this instance because it
serves to render explicit its irreducibility to either the sensible or the intelligible. Rather, in the production of sense as stammering translation, each
always invests the other: an intimate entanglement of sense and sensibility, of
meanings without sense and sense without meaning in an imbrication of the
material and the semiotic that always far exceeds any reduction to the words
spoken by human animals alone.

In this, we are beginning to understand how *all* forms of sense-making
depend upon the installation of *technicity* as and at the origin. As we shall see,
it is this originary technicity of being which renders untenable any further
recourse to the myth of a 'natural' pathic animal communication, and which
ultimately renders unacceptable the murderous ideology of the undying

---

[17] On the unsublatable excess of the always already (no) more 'example of example' that
disarticulates Hegel's reading of sense-certainty, see Andrzej Warminski's 'Reading for
Example: "Sense-Certainty" in Hegel's Phenomenology of Spirit' in *Diacritics* 11 (1981),
83-96.

animal. To understand this, however, we must continue along the trail of Nietzsche's incomparable and unclassifiable 'first' image.

Zoogenesis (1): the whir of technological being

As that which marks our coming into being, all sensitive bodies have thus already fallen away into the metaphoricity of sense, a fall that is also always an emergence, a coming to one's senses and thence to one's 'self'. Moreover, insofar as this by definition involves the taking of something *as* something else, Nietzsche thus argues that the 'as'-structure, rather than being the exclusive property of the human-Dasein, is instead the common condition of *all* forms of sensing, from the sensation of warmth to the scent of a lover, from the compound sense of winter's approach to the anxiety of homelessness.

Staying with Nietzsche's unique 'first' image, while we know this refers to the sensing of being *as* such, and thus of the taking place of language, we also know that the inaccessible X of the originary 'acquaintance' can never itself make sense. Consequently, Nietzsche's primary image can only be a sense – a translation and thus a *remarking* – of the taking place of the 'as' which has necessarily escaped. Here, it is important to recognize that such numerical markings as employed by Nietzsche are *grammatical*, and not genetic.[18] The 'original, unique and individual experience' is, in other words, that alien, uncanny transport that gives a being to apprehend the wonder that beings *are* in the obdurate materiality of their withdrawal. The 'first' image, in other words, refers to the event of *zoo-genesis* in which the creative attunement of Heidegger's 'profound boredom,' rather than belonging to Man alone, is instead an event shared potentially by *every* sensitive being. This has profound consequences, not least of which is the fact that the sense only of the reserve of being as such in the withdrawal of sense, that is, *of being considered in its being*, is considered by many to be the defining movement of philosophy itself – thus throwing into doubt the worn-smooth truism that only the human animal 'does' philosophy.

Moreover, as the condition of possibility for the abysmal generalization of the image, this sense of that which escapes is necessarily a pure perform-

---

[18] By contrast, Vanessa Lemm in *Nietzsche's Animal Philosophy* reads Nietzsche's ordinals as genetic, rather than grammatical. Such a reading, however, necessitates the erroneous reduction of Nietzsche's notion of memory, which he *explicitly* extends to all living beings as we shall see in a moment, to that of *human* memory alone (and which is thus 'inseparable,' according to Lemm, from the 'transposition (*Übertragung*) of an intuited metaphor into a *word*' (135, emphasis added).

ative. It refers, in other words, only to itself, and thus to its fantastic masking of the abyss. This follows from the fact that, for any image to 'make sense,' that is, for any image to be apprehended *as* an image, it must, upon its 'first' appearance, always already be repeated. To understand this, however, it is necessary to return to Derrida's notion of *iterability*, as discussed briefly in the previous chapter.

Iterability, we recall, as the possibility of repetition, is the structural characteristic that permits any mark, any grapheme, any phoneme, indeed, any sense-experience whatsoever, to function ritualistically as language. At the same time, however, iterability determines that every production of sense is necessarily subject to dissemination, to the *dérive* of meaning, insofar as repetition necessarily divides its indivisible essence in a double movement of protention and retention. It is this, moreover, which ensures that every production of 'sense' is always already a *re*production. It would not be possible, for example, to apprehend something as 'red' without a prior sense of 'redness,' simply because 'redness' would not be perceivable as such. Hence, to recognize 'red' not only requires its differentiation from everything 'not-red,' which thus situates it within a language in general, but such recognition also requires the recollection of previous manifestation(s) over time, and thus at once the possibility of future manifestations. Iterability, in short, is the condition for 'an idealization that permits one identify it as the same throughout possible repetitions' (Derrida, *Specters*, 200). Consequently, the specific context of a given sense of 'red' is already dependent upon past and future manifestations, thus ensuring that any notion of indivisible presence is necessarily interrupted. In this way too, the iterability of a recognized sense at once marks a sense of the *temporal*, with 'sense of time' being understood as the multiplicity of local economies which constitute the 'time of sense.'

Hence, what for Nietzsche is the metaphoricity of sense is perhaps better understood as the *re-cognition of sense*: cognition, the process of 'knowing' in the broadest sense, here recalling the tropological movement by which sense is *produced*, a production which the prefix marks out as already a *re*production. In summary, the singular encounter *as such* necessarily escapes in the recognition of the perceptual metaphor *as* image, that is, in the sense of sensation *as* sensation, of sense *as* perception and affection.

From this, it thus follows that a recognized image, in addition to being a reiteration and thus a temporalization, is thus at once what Heidegger calls a 'destructive observation.' This is because, in being always reiterated, a given image inevitably congeals, becomes sedimented, insofar as any production of sense must ignore differences between singularities. Indeed, as Nietzsche makes clear, recognition requires a violent equation, one that omits or forgets the various aspects in which specific experiences are unequal (TL, 83). Only through the violence of omission, in other words, can 'the traces continue to function in the absence of the general context or some elements of the context" (Derrida, 'Strange Institution', 64). Recognizing an image – *making sense* – is thus always both habitual and conventional.

All of this leads us to the conclusion that, insofar as the giving (of the) *as such* to recognition is already a calculation, there can thus be *no recognition of recognition as such*, no sense of the *reproduction* of sense, and thus no absolute distinction between the sensible and the intelligible. That 'it gives' is, in other words, given up in the recognition of its been given – its taking place at once obscured by its having taken place – a giving which, as we saw in the previous chapter, is at once the gift of finitude, of death. Hence, the *stammer* of recognition dissimulates both *what* it shows and *that* it shows.[19]

In every *sense* then, that which is encountered is defaced as it at once defaces that which encounters, its destructive observation reproduced behind our backs, so to speak. A machinic rumbling, both before and beyond, it now becomes clear why philosopher Avital Ronell (who has written extensively on both Heidegger and Nietzsche in conjunction with such apparently diverse subjects as testing, stupidity, and technology) describes 'boredom' – that profound zoogenetic operator – as an 'affect closest to the isolated whir of technological being' (*Test Drive*, 232). Differentially sited and cited, *perception is thus always already apperception, which is nonetheless irreducible to cogitating activity.*

Here, then, we have two distinct yet indissociable sites of non-sense. On the one hand, there is the necessary withdrawal of being as such that is the condition of possibility for the production of sense (the *taking place* of language). On the other, there are the singular differences of a given sense-experience that are necessarily and violently effaced in its recognition (language having already *taken place*). We can see, in other words, only because we are blind, can hear and feel only because we are deaf and unfeeling. This distinction is extremely important, in that it is the former which retains the potential to interrupt the latter, and is central to my thinking in the next chapter.

For the moment, however, it is sufficient to note that it is the iterability of the image which, in its having always taken place, already situates beings in and as language. Futhermore, it is iterability that ensures the reproduction of *materialization*. Heidegger, as we saw earlier, introduces the notion of *body-*

---

[19] In *On Time and Being* (1969), Heidegger names this stuttering of sense *presencing* (*Anwesen*).

ing [*das Leibende*], which refers not to physical bodies, but to the reproducing or performing of material form in an as which 'what we call the body' comes to appear (*Nietzsche*, III: 79). As I suggested, this materialization is the putting to work of a machinery of materiality through which a contour is (re)produced – a contour and thus a distinction which is, I should now add, at once the (re)inscribing of a *limit*. Finally, it is only by way of the habitual effacement of difference, that is, through the idealization of iterability by which historicity is constituted, that *beings* are able to *be*. As Nietzsche insists, the production of relatively stable contextual elements such that allow a body to 'live with any repose, security, and consistency' are completely dependent upon 'the petrification and coagulation of a mass of images' (TL, 86).

One should reiterate, however, that for Nietzsche this habitual petrification and coagulation of images characterizes the entire 'weaving together' of beings, for whom this 'ability [*Fähigkeit*] for creation (formation, invention, imagination) is their fundamental capacity. … Immense amounts of such habits have finally become so solid, that *species* live in accordance with these orders.'[20] Such, he continues, is *memory*, understood as 'the quantity of all experiences of all organic life, alive, self-ordering, mutually forming each other, competing with each other, simplifying, condensing and transforming into many different unities. There must exist an inner *process*, which proceeds like the formation of concepts [*Begriffsbildung*] out of many singular cases [*Einzelfällen*].'[21] Ultimately, the tropology of sense is not *substitution*, but rather *constitution*, of being, thus rendering untenable any further recourse to the myth of a 'natural' pathic animal communication – a myth upon which has been constructed the ideology of the undying animal. Hence, with his notion of the image, Nietzsche is thus proposing an extraordinary and originary *biosemiotics*. Moreover, once we move beyond the limits imposed upon Nietzsche by the history of its conception, we discover a biosemiotics that, in requiring neither an organism nor even an *organicism*, is considerably more radical than its contemporary incarnations.[22]

---

[20] Nietzsche, *Kritische Studienausgabe*, 11:34; cit. Lemm, *Nietzsche's Animal Philosophy*, 25.

[21] Nietzsche, *Kritische Studienausgabe*, 11:26; cit. Lemm, *Nietzsche's Animal Philosophy*, 134. Famously, in the second of his *Untimely Meditations*, Nietzsche would seem to have completely changed his mind when he states that 'the animal lives *unhistorically*' and thus exists in a constant state of forgetfulness (UMII, 61). As we will see during the discussion of 'prehistorical mnemotechnics' in chapter nine, however, I would suggest that what Nietzsche terms 'the animal' here does not in fact refer to other living beings, but is rather a *figure* of that which can take no figure.

[22] On biosemiotics, see, for example, Jesper Hoffmeyer, *Signs of Meaning in the Universe* (Bloomington: Indiana University Press, 1996); Thomas A. Sebeok and J.

Furthermore, the Nietzschean image utterly transforms our understanding of the *brain*. In place of traditional conceptions of a centralized exchange or central computer, the Nietzschean brain is necessarily a supple, differentiated configuration of 'bodyings', at once constituted and transformed in and as reiterated 'encounters'. It is thus far from incidental that contemporary neuroscience is proving this to be precisely the case, that the brain is in fact the accumulation of a differential network of billions of neuronal synapses that somehow *remember* the reiterated stimulation of internal and external encounters. The synapse, in other words, is the locus of a trace that can transform itself through repetition of a past function. In this, every brain is formed and reformed through its own unique history, by way of its own nonsubstitutable memory, a memory marked by the self-transformation of various neuronal connections that make up the infinitely diverse and plastic 'work' of the brain's ongoing self-cultivation.[23] Indeed, Nietzsche's description of memory cited above accords uncannily here, lacking only the plasticity of neuronal synapses in the conception of its 'inner process'.

The politics of sense

In a somewhat schematic summary then, an image – the tropological making sense of sense – is a singularly situated contraction of reiterated habitual sense-components within a relational structure. Such sense-experiences consist of a utilitarian and conventional selection or cutting out, that is, an habitual *interpretation* of meaning, according to its use within dominant social relations. Sense, as a result, presupposes relations of power.

Making sense, in other words, is already political. Philosopher Gilles Deleuze and psychoanalyst Félix Guattari, from whom we will be hearing a good deal more over the course of this book, make this clear in their gloss on the notion of *opinion* – a notion which, understood in the context of this text, can never belong exclusively to the human, and which will be further developed when we turn to Nietzsche's definition of truth in the following section:

Umiker-Sebeok, *Biosemiotics: The Semiotic Web* (The Hague: Mouton de Gruyter, 1991); and Wendy Wheeler, *The Whole Creature: Complexity, Biosemiotics and the Evolution of Culture* (London: Lawrence & Wishart, 2006).

[23] On this, see Catherine Malabou, *What Should We Do with Our Brain?*, trans. Sebastian Rand (New York: Fordham University Press, 2008), especially pp.15-31 and pp.55-77; and Antonio R. Damasio, *The Feeling of What Happens: Body and Emotions in the Making of Consciousness* (New York: Harcourt, Brace & Co., 1999), pp.169-172.

We pick out a quality supposedly common to several objects that we perceive, and an affection supposedly common to several subjects who experience it and who, along with us, grasp that quality. Opinion is the rule of the correspondance of one to the other. ... It extracts an abstract quality from perception and a general power from affection: in this sense all opinion is already political (*What is Philosophy?*, 144-5).

How being, and *a* being, *makes* sense can thus be considered sociopolitical throughout. In this, the habitual forgetting or omission of specific differences, just as much as the recognition of the supposedly common, reproduces relations of power through the production and reproduction of norms.

The recognized image is therefore already an 'image-*concept*,' proceeding as it does 'like the formation of concepts out of many singular cases.' Thus, writes Nietzsche, after the image 'has been generated millions of times and has been handed down for many generations ... it acquires at last the same meaning ... it would have if it were the sole necessary image and if the relationship ... were a strictly causal one' (TL, 87). For every sensitive being therefore, such tropes are machines of calculation and repetition that, beyond and before any 'I,' habitually order the sense of the world. It is, in Heideggerian terms, to be thrown [*Geworfenheit*] and falling [*Verfallen*] into opinion, that is, into the *doxa* of the everyday, as its existential-ontological constitution.

Language, society, politics, concept formation, all of which for so long have being considered the privilege of the human, can thus no longer be denied to other animals. Furthermore, the originary technicity of being necessarily dismantles the traditional distinction between human *response* and animal *reaction*.[24] From Aristotle onwards, this binary pairing has been employed to reduce 'animality' to a collection of mechanical drives and purely reactive instincts against which the would-be autonomous human response can thence be constituted. In this way, as we saw with Heidegger, all other animals are posited as locked within an environment which they are instinctively conditioned to read, yet without ever responding to beings *as* beings. Ultimately, what this comes down to is the paradox of perception without cognition, that is, the impossible act of 'reading without language.' Rather, as we shall see in later chapters, there can be no determinable limit distinguish-

---

[24] On this, see Nietzsche, *The Gay Science*, §333. Derrida too, as is well known, has set about deconstructing this binary is a number of places; see, for example, 'And Say the Animal Responded?' in *The Animal That Therefore I Am*, 119-140. Also in this context, see Bruno Latour's deconstruction of the division between facts and values corresponding to the modernist Constitution which renders incommensurable the houses of (nonhuman) Nature and (human) Culture in 'A New Separation of Powers' in *Politics of Nature*, 91-127.

ing reaction from response, just as there can be no absolute dividing line between animal instinct and human will.

While this response-reaction dichotomy has a long and illustrious philosophical history, in passing it is sufficient to gesture towards just one consequence of its ongoing deconstruction, one requiring a vast and painstaking analysis to unpack. To no longer be able to posit nonhuman animals as reactive mechanisms is necessarily to refuse the notion of 'premeditation' that determines a *responsible*, that is, a *guilty subject*, upon which stands the entire humanist-juridical discourse. Put simply, if animals respond, or humans react, then the 'responsible' intentional subject before the law becomes indeterminable. One can thus understand the considerable significance invested in its maintenance, as well as the centrality of the nonhuman animal to its ongoing deconstruction.

The truths of men

It still remains for us to ask Nietzsche, however, as to the difference, if any, between human and nonhuman metaphoricity of sense, and in particular as regards the predominantly human sense of *verbal* language.[25] In answer to this question, Nietzsche argues that there is indeed a difference between humans and other animals: 'Man' alone bears the mark of *marking out*, that is, of the exclusion and externalization of 'the animal,' in order to produce the proper, albeit empty concept of 'Man' itself.

At this point, however, Nietzsche appears to contradict himself. As we have seen, nonhuman animals cannot be excluded from the metaphorical displacement from the *as such*, and thus from the coagulated mass of image-concepts and their habitual conjunctions and combinations such as allow them 'repose, security, and consistency.' Moreover, in their various ways of making sense, all sensitive beings are necessarily social and political, and thus take part in the positing of castes and degrees, that is, of subordinations and clearly marked boundaries. However, for Nietzsche, it would seem to be exactly this which marks out the human from the nonhuman animal. 'Everything which distinguishes man from the animals,' he writes, 'depends upon this ability to volatilize perceptual metaphors in a schema, and thus to dissolve an image into a concept' (TL, 84). It is such schemata, he continues,

---

[25] It should be noted that even the distinction of 'verbal' language alleged to be uniquely human is increasingly being erased, resulting in a number of dramatic u-turns among eminent linguists.

which then allow for 'the construction of a pyramidal order according to castes and degrees, the creation of a new world of laws, privileges, subordinations, and clearly marked boundaries … the regulative and imperative world' (84). Reading this section more closely, however, in the hope of chasing down the difference which situates a man's mode of translation as different to that of every other animal, one discovers this difference does not in fact consist of man's having the *word*, and thus the concept, but, quite simply, in man's having of *truth*.

Upon first glance, such a division comes as something of a shock, appearing as it does to unambiguously reiterate the long familiar metaphysical gesture which allocates, and thus defines, man and man alone as the site of teleological reason. This is, however, simply impossible according to Nietzsche's logic for several reasons. First of all, insofar as the word 'is not supposed to serve as a reminder of the unique and entirely individual original experience to which it owes its origin' (83), the word is therefore already a word-*concept* and thus excluded from the singular 'truth' of being as such. Indeed, as the site of an habitual recognition that ignores difference in order to let 'the traces continue to function in the absence of the general context,' the word is merely a specific subgenre or subcategory of the image in general.

Moreover, within the machinery of habitual recognition word-concepts are inseparably entangled with specific image-concepts, the latter composing the overwhelming majority of the human animal's tropological functioning of perception and affection. Think, for example, of kinesic and paralinguistic communications such as facial expression, posture, tone of voice, movement and stillness, respiration, muscle tensity, even peristalsis. All of these corporeal 'expressions,' insofar as they are iterable and/or are read as such, function at the nonverbal 'animal' level of the Nietzschean image and are thus, for the most part, interpreted and taken account of outside of the magical sphere of the conscious Cartesian 'I.' This in itself strongly argues against the claim that human verbal language evolved to replace crude, so-called 'animal' language in that, if this were the case, then the evolving of this new, more efficient method would have resulted in the decay and disuse of 'animal' language among humans.[26]

---

[26] Indeed, it can be argued that verbal language also serves to distract from, or mask, kinesic and paralinguistic dissemination, and can do so only because it is considerably *less* efficient. Emil Menzel has shown, for example, that not only are chimpanzees 'masters of gestural subtlety,' but also that the most dramatically *humanoid* of their gestures are made only 'by the most infantile and inexperienced animals' – the use of which decreases as the young chimps gain experience, and thus subtlety (Noske, *Beyond Boundaries*, 148).

Given this, and despite being termed a 'second' stage, that which for Nietzsche marks out the human does not therefore bear the mark of a teleological progression. Once again, it should be clear that Nietzsche uses the ordinal here solely as a *grammatical*, and not genetic, marker. This stage, in other words, comes second in the ordering of the paper and consists simply of another *way* or another *mode* of inhabiting and being-inhabited by generative structures of meaning. Being-human, therefore, inheres in its *way(s) of inhabiting the abysmal technicity of language*. Moreover, such way(s) of being, while discontinuous with the enormous diversity of other ways of being inhabited by other animals, nonetheless always retain at least the potential to be shared across overlapping zones of indecipherability or undecidability. Take, for example, the 'meaning' accorded on both sides to the event of an aspirated breath, or the significance of an uncanny stillness as sensed by several animals of vastly differing species.

Borrowing here an exemplary nonhuman being from amongst Nietzsche's extensive bestiary, we thus find that, while 'being-gnat-in-the-world' necessarily remains discontinuous to the plurality of ways of being-tiger, being-bird, or being-plant (or rather, being *this* 'tiger', *this* 'bird', or *this* 'plant'), for Nietzsche there is nevertheless no *ontological* difference dividing sensitive-beings-in-the-world, no difference in *essence* between 'the human' and 'the animal' as there is for Heidegger. Indeed, writes Nietzsche, 'if we could communicate with the gnat, we would learn that he likewise … feels the flying center of the universe within himself' (TL, 79). Here, the nature-culture divide breaks down utterly, the 'natural' – whether considered as concept or word, as image or symbol, signifier, signified or referent – being henceforth transformed into something fantastical, some truly fantastic thing which is not a thing, which *is*, and *is nothing*.[27]

Nonhuman animals, in short, apprehend a world in ways both similar and dissimilar to those of human animals. As a result, it is no longer possible to justify human exceptionalism on the basis of language and world. Indeed, as Nietzsche's philosopher-gnat would tell us, it is no longer even possible to justify an anthropological *privilege*:

This is not to suggest, however, that verbal distraction is a uniquely human trait.

[27] At times, however, Nietzsche suggests that anthropogenesis 'takes place' only when man (who is not yet 'Man') banishes 'the most flagrant *bellum omni contra omnes* [war of each against all]' in order to live socially (TL, 81). In this, Nietzsche in fact falls foul of the nature-culture dichotomy which his own text is in the process of rendering inoperative. As Donna Haraway acutely remarks, '[t]he naturalistic fallacy is the mirror-image misstep to transcendental humanism' (*When Species Meet*, 79).

the insect or the bird perceives an entirely different world from the one that man does, and that the question of which of these perceptions of the world is the more correct one is quite meaningless, for this would have to have been decided previously in accordance with the criterion of the *correct perception*, which means, in accordance with a criterion which is *not available* (TL, 86).

Inhabiting verbal language, the habitual world of words, is simply one way of being among many, one more way of being in difference. As we shall see in the next section, being no closer and no further – both spatially and temporally – from being *as such*, it neither precedes, nor is subsequent to, any other translative displacement. And even as far as the word itself is concerned, can we so easily exclude nonhuman animals from its purview? In reiterated giving voice, in the call calling for a response, in declaration and in warning, but also in the gesture of a paw or claw, do not certain other animals name or sign an image that is recognized, and thus shared, by another?

All too clearly, we have not yet located the 'truth' that marks the human out from other animals. Both the word in particular and the image in general are necessarily dissimulations, habitual formations which, in permitting repose and security to human and nonhuman animals alike, allow us to live and work together. Nevertheless, argues Nietzsche, it is exactly here that the difference is found, albeit without being founded, in that it is *only* Man who invents –

> a uniformly valid and binding designation ... for things, *and this legislation of language likewise establishes the first laws of truth. For the contrast between truth and lie arises here for the first time.* The liar is a person who uses the valid designations, the words, in order to make something which is unreal appear to be real. ... He misuses fixed conventions by means of arbitrary substitutions or even reversals of names. If he does this in a selfish and moreover harmful manner, society will cease to trust him and will thereby exclude him (TL, 81, emphasis added).

'Truths,' continues Nietzsche, are thus habitual duties 'which society imposes in order to exist,' to wit 'to be truthful means to employ the usual metaphors' (84). In other words, by imposing certain habitual duties subsequently established as 'truths' so as to safeguard its continued existence, a given social order ultimately gives rise to 'a moral impulse in regard to truth' (84). Only here, claims Nietzsche, only with the manifestation of a *moral* impulse to truth, and thus of the exclusion of the lie on the basis of an alleged immorality, does 'man' appear, and as different from the nonhuman animal. The specificity of Man, in short, emerges in the moment when any refusal to acquiesce to the conservative demands of a given social order is deemed a lie and at once equated with immorality. By contrast, whereas a nonhuman animal may indeed make something which is unreal appear to be real, may well misuse fixed conventions and perhaps even be socially ostracized as a result, he or she cannot, however, lie in an *immoral* (or indeed, moral) sense, but only in an *extra*-moral [*aussermoralischen*] sense.

The truths of men are, in short, 'illusions which we have forgotten are illusions', dissimulation being the very condition of reason itself (84). Upon the abyss, 'rational man' thus legislates; he universalizes and, in so doing, constructs 'values' – values that, in secretly maintaining a given ordering of power, habitually serve to exclude and demonize. Here, argues Nietzsche, resides the difference between human and nonhuman animals: the difference between the reactive legislation of an illusory moral truth and the aesthetic constitution of meaning. The difference, in short, between the Law and making sense.

Being-animal, therefore, is to be exposed across machines generative of meaning, and yet to be without or before the Law in a double sense. An animal, in other words, exists *sovereignly* insofar as she is not subject *to* the Law but, precisely because she is not recognized as a subject *of* the Law, nonetheless finds herself utterly subjected.[28] Indeed, the animal stands before the Law not like Franz Kafka's man from the country, but rather as a prisoner-supplicant of the Kafkan penal colony who must learn man's Law by her wounds, by its being written over, into, and through her body.[29]

However, given that 'man' is nothing but the appearance of the lie within the concept of truth, it must be remembered that it is not simply truths that are illusions, but also the phallogocentric superiority of 'Man' himself. Indeed, Kafka demonstrates just this through the conjuncture of animals and law in his short story 'Investigations of a Dog', as we will see in the next chapter. Utterly without foundation, man necessarily builds his edifice of concepts only 'from himself', and in so doing constructs a world 'more solid, more universal, better known, and more human than the immediately perceived world' (TL, 84). Man's truths, in other words, are 'thoroughly anthropomorphic', and thus can never be 'really and universally valid apart from man' (85).

---

[28] On this double sense of 'outlaw', see Derrida, *The Beast and the Sovereign* (2008).

[29] See 'Before the Law' and 'In the Penal Colony'. For Kafka, the Law, inscribing innumerable yet indistinguishable deaths between which the 'ignorant onlooker would see no difference', remains indecipherable to the end, and whose monument is a death-machine that can no longer be maintained ('In the Penal Colony', 170).

Dogmatic legislation and artistic conduct

Having located the difference between 'man' and 'animal' as between the imposition of Law and the creation of sense, it still remains for us to see what possibilities, if any, for thought and being this in turn opens up. First of all, it should be noted that, insofar as nonhuman animals similarly require an 'inventive intermediate sphere and mediating force' (TL, 86), they are necessarily *no closer* to the immediate perception of the singular situatedness of being as such, that is, no more and no less 'originary' than the rational man with his moral schema. Consequently, Nietzsche is by no means advocating a 'return' to some kind of preverbal, quasi-natural state before the Law, as this would be to advocate a turning at once impossible and nonsensical: impossible insofar the human takes place only in and as the legislation of truth; nonsensical insofar as it would constitute a move only from one lie to another, both of which are 'equally' displaced from the unique, individual and original relation (although no calculation, of course, could ever measure this incommensurable proximity and distance of equality). Indeed, given that any one vehicle or any given genre of translation can never be more truthful than a second, one can no longer lay claim to such absolute judgments of value.

Clearly then, Nietzsche is not suggesting a simplistic binary inversion, that is, a direct exchange of valence, which would serve only to reinscribe the human-animal division. Rather – and this is absolutely central to my thinking throughout this book –, what Nietzsche gives us to think is a way of being (human) with others who do not share our language, who are neither Socratic nor Heideggerian reflections of ourselves, but are rather those others with whom or with which neither consensus nor essential disclosure is possible.

As we know, every interpretation, that is, every *sense*, is always a *misrecognition* insofar as it entails the non-recognition, and thus the effacement, of the singular encounter as such. However, while the displacement into metaphor indeed ensures that there can only ever be translation without identity, it is also the case that the tropological displacement can never leave that which it translates without ceasing to be its vehicle. The reproduced sense, so to speak, must always *touch* (on) the passage and transmission that is the bodying of its originary laying claim. It must, in other words, always be with, and in this the effaced materiality of the encounter necessarily remains, like a specter compelled to return by the violence of its exclusion.

When habit petrifies into *dogma*, when *legislation* displaces translation, however, a different mode or scheme of misrecognition comes into operation, one which in fact *predetermines* the sense of a given encounter. In other words, the exposing of being as such is misrecognized in the strong sense, insofar as the sense of the encounter is produced *prior to* that encounter's incidence and maintained with absolute inflexibility. *As such*, the encounter is thus essentially prevented from taking place: *I see without having being seen, I touch without having been touched.* Detached from that which gives itself to be interpreted, interpretation ceases to be interpretation and thus becomes Law. It is this latter misrecognition which, according to Nietzsche, is the mark of the human: the falling always into the *transcendental*. A brief comparison with Hegel proves helpful here. Like Nietzsche, Hegel too argues that the *concept* 'exists in the animal,' but that only the *human* concept can exist 'in its fixed, independent freedom,' that is, as a transcendental ideal.[30] The difference between the two thinkers, however, lies in the fact that, for Hegel, it is the *animal* who is rendered 'sick' and 'anxious' as a result.

We must pause here a moment, however, insofar as this last point requires the insertion of a short coda: in following the argument being explored here, it is essential to bear in mind that misrecognition (understood equally in its strong sense of predetermining the sense of an encounter) can be confined neither to human nor nonhuman egological consciousness, nor to human verbal language. Indeed, to do so in the latter case would ultimately serve only to reinstall a traditional human-animal distinction based upon a properly human belief in God.

The specific difference outlined by Nietzsche then, is that of the moral legislation of truth common to human ways of being, rather than misrecognition *per se*, although even here one can by no means rule out the possibility *a priori* of there being other ways of being similarly 'morally impulsive' amongst nonhuman beings. Indeed, Derrida makes precisely this point when he argues in *The Beast and the Sovereign* that 'where there is transgenerational transmission, there is law, and therefore crime and peccability.'[31]

It is in the face of the falling-surfacing of language that Nietzsche proposes his notion of a vigilant and recursive *artistic conduct*, that is, a conduct defined by its affirmative response to the inartistic, reactive violence of misrecognition. A truly artistic conduct, in other words, consists of a responsive and responsible way of being-with that leaves itself open to the possibility of uncanny zoogenetic transport preserved in the singularity of every encoun-

---

[30] In fact, it is possible to read Nietzsche's entire essay as a revaluing of this sentence from the *Encyclopedia of the Philosophical Sciences in Outline and Critical Writings* (cit. Benjamin, 'What if the Other were an Animal?,' 67).

[31] *The Beast and the Sovereign* I,106. Transgenerational nonhuman transmission is a major consideration of this book, ultimately taking on specific focus in the discussion of Bernard Stiegler in the final chapter.

ter. Hence, to conduct oneself artistically is, in the face of blind universals, to open one's 'self' to the affirmation of a transmission and passage which, exceeding the transcendental, is always yet to come.

Zoogenesis (2): encountering the *Übermensch*

Nietzschean 'conduct' then, refers to a way of being that directs itself toward the 'original, unique and individual experience' that is a sense of the *taking place* of sense prior to its recognition. Only by way of such encounters, argues Nietzsche, can 'unheard-of relations' and 'forbidden metaphors' emerge into being (TL, 90). While this will form the subject of the second part of this book, we must here pause briefly to further consider Nietzsche's notion of 'individuality'. As we have seen, 'individual' refers neither to a preexisting substance nor to a unique identity, but rather to a transformative event and an experience of transformation. As such, the Nietzschean individual does not *live*, does not *exist*, but rather 'is' that which exceeds every determinable form. It 'is,' in short, that which *out-lives* [*überleben*].[32]

In a very fine reading of the Nietzschean individual to which we shall return in due course, philosopher Werner Hamacher takes this further by making explicit the fundamental relation that links the *individual* to the *overman* [*Übermensch*]. The individual, he writes, is never a social or psychic form of human existence. Instead, it marks 'the *announcement* of the *Über-mensch*' ('Disgregation of the Will' 159; my emphasis). 'Individuality' thus *announces* the overhuman, that is, it articulates and makes known at the same time as it prepares for and proclaims its coming. Moreover, insofar as it *outlives* everything that lives, individuality announces too that the overhuman is necessarily both posthuman and posthumous.

From this preliminary encounter, an introductory sketch awaiting its full development in the next chapter, we begin to gain a sense of Nietzsche's infamous überhuman as *the calling into being of the individual event of its own announcing*. Withdrawn from all recognition and therefore exceeding all specular delimitation, the posthumous *Übermensch* interrupts the staging of Heidegger's fabulous anthropo-magical mirror in a silent announcing that necessarily out-lives any enclosure of the properly 'human'.[33] Artistic con-

---

[32] On Nietzsche's notion of *überleben*, see *Beyond Good and Evil*, sections 210-212.

[33] In addition to Hamacher on outliving as *living-on* (*sur-vivre*), see Jacques Derrida 'Living On' in Harold Bloom et al. *Deconstruction and Criticism* (New York: Continuum, 1979), 75-176.

duct thus names a way of being-together-in-the-world that remains vigilantly attuned to the possibility of such individual announcements, a *conducting toward* a creative forgetting of being in which something comes to be that which it is as such: 'Invention,' writes Nietzsche, 'beyond the limits of experience' ('The Philosopher,' 53).

We must not forget, however, that humans, being such clever beasts, *invented* knowing and thus *invented the division* between humans and other animals. Here, despite, or rather because of, the injustice of any such division, we must therefore always return – inexorably, inescapably – to the destructiveness of every observation regarding ways of being other to our own, that is, of a 'talking as if' in which the other *of* nonhuman being (both its 'otherness' in relation to human animals and the différance constitutive of being as such), is, in a stammering catachresis, written over by way of all too human (pre)conceptions. Nonetheless, we can at the same time follow Derrida when he says of the 'nonsubstitutable singularity' of any given animal that 'Nothing can ever rob me of the certainty that what we have here is an existence which refuses to be conceptualized [*rebelle à tout concept*]' (*The Animal*, 9). Here, despite the obvious irony, Derrida is making the important point that a given animal does not simply *escape* conceptualization, but rather by her very existence *refuses* it. She gives herself, in other words, only as *the sense of that which exceeds sense*, one individual among the infinite diversity of individual ways of being that are in themselves indecipherable and undecidable spaces in the putatively secure edifice of the certain world. *Any thinking encounter with animals, it thus becomes clear, takes place in this tension between genesis and destruction.*

Ways of being in language are such that they can never be securely delimited. Indeed, they presuppose as their condition fluid overlaps and abrupt jagged edges – a condition that is at once the possibility of ethical response. Artistic conduct is a way of conducting one's being toward that possibility, toward that which exceeds a given ordering of sense. It is, and this will be our subject in the next part, to open one's habitual way of being to the arrival of truth, and one's self to apocalyptic transformation. Such is the affirmation of life: not only to be exposed to the creative withdrawal of being as such, but to *rejoice* in the encounter, as indeed Lewis Carroll's Gnat, that untimely cousin of Nietzsche's gnat-metaphysician, expects of Alice, from whom he awaits a *response*.

Conclusion: on the deaths of animals

Above all else, it is thus imperative to disclose another way to give death, and to the giving of dying, to animals. To *give death to other animals*: the gift of and the giving that is the shared finitude of living beings. Only then will the monstrous hubris of an unthinking utilization and consumption of fetishized corpses itself become unthinkable.

Finitude, put simply, is the condition of possibility for any thinking encounter. When Heidegger excises the 'merely living' from living *being* as such, it is finitude which is elided – rendered imperceptible, made nonsense – by an unthought 'truth' that overwrites other bodies. Such is the paradoxical ellision that calculates nonhuman animals as undying and thus killable. That death is an exclusively human privilege is patently absurd, a privilege that itself must be done away with. At the same time, however, death is not simply something that 'we humans' can, with the implicit self-congratulation of *noblesse oblige*, confer upon others, as if posthumously awarding a medal to a particular animal for services on the battlefield. Death and dying is not some-*thing*. At best, to give *this* death is to bear witness, to attest. It is to respond, albeit always inadequately, to this death of this – singular, nonsubstitutable – other animal.

Contrary to the secular salvation dreams of Enlightenment instrumentality, no animal (in the broadest possible sense) can die in the place of another. In this sense therefore, it is indeed the case that dying can be neither given nor taken away. However, throughout this first part I have attempted to show that it is nonetheless a fact, as Derrida insists in *The Gift of Death* (1992), 'that it is only on the basis of death, and in its name, that giving and taking become possible' (44). This is a death which, doubly abysmal, confounds every attempt to separate interior from exterior and organic nature from technological artifice. Finitude, in other words, presupposes both an abysmal structure of language that exceeds any reduction to the verbal, and an abysmal bodying that exceeds organismic delimitation. Put simply, all living beings, being finite, share the iterability of language and the singularity of being-there.[34]

By refusing to elide the nonsubstitutable deaths of nonhuman animals, a responsible way of being-with other animals becomes possible, one that affirms *a priori* the shared potential for unheard-of encounters that give rise to radically new, hitherto unimaginable bodyings. Such thinking thus moves

---

[34] On this doubled abyss of language and bodying, see also Cary Wolfe's 'Flesh and Finitude: Thinking Animals in (Post)Humanist Philosophy' in *SubStance* #117, 37:3 (2008), 8-36.

beyond both traditional humanist and Heideggerian überhumanist meta-physics, and toward the necessity of always again rethinking that destructive observation which is, of course, the very interpreting of something as such that Heidegger denies to his fabulous animal.

In concluding this first part, it is thus clear that, if we are to become both responsive and responsible, no matter how inadequately, within the midst of a largely unremarked global slaughter, it is absolutely imperative that post-humanist philosophy think both the finitude and the nonsubstitutable deaths of other animals. Such is to think the sharing of each other and of the world, always already separated by the greatest possible proximity.

Part Two. Encounters

Introduction to Part Two

We discovered in the previous chapter that Heidegger's analysis of 'the essence of animality' serves ultimately as a fabulous anthropo-magical mirror, one that renders visible the essence of human being which being-human itself renders invisible. In so doing, he constructs a specular, introspective relation outside of which nonhuman animals are reduced to phantom individuations which, constituted as beings only in the looking-glass of the Dasein, are brought-to-appearing for no other reason than as puppets that man gives itself to see. Within its specular captivity, the way of being-human thus remains corralled within a circle that excludes every other 'who' or 'which' who does not share 'our' language. As such, Heidegger forecloses any potential opening to a radical alterity: becoming-other, by definition, being a moment and a movement in which 'I' can no longer recognize 'my' reflection.

While such destructive misrecognition necessarily limits 'the human' as regards both what it is and what it can do, the work of Heidegger nonetheless remains essential if we are to step beyond the mirror, and beyond the human-animal dichotomy upon which it depends. Indeed, only *with* Heidegger does it become possible to fully disclose the extramoral imperative to which Nietzsche's thinking of 'active forgetting' responds, as we shall explore in more detail in this part and throughout.[1]

Nonetheless, as we know, Nietzsche's originary technicity of sense affirms precisely that excess which Heidegger seeks to constrain within an exclusively humanist frame, and in so doing extends worldhood to the living in general.

---

[1] I am thinking primarily not only of Heidegger's analyses of bodying and of the creative event of profound boredom, which have already been considered in some detail, but also more generally of the enriching of the concept of time (or, rather, of time-space) leading to the analyses (from *Contributions to Philosophy (Of the Event)* onward) of *das Ereignis* and of the moment of transition [*Augenblick*] between that which is no-longer and that which is not-yet. Finally, we must not overlook the profound importance of Heidegger's identifying of the metaphysical determinations of the human-animal relation, and thus of both the possibility and the necessity of breaking with them.

Constitutive technicity, in other words, affirms that the alien creative transport which gives a sense only of the reserve of being as such is a transport potentially shared by every living being – never *anthropo*-genesis, in short, but always *zoo*-genesis. Moreover, it is this same originary technicity which, as we have seen, not only derails every judgment of absolute truth and value and interrupts any hierarchy of proximity, but also excludes *a priori* both vitalism and biological continuism, as well as the possibility of an essential distinction dividing any one species from all others. Finally, originary technicity puts out of the question any notion of representationalism, and thus any narcissistic form of identity politics which posits an *a priori* essence in seeking to inscribe a determining homogeneity within impermeable borders.

Put simply, originary technicity demands the affirmation of an encounter with another whose language 'I' do *not* recognize. This unrecognizable other is, however, *every* other, and thus not only is essential disclosure rendered impossible, but so too is *consensus*. Hence, originary difference reveals the groundless injustice of liberal contract theory and related arguments of 'tolerant' multiculturalism, all of which depend upon an exclusion that functions to animalize all those others whose language 'I' (or 'we') do not recognize.

At the same time, the concept of language ceases to be the privileged site from which one can, in sovereign fashion, exclude the Other on the basis of lack, that is, by way of an attribution of mute bestiality. In contrast, as we shall see, the imperative of active forgetting is nothing less than *invention*, the supremely creative event the call of which shatters the mirror and at once the psyche by way of an **animal encounter**. This should *not*, however, be understood as a call to dutifully "encounter animals" in the sense of 'bettering oneself' by taking responsibility *for* an animal, nor should it be understood as a prescriptive instruction to somehow 'commune with nature,' both of which presuppose a prior substantive human subject, and thus an unthinking human-animal distinction.

Rather, remaining with the notion of responsive conduct in relation to what I have described as the sense only of the taking place of sense, we can now better understand why Nietzsche insists that man 'grows dumb' before such 'intuitions.' As prior to recognition, there can therefore 'exist no word' with which to name such an encounter (TL, 90). Nevertheless, continues Nietzsche, all is not lost: chance may yet call forth a 'creative correspondance [*schöpferisch zu entsprechen*]' which shatters the conceptual barriers of habit (90). Having being rendered dumb, stripped bare of habitual concepts by an animal encounter, this shatteringly creative co-respondance can thus only come into being, as Nietzsche insists, 'in forbidden metaphors [*verbotenen*

Metaphern] and in unheard-of combinations of concepts [unerhörten Be-griffsfügungen]' (90).

The question that will occupy this part is therefore quite simple: how might this unheard-of relation be approached, a relation which, while not yet even sensed, is paradoxically already forbidden? How, in short, might one recognize the unrecognizable? It is in the context of this question alone that I will engage here with the otherwise disparate discourses of Nietzsche, Franz Kafka, Jacques Derrida, Karl Marx and Jacques Rancière.

The forbidden, unheard-of Nietzschean figure is hugely important here, naming as it does a metonymical *prosthesis*, that is, a bandage and a mask of disconcealment that holds the place of that which cannot be recognized. In this, it does not make sense, but rather only makes sen*sible*, and in so doing stages a correspondence which inscribes an aberration within the order of things. In this way, as we shall see, inventions 'beyond the limits of experi-ence' come to take place in the spacing, in the *play*, between the twin pillars of nihilism. Between, that is to say, the positing of suprasensory ideals and the parodic play of self-interest. Such, I argue here, are those monstrous-ly 'improper' metonymies which announce themselves as the deafening yet inaudible fanfare that throws Kafka's young dog from his senses, as the 'world-historical necromancy' which exalts the struggles of what Marx calls 'the spirit of revolution,' and as the 'cross' or 'wrong' name of Rancière's rev-olutionary performative.

A fabulous tale of dancing dogs will hopefully illuminate this further.

3. Making Sense beyond Species

Investigating Dogs with Kafka and Nietzsche

A more advanced physiology will surely confirm that the artistic force inheres our
becoming, not only in that of the human being, but also in that of the animal.
Friedrich Nietzsche, *Kritische Studienausgabe*

The Word of Dog

In an attempt to account for a life largely spent seeking to understand the caesura passed over in silence between, on the one hand (or paw), how one desires to live and, on the other, how one is actually compelled to live by the laws and institutions that bind the *socius*, the elderly canine narrator of Franz Kafka's 'Investigations of a Dog [*Forschungen eines Hundes*]' (1922) is first of all compelled to recall the compulsion which underlies his own research [*forschung*] and his ceaseless desire for understanding. He must, in short, call forth the event of his own coming to be – the very moment when, thrown into the 'peculiar openness' of critique, the young dog he will have been ceases to be. Insofar as this young dog is, and yet is not, the investigator himself, the autobiographical narrative which follows is thus equally an *hetero*biography, that is, an accounting and a recounting of an other that I am.

The apocalyptic transformation of young dog to investigator exemplifies here the maddening zoogenetic displacement to be traced throughout this part, an example which in turn calls forth parodic ghosts and revolutionary spirits, which calls last men to account and corpses to outlive. Somewhat paradoxically, however, this uncanny displacement of the dog-investigator at the same time constitutes an example of that which can essentially have *no* example. Nonetheless, it is an exemplarity that allows one to tell, to narrate, a story; one which therefore constitutes yet another exemplary fiction: a *fable*, so to speak.

Only a careless reading, however, would classify Kafka's text within the traditional genre of the fable. In fact, such an anthropocentric reading is explicitly undone from the start. Dismissive of the other 'wretched, limited, dumb creatures who have no language but mechanical cries' (279), the investigator reduces *all* other animals to an homogeneous mass bound only by 'the basest [*gemeinste*] of interests' giving rise to 'conflict and hatred' (279). Hence humans too, lacking canine language and thus those canine social institutions geared towards being together beyond all division, are necessarily 'wretched.' This explicit *cani*centrism, and the humanist outrage it provokes, thus parodically calls into question that very anthropocentric hubris which presumes the possible reduction of animal figures to the simple, remainderless anthropomorphisms of moral education.

Prior to his emergent transformation, the investigator recalls enjoying a perfectly ordinary youth, that of an unremarkable and pleasurable life passed in the senselessness of the everyday, 'blind and deaf to everything' (280). Happily lacking any sense, in the dark, one day however, he becomes the sudden focus of an unimaginable brightness. Within this brightness, the young dog finds himself abruptly recalled to the singular situatedness of his being-there, whereupon seven strange dogs appear before him, conjured as if out of the darkness and accompanied by terrible, unrecognizable sounds. These dogs, insists the investigator on behalf of his youth, are doubtless 'dogs like you and me' and yet, at the same time, they are somehow not dogs at all:

> I regarded them by *force of habit* simply as dogs … but while I was still involved in these *reflections* the music … literally knocked the breath out of me and swept me far away from those actual little dogs, and quite against my will, while I howled as if some pain were being inflicted upon me, my mind could attend to nothing but this blast of music which seemed to come from all sides, from the heights, from the deeps, from everywhere, surrounding the listener, overwhelming him, crushing him, and over his swooning body still blowing fanfares so near that they seemed far away and almost inaudible. And then a respite came, for one was already too exhausted, too annulled, too feeble to listen any longer; a respite came and I beheld again the seven little dogs carrying out their evolutions, making their leaps (281-2, my emphasis).[1]

---

[1] The German text reads as follows: *[M]an beobachtete sie gewohnheitsmäßig, wie Hunde … viele von solcher oder ähnlicher Art kannte ich, aber während man noch in solchen Überlegungen befangen war, nahm allmählich die Musik überhand, faßte einen förmlich, zog einen hinweg von diesen wirklichen kleinen Hunden und, ganz wider Willen, sich sträubend mit allen Kräften, heulend, als würde einem Schmerz bereitet, durfte man sich mit nichts anderem beschäftigen, als mit der von allen Seiten, von der Höhe, von der Tiefe, von überall her kommenden, den Zuhörer in die Mitte nehmenden, überschüttenden, erdrückenden, über seiner Vernichtung noch in solcher Nähe, daß es schon Ferne war, kaum hörbar noch Fanfaren blasenden Musik. Und wieder wurde man entlassen, weil*

Here, then, between the young dog he was and the investigator he will become, we are able to locate the interval *as such*, the extreme passivity of its apocalyptic instant marked by a rupture in and of the first person narrative. Thrown from his self by the music of everywhere, nothing remains of the youth but the violent seizure of attunement: 'my' mind, the seat and site of the 'I,' being radically displaced onto the 'he' or 'it' of a swooning, overwhelmed listener, an utterly helpless auditor who is at once the third-person *par excellence*.

Driven 'out of [his] senses' (284) and thus nothing but an intoxicated interval between first-persons, in this moment Kafka's narrator is necessarily alien to any and every 'I.' It is, precisely, event as dis-*orientation* of the 'I,' its caesura marking the opening of a new *path*, a new *way* of being. Consequently, however, for the 'I' that comes into being only *following* the event, its founding intervallic existence cannot be *re*called, but rather can only be called forth *as* another, that is, as *he* or, better, as *it*. This momentary displacement into the third-person thus marks an absolute discontinuity. The investigator can never say of himself 'I *am* other,' but only that 'I' *is* other, is another. No longer a youth, the investigator emerges anew: *I* was a child, *ich war ein Kind*, recalls the investigator of his new, posthumous self.

One of Kafka's most astute readers, Maurice Blanchot notes how Kafka's texts teach us 'that storytelling brings the neutral into play … kept in the custody of the third-person "it" [*il*], an "it" that is neither a third person nor the simple cloak of impersonality' (*Infinite Conversation*, 384; trans. modified). Rather, it is the neutral 'it' that permits us to feel that the accounting is not being recounted by any*one* and which, moreover, interrupts the subjects of the action, causing them to 'fall into a relation of self-nonidentification' (384):

> Something happens to them that they can only recapture by relinquishing their power to say 'I.' And what happens has always already happened: they can only indirectly account for it as a sort of self-forgetting, the forgetting that introduces them into the present without memory that is the present of narrating speech (384-5).

The 'it,' adds Blanchot in a footnote, designates 'its' *place* as 'both the place from which it will always be missing and that will thus remain empty, but also as a surplus of space, a place that is always too many' (462n2). The neu-

---

man schon zu erschöpft, zu vernichtet, zu schwach war, um noch zu hören, man wurde entlassen und sah die sieben kleinen Hunde ihre Prozessionen führen, ihre Sprünge tun ('Forschungen eines Hundes').

tral 'it', in short, is a mark or a placeholder of 'the intrusion of the other …
in its irreducible strangeness,' a strangeness, an *uncanniness*, which Blanchot
elsewhere describes as both *spectral* and *ghostlike* (385). As we shall see, it is
this intrusion, this imposition of an empty surplus, which marks the Kafkan
encounter beyond any sense of species. Such, then, is the demand of ontological disorientation, a demand in and as which a young dog ceases to be in
having always already become an investigator.

Coming into his senses and yet sensing only the senselessness of their
address, the investigator feels constrained to offer assistance to the seven *actual* dogs before him. With 'good manners' [*guten Sitten*] that in the original German are also 'good morals,' he thus greets the dogs and, in so doing,
recognizes them *as* dogs. Incredibly, however, this attempted recognition is
refused in what is, quite simply, the greatest possible offence within the social
domain. This extraordinary breach of custom and habit not only places the
other dogs beyond all *sense* but also, and as a result, beyond even the certainty of *specie*: 'Perhaps they were not dogs at all? But how should they not be
dogs?' ('Investigations,' 283).

Upon receiving this monstrous affront to proper sense, another constraint abruptly makes itself felt on the body of the investigator: 'a labyrinth
of wooden bars … arose around that place, though I had not noticed it before' (282). As a result of his becoming-other, in other words, a previously
insensible limit manifests itself to the investigator *as* a limit, that is, *as* a sensible constraint. He senses, in short, the limit of good sense, and of its 'proper' reproduction. In this way, the contingent limit of sense becomes sensible
precisely *as* contingent, and all sense certainty is necessarily lost as a result: 'it
is too much to say that I even saw them, that I actually even saw them' (281).

Experiencing a brief respite from the violence of the encounter, overcome
by the anxiety of absolute uncertainty and at the same time forcefully constrained by this terrible and, as it transpires, *criminal* affront to proper sense,
the investigator calls desperately upon God to restore divine order. The dogs,
he exclaims to the heavens, are 'violating the law [*das Gesetz*]'"(283). Here,
in a final vain attempt to repudiate the refusal of recognition, the investigator
falls back on the certain gaze of judgment, disavowing their monstrous affront to good sense by reducing it to a mere symptom of *shame* [*Schuldgefühl*]
in having their sinful *nakedness* witnessed. The investigator, in other words,
falling back upon precisely that sense traditionally denied to all animals but
one, attempts to dispel his intense anxiety by way of *ressentiment*, externalizing the uncannily intimate alterity of the encounter as a manifestation of the
other dogs' fallen status.

Let us, along with Kafka's investigator, pause here for a moment to get our breath. The extraordinary encounter has thrown up a cluster of interrelated figures, concepts, and images that are important to our own investigation – namely, uncanniness and sense-certainty; violation, judgment and the gaze; and shame, sin and nakedness. Here, too, one senses the presence of Sigmund Freud, a contemporary of Kafka's whose psychoanalytic works he knew well. Indeed, both Kafka and Freud occupy a crucial 'in-between' position, not only in historical and intellectual terms between Nietzsche and Heidegger, but also through a certain impropriety of genre that opens itself to the critical question of *style*. Indeed, it is not by chance that Freud, in his curious yet compelling study of 'The Uncanny' published in 1919, employs one of E. T. A. Hoffmann's 'fantastic narratives' in order to elucidate various points of interest for psychoanalysis – an apparently paradoxical move for what was then an emergent discipline struggling to establish its reputation as an orthodox science. Indeed, argues Freud, it is precisely because that which is uncanny withdraws and thus conceals itself it can therefore only be approached obliquely via its effects, that is, only through its fantastic, monstrous figures. Recalling our guiding question for this part – how might one recognize the unrecognizable? –, this would suggest an answer may be found in the relay between philosophy and the monsters of literature.

Returning to the investigator, his attempts to efface the madness of the encounter all come to nothing as once more the terrible music irresistibly imposes itself. Arising 'without variation from the remotest distance' (284) which is at once the most near ('fanfares so near that they seemed far away'), this dreadful music spins the known world on its axis. In so doing, it sweeps away all possibility, if not the hope, of the investigator being returned to the deafened and deafening respite of the everyday. 'Was the world standing on its head?' he cries. 'Where could I be? What could have happened?' (284).

It is right here, as we shall see, in being anxiously impelled across the furthest proximity to make sense of that which is without sense, and thus to construct an autobiographical narrative which must narrate precisely its own impossibility, that the cries of the investigator call forth an intensive correspondence with certain 'biographical' texts of Friedrich Nietzsche and Jacques Derrida. He calls, that is, to Nietzsche's preacher of the overhuman, who cries in his turn, 'What is happening to me? … What? Has the world not just become perfect?' (*Zarathustra*, 288), and to the little female cat whose bottomless gaze is fixed upon Derrida's nakedness. In exploring these uncanny animal encounters, and as the investigator's account exemplifies, I will thus argue that they can only take place 'under the species of the nonspecies, in the formless, mute, infant, and terrifying form of monstrosity' (Derrida, 'Structure, Sign and Play,' 370).

Thinking through great nausea

Here, we begin to approach our central question, this Kafkan, this Nietzschean question: how might the unrecognisable and unheard-of relation be recorded? How might the senseless interval come to make sense, perhaps even to *create* sense? How might the as yet formless form of monstrosity come to be manifest, given that its sense can only be that of the taking place of sense prior to its recognition? How, in short, might one recognize the unrecognizable, think the unthinkable?

For Nietzsche, as we know, it is a question of an artistic response to the reactive violence of habit and moral calculation. Only then does that which habit renders insensible become manifest, only then does the demand of that which 'has no name as yet and hence cannot be mentioned although it stares us all in the face' become perceptible (*The Gay Science*, §261). Such, then, is the unheard-of co-respondence which marks the 'unique and entirely individual original experience' that 'is' being as such in an *announcing* which exceeds every determinable form (TL, 83). It is, put simply, the event of the arrival of *truth*, understood as the dis-*covering* of that which *is*, but *is* hidden.

Such an announcing is located, Nietzsche tells us, in the spacing, the play, *between* the two forms of nihilism. Between, that is, the rational man who negates the world in positing suprasensory utopian ideals, and the last man who, recognizing that truth and value are all too human constructions, negates the world in advocating the parodic play of cynical self-interest.[2] Instead, its interval, its interruption, moves *before* and *beyond* nihilism's 'great nausea' (*Genealogy*, II:24) as the moment in which a being opens itself to that which has been excluded in the production of sense and thus value and, in so doing, is transformed utterly. Hence, *neither being exists prior to their unheard-of relation*, but rather are *created* 'in' the encounter.

Such a becoming-together necessarily manifests itself by a 'forbidden' *phrasing*, one which shatters the conceptual shackles that order the sensible world by reinscribing that which has been elided by habitual recognition. The manifest phrasing, in other words, discloses a lacuna within the known, thus interrupting the proper ordering of a certain state of affairs. One thus begins to understand why, even though it is *as yet* unheard-of, it is nonethe-

---

[2] See, for example, *The Gay Science*, §346.

less *already* forbidden. As an aberration within the order of things, moreover, it necessarily bears the mark of monstrosity.[3]

Openness and fidelity to such encounters that open a space and a time for the coming into being of previously foreclosed relations thus constitute the core of Nietzsche's ethical aesthetic (we shall further explore the meaning of 'fidelity' in this context in later chapters). In short, the ethical imperative, an imperative that marks every living being as *living*, consists in opening up differential temporalities of materialities and potentialities. The artistic and ethical thus coincide in the refusal to allow life to harden in one configuration, in a single sclerotic possibility. It is to grant life, as Heidegger says, 'its inalienable right to become' (*Nietzsche*, II:126).

Following the event of creative metamorphosis, as we shall see, Kafka's canine investigator comes to inhabit just this Nietzschean notion of responsive and responsible conduct. Such is a conducting of one's self openly towards an autocritical imperative that returns eternally, thus remaining faithful to a permanent revolution that ever questions and, in so doing, *creatively* transforms.

This is not to suggest, however, that through such conduct the singularity of the encounter *as such* is in some sense disclosed. Rather, in announcing only an unnameable monstrosity, the encounter has always already withdrawn. And yet this withdrawal is synonymous with *creation* in that it calls forth, as the mark or trace of withdrawal, the formless form or improper figure of a 'senseless' metonymy. Here, then, we come up against the inherent constraint and contradiction of *invention* itself.[4] On the one hand, insofar as the 'senseless' metonymy brings to the senses the delirious mute call of that which the habitual reproduction of sense renders insensible, this placeholding figure must explicitly refuse any and all identity. On the other hand, however, in being called forth to hold open the space of the 'new,' such an improper placeholder must, in order to be recognized or even *sensed*, 'materialize' in the borrowed costume of the old. While this will be explained further in the next chapter, for the moment we can say that the figure called forth by the encounter's withdrawal is thus constrained to *dress improperly*. Moreover, as we shall see, this constraint is both the condition of every revolutionary invention and that which ensures its parodic, nihilistic recuperation. Furthermore, I will argue, it is exactly this creative becoming of what, for strategic

---

[3] On this, see Michel Foucault's lecture from 1975 in which he argues that the (human) monster 'combines the impossible and the forbidden' and as such 'violates the law while leaving it with nothing to say' (*Abnormal*, 55-79 (56)).

[4] On the inherent paradox of invention, see Jacques Derrida, 'Psyche: Invention of the Other' in *Psyche: Inventions of the Other*, Volume I, 1-47.

reasons, I am calling an animal encounter, which renders it *un*thinkable that living beings can be put to death with impunity. That is, in contrast to the dissimulating 'nakedness' of the 'pure' concept, it is only in the thickness and impropriety of its dress – its inbetweenness – that the chance *address* from another might arrive to interrupt the murderous theatrics of animalization.[5]

'Nakedness,' as we have seen, implies the reactive authority of judgment for Kafka's investigator. Indeed, it is the very 'nakedness' of truths that function to place the apodicity of authority beyond question. Finally, the possibility of being naked constitutes yet one more of those 'propers' which supposedly separate the human from the nonhuman animal. Playing on these figures somewhat, I suggest that, inasmuch as the revolutionary placeholder remains *between* senses, that is, so long as it remains improperly dressed, it is therefore '*animal*.' By contrast, this animal figure ironically becomes '*human*' the moment its obscure thickness congeals into the apparent transparency of habit. Such transparency which is, in other words, the naturalising and thus normative function of 'nakedness.'

Thinking nonsense

To recap, we have seen that the tropology of sense is not substitution but rather *constitution* of being, every passion being an act of interpretation and every action dependent upon a passive infolding of externality. Further, this blinding, deafening, benumbing reproduction of sense places *every* living being 'in' language, presupposing as it does machines of habitual recognition inhabited by power that are both constitutive of bodyings and coextensive with material*iz*ation. As feminist philosopher Judith Butler writes in her important early text *Bodies That Matter* (1993), we must not think of 'matter' as a simple site or surface, but rather as a *process* of materialization that, with iterability as its condition, 'stabilizes over time to produce the effect of boundary, fixity, and surface *we call* matter' (9; emphasis added). Hence, while the fixity of a body is indeed fully material, its material*iz*ation by contrast must be thought 'as power's most productive effect' (2). Indeed, the clearly bounded structure of 'the organism' is just such an effect, the very obviousness of which being the gauge of its investiture with power relations.

In this process of *materialization*, then, a process that is at once the *idealization* of iterability, the singularity of a given being is violently covered over,

---

[5] See, for example, *The Gay Science*, §352. Also, see 'Nakedness, Dress' in Sarah Kofman, *Nietzsche and Metaphor*, 81-100.

disciplined and reserved in the very act of making sense. At the same time, however, the *im*mediate perception of a uniquely situated relation of being equally necessarily reserves itself *as* withdrawn, and in so doing remains to haunt every ideality as the spectral trace within every repetition. Such is the 'pure reserve' of unlivable excess which outlives every determinable form.[6]

We are thus returned to those two distinct but indissociable sites of non-sense considered briefly in the previous chapter. On the one hand, we recall, there is the necessary withdrawal of being as such that is the condition of possibility for the production of sense (the *taking* place of language) and, on the other, there are the singular differences of a situated encounter that are violently elided in the recognition of its sense (language having already *taken* place). In one sense, then, while the impossible event of *infinite* being as such necessarily withdraws in the everyday *finite* state of affairs, it is nonetheless the former which effaces itself in and as the latter. At the same time, however, these two sites, the finite and the infinite, are absolutely heterogeneous, in that the act of making sense is necessarily marked by a sense of the tempo-ral, that is, by an historically contingent time of sense. In the taking place of language, therefore, being as such is already *no longer* perceptible in its being recognized, whereas insofar as language has nonetheless already taken place, being as such is always *not yet* perceptible, the reserve of pure potentiality.

Given power's investiture in the habitual effacement of difference that constitutes the possibility of making sense, the unlivable excess of pure re-serve can necessarily be 'actualized' – as we saw with both Heidegger and Nietzsche in the previous chapter – only *as* withdrawn. It manifests itself, that is to say, *as* meaning without sense (content) and as sense (sensibility) without meaning. As the sense only of being without sense, of the singular laying claim of being as such, it is thus a purely formal telling only of itself, one which exceeds every structure of meaning upon which its affective man-ifestness nevertheless depends. In this way, the call of an impossible, singu-larly situated encounter potentially comes to be heard. A call that compels a becoming-other which cannot be predicted from within the everyday state of affairs it interrupts, and which in so doing violently dis-locates the certainty of being the 'I' that 'is,' the latter referring both to the secure sense of self *as* self, *and* to the surety of repose within the world. We can now understand

---

[6] This event of singular reserve is, as Deleuze and Guattari write, 'the part that eludes its own actualization in everything that happens. The event is not a state of affairs. It is actualized in a state of affairs, in a body, in a lived, but it has a shadowy and secret part that is continually subtracted from or added to its actualization … it is a virtual that is real without being actual, ideal without being abstract … The event is immaterial, incorporeal, unlivable: pure reserve' (*What is Philosophy?*, 156).

why Kafka's investigator, emerging into being in response to just such a call, finds himself immediately thrown outside of "the ordinary, calm, happy life of every day' ('Investigations,' 286).

Moreover, in being thrown thus, the canine investigator is thrown into an antagonistic relation with the everyday that, according to Heidegger, presupposes a specific *critical* ability, termed *krinein* by the Ancient Greeks, 'which is always decision' and by which 'the human being is lifted out of mere captivation.'[7] Kafka's dog, however, punctures such exceptional hubris not merely because he explicitly bodies a critical capacity in nonhuman form, but also because it is a capacity to which, in coming to be, he has being *thrown* by way of an encounter that has neither will nor *conscious* decision as its condition. As such, implicit to Kafka's 'Investigations' is the claim that the inventive, evental disorientation of sense does not presuppose human consciousness, nor indeed *any* form of egological consciousness. Here, then, Kafka affirms Nietzsche's claim that a 'more advanced physiology' – and *physiology* is absolutely correct here – 'will surely confirm that the artistic force inheres our becoming, not only in that of the human being, but also in that of the animal' (albeit with the proviso that 'the animal' here must be considered synonymous with 'life in general,' a concept itself riven with uncertainties and impossibilities).[8]

Conditioned by neither will nor conscious decision then, the encounter, withholding itself in giving itself, is rather that which both *exceeds* recognition and is always *prior to* recognition – its madness of originary composition the spectre of pure potentiality haunting every actualization. Hence, the specter is double: on the one hand, the specter of all that has been foreclosed by a caricatured materialization coextensive with its investiture with power and, on the other, the spectral 'truth' of originary composition prior to any recognition as truth. The spectre 'is,' in short, the unlivable that outlives.

Violently dislocated by the encounter, exposed in and as what Giorgio Agamben describes as 'the suspension and withholding of all concrete and specific possibilities' (*The Open*, 67), the self-certain 'I' is thus thrown from itself *to* existential anxiety. This is not, however, the *experience* of the disconcealing of pure potentiality as Agamben claims, but rather pure potentiality *as such*, and thus precisely that which (an) 'I' can never experience. Originary being-with prior to any recognition, and thus always prior to the constitution of the 'human' or the 'nonhuman,' is (and *is* not) absolute *inter*,

---

[7] Heidegger, 'On the Essence and Concept of Φύσις in Aristotle's *Physics* B, I' in *Pathmarks*, 183-230 (202).

[8] Nietzsche, *Kritische Studienausgabe*, 7:19; cit. Lemm 133.

that which 'is' *no longer and not yet*. Put more simply, in the infinite materiality of pure *potentiality*, nothing can possibly *be*. Such, then, is the uncanny nonplace of the event: at once the reserve of the infinite *not yet* in its taking place which, in having nonetheless already taken place, is always *no longer* in every actualization. Being as such is, in short, the im-possibility of being.

Following the apocalypse

As the impossibility of possibility, infinite materiality is thus necessarily atemporal, ahistorical: *untimely*. The other of time, and thus heterogeneous to every state of affairs in which an 'I' comes to be thrown, the disposing of being as such 'is' therefore a maddening interlude *from* which an 'I' can only return *to* anxiety, but never experience *as such*.

It is this 'moment' of being thrown from infinite senseless madness to the 'there' of a previously unrecognisable 'I' which Derrida attempts to recall in a well-known passage from *The Animal That Therefore I Am* (2006). Here, he relates the story of how, naked in his bathroom one morning, he encounters the 'bottomless gaze [*regarde sans fond*]' of his female companion cat in 'an instant of extreme passion' (12), one which –

> offers to my sight the abyssal limit of the human: the inhuman or the ahuman, the ends of man, that is to say, the bordercrossing from which vantage man dares to announce himself to himself. And in these moments of nakedness, as regards the animal, everything can happen to me [*tout peut m'arriver*], I am like a child ready for the apocalypse. *I am (following) the apocalypse itself* [*je suis l'apocalypse même*], that is to say, the ultimate and first event of the end, the unveiling and the verdict (12).

While there have been a number of recent interpretations of this passage,[9] they have generally tended to focus on the *gaze*, whilst overlooking the interrelation of the 'I' and the apocalypse in the play of '*am* [*suis*]' and '*follow* [*suis*]'.[10] Such an omission, however, elides the very trace of that encounter

---

[9] See, for example, Matthew Calarco, *Zoographies: The Question of the Animal from Heidegger to Derrida* (New York: Columbia University Press, 2008), 121-126; Cary Wolfe, 'In the Shadow of Wittgenstein's Lion' in *Zoontologies: The Question of the Animal* (Minneapolis & London: University of Minnesota Press, 2003), 1-58; and Donna J. Haraway, *When Species Meet*, 19-23. See also Leonard Lawlor's particularly interesting reading of the bathroom scene (74-7), which is the highpoint of his book *This Is Not Sufficient: An Essay on Animality and Human Nature in Derrida* (New York: Columbia University Press, 2007).

[10] As David Wills' translation makes clear, Derrida plays throughout this passage on the shared first-person singular present form of the verbs *être* (to be) and *suivre* (to

which is otherwise being sought. In this animal encounter (in the double sense here of an animal encounter *with* a nonhuman animal), the nonsubstitutable singularity of this female cat opens itself beyond itself in being given outside of the constitutive outside of the properly human. It is in this instant of extreme *passion*, of absolute receptivity, that everything can happen but within which no *one* possibility, no *one* configuration, can be *actualized*.

The encounter, that is to say, 'takes place' in the pure potentiality of the *not yet taken place*, within the apocalyptic suspension of every actualized possibility, but as such can only be called forth by an 'I' insofar as its encounter 'is' *no longer*. In other words, insofar as I *am* the apocalypse [*je suis l'apocalypse*], this necessarily precludes every 'I' [*je*], and inasmuch as I *am* [*suis*] this possibility, 'I' can thus only ever *follow* [*suis*]. An 'I', in short, comes back to find itself only in the anxious trace or mark of the encounter's having already taken place, hence 'I' necessarily *follows* the apocalypse [*je suis l'apocalypse*].[11]

Moreover, this *marking*, this trace of absolute dislocation, necessarily re-marks – i.e., makes manifest – that which was previously foreclosed: a *manifesto* and a *manifestation* in the most literal sense. Such is the proclamation and appeal *as yet* without meaning, a sense that is *as yet* without sense, but which nonetheless violently calls into being its own monstrous and terrifyingly unpredictable becoming. This affective perception of the 'without sense', that is, the sensing of some 'thing' or, better, some *relation*, hitherto denied sense and thus articulation, quite simply marks the obdurate emergence into being of that which has otherwise been refused admission by the dominant structures of intelligibility-materialization. In response, the 'I' necessarily comes back to itself otherwise, obligated to a call which, exceeding all knowledge, thus refutes every certainty and surpasses self-understanding.

Further, insofar as it has already withdrawn in sounding its manifesto of the unheard, the encounter thus ever again preserves its infinite potentiality. The event, in other words, remains forever to come and thus to eternally return in that it gives itself only as the trace of the future anterior, namely that which *will have been attested to* by the anxiety of its 'sense without sense'.

---

follow), both of which produce *suis*. Thus 'je *suis*' can mean either *I am* or *I follow*, or, as here, both at once.

[11] On the normative yet paradoxical relation between nudity, shame, and guilt, see Derrida, *The Animal*, 4ff. Particularly interesting in the context of this bathroom encounter is the absolute uncertainty of both sexual and species difference, Derrida being unable to say, with the bottomless gaze of the female cat focused upon his genitalia, if he is naked and ashamed *like* an animal, that is, *like* a beast or, instead, *like* a man. It is a passage which I hope to engage with in more detail at a later date.

Hence, in Nietzsche's parable of the eternal return "At Noontide," Zarathustra is, like Kafka's investigator, similarly thrown both from and to his senses in a violent seizure of attunement.[12] 'I know not how,' Zarathustra admits, 'it inwardly touches me … it compels me.' Such is the uncanny, utterly disorientating intoxication of the fall into the well of eternity, into the 'serene and terrible noontide abyss' of the world's singular perfection that is the 'golden round ring' of being as such. Upon coming to his senses, having being turned about in being turned towards the radically new, Zarathustra finds his self transformed, all prior certainty destroyed: 'I spoke once and thought myself wise. But it was a blasphemy: I have learned *that* now' (288). There is, moreover, nothing of the *human* in such Nietzschean encounters. Instead, Zarathustra, the prophet of eternal return and the overman, only ever encounters other animals in the 'noontide abyss,' that is, in that interval of 'glowing midday' which throughout *Thus Spoke Zarathustra* 'unleashes an essential image-generating force' (Heidegger, *Nietzsche,* II:46).[13]

In summary, then, the address of an animal encounter marks the emergence into being of a relation which has been foreclosed within a given state of affairs, and which thus exceeds a body's capacity for recognition. Unheard-of, forbidden, and unmentionable, that which cannot 'make' sense is thus compelled to announce itself only as a sense of the without sense. *It proclaims, in short, that the fact that this way of being-together has no sense is itself an issue. In this way, the foreclosure or forbiddenness of its sense is performed.* It is a performative, moreover, which at the same time discloses the limit not only as limit, but as *contingent* limit. Enacting thus the prison of enclosure and delimitation, its questioning of enforced limits is therefore indissociable from its remarking of the eventual withdrawal of being as such.

Invention of monstrosity, monstrosity of invention

Having thus explored how an unrecognizable other comes to impose itself within a given state of affairs, we focus in this penultimate section on the necessary *monstrosity* of its coming. In the final section, I will then consider the implications of such creative monstrosities for liberal ideology and for the staging of animalization, before concluding with a deafening yet inaudible

---

[12] Nietzsche, *Thus Spoke Zarathustra*, 287-9.

[13] 'Image,' it should be remembered, is for Nietzsche the discontinuous tropological vehicle that makes *sense*, and hence I read Heidegger here as referring to the inventive *genesis* of sense.

fanfare, arriving simultaneously from the most near and the most far, which throws a young dog into the 'peculiarity' of critique.

As we have seen, an encounter in its withdrawal traces the scene of a prior exclusion. The mark of a present-absence and an absent-presence, its ghostly apparition announces the coming into being of *spacing* and *articulation*. Put another way, the sense of its void marks the opening of a space of invention in which what is foreclosed can potentially come forth. Nonetheless, as the coming into being of something unrecognizable, of some unthinkable 'thing' which cannot be, such an invention is necessarily monstrous in being absolutely alien to all that is.[14] For Nietzsche, this is supreme creative event: in and as the *active forgetting* of the encounter's extreme passivity, the foreclosed and forbidden make sense in becoming monstrous.

Simply put, this marks the emergence of an entirely new being – the creation, that is, of a *transductive* being, i.e., one in which the 'elements' of its unheard-of combination do not precede their relating, but rather can only be discerned retrospectively. *The terms constituting the relation, in other words, do not exist prior to their relation.* As such, the 'unheardness' of this literal 'becoming-together' is not that of the construction of an unfamiliar portmanteau, nor the estranging production of a surrealist montage. It is not a case, in other words, of simply placing together two or more elements in an unfamiliar relation – a calculation whose very unfamiliarity depends upon the *prior* sense of those elements being recognized as disparate. Rather, we can *only* say that such a being is composed of *not* the I that I was, and of *not* the other that he/she/it was. This is exemplified for us by Kafka's canine hetero-autobiography: conducted through the encounter's apocalyptic ordeal, a relation is staged between *not* the young dog that 'I' was and *not* the 'actual' dogs that they were. It is only *following* this relation, however, that the Investigator comes to be discerned as one of the elements in its creation. As such, the Investigator in no sense *pre*cedes the event of their becoming-together. Rather, the encounter confers a way of being from which he always *pro*ceeds.

In summary, while it is indeed the case that every 'attunement' by which beings are always outside themselves is irreducible to its elements, here, by contrast, the elements as elements do not exist prior to their attunement. Rather than preceding its call, the 'I' (which, again, cannot be restricted to an egological consciousness) is always constituted anew in and as the address,

---

[14] On the necessary impossibility, and thus monstrosity, of invention, the reader is once again referred to Derrida's 'Psyche: Invention of the Other', a text which is fundamental to an understanding of his philosophical project.

just as that 'other' which is made manifest in being so marked does not pre-exist this relation *as such*.

Beings, therefore, do not precede the originary being-with or *Mitsein* that 'is' being as such. Rather, as the condition of possibility for all individuation, it is being-with that precedes identity and substance.[15] The post-apocalyptic 'other-I' thus comes to *body* (in the Heideggerian sense of passage and transmission) a transformed relationality, an intensive, maddening relation of forces.[16] Put another way, the 'other-I' becomes 'animal' in the sense that there can be nothing recognisable, nothing properly human or, indeed, properly canine in the attunement of an intensive composition that has no meaning.[17]

Put simply, one only ever *calculates* the human. That is to say, 'the human' is made calculable by way of a discursive abstraction constructed through the forgetting of particular contours and site-specific phenomena; one more conceptual husk transferred to the Nietzschean land of 'ghostly schemata.' An animal encounter, by contrast, interrupts the most proper of human properties twice over: on the one hand, as a nonhuman moment that exceeds every stable delimitation of the self and breaches every fixed contour of the body and, on the other, as an inhuman movement through the technicity of language. In and as the encounter, a new yet historically contingent being is created: a monstrosity 'under the species of the nonspecies' that demands only its own impossible possibility. Here, then, Nietzsche's claim in section 958 of *The Will to Power* to 'write for a species of man that does not yet exist' takes on a clarity and a force hitherto obscure. Similarly, the distinction between 'nonhuman' and 'inhuman' is also clear: '*non*human' refers to all those billions of singular living beings who, while other than human, are nonetheless similarly *constituted* by the making of sense, whereas 'inhuman' refers to the a-human *machinery* of sense, the structure of language, which *constitutes* every living being.

In calling forth a radically new being, the animal encounter inevitably interrupts the regulative economies which otherwise *determine* a response (or, rather, a reaction). As an inscription of pure language in and as its withdrawal, it equally necessarily can neither be said nor shown as it 'is,' but rather

---

[15] What I am calling the animal encounter, it should be clear, has therefore nothing to do with a human imitation of a nonhuman other, an *imitation* which thus presupposes prior identity.

[16] On this, see what Deleuze terms 'nonorganic vitality' in 'To Have Done with Judgment' in *Essays Critical and Clinical*, 126-135 (131).

[17] Such a composition, moreover, may irretrievably exceed a future reinscription of meaning, as we will discover in chapter five.

can only be indicated precisely where and when it is not. In this, the trace of the encounter's withdrawal readily translates into rhetorical terms as the site of both an apostrophe and an ellipsis, that is, at once relentless address and disclosure by concealment.

As we know, this elliptical apostrophe marks the opening of a space of recognition to-come, which is another way of saying that it marks an opening in and of everyday *time*. Linear temporality, as we have seen, is produced by the idealization of iterability such as permits the identification of the same throughout possible repetitions, and which is indissociable from the sedimentation that constitutes historicity. Allowing of no identification, however, the call of the encounter necessarily disrupts this linear temporality, marking an abrupt breakdown in its otherwise smooth functioning. In this way, the trace of the withdrawal of being as such constitutes a *purely temporal irruption* within the everyday *spatialization of time* (i.e., temporality constructed as a linear series of discrete and bounded 'now's'). As a result, if the call without sense is to constitute an effect in the world of beings, it has no choice but to don a prothestic from the past. Only then might that which is not possible become sensible, and only then might both the calculability of linear time and the previously self-evident propriety of the prevailing order be thrown into question. Uncanny historical prostheses, therefore, will be the subject of our next chapter.

Before moving on to the concluding section, I feel it is important to reiterate once again that what I am calling the *animal* encounter can never be restricted to the *human animal* alone. Rather, whatever her, his, or its ways of being, no nonhuman animal may be refused its disorientating, creative potential, just as no nonhuman animal may be refused time or historicity.[18] This, as will hopefully be clear, follows from the simple fact that all living beings habitually make sense – this is what being alive means. Indeed, there can be no doubt that the vast majority of monstrous creations called into

---

[18] This specificity, however, is not to suggest that nonhuman animals are therefore excluded from *historiology*, of which one example will for the moment suffice. In 1919, farmers attempted to murder 140 elephants from the South African park of Addo, of which between sixteen and thirty survived. Even today, recounts Barbara Noske, the Addo elephant group is 'mainly nocturnal and responds extremely aggressively to any human presence ... they obviously have transmitted information about our species even to calves of the third and fourth generation, none of whom can ever have been attacked by humans' (*Beyond Boundaries*, 111-2). These elephants are thus 'the cultural heirs of the fear and hatred among their ancestors for our species' (155). This also, in reference to Derrida's point regarding the necessary link between transgenerational transmission, law, and therefore crime and peccability, appears to mark an elephant social *taboo*.

being by inter- and intra-specific encounters never once cross paths with a human way of being.

Exclusions and inaugural citations

Where, then, does this notion of monstrous invention leave nonhuman animals in relation both to the economy of animalization and to the ideology of liberal individualism? Most obviously, its mute announcing addresses itself to those founding exclusions upon which the 'inclusive' ideology of liberal consensus depends. Or, in more general terms, it addresses every body habitually excluded in the ordering of a given state of affairs.

More than this, however, its anarchic call to *dis*order in fact renders perceptible the whole murderous theatrics of animalization, that is, the machinic reproduction marshalling what, in the Introduction, I called *the economy of genocide*. Animalization, as we have seen, consists of the reductive reconfiguration of a constructed identity as 'animal' which, figured along a humanist teleological dialectic, is thus considered synonymous with 'subhuman'. More bluntly, it is the institutional reproduction of materialization, determined within dominant relations of power, by which singular situated 'bodyings' are written over and thus excluded from making sense – an economy which, in the modern era, is largely reducible to the exploitive demands of capitalism. In its disconcealing of these ideologically dissimulated machinations, therefore, the animal encounter is *necessarily opposed to capitalism*, be it national or international, intellectual or biomedical, or as regards the 'simple' economics of subsistence.

While this will be explored in detail over the following chapters, it is already clear that, within the terms laid out in this book, the movement of sedimented traces by which other bodies are constituted as killable must be understood as a *reactive* ordering of the sensible. In this, an habitual *mis*recognition is produced which, in dogmatically predetermining the sense of an encounter prior to its taking place, essentially prevents that encounter from taking place, whilst at the same time reproducing the 'proper' limit of the human collective. In contrast to the tropological displacement of animalization, however, the call without sense is the call of and to tropes *which function in precisely the opposite direction*. Rather than reductive metaphors and anthropomorphisms of 'proper' identity, they mark instead the coming into being of improper animal relations which make it *un*thinkable that other living beings – whether human or nonhuman – can be put to death with impunity.

Described above as 'uncanny historical prostheses' through which the untimely call without sense becomes sensible and thus capable of constituting a worldly effect, such tropes are, moreover, dependent upon the positing – at once creative and destructive – of a particularly Nietzschean *irony*. As that which, quite simply, cannot mean what it says, it thus follows that only just such an ironic figure can perform – and hence form, that is, materialize or manifest – that terrifying demand and meaningless compound that marks only the sense of exclusion. Furthermore, insofar as this uncanny prosthetic figure must be both inaugural *and* citational, its very impossibility discloses the paradox of invention itself – that of being absolutely other to what is possible whilst at the same time reiterating what has already been in order that its invention be recognized.

For an example of this impossibly improper figure, a figure whose very impropriety in a strict sense renders *every* example impossible, we need only to recall the neutral 'it' of Kafka's overwhelmed listener, exposed in the zoogenetic interval between young dog and investigator. As we have seen, the narrator of Kafka's heterobiography comes into being following an intoxicated rupture between first persons, a breach of timespace which, as such, takes neither space nor time. Prior to sense, this caesura 'is' a nonmoment which essentially does not take *place*, and thus there can be no *sense* of the encounter with what may or may not be seven dogs in and as which the investigator has already come to be. For this reason, the narrative 'I' can never *recall* the event of its constitution, but rather only *call it forth* by way of a placeholding marker – in this case the neutral third-person 'it.'

Nevertheless, this is not to say that the encounter henceforth *remains* indescribable. Rather, I have argued, its call without sense is precisely the *opening* of a space allowing that which 'has no name as yet and hence cannot be mentioned' to become an affective worldly entity. The question, then, is how does the investigator-narrator *re*-enact the event? How, in other words, does a body *reconstitute* its purely formal trace of nothing that is being, and which is not nothing? How might one re-articulate that which, in its calling forth or conjuring up of a nonmoment in which 'I' is utterly other, is both the condition of possibility of autobiography *and* that which renders all autobiography impossible? Such are the questions that will occupy us for the remainder of this chapter and all of the next.

The investigator, we discover, can *articulate* the encounter only by *conjuring up an impossible simultaneity*: that of a violently *in*audible blast of sound, of determined silence full of a strident, ear-rending music that comes from the most near which is at once the most distant.

> [The seven dogs] did not speak, they did not sing, they remained generally silent, almost determinedly silent; but from the empty air they conjured music. Everything was music, the lifting and setting down of their feet, certain turns of the head, their running and their standing still ... this blast of music ... seemed to come from all sides ... blowing fanfares so near that they seemed far away and almost inaudible ('Investigations,' 281-2).

Just as the neutral 'it' holds the impossible grammatical place of the (non) subject, we thus find that the animal encounter takes on an improper metonymy which *holds* and *marks* the place of the impossible (non)event. It is, in other words, to 'clothe' an event which has neither spatiality nor temporality and which disrupts *without limit* the autobiographical narrative. Here then, is the borrowed costume, the senseless 'dressing' of an improper metonymy: such is the silent *and at once* clamorous music without which 'the creative gift' of the canine race cannot be made to make sense, cannot be *heard* (281). The improper, placeholding metonymy, in other words, marks a deafening interval within the deafness of the everyday.

4. 'We are all German Jews'

Dressing Improperly, 1968

Introduction

The guiding question of this chapter, as we know, concerns the way in which the untimely call without sense takes on a borrowed costume in order to constitute intra-worldly affects. This will be explored directly through an explication of the political force of the performative 'We are all German Jews' [*Nous sommes tous des juifs allemands*] as enacted in France in 1968, paying particular attention to its relation to what political philosopher Jacques Rancière calls *assujetissement* or 'subjectivization.'

Put simply, I will argue that only by taking on the 'technical prosthesis' of just such a borrowed costume might an encounter's demand come to be preserved, a preserving which makes possible the chance of *fighting a dominant power for the past*. Historically contingent, the ghostly announcing of the encounter in this way takes on a *material* form. A coming to being which, in its staging of an intensive metonymic co-respondence with the past that counters all historicist reduction, thus enables it to impact in and upon the world by putting to work otherwise the machinery of sense. As such, these tropes function in *precisely the opposite direction to animalization*, producing a rupture in the economy of genocide.

The apocalyptic encounter, as we have seen, interrupts the linear time of the everyday, with its mute call marking its opening as the *taking* place of time. The 'preserving' metonymy, by contrast, insofar as it has always already *taken* place, thus *constitutes its own* time and space. In this way, that which the prevailing order must exclude is reinscribed as the outside of that order and thus, outside of consensual reflection, as a division *within* that ordered state. This is not to suggest, however, some kind of transcendence of the everyday. Rather, the revolutionary positing of an improper, placeholding metonymy, as a catachrestic reinscription which refuses subsumption to the Same, is necessarily immanent to sedimented power relations. This is simply because the passivity of our being-thrown must already preserve the possibility of just such a chance encounter of material imposition – the chance, in short, of disrupting the habitual *re*production of sense.

Rancière: the most near at once the most distant

One of the few political theorists to take serious account of deconstruction, Jacques Rancière too is concerned with the staging of a revolutionary performative that enables those who do not 'count' to confront the prevailing order that otherwise excludes them. In this, Rancière's position is, as we shall see, closely allied to my own. In other ways, however, our positions are diametrically opposed. First of all, the evental encounter is, for Rancière, an *essentially* human affair dependent upon 'the desire to engage in reasoned discourse' which thus disqualifies all nonhumans as potential participants.[1] Secondly, and perhaps as a result of these differing starting points, we reach different conclusions regarding the relation of the event to the revolutionary performative, as this chapter will show. Nevertheless, the proximity of Rancière's position will hopefully serve here to further clarify my own.

According to Rancière, *policing* or *policy* is the arranging of 'that tangible reality in which bodies are distributed in community' (*Disagreement*, 28). *Politics*, however, concerns 'whatever shifts a body from the place assigned to it or changes a place's destination. It makes visible what had no business being seen ... it makes understood as discourse what was once only heard as noise' (30). Hence, given Rancière's further claim that thinking is always a '*re*thinking' – understood as 'an activity that displaces an object away from the site of its original appearance or attending discourse' ('Dissenting Words,' 120) – it thus becomes clear that for Rancière the task of philosophy is itself necessarily political, and vice versa.

Philosophy and politics, in other words, are united through the notion of active *restaging*, or *assujetissement* (subjectivization), that is, the process by which those 'outcasts' who are 'denied an identity in a given order of policing'

---

[1] This was Rancière's response to the question as posed by Jane Bennett at a conference at Goldsmiths College in 2003. See Bennett, *Vibrant Matter: A Political Ecology of Things* (Durham & London: Duke University Press, 2010), 106.

thus come to be perceived as viable discursive beings (Rancière, 'Politics,' 61). In short, political philosophy (either term being technically redundant) consists of making sensible that which is insensible within a given state of affairs. Hence, political (or philosophical) *activity* is the coming to be sensible of any and all bodies rendered invisible and voiceless within, and by, a given police order. The question then, is *how*, and under what conditions, those 'bodies' which, reproduced as invisible, senseless noise according to a historically contingent 'distribution of sensible,' are suddenly able to *make* sense, and thus affect a world arranged in such a way as to make this very act impossible.

The movement or process of politics, argues Rancière, never consists of 'an act of an identity' ('Politics,' 60). Rather, it requires 'the formation of a one that is not a self but is the relation of a self to an other' (60). As such, he continues, this 'process of disidentification' is necessarily dependent upon a trope 'that links the name of a group or class to the name of no group or no class, a being to a non-being or a not yet being' (61). This does *not*, however, 'mean the assumption of a different identity or the plain confrontation of two identities' (62). In other words, it can be neither a *metaphorical* claim to another's identity (whether directly or as their representative), nor an unfamiliar juxtaposition of two recognizable identities, a calculated relation whose very unfamiliarity, as we know, depends upon the prior sense of its elements being recognized.

Instead, writes Rancière, such an 'impossible identification' takes place only as 'an interval or gap: being *together* to the extent that we are *between* – between names, identities, cultures, and so on' (62). It is, in other words, a being-together in and as a relation to an other that is *not*, or *is not yet*. Such a relation, as we have seen, consists in the creation of a *transductive* being – what Rancière calls a 'heterological enactment' being synonymous with the enacting of an *improper metonymy* whose elements do not precede their relation. Only in this way can 'identification' be at once 'the denial of an identity given ... by the ruling order of policy' (64). This impossible identification, moreover, has *iterability* as its condition. This is because it is iterability which ensures that the dissemination of a 'series of words' cannot be controlled, insofar as any such series is 'equally available both to those entitled to use it and those who are not' ('Dissenting Words,' 116).[2]

---

[2] Rancière, however, would argue that it is what he calls *literarity* – rather than iterability – which ensures such dissemination while at the same time reserving it for the human alone. See 'Dissenting Words,' 115. For a critique of Rancière's literarity, see my paper 'Philosophers and Their Animals: Between Derrida and Rancière' which can be accessed at: http://www.zoogenesis.wordpress.com/2011/12/22/philosophers

While Rancière inexplicably restricts improper identifications to the users of *words* alone, we can nonetheless agree with his assertion that such het-erologies are nothing less than the 'creative activity of invention' allowing for 'a redescription and reconfiguration of a common world of experience' (116). For Rancière, this is exemplified above all by the affirmation in 1968 of an impossible identification with a number of Algerians beaten to death and dumped in the Seine by the police seven years earlier. 'We could not,' he writes,

> identify with those Algerians, but we *could* question our identification with the 'French people' in whose name they had been murdered ... we could act as polit-ical subjects in the interval or the gap between two identities, neither of which we could assume. The process of subjectivization had no proper name, but it found its name, its cross name, in the 1968 assumption 'We are all German Jews' - a 'wrong' identification ('Politics,' 61).

Here, then, there are a number of similarities between what Rancière un-derstands as the process of *assujetissement*, and what I am calling the move-ment of *zoogenesis*. Despite this, a number of difficulties remain concerning Rancière's accounts of the positing of an impossible identification. In the first place, Rancière does not give us to understand exactly *how* that restaging comes to be, nor of the efficacy of its becoming. He does, however, suggest that *assujetissement* consists not simply of 'unentitled' speech acts, but also of a *mimicking* of the existing discourse of power, for which the secession of the Roman plebeians serves as his primary example. Thus, states Rancière in his analysis of the act of secession, it is 'necessary to invent the scene upon which spoken words may be audible, in which objects may be visible, and individu-als themselves may be recognized' ('Dissenting Words,' 116). Such an inven-tion, he argues, establishes another distribution of the sensible by executing 'a series of speech acts that mimic those of the patricians' (*Disagreement*, 24).

It is difficult to know if this is exactly the *same* process of subjectivization as 'We are all German Jews,' but it is nonetheless clear that it similarly in-volves the invention of an improper metonymy, the positing of the same 'we are and are not.' Such a performative, however, points to a *prior* coming to one's senses otherwise which, *only in its having already taken place*, at once calls forth the mimicry. That is to say, the plebeians' coming to a sense of themselves as beings whose 'right' to make sense has been previously elid-ed, and thus of a division within the State, must have *already* taken place. In other words, what Rancière omits from his account is the posthumous, post-apocalyptic sense of being without sense that *constitutes the call and the manifesto* – the *assujetissement* – which necessarily *precedes* any such place-holding 'prosthesis.' He fails, that is, to elaborate the prior *condition* of the restaging that is the 'cross' name.

Hence, for Rancière a restaging is that uniquely human speech act which, by making sensible the previously insensible, shifts a body outside ordered distribution. However, I would argue that this political restaging is rather the *preservation* of the encounter's call. The meaningless metonymic placeholder, in other words, constitutes the time and space of an encounter which has *already* taken place, and which is staged by a being who has *already* come into being *outside* of an ordered state of affairs. I shall endeavor to clarify this further in the next section through the frame of Rancière's privileged example.

'We are all German Jews'

In order to understand the efficacy of the improper metonymy 'We are all German Jews,' it is necessary to focus not solely on its positing, but also on that which constitutes its condition of possibility. First of all, its *chance* paradoxically resides in the very relations of power it puts into question. This is because the excess of an encounter is always and only that which exceeds the proper identification demanded by the process of recognition that is both institutionalized and historically contingent. Here, then, a singular encounter with the abject materiality of the dead Algerians comes to dislocate the recognisable 'I.' The anxious call, in other words, of its insensibility and at once the sense of its sense having being effaced, dis-locates the sense of a delimited self exposed within a shared community affect, in this instance 'the French people.' This 'sense without sense' can necessarily mark only its absence of content in its being *prior* to any possible referent and thus, in its interruption of the habitual interpretations inhabited by dominant relations of power, 'I' comes to be other, falling in the interval between two identities: no longer a recognisable 'I' and not yet a recognisable other. Hence, that which Rancière neatly describes as 'the paratactic logic of a "we are *and* are not"' ('Politics,' 62) can be understood as synonymous with the phrase 'I *is* other.'

In short then, being *this* being encountering an excessive withdrawal of sense in the singularity of its being-there-in-relation to the murdered Algerians, forces its 'I' *from* the self-certainty of familiar repose, and *to* that anxiety which marks, and is indissociable from, the impossible irruption of the as such, of the *taking* place of sense, within the everyday.

All this, therefore, is prior to the actual positing of an improper metony-my that rather *preserves* that monstrous call of a time and space to come. A preserving, in other words, of 'the advent of thinking for those who were not initially destined to think' (Rancière, 'Dissenting Words,' 121). Insofar as the encounter can be apprehended only *as* meaning without sense (content) and *as* sense (sensibility) without meaning, its *making* sense permits only and always an inaugural *citation*, an ironic positing whereby the unheard-of combination becomes sensible. Explicitly put *in the place* of that unnamea-ble which withdraws, such a meaningless placeholder unequivocally refuses identity, mimesis, and surrogacy. Instead, it preserves the having come to being of a space and a time of becoming which, while (the) outside of a given state of affairs, nevertheless resonates *within* that state of affairs.

With the aim of further clarification, it is helpful to pause a moment to recall the fine exegesis of the notion of the monster provided by philosopher and historian Michel Foucault. In a lecture from 1975, Foucault argues that the monster is 'essentially a legal notion … since what defines the monster is the fact that its existence and form is not only a violation of the laws of soci-ety but also a violation of the laws of nature' (*Abnormal*, 55-56). As such, he continues, the monster is the *limit*, 'the point at which law is overturned and the exception that is found only in extreme cases. *The monster combines the impossible* [i.e., *unheard-of*] *and the forbidden*' (56, emphasis added). Even more, the monster effectively *silences the law*, insofar as the latter finds itself incapable of offering a *legal* response to its violation. Unable to employ itself to protect itself from the challenge posed by monstrosity, the law is thus com-pelled to respond, as Foucault notes, with either 'violence, the will for pure and simple suppression, or medical care or pity' (56). The monster, in short, is 'a breach of the law that automatically stands outside the law' (56).

Monstrous and unnameable, the call without sense must therefore take on a borrowed costume if it is to hold its place beyond the law. It must, in other words, take on the appearance of the old – its languages, senses, styles, and conventions – in order to compose an improper past-future *metonymy* which marks or, rather, holds the place of, the irruption of the new in its being posited within contexts where it has not previously belonged. In so doing, its inaugural citation necessarily interrupts the economy of substitu-tion, that is, of *metaphor* as understood within the discipline of rhetoric as an identification of one thing with another (this is that). Only in this way is an opening of the time-space of the new preserved.

In this, 'We are all German Jews' is an intensive, nondialectical corresponding with the past, that is, it possesses neither a proper nor a figurative *sense* but only the intensity of beings improperly resonating together, past and future. The dislocating trace, in order to preserve its own time-space to come, thus calls to an *untimely* deterritorialization of sense which, dependent upon the fact that the context of a phrasing is never fully determined, thus functions as a catachrestic reinscription.[3] The 'impossible' sense of the enactment 'We are all German Jews' thus constitutes at once an intensive relation and a restaging, and it is through the prosthesis of such a borrowed costume that the necessary countersignatures of recognition are gained.

Taking on the clothes of improper metonymy, the mute manifesto of a content-less relation – described by Rancière as 'being together to extent that we are *in between*' ('Politics,' 62) – thus *comes into being*, becomes manifest. Hence, the 'borrowed costume' can be neither an imitation of, nor a calculation 'for the benefit of' or 'on behalf of,' that *with which* it comes to be, which would presuppose a prior identity. It is, in Rancière's words, neither the 'assumption of a different identity [n]or the plain confrontation of two identities' (62).

However, if we are to understand the *efficacy* of this placeholding, it is necessary to leave Rancière behind for a moment and turn instead to what Karl Marx calls *the recovery of the spirit of revolution*. Here too, amid another turn of revolution and attended by the walking ghosts of nihilistic parody, we discover a point of contact, a correspondence between Marx and Nietzsche in an announcing of the *Übermensch* that outlives every determinable form.

The spirit of revolution

In the famous opening passages of *The Eighteenth Brumaire of Louis Bonaparte* (1852), Marx writes of those bodies which, never the liberal subjects of free will, instead find themselves only in being displaced, never making history 'under circumstances they themselves have chosen, but under circumstances directly encountered, given and transmitted from the past' (146).[4] The relation of a body to the world is, in other words, delimited by the idealization of iterability, that is to say *historicity*, and thus the making of sense always *precedes* the exposing in and as which a being comes to be. As a result,

---

[3] Hence the plebeians can only catachrestically mimic, and in so doing transform, an improper positing in order for it to be recognized.

[4] Translation modified here and throughout. See also Derrida's important reading of these passages from *Eighteenth Brumaire* – a reading to which my own is clearly indebted – in *Specters of Marx*, 133-145.

'making history' is at once the necessity and the impossibility of the new:

> The tradition of all the dead generations weighs like a nightmare on the minds of the living. And, just when they appear to be engaged in the revolutionary transformation of themselves and their material surroundings, in the creation of something which does not yet exist, precisely in such epochs of revolutionary crisis they anxiously conjure up [*beschwören sie ängstlich*] the spirits of the past to their service; they borrow from them names, slogans and costumes so as to stage the new world-historical scene in this venerable disguise and borrowed language (146-7).

Employing the example of The French Revolution's catachrestic donning of Roman costume, Marx here describes the necessity of borrowing the appearances of the past – i.e., its languages, genres, poses, conventions, etc. – in order for that transformation to be *staged*. A borrowing, moreover, which is *subsequent* to the revolutionary transformation which has already 'appeared.' In other words, in order for the new to stage its – until then – only *potential* efficacy in the world, it must improperly take on, i.e., *restage*, costumes borrowed from the past. This theatrical disguise is, quite simply, *the condition of historical action itself*. Without it, the revolutionary potential inherent in every living being can produce no material affect whatsoever. It is also another way of stating the impossibility of the 'appearing' coming to be *as such*.

Material transformation thus occurs only with a reconfiguration of both an earlier time and another language, that is, with a reactivation of spectral sediments, in what is the anxious process of 'world-historical necromancy [*Totenbeschwörung*]' (147). In these revolutionary restagings,

> the resurrection of the dead served to exalt the new struggles, rather than to parody the old, to exaggerate the given task in the imagination, rather than to flee from solving it in reality, and to recover the spirit of the revolution, rather than to set its ghost walking again (148).

Here, then, Marx is clearly suggesting there are two, very different ways of restaging the past. On the one hand, we have an anxious conjuration from unnameable monstrosity to resurrected corpse which, insofar as it exalts the new, recovers the revolutionary spirit. On the other, however, we have recourse to the walking ghost of parody, a restaging of the old which nonetheless flees the task of bringing the new into reality. While I will return to this notion of a parodic restaging in the next section, it is already clear that, for Marx, only through the former might that which does not yet exist come into being, and do so in the guise of those who are no longer.

With this lively restaging of a corpse, and of the need to dress the revolutionary spirit in the clothes of the old and dead, we are recalled to Nietzsche's affirmative *response*. As we have seen, such a response improperly stages the singular, unheard-of relation which does not live but rather only *out-lives* [*überleben*] every determinable form. It is this response which *materializes* the silent announcing of that which survives the properly human, and which Werner Hamacher acutely contends comes to be 'only in the form of one who, having outlasted the death of its type, has returned to haunt the living: a living corpse' ('Disgregation,' 159, emphasis added). The posthumous, posthuman corpse thus out-lives its type and genus insofar as it exceeds its proper sense and limit. Having finitude as its condition, and hence a technics as and at the origin of life, we recall its 'dangerous' reiteration is that arriving of truth which interrupts all life, and by which life out-lives itself.

In this, we can better understand how the affirmative turn of the phrase 'We are all German Jews,' in that it returns as a *living* corpse, comes to interrupt the given state of affairs. It announces, in other words, the return of the repressed Algerian corpses in their being raised (again) and catachrestically posited within contexts where they had not previously belonged. In this way, they 'out-live' their proper sense, that is, they outlive their habitual, institutionalized actualization in a given state of affairs. Hence, it is the death machine of living being which, as both the condition of possibility of proprietary norms and of their 'out-living,' thus enables the shattering return of the oppressed. *Such is a conjuration from unnameable monstrosity to resurrected corpse as a calling upon death to summon the future and invent the impossible.*

Ghosting the revolution

It remains, however, to understand the distance and at once the proximity of this revolutionary necromancy to the walking ghost of parody. Here, it becomes necessary to recall, this time with Marx, Nietzsche's specular figures of nihilism.

Perhaps unsurprisingly, given both the tropological machinery of sense and the elliptical apostrophe of the call marking the zoogenetic translation, the key to the difference between Marx's revolutionary spirit and that of the walking ghost lies in their *tropes*. On the one side, we have the living corpse of catachrestic repetition and, on the other, *parody*. Parodic citation is, as we have seen, one of the two forms of nihilism Nietzsche seeks to move beyond. Figured by the 'last man' as the advocate of the cynical play of relativism, parody consists of a play with habitual values in such a way as they become ghostly remains, their value to the last man being merely their usefulness and exchangeability vis-a-vis the selfish manipulation of others. In this, parody plays with *recognized* sense in a calculated game of exquisite corpse. It is this ghost of parody which Marx locates in the bourgeois society of post-revolutionary France:

> Bourgeois society was no longer aware that the ghosts of Rome had watched over its cradle, since it was wholly absorbed in the production of wealth and the peaceful struggle of economic competition … And its gladiators found in the stern classical traditions of the Roman republic the ideals, art forms and self-deceptions they needed in order to hide from themselves the limited bourgeois content of their struggles and to maintain their enthusiasm (*Eighteenth Brumaire*, 148).

Parody, a game which plays with ghosts so as to always reproduce an ashen corpse, is that which remains when the revolutionary restaging comes to be *a part of*, rather than *apart from*, a given state of affairs, *its sense having being reappropriated to economic interest* and its re-investiture of power effaced. Moreover, because of the necessary idealization of iterability, such a reinscription *must always already accompany the recovery of the revolutionary spirit*. Its cynical parody, in other words, emerges concurrently with the revolutionary living corpse, and with which it remains forever indissociable. Hence, while the evental spirit discloses the truth of what arrives – the revealing of that which *is*, but is hidden –, parody at once re-*covers* this truth.

In this way, the last man and the walking ghost, the discovery and recovery of truth, together figure the utilitarian sedimentation by which a dominant power both conserves and exploits its position. Indeed, given that parody's 'still undrained, still unexhausted decay' lives on' (Hamacher, 'Disgregation,' 160) in this way, we can now fully appreciate the Nietzschean injunction towards an eternally returning autocritique.

Outliving the language of revolution

For Marx, having witnessed 'the ghost of the old revolution' which, from 1848 to 1851, 'knew no better than to parody' (*Eighteenth Brumaire*, 148 & 147), the circumvention of the indissociability of the revolution and its ghost could thus only be the most urgent of all concerns if the working class revolution is to *permanently* succeed. In this early stage of Marx's project therefore, one discovers a fundamental difference between his conception of 'ideology' and Nietzsche's notion of 'metaphysical fictions.'[5] Put simply, whereas Marx's world is hopeful for the future but joyless in the present, Nietzsche's world, given that the overhuman remains always to come, is bereft of hope for the future but potentially filled with joy in the present. Consequently, for the young Marx revolutionary politics must inevitably concern itself with the macro-level of world history, contrasting sharply with Nietzsche's genealogical focus upon micropolitical conflagrations.[6] While opposites in one sense then, it is nonetheless the case that both worlds are filled with fetishes and illusions that must be over-come (Marx) or under-gone (Nietzsche).

In seeking to maintain the exalting automanifestation of the revolutionary spirit by somehow pre-empting its cynical hollowing-out in the guise of parody, Marx turns to the example of language itself. It follows from our argument thus far that, in order to avoid the reiteration by which the improper metonymy of the revolutionary citation becomes its own ghost, it must be utterly *dis*continuous with the past. Only then does it refuse the possibility of reiteration. Hence, writes Marx, it is necessary to be fluent in *the language of revolution*. In contrast to the beginner who, having learned a new language, still always translates it back into her mother tongue, the fluent revolutionary must 'appropriate the spirit of the new language,' an appropriation that can be considered complete only when she 'can manipulate it without reference to the old' (*Eighteenth Brumaire*, 146-7). The improper metonymy by which the future revolution preserves itself must, in other words, *no longer relay* the old, must no longer be haunted by the past from which it is excized in being transformed.

In this way, the power of a revolutionary positing must be utterly, i.e., *permanently*, discontinuous with any possibility of making sense within the state

---

[5] This is not to say, however, that the impossibility of circumvention is not disclosed by the later Marx. The dislocation of the intending subject, for example, as in the famous 'personification' of capital (*Capital* I:253-4 and III:403), necessarily demands a critique that remains vigilant to an originary technics. On this 'spectrality of the rational' see, along with Derrida's *Spectres*, Gayatri Chakravorty Spivak, 'Ghostwriting' in *Diacritics* 25:2, 65-84; and *A Critique of Postcolonial Reason*, 76-84.

[6] The historian, writes Foucault in 'Nietzsche, Genealogy, History' (1971), offers possible alternate identities that are more substantial and individualized, but only the genealogist knows what to make of this masquerade by pushing it to its limit until, with the coming of the great carnival of time, masks are constantly reappearing that are no longer 'the identification of our faint individuality with the solid identities of the past, but our "unrealization" through the excessive choice of identities' (*Language, Counter-Memory, Practice*, 161). Perhaps then, and here Foucault cites Nietzsche in *Beyond Good and Evil*, 'we can discover a realm where originality is again possible of parodists of history and buffoons of God' (161). It is in this context too we must think of Nietzsche as Dionysus, Nietzsche as Zarathustra, Zarathustra as Dionysus, etc.

of affairs it interrupts. It can, in Marx's words, 'only create its poetry from the future, not from the past. ... There the phrase transcended the content [*die Phrase über den Inhalt*]; here the content transcends the phrase' (149). This, however, is simply not possible. Rather, for the 'phrase' to be effective in the world, for it to *make sense*, it *must* relay the past, inasmuch as the making of sense in fact depends upon the indissociability of spirit and ghost as the very condition of its being-constituted. The 'phrase,' in other words, is the having taken on of a materiality, an expropriation of form which, as with all forms, necessarily constitutes a mask. Such is the manifest dissimulation necessary to effect an efficacious restaging, and in this the improper metonymy must always transcend the content.[7]

Hence, whereas for Marx the revolutionary transformation is appropriated when 'the new' is no longer marked in its difference and deferral, it is rather the case that this appropriation marks the *cooptation*, the re-covery or reinscription, of its interruption within a state of affairs. It is the moment, in other words, when the idealization of the phrasing allows for its parodic manipulation. Once again, in becoming 'naked' – becoming '*human*' in the figural sense I am employing it here – its excluded sense is *disguised by an apparent transparency*. Such is the walking ghost, a congealed clarity which dissimulates the impropriety of the 'animal' encounter's address.

In summary, the revolutionary phrasing is the preserving of an encounter which, in borrowing the old clothes of the past, enacts a restaging in which the new-old language *refuses* to make sense. *This refusal is absolutely crucial to the argument being explored throughout this book.* Insofar as it remains between senses in this way, it *both no longer and not yet makes sense*, but rather constitutes a time-space of intensive correspondence. The sense of the materiality which exceeds its placeholder is thus, in Marx's terms, the content *outliving* as its phrase. Its power, in common with the indiscipline of 'animal studies' itself, resides in the *between* of sense, an indecipherable intervallic zone between negation and sublation which ruptures any possibility of synthesis.

The refusal to make sense, the no longer and not yet of meaning, thus constitutes the opening of desire to an infinity of non-consummation.[8] Two

---

[7] The term 'phrase,' it must be recalled, does not necessarily refer to a *human* speech act, or even to a *speech* act, and thus it is important to hear within it many other kinds of phrasings, that is, other and others' ways of *spacing*.

[8] As can be seen most clearly in the 1962 lecture 'Time and Being,' Heidegger's key notion of *Ereignis* (event) constitutes an attempt to bring together the *no longer* and *not yet* in the instant of transition [*Augenblick*]. Thinking with Heidegger is, I would argue, essential for reading Nietzsche, and vice versa, as only with Heidegger can we fully

important corollaries are immediately evident: first, that *desire can no longer be limited to human animals alone*; and second, that this refusal of recognized sense *functions in the field of politics as the ever-renewing promise of emancipation*.

However, as we have seen, this revolutionary phrasing must *at once become its own ghost*. Becoming naked, transparent, the impropriety of its mask necessarily falls away, slides into the habitual, losing itself to the nihilistic parody of the last man. In *Specters of Marx*, Derrida puts this perfectly when he states that as 'soon as one identifies a revolution, it begins to imitate, it enters into a death agony' (144).

Viral micropolitics and genealogical conflagrations

Returning to Rancière, we can now understand why the phrase 'We are all German Jews' – 'the validity of which … rest[s] entirely on the capacity to overturn the political relationship between the order of designations and that of events''' (Rancière, 'Dissenting Words,' 114) – exists only as an intensive corresponding. It is not, in other words, a *synthesis*. Rather, it is a *placeholder* whose invention both marks and is marked by its intensity in holding open the 'place' of the interval from and to which a being is recalled otherwise. Hence, as Rancière argues, the name always *finds itself*, that is, finds its 'cross' or 'wrong' name ('Politics,' 61).

The improper metonymy is, in short, a *prosthesis*, a bandage and a mask of disconcealment which, making no sense, rather enacts an intensive resonance that is a making sensible. Whereas Rancière argues that the *event* of *assujetissement* or "subjectivization" is identical with the prosthetic declaration, it is rather the case that *assujetissement* refers to that which is *called forth* by the disorientating withdrawal of an *anterior* event, that of the animal encounter. Staging in this way an intensive metonymic correspondence with the past that constitutes its own time-space, the improper metonymy thus reinscribes *as* its divisive outside that which the prevailing order must exclude. It is, in other words, the staging of an unmentionable relation which, as Rancière attests, 'is not a place for dialogue or a search for a consensus' (62).

In contrast to a reasonable application on the basis of prior identity, the performative affirmation of an improper metonymy demands only those affirmative countersignatures by which that exclusion is recognized. Its phrase

---

appreciate the thinking of the event otherwise left implicit in Nietzsche.

resonates, intensifying and coalescing in an opposition, imposing its own sense differently and at once interpellating other beings which come to be insofar as they share the disorientating call of its encounter. This transformative force is not linear, that is, it does not 'catch fire.' Rather, its efficacy is the chance affect of a feverish disposition that may flare up in local conflagrations in and as an inhuman multitude inflamed by the prevailing order's refusal to recognize its sense. Aesthetic in the Nietzschean sense of being before and beyond any notion of taste and judgment, it is thus *necessarily* political in that it is other to the dominant culture of *recognized* value. It is, in short, the coming into being of a nonreactive, affirmative micropolitics that allows for a political ethics insofar as it operates without any kind of transcendence, that is, without any overarching control from above.

Moreover, the resonance of the phrasing is at once the opening of the space of a Nietzschean *genealogy*, of its mapping of a site of exclusion, in that by becoming sensible it at once marks its prior *non*sensibility. That is, the placeholding phrasing makes legible its prior exscription from sense as an – *hitherto imperceptible* – operation of power. Hence, the inscription of the new at once makes possible a genealogical rearticulation which, in that making sense of a prior exclusion makes perceptible the economic interest concealed within the parodic citation of habitual values, calls others to an encounter with the force of the reinscribed exclusion.

In this way, the phrasing 'We are all German Jews' is not only the arrival and dissimulation of truth, not only the placeholder of a new encounter, not only the creation of a monstrosity at the limit of sense, but also the opening of a genealogical time-space in which the investment of power in the prior exclusion of the newly sensible Algerian bodies can be rendered legible. *It potentially makes perceptible, in other words, the local theatre of animalization, and thus the machinery of constitutive exclusion.* In summary, the improper metonymy enacts a restaging that resounds with future encounters at the same time as opening a space of revaluation within historiological discourse.

Conclusion: from a happy life to a joyful one

We have now explored in some detail the three stages that together make up the movement of *zoogenesis*. Beginning with the senseless address of an *animal encounter* in response to an ethical demand, a new transductive being is called into existence; a being which, insofar as its prosthetic *placeholding metonymy* remains *between* sense, opens the site of a potential politics of resistance. It is a movement, furthermore, in two directions: at once the opening of a time-space of recognition to come, *and* the opening of the past as the future by a rethinking of what takes place today. In other words, if we are to fully understand the efficacy of 'We are all German Jews' – or indeed any such improper metonymy – it is necessary to respond to the specific demands of its coming into being. One must, in other words, consider such questions as, what investment of reproduction rendered its prior insensibility? What *use* does such an elision serve? Which figures organize the effect of foreclosure? and so on.

The space of genealogy is thus the chance to interpret and evaluate, in Deleuze's words, the 'truth of a thought ... according to the forces of power that determine it to think and to think this rather than that' (*Nietzsche and Philosophy*, 97). As such, in disclosing 'what forces are hiding themselves in the thought of *this* truth, and therefore what its sense and value is' (97), the genealogical space thereby offers a radical political historiology in that the making sense of the previously insensible demands an oppositional stance to the state of affairs that reproduced its exclusion. It is, in short, the redoubled space of *respond-ability*: the excessive recursivity between concept and singular experience, between deafness and the inaudible clamor of being-with. Only here, in and as this redoubled space, resides the potential of an emergent trajectory of escape.

At last then, in concluding this part let us consider once more the example of Kafka's investigator which which it began. The investigator, we recall, having come to his senses following the intoxicating expropriation of the 'I,' comes to a self that senses itself constrained by previously insensible limits. However, in the same instant that the youth becomes an investigator, he is also, in being-thrown into the 'peculiarity' of critique, irredeemably displaced from the 'happy life' of the everyday. The animal encounter, in other words, calls *forth* the investigator and at once demands *from* the investigator an indefatigable, unending pursuit that is nothing less than an unending critique of theology, economics, politics and philosophy.

No longer insensible to the impositions and exclusions of knowing, the investigator ultimately finds *himself* potentially marked out for social exclusion: 'my peculiarities [*Sonderbarkeiten*],' he writes, 'lie open to the day' ('Investigations,' 279). In following the apocalypse, he can maintain with his silence neither the nostalgic reactive longing for ecstatic communion, nor the quietism of consensus that serves only to maintain the status quo. Rather, having become other, the investigator is paradoxically compelled to always seek instead those irresistible [*unwiderstehlich*] encounters that 'drive us again and again, as though by sheer force, out of our social circle" (280). He is compelled, in other words, to open his self to those encounters which drive us beyond our all too canine, all too human limitations and, indeed, beyond and before every proper delimitation of species. He is, moreover, and in spite of the grave risks involved as we shall see, compelled to do so joyfully.

Part Three. Ethics and Power

The 'unrecognizable,' I shall say in a somewhat elliptical way, is the beginning of ethics, of the Law, and not of the human. So long as there is recognizability and fellow, ethics is dormant.

Jacques Derrida, *The Beast and the Sovereign*

Whoever heard of an ironic ethics? Not an unserious question, for it may be the case that ethics can only be ironic, untimely, disguised and failing.

Avital Ronell, *The Test Drive*

Introduction: the fatal risk of the untimely

In the preceding chapters, we have seen that, like every concept, 'the human' is a discursive abstraction constructed through the forgetting of difference and, as such, is reproduced to a degree as necessary and uniform. As a consequence, as Nietzsche tells us, 'humanity' is 'actually *made* calculable,' a calculability which has as its most fruitful effect 'the *sovereign individual*, like only to himself' (*Genealogy*, II:2). This indissociability of the violence of making-calculable and the effect, and the efficacy, of sovereignty, should certainly give us pause. Another way of saying this would be that to be human is to come into being within, and as a consequence of, the vast machinery of making-sense-ability which conditions the visibility and viability of each and every social being. All social beings are, in short, the result of habitual practices of long-standing cultural formations congealed in and as the languages they inhabit and which inhabit them. This 'already-there' which, prior to its effect, already divides the indivisibility of the sovereign 'I' thus ensures the active-passive production and reproduction of norms determined by dominant relations of power.

Amid the vast array of contemporary studies deconstructing the 'normalizing' function of various cultural formations, however, the machinations of one particular norm remain all too often unthought, with the result that its global death machine continues to function largely unopposed. Such is the normalizing anthropocentrism which unthinkingly identifies the machinery of the already-there with *human* language, *human* culture, and *human* history alone. It is essential, therefore, that the notion of the already-there be freed from its stifling association with human exceptionalism, and be extended instead to every sensitive being.

The stakes of this hospitable extension are huge. As we have seen, it is originary technicity – the 'already' of every 'there' – which holds in reserve the space of ethical response, and which permits of the chance calling forth of improper, transforming metonymies that breach the enclosures of property and propriety. Hence, to extend originary technicity to nonhuman beings is to include every living being within the ethical domain. Ethics, it has further been argued, only begins in a movement beyond that which can be determined. For the human animal, for example, ethics can begin only in a disidentification with the radical alterity of a *non*human or *in*human being which marks, and thus interrupts, the measure and the limit of humanity.

More specifically, however, 'the ethical' is precisely that which withdraws in the opening of a politics as its actualized supplement. In this, the *politicity* of an animal encounter resides in the impossibility of preserving its call without redressing its insensibility within the clothes of the sensible, this latter being a reactive concealment which paradoxically marks its becoming naked. In contrast to Rancière then, a phrasing remains political only insofar as it no longer and not yet makes sense, thus making explicit the impropriety of its costume and hence the unnameable absence it names. Insofar as the already-there remains as its condition of possibility, however, there can be no guarantee that such a placeholder will gain the necessary countersignatures of recognition. Rather, every ethical encounter brings with it the *risk of becoming-unrecognisable within the structures of meaning that reproduce viable ways of being*. It is this risk of a potentially fatal withholding or withdrawal of recognition that will be explored in the next chapter.

This withholding of recognition, it will be argued, in fact neutralizes the ethical encounter through a doubling of 'outsides.' As we have seen, the materiality of the atemporal outside imposes itself in the chance of an animal encounter, and in this opens *to* the unnameable outside of a given state of affairs which nevertheless resonates improperly *within* that state. In contrast to, and yet indissociable from, such an encounter, the withdrawal and withholding of making-sense-ability displaces and confines the maddening event to an 'outside' constituted *within* a given state of affairs. In this way the internal 'outside' serves as both the limit *of* normativity and the limit *to* normativity. It is, in other words, a conserving reaction which doubles and at once disavows the animal encounter by reinscribing it 'inside' an 'outside' constituted *by* a given state of affairs, and which constitutes the limit and the legitimate *of* that state.

Such reactive socioeconomic, political and material displacings range from social exclusion, ridicule, prejudice and hatred on the one hand, to the full-scale mobilization of the juridico-medical machinery with its physical confinements and judgments of criminality, deviancy, pathology and madness on the other. Being judged, whether officially or not, to be 'mad,' as lacking the ability to make sense and thus 'outside' of the social constraints determined by the already-there, is thus to be displaced *within* an 'outside' constituted only in opposition to the 'inside' of a given state of affairs. In this, the neutralizing displacement of the encounter to the confines of the 'outside' of reason can be seen to mirror the maddening displacement and extreme passivity of the encounter's apocalyptic interval.

More than this, as we shall see, it is within this contested space of recognizability, the unrecognizable, and the withholding of recognition, that an essential link is revealed between the neutralization of an animal encounter, the necessary dormancy of any so-called ethics based upon similarity and familiarity, and the genocidal economy of animalization which functions to exclude other beings from the ability to make sense.

In this context, it thus comes as no surprise to find the discourse of madness paradoxically linked to that of *domesticity*, that is, to the home and to the everyday, in that madness consists of an interruption of the *foreign*, of the unrecognizable, *within* the familiar. In Plato's *The Sophist*, for example, the Foreigner fears that, in being outside of common (i.e., *communal*) sense, he will be judged mad. Doubling the immigrant's fear that he or she will be unable to make sense in the language of another, the Foreigner in particular fears that he will be considered mad insofar as he represents a challenge to the paternal *logos* by suggesting that nonbeing, that whose being is not there, nevertheless *is* (or *has*) being. He fears, in other words, being condemned as contrary to its truth of being-there. Similarly, to respond to the demand of an animal encounter is to risk *becoming* a stranger or a foreigner at home, an internal exile or even a domestic terrorist. It is to risk becoming an asylum seeker and at once to risk the asylum.

Against this, however, I argue that *every living being is always already seeking asylum within the domestic, and yet each is constitutively foreign to the 'there' of its singular being.* Consequently, every living being demands hospitality and yet, insofar as hospitality demands an autonomous sovereign decision, every living being is incapable of offering it or, rather, is able to do so only inadequately. It is an inability and an insufficiency, moreover, which in addition renders both unjust and unjustifiable the liberal-Aristotelian contractual argument that seeks to exclude nonhuman animals from the ethical domain on the basis of an alleged inability to reciprocate.

Butler's human and Burroughs' centipede

In the first chapter of this part, I seek to illuminate the obscure region within which other animals dwell in the philosophy of Judith Butler. In so doing, I show why the inclusion of nonhuman animals is fundamental to the ethical domain as, without it, the normative privileging of the white Western heterosexual human male is inevitably reinforced. Through a critical engagement with Butler's work, I argue that a subject does indeed come to be as the result of reiterated practice propagating sameness and identification as and at the junctures of multiple 'outsides.' However, in contrast to Butler, I maintain that 'the human' is never the simple *effect* of regulatory reproductive power, but rather that 'humanness' is itself a regulatory norm – a norm, moreover, through which all other norms must pass in order to reproduce themselves as 'natural.' As a result, I argue, ethical responsibility demands that an 'I' open its self to the risk of being judged socially non-viable and thus *non*human, as exemplified here by the life – and untimely death – of Venus Xtravaganza.

In chapter six I trace some of the implications of this through various related readings of the wild-tame and timeless-timebound dichotomies. My primary references here are the late texts of the North American novelist William S. Burroughs, which have been chosen not only because of their explicit engagement with human-animal relations but, more importantly, because they follow from an animal encounter which, according to Burroughs, saved him from 'a deadly, pervasive ignorance' (*Cat Inside*, 46). In this way, I aim to demonstrate that, without an excessive hospitality, the entangled hegemonies of oppression are inevitably repeated and thus reinforced. I thus argue that, while for Burroughs the valorized timelessness of the wild makes possible an animal-Love which transcends pain and conflict, in fact the restriction of love to some, but not all, nonhuman animals inevitably serves only to reiterate a logic of domination, as evidenced too in the complementary reading of Deleuze and Guattari's notion of 'becoming-animal.'

Such a logic or *logos* is, in short, dependent upon the exclusion of the *alogon*. It depends, that is to say, upon the entangled exclusions of madness, of animals, and of the foreign within the domestic. Consequently, I argue in the 'Centre Piece' that follows this part, the beginning of ethics resides within the detested figure of the Burroughsian centipede, to whom a welcome must be offered if Burroughs' thinking of the posthuman is to escape its masculinist, imperialist logic.

5. Domestic Scenes and Species Trouble

On Judith Butler and Other Animals

Introduction: Crossing out the Animals

In the film *Paris is Burning* (1990), director and producer Jennie Livingston vividly documents the Harlem drag balls between 1987 and 1989, in which African-American and Latino men compete in a variety of categories such as 'executive', 'schoolboy/girl', and 'town and country', all of which are judged according to the single criterion of 'realness'. One of the balls' participants defines this as the attempt to become 'a real woman, or a real man – a *straight* man' – by 'erasing all the flaws, the mistakes'. 'Realness' in this context thus rests on an ability to 'pass' as 'the real thing', that is, the ability to attain a certain believability through the reiteration of various social norms that together produce the *effect* of naturalness. At the same time, however, the very possibility of passing *as* real, that is, of artfully reconstituting an apparently natural effect, inevitably serves to *de*naturalize those very same norms which otherwise compel belief and thus apportion 'realness'. It is here, at this intersection of the natural and the unnatural, of the real and the artificial, that the figure of Venus Xtravaganza emerges as a compelling focal point of what is a problematic but nonetheless fascinating film.[1]

A light-skinned Latina who 'passes' as both white and female, Venus desires above all a comfortable white domesticity. White girls, she says, get everything they want. For Venus, the only way of accessing this idealized domestic scene is by transforming herself into a 'complete' woman: 'I want

---

[1] On the problems of Livingstone's 'phallic' position of promise behind the camera see bell hooks 'Is Paris Burning?' Z, Sisters of the Yam (June 1991), which in turn is further discussed by Butler in *Bodies That Matter*, 133-7.

a car, I want to be with the man I love, I want a nice home, away from New York where no one knows me [i.e., in middle-class white suburbia]. I want my sex-change. I want to get married in church in white.' It is not enough, in other words, for Venus to pass as white and female only at the Harlem balls. Rather, if this domestic ideal is to be realized, she must be able to pass all the time and in the most intimate of situations. This desire to be, and to desire the desires of, a wealthy white heterosexual woman is precisely the desire not to be excluded as foreign or unnatural. A passionate yet mundane desire that contrasts shockingly with the revelation of her murder as an addendum to the film.

As a prostitute presumably killed by a male client upon discovery of her male sexual organs, Venus is thus murdered for her supplemental 'incompleteness,' for the foreignness that has always already invaded both the dream of the domestic and the domestic itself, the manifestation of which puts at risk her viability as a human being at the hands of a patriarchal order. Indeed, it is by no means incidental that her strangled body was eventually discovered stuffed *under* a bed – the place of an animal – in a cheap hotel room. Her murder thus all too clearly bears on the gap between the phantasmatic 'realness' performed during the balls, and the equally phantasmatic morphological ideal produced by the inculcation of hegemonic norms within society at large.

In order to better understand this process by which hegemonic norms either constitute, or refuse, a certain effect of 'realness,' the *oeuvre* of feminist philosopher Judith Butler is indispensable. Moreover, her core notion of *performativity* promises much for the development of animal studies. Despite this, however, her work has been largely overlooked in this area – in the main, I believe, due to the erroneous belief that performativity refers only to human verbal language, leading many to dismiss it as some sort of linguistic constructionism which therefore ignores all 'natural' material and biological strata.[2] Given that the opposite is in fact the case, I hope the following goes some way toward rectifying this error.

Having said this, however, Butler's own ambivalence regarding the place, or otherwise, of nonhuman animals does not make this task any easier. The aim of this chapter is thus twofold: first, to illuminate this obscure region in

---

[2] There are, to my knowledge, a couple of notable exceptions: Kelly Oliver's *Animal Lessons: How They Teach Us to Be Human* (New York: Columbia University Press, 2009), which briefly deals with Butler's work in relation to nonhuman animals; and Chloe Taylor's 'The Precarious Lives of Animals: Butler, Coetzee, and Animal Ethics' in *Philosophy Today* (2008), 52, 60-72 (I thank the anonymous reviewer at JCAS for drawing my attention to this latter paper).

which other animals dwell within Butler's philosophy and, second, to thereafter further elucidate how the reproduction of 'killing ideals' function to deny the humanness of Venus Xtravaganza and, in so doing, open the space for an apparently 'morally legitimate' putting to death. In this, we will also see why, in any critical engagement with the so-called 'question of the animal,' *humanness* too must be put into question, as only then does it become possible to understand how speciesism – marked fundamentally by the *killing*, rather than the *murder*, of nonhuman animals – forms the excluded support of myriad other structural exclusions, from racism and sexism to homophobia and classism.

I begin by considering Butler's important early text *Bodies That Matter* (1993), in which she lays out her political philosophy of the performative. Therein, Butler argues that the apparently 'free' subject of secular humanism is rather the result of a regulatory network of inculcation which – by way of various 'phantasmatic' ideals that serve to exclude women, people of color, and the poor – thus ensures the continuing hegemonic privilege of the white 'Western' heterosexual male. Butler's list of constitutive exclusions, however, is *itself* marked by exclusion, that is, by the exclusion of nonhuman animals. Indeed, this exclusion is made all the more ironic insofar as it is in large part thanks to the theoretical interventions of Butler, among others, that we now find ourselves in a position to recognize that the critical reinscription of nonhuman animals within those very places where admittance has thus far been refused is absolutely crucial if we are to transform the current regime of exploitation.

To this end, I focus throughout on the contestation of one particular claim, initially proposed by Butler in *Bodies That Matter* and reiterated in a number of later texts: that the 'human,' being neither substance nor specie, is simply the aggregate *effect* of regulatory reproductive power. Against this, I argue that 'the human' is never a cumulatory effect, but it is rather that '*humanness*' is itself a regulatory norm constituted through species difference, just as 'whiteness,' for example, is a regulatory norm constituted through racial difference. 'Humanness,' moreover, is a norm through which all other norms – of race, gender, class, sexuality, and so on – must pass in order to reproduce themselves as 'natural.' Think, for example, of the privileged sexuality accorded to the ideal of 'whiteness' so desired by Venus Xtravaganza, a privilege that can never be fully understood without recognising the concomitant displacement that shifts nonwhite sexuality toward 'animality.' Only then can we understand the fatal 'crossings' performed by Venus, and only with this understanding might we thenceforth begin to dismantle the racist, sexist, and speciesist network of privilege that resulted in her death. While a redress of this exclusion clearly points to the importance of thinking (with) animals for radical thought, it should also be noted from the outset that, in a very real sense, Butler herself calls for the clarifications contained herein, as we shall see when considering the ever-increasing ambivalence toward other animals that marks her later texts. As such, this chapter is itself ambivalently positioned somewhere between critique and dutiful response.

Phantasms, the Human-effect, and Ineffectual Animals

To begin, it is necessary first of all to understand the process by which 'phantasmatic ideals,' imposed by the reiteration of regulatory norms, come to be naturalized. Take, for example, the *activity* of gendering. As Butler explains in *Bodies That Matter*, such an activity both precedes the willing subject of the secular humanist tradition, and is at once 'the matrix through which all willing first becomes possible' (7). Consider, she continues, the medical interpellation which –

> shifts an infant from an 'it' to a 'she' or a 'he,' and in that naming, the girl is 'girled,' brought into the domain of language and kinship through the interpellation of gender. But that 'girling' of the girl does not end there; on the contrary, that founding interpellation is reiterated by various authorities and throughout various intervals of time to reenforce or contest this naturalized effect. The naming is at once the setting of a boundary, and also the repeated inculcation of a norm (7-8).

The subject, according to Butler, is the singular yet ventriloquized nexus of a network of such inculcations, constituted in the intersection of various phantasmatic ideals reproduced by regulatory norms with the result that the very materiality of the body 'will not be thinkable' apart from the materialization of these norms (2). Furthermore, each of these norms 'require and deploy each other for the purpose of their own articulation' (18). Hence, the practice of gendering, to stay with Butler's example, requires that it simultaneously deploy racializing and heterosexualizing practices. Mutually supporting, there exist no independently articulated norms but only imbricated 'hegemonies of oppression' (132). As a result,

> [a] convergent set of historical formations of racialized gender, of gendered race, of the sexualization of racial ideals, or the racialization of gender norms, makes up both the social regulation of sexuality and its psychic articulations. ... Hence, it is no longer possible to make sexual difference prior to racial difference or,

for that matter, to make them into fully separable axes of social regulation and power (181-2).

In short, reiterated practice is productive power: 'the power to produce – demarcate, circulate, differentiate – the bodies it controls' (1). It is this regulatory activity which, insofar as it both precedes and enables the materialization of the willing subject, leads Butler to claim that 'the matrix of gender relations is *prior to* the emergence of the "human"' (7, emphasis added). The 'human', by contrast, is merely the aggregate *effect* of regulatory reproductive power. It is here, however, that Butler's analysis loses its cohesion, in that such a claim actually effaces the relations of power it seeks otherwise to disclose.

It is rather the case, as Butler in fact gestures toward in her discussion of Plato's *khōra*, that 'humanness' is itself a regulatory norm, a reiterated practice of *human-ing* which similarly requires and deploys every other norm for the purpose of its own articulation. Hence, equally important in the discussion of gendering activity is the imperative to also consider – and not as something external or separate – that 'other' matrix through which the majority of nonhuman animals are rather *refused* that shift to gendered being. Only once consideration is extended in this way does it become possible to understand the meshed machinery that opens the possibility of a *refusal* or *withdrawal* of gender, and which at the same time necessarily relegates the 'improperly' gendered human being to the status of an animal. Hence, only when 'humanness' is understood as a regulatory norm imposing murderous, phantasmatic ideals through the mechanism of species difference can we understand the enactment of the specific withdrawal or withholding of recognition from Venus Xtravaganza, a withdrawal which ultimately serves to neutralize the subversiveness of her 'crossing.'

In practice, the naturalization of speciesism in Butler's text both traces and effaces an unmarked-but-marking receptacle through which all other norms must pass – an effacement that serves precisely to *produce* this apparent effect of 'the human.' This is not, however, to make species difference prior to, or more fundamental than, sexual, racial, or any other regulatory difference. Rather, as we shall see, species difference serves to 'ground' all the other norms at the same time as it is reciprocally 'grounded' by them. For this reason, it is necessary to extend Butler's convergent sets of historical formations beyond the imbrication of gender, sexuality, and race, so as to include such convergent sets as the animalization of racialized gender, the racialization of human norms, the normative sexualization of animality, and so on. Indeed, unless we attend to this imbrication of a speciesist reproduction of difference along and within racist, sexist, homophobic, and classist norms, those 'hegemonies of oppression' which critical discourse seeks to challenge may instead be unwittingly reenforced.

While Butler does subsequently touch upon the mechanism of negative displacement whereby a targetted human or human grouping is 'relegated' to animal status, her repeated invocation of the human as an aggregate effect ensures that the economy undergirding this displacement remains frustratingly obscure. Thus in *Precarious Life: The Powers of Mourning and Violence* from 2004, Butler once again claims that 'there are racial and ethnic frames by which the recognizably human is currently *constituted*' (90, emphasis added), while simultaneously arguing that it is imperative that we ask how 'the human' works, 'what it forecloses, and what it sometimes opens up' (89). Indeed, on occasion Butler even refers to a 'norm of humanness' (98), acknowledging too that the reproduction of the 'enemy' as 'less than human' involves 'a reduction of these human beings to animal status' (78). Butler, however, all too quickly glides over this issue, one result of which being that her analysis of the mechanism by which those illegally imprisoned in Guantanamo Bay come to be constituted as 'dangerous' remains – like her analysis of the murder of Venus Xtravaganza – necessarily incomplete.

Similarly, in her recent book *Frames of War: When is Life Grievable?* (2009), Butler yet again writes of the 'the civilizational and racial norms by which the human is constituted' (93). Nevertheless, by now the specter of the excluded animal is increasingly making its (non)presence felt from within the margins of her discourse. Butler acknowledges, for example, that 'there is no firm way to distinguish in absolute terms the *bios* of the animal from the *bios* of the human animal' (19). This fundamental insight is immediately disqualified, however, insofar as Butler concludes from this only that 'animality' is therefore 'a precondition of the human' (19). With this, she thus reinstitutes the very distinction just dismissed as untenable in that, given that the human has animality as its *pre*-condition, its animal status is therefore that which is *transcended* in becoming human, an event synonymous with the emergence of the human into the realm of pervasive social relations that form its actual, and thus exceptional, conditions. Put simply, Butler is here reiterating a central tenet of humanist dogma in claiming that the human comes to be only in transcending the state of (animal) nature.

Ultimately, the vacillation between aggregate effect and constitutive norm reveals itself in the uncertainty with which Butler views her own theoretical position, as when she states in *Precarious Life* that 'I may seem to be positing a new basis for humanism. That might be true, but I am prone to consider this differently' (42). This hesitancy, put simply, can only be resolved by recognizing as fundamental the place and status of nonhuman animals. In order to fully appreciate the stakes involved, it is necessary to return once more to the founding principles as laid down in *Bodies That Matter*.

To begin with, insofar as Butler refuses to think with nonhuman animals, she is thus compelled to invoke the empty yet foreclosed domain of 'the in-human' as the constitutive outside of the human, an invocation that remains more or less constant throughout her work.[3] Instead of a simple and narcissistic reversal, however, it is rather the indecipherable nonhuman animal, traditionally synonymous with irrationality, with dumb nature, with the alogon, who haunts the boundaries of the properly human 'as the persistent possibility of their disruption and rearticulation' in both producing and threatening 'the more and the less "human"' (*Bodies That Matter*, 8). This latter, it is clear, requires some sort of continuum that the inhuman simply cannot provide. Indeed, particularly telling in this regard is Butler's later claim that once a body is produced as less than human, and is thus no longer apprehended as a 'life,' the *murder* of such a body can thereafter never take place (*Precarious Life*, 147). Put simply, killing ceases to be murder only when the murder involves a 'mere' animal – the 'enemy' to be slaughtered may indeed be figured as 'inhuman,' but it is always as animals that they are killed.

This becomes even clearer when we consider Butler's claim that 'the examples of those abjected beings who do not appear properly gendered' serve to demonstrate that 'it is their very humanness that comes into question' (*Bodies That Matter*, 8). This is indeed a crucial point. However, if the human is only ever the result or *effect* of the appellation and inculcation of gender and other norms, as Butler also claims, then an improperly gendered being (as cause) can never in fact result in the effect of humanness, meaning therefore that humanness can neither be *questioned* nor *withdrawn*, neither allocated nor retracted, degraded nor elevated, in that such a body can never have *appeared* human in the first place.

Rather, it is only once we realize that 'humanness' is also a regulatory norm which, through the inculcation of viable ways of being, reproduces itself by way of the constitutive outside of 'the animal,' that the coincidence of

---

[3] Subsequent to *Precarious Life*, in *Giving an Account of Oneself* (2005) Butler fleshes out – so to speak – the concept of 'the inhuman' to some degree through an engagement with Theodor Adorno. Nonetheless, it remains conveniently empty of specific content and thus open to the multiple valences Butler finds in Adorno – an emptiness which in turn reveals the violence undergirding its instrumentalized relation. In *Frames of War*, Butler again maintains that the inhuman functions as the constitutive outside through which the human, understood as both value and morphology, may be both 'allocated and retracted' (76).

improper gender and questionable humanity can be understood. Similarly, it is only by way of the constituted opposition between the human and the animal that we can understand, and thus question, the sexualization mutually articulated by the 'killing ideals' (125) of race, for example, as with the privileged sexuality accorded to the ideal of whiteness as noted above.

In her introduction to *Bodies That Matter*, it might seem that Butler in fact pre-empts just this criticism when she states that 'any analysis which foregrounds one vector of power over another will doubtless become vulnerable to criticisms that it not only ignores or devalues the others, but that its own constructions depend on the exclusion of the others in order to proceed' (18). She then counters this future criticism with the point that 'any analysis which pretends to be able to encompass every vector of power runs the risk of a certain epistemological imperialism which consists in the presupposition that any given writer might fully stand for and explain the complexities of contemporary power. ... [T]hose who claim to offer such pictures become suspect by virtue of that very claim' (18-19). Here, however, I make no such claims to certainty and/or completeness, but aim only to demonstrate that, if one wishes to even *begin* to approach the complexities of contemporary power, one cannot *not* include the question of speciesism, the inscription as excluded of nonhuman animals being necessarily indissociable from gendering, racialising, and sexualising activities. Indeed, Butler herself cannot continue without recourse to the animal, and it is this which raises the ambivalence that threatens to explode her discourse from within.

The animal, in other words, is essential to the hierarchical functioning of 'the more and the less,' in that 'the animal' is always the least of the less, the negative pole to be transcended – more and less – along a humanist teleology which reaches its apotheosis in the phantasmatic ideal of the white human male. Only once this is recognized does it then become possible to understand how the machinations of power legitimize the slaughter of human animals by way of the prior 'animalization' of a specifically targetted human or human grouping, a reconfiguration that strips its target of a fully human status and, in so doing, constitutes a non-subject that can thereafter be killed with impunity. Again, one thinks here of the Nazi demonization of Jews as *Saujuden* ('Jewish swine'), or of Lynndie England parading around Abu Ghraib with an Iraqi prisoner on a dog leash. Indeed, to reduce a singular, nonsubstitutable living being to an essential identity which is in turn reconfigured as 'animal' - what I earlier described as the economy of genocide - is precisely the process that Butler describes as the reductive imposition of an *unlivable* identity.

Ultimately, the complex differential articulation of regulatory norms necessarily constitutes women, people of color, lesbians, gays, bisexuals, transsexuals, the poor, and so forth, as 'more' and 'less' human, and thus at once as 'more' and 'less' animal. The naturalization of heterosexuality, for example, depends upon the normative sexualization of animality (paradoxically utilising an unremarked biological continuism). Or again, the alleged mis*andry* of the lesbian – in which 'a lesbian is one who must have had a bad experience with men, or who has not yet found the right one' (*Bodies That Matter*, 127) – crosses with the alleged mis*anthropy* attributed to anyone concerned with the exploitation, torture and extermination of nonhuman animals (animal activists, it is invariably alleged, must hate humans as a result of social deficiency). Following Butler, such diagnoses presume, on the one hand, that lesbianism 'is acquired by virtue of some failure in the heterosexual machinery, thereby continuing to install heterosexuality as the "cause" of lesbian desire' (127) and, on the other, that animal concern is acquired by virtue of some failure in the machinery of anthropocentrism, thereby continuing to install human exceptionalism as the 'cause' of animal concern. One thinks here, for example, of love for a nonhuman companion animal being reconstrued as deflected desire for a (human) child.

In this way, both humanist and heterosexual desire are thus always constructed as 'true', whereas animal concern and lesbianism are 'always and only a mask and forever false' (127). Within this economy too is found the reactive subordination in which concern for nonhuman suffering is deemed offensive to man – as degrading to both his exceptionality and his interiority – and dismissed as an immoral deflection of 'more pressing' human concerns. Here then, one can clearly perceive the importance of animal studies in that, by way of its central notion of intersectionality, it thus seeks to challenge the 'hegemonies of oppression' in all of its articulations.

We should not be surprised, therefore, that in Butler's text the displacement and denigration of species difference to that of a mere 'effect' has serious consequences – as acknowledged by Butler herself, albeit only negatively in the context of *sexual* difference. It is the claim of a fundamental priority for sexual difference over racial difference which, she writes,

> has marked so much psychoanalytic feminism as white, for the assumption here is not only that sexual difference is more fundamental, but that there is a relationship called 'sexual difference' that is itself unmarked by race. That whiteness is not understood by such a perspective as a racial category is clear; *it is yet another power that need not speak its name*. Hence, to claim that sexual difference is more fundamental than racial difference is effectively to assume that sexual difference

is white sexual difference, and that whiteness is not a form of racial difference (*Bodies That Matter*, 181-2, emphasis added).

In the same way therefore, to claim an equal and fundamental primacy of human differences presupposes that the relationships named in this way are themselves unmarked by species, thus effectively assuming that sexual and racial differences are *human* sexual and racial differences, and that human-ness is not a form of species difference. It is to assume, in other words, that the constitution of 'the more or the less' human (and simultaneously of 'the more or the less' animal) is itself unmarked by racial and sexual differences. In short, the humanist ideals of the 'West' are assumed to be prior to, and thus untouched by, racial, sexual, and species differences – an assumption which, as we will see in the next part, thus reiterates the Platonic economy of xenophobic masculinist reason. We can also see that Butler's attempt to preempt criticism by way of the impossibility of completeness does not, by virtue of her own logic, apply here.

The Foreign in Place and the Madness of Power

The stakes of this exclusive operation are disclosed most clearly by Butler herself in her critique of Luce Irigaray's reading of the *khōra* in Plato's *Timaeus* (not by chance the only place in *Bodies That Matter* where, to my knowledge, Butler attends – if only briefly – to nonhuman others). Whereas Irigaray identifies the 'elsewhere' of the *khōra* with the founding exclusion of the feminine, Butler points out that Irigaray must therefore exclude all those 'other' others similarly excluded from the economy of masculinist reason:

> Plato's scenography of intelligibility depends on the exclusion of women, slaves, children, and animals, where slaves are characterized as those who do not speak his language, and who, in not speaking his language, are considered diminished in their capacity for reason. ... This domain of the less than rational human bounds the figure of human reason, producing that 'man' as one who is without a childhood; is not a primate and so is relieved of the necessity of eating, defecating, living and dying; one who is not a slave, but always a property holder; one whose language remains originary and untranslatable (48).

For Plato, as Butler makes clear, it is the speechless – and thus irrational – being who must be excluded in crafting the 'imaginary morphology' of masculinist reason. In this, the dumb animal – embodied, enslaved, and without property – is thus the utterly other, the absolute outsider. The specter, in other words, of an indecipherable and unmasterable materiality, a dreadful eating, dying, living, and defecating unintelligibility. Terrifying, monstrous, 'the animal' never stands before 'the human' in the relation of a simple *reversal* of intelligibility (i.e., as the inhuman), but rather marks its very limit and, as such, constitutes the site of a terrifying potential identity which, in being imposed, ultimately renders the Other both indecipherable (and thus outside of 'civilized' sociality) *and* monstrous (and thus outside of 'the human').

In this way, the undecidable limit that is 'the animal' falls back upon those 'other' human animals, an economy indissociable from the constitution of the property of the liberal humanist subject. Thus, while Butler points out that the 'materialization of reason … operates through the dematerialization of other bodies,' the feminine being that which is itself undifferentiated but which contributes to the contouring of things (*Bodies That Matter*, 49), the figure of the abject nonsubject without which this dematerialization could not be reproduced rather remains always that of 'the animal' as undifferentiated Nature. It is this, moreover, which always again reserves the potential to animalize 'other' humans and thus render them killable – or, in Butler's terms, nonliving and thus non-grievable – in displacing them 'backwards' along the familiar humanist teleological dialectic. A dialectic which, as we have already seen, Butler reiterates insofar as she makes animality a precondition of humanity. This has extremely serious implications, insofar as its reproduction of the humanist paralogism simultaneously serves to ground, in its appeal to an evolutionary *tēlos*, the reconfiguration of 'other' humans *as* irrational, that is, *as* subhuman animals – be they primitives, idiots, or lunatics – in opposition to normative speciesist rationality.

This mention of primitive idiocy or subhuman lunacy thus brings us into the vicinity, the proximity, of madness, and here too we share our concerns with Butler. However, it is the animal, even more than the idiot (with whom the animal nonetheless retains an intimate relation), who points to a privative relation to language. In her examination of stupidity, philosopher Avital Ronell describes the idiot as a being who 'unleash[es] only muffled signals of original erasure' (*Stupidity*, 253). Yet, there can be no idiot without the animal who, with her alleged lack of language and thus ontological memory disorder, is the most idiotic of idiots, the constitutive outside of reason and thus also of idiocy – the idiot representing a deprived relation *to* language, rather than a deprivation *of* language. Hence, it is not idiocy, as Ronell contends, but rather the animal who fallaciously 'commences in disfigurement, as the mutilation over which the philosophers tried to write in an attempt to restore the proper, the literal, what is proper to man' (253). The notion of idiocy, of the subnormal or subhuman, thus employs regulatory norms constituted through species difference in ways that mutually articulate other regulatory norms such as 'whiteness' and 'maleness.' Think, for example, of the institution of racialized Intelligence Quotient tests as a method of regulating immigration into the US, the application of which being so designed as to ensure that a high percentage of nonwhite, non-European applicants would register at the 'moron,' 'imbecile,' or 'idiot' levels – categories in turn overdetermined with notions of overt and perverse sexualization, including incest and bestiality, resulting from an alleged animal primitiveness that supposedly leaves people of color at the mercy of their 'uncivilized' drives.[4]

Outside, yet undecidably so, of the exclusive property of the human, the absolute idiocy of the instinct-driven animal – the irrationality of the beast – thus relates at once to the domain of the domestic, to 'animal' reproduction and to the foreigner who contaminates that properly civilized domesticity. The xenophobic Platonic exclusion, writes Butler, operates through the reproduction of 'those considered less rational by virtue of their appointed task in the process of laboring to reproduce the conditions of private life' (*Bodies That Matter*, 49). Here, Butler thus draws attention to the animalization of both reproductive and domestic labour. In the former category, we find the exclusion from masculinist reason of women thus confined *within* the domain of the domestic figured by the 'animality' of reproduction. In the latter, masculinist reason excludes all those other beings who, outside within the domestic, are thus construed as foreign to reason, i.e., slaves, immigrant workers, and children, as well as certain other so-called 'food' and 'working' animals. Labouring only to reproduce the same of masculinist reason – albeit without leaving their mark – , the twinned categories of the domestic and the domesticated are thus, by way of nonhuman animals, constituted as that which improperly and unintelligibly reside within the domain of the properly human precisely as the condition of its reproduction.

As we have seen, the unintelligible animal marks the constitutive outside of the human norm, and thus the site of an identification which, when *externally* imposed, is always to be dreaded.[5] At the same time, however, the

---

[4] On this, see Stephen J. Gould, *The Mismeasure of Man* (New York: Norton, 1981).

[5] In the *Republic*, for example, Plato claims that the 'despised' manual workers are 'apes' insofar as they are naturally weak in reason and thus condemned to serve their most base and beastly instincts (590a-591c). Interestingly, according to Plato the biggest threat to the security of his plutocratic *Republic* is the emergence into the *polis* of the 'instinct' or 'urge' for democracy that is naturally shared by all those foreign to reason, the most dangerous symptom of which is a 'sensitivity' toward the enslavement and exploitation of other animals. On this, see my paper 'Cannibals and Apes: Revolution in the *Republic*,' which canbe accessed at: http://zoogenesis.wordpress.com/2012/07/03/cannibals-and-apes-revolutionin-the-republic/

animal must remain within the properly human as the trace of 'its' denial. Animals remain, in other words, as the foreign residing within human property, inscribed as excluded within the uniform and calculable reproduction of the Same. Already within the domestic scene through which the human is reproduced, 'man' has no choice but to share his home, his place, with 'the animal' and, indeed, with other animals. Exceeding all recognition and yet sharing our space and taking our time, animals are thus the most distant in the closest proximity. Recalling us once again to that 'proximal distance' found in both Blanchot and Heidegger, animals are, in short, the always with us that are not 'us.'

It is for this reason that the question of ethics must begin with nonhuman animals. In part, I would suggest, Butler is ultimately unable to fully articulate the normative mechanism of exclusion as a result of the influence of Emmanuel Levinas's ethical humanist philosophy on her own thought subsequent to Bodies That Matter.[6] The problem, as I see it, rests with the fact that Levinas limits his thought to the two poles of humanization and dehumanization, when it is only by admitting the 'animal' that critical thinking stands a chance to interrupt the process by which life is withdrawn from the living. It is here, in this indecipherable domain, where we will discover those beings to whom, and perhaps first of all, we owe a responsibility and a response to the shared precarity that marks the community of the living *in general*. It is, in short, to affirm our being-together outside of any exclusive hierarchy by which the value of other beings is unthinkingly rejected and abjected, and thus to resist as far as possible the imposed violence of the subject-formation that necessarily precedes every 'I.' By contrast, an ethics which presupposes 'the human' as at once its condition, effect, and unmarked category is an error which in practice ensures that ethics can never begin.

Crossing out the human: Venus, the slaughter of an animal body

Having understood the necessity of 'admitting' other animals within the ethical domain, we are now in a position to reconsider the mechanism through which the death of Venus Xtravaganza is articulated.

---

[6] Levinas's ethical philosophy of the 'face' is considered in detail in the concluding part of *Giving an Account*; in the concluding essay of *Precarious Life*; and again in the concluding essay entitled 'The Claim of Non-Violence' in *Frames of War*. Moreover, immediately following Butler's analysis of the human as a 'shifting prerogative' in the long essay 'Torture and the Ethics of Photography' in *Frames of War*, Levinas's notion of the face is yet again invoked.

In essence, the murder of Venus Xtravanganza offers to view a 'limit case' of the human and, in so doing, renders perceptible the otherwise habitual hegemonic operation of normative frames. As Butler writes, this is a 'killing that is performed by a symbolic that would eradicate those phenomena that require an opening up of the possibilities for the resignification of sex' (*Bodies That Matter*, 131). Nevertheless, it is never *only* a question of sexuality:

> If Venus wants to become a woman, and cannot overcome being a Latina, then Venus is treated by the symbolic in precisely the ways in which women of color are treated. Her death thus testifies to a tragic misreading of the social map of power, a misreading orchestrated by that very map according to which the sites for a phantasmatic self-overcoming are constantly resolved into disappointment. If the signifiers of whiteness and femaleness – as well as some forms of hegemonic maleness constructed through class privilege – are sites of phantasmatic promise, then it is clear that women of color and lesbians are not only everywhere excluded from this scene, but constitute a site of identification that is consistently refused and abjected in the collective phantasmatic pursuit of a transubstantiation into various forms of drag, transsexualism, and uncritical miming of the hegemonic (131).

It is not enough, as Butler here makes clear, merely to *mime* the hegemonic, albeit illegitimately – an assertion which recalls our earlier discussion of political eventuation in the context of the mimicking by the Roman plebeians of the existing discourse of power. It remains unclear, however, how the positing of what Butler calls 'resignification' can be differentiated from just such an uncritical miming other than by taking account retrospectively of its effects. And yet, it is the very moment when the improper reiteration of 're-significance' becomes accountable – that is, when it becomes calculable and transparently sensible – which marks the neutralization of the encounter by the dominant order. Accountability, in short, marks the fact that the improper relation has ceased to manifest itself, that is, has ceased to *matter*. It is no longer the injunction of what is most undeniably real. By contrast, the revolutionary mark of an encounter is not its resignification, but rather the anxious obduracy of its being *between* sense, that is, the mark of its indecipherability and thus its exclusion.

Moreover, and for the reasons already discussed, Butler leaves unmarked here the question of what constitutes viable ways of being *human*. However, given the mutual articulation of regulatory norms, the de-naturalization of both race and gender enacted by Venus must at once de-naturalize the constructed domain of the properly human. Paradoxically, Venus here falls prey to the murderous judgment, both homophobic *and* misogynistic, of '*un*naturalness' (of being a 'freak of nature'), which thus falls back upon an unremarked biological continuism. As we know, the naturalization of human heterosexuality depends upon the normative sexualization of animality (long used by men to excuse anything from rape to hunting), hence the exclusion of homosexuality from the activity of 'human-ing' moves by way of a constructed 'unnaturalness' that depends upon an apparently 'natural' human animality or, rather, upon the reproduction of sexual activity as essentially *animal*, and thus in a sense not 'human' at all.

The reproduction of Venus as 'unnatural', in other words, paradoxically depends upon her exceptional humanness so as to withdraw from her that very status of 'humanness'. At the same time, however, the conservative judgment which ends with her murder-slaughter depends equally upon a human-animal distinction which *denies* to humans another putatively 'natural' animal sexual and reproductive activity, that of the potential retained by certain nonhuman animals to change their 'biological' sexuality so as to gain social advantage. In this way, Venus Xtravanganza finds herself doubly displaced between the 'naturalness' and the exceptionalism of 'the human'.

Venus is thus murdered for both her unnaturalness *and* her animality, an 'unnatural animality' which fatally crosses with white, masculinist notions of her being a prostitute and both (and neither) a Latina and a woman. In potentially putting into question what it means to be properly human and, consequently, properly *animal*, Venus – described by her House mother as being too *wild*, as always taking too many risks – thus at once risks performing an abject and 'unnatural animality' which, displacing her inside the 'outside' of the human domain, withdraws from her all human rights and protections. As Butler writes,

> The painfulness of her death at the end of the film suggests as well that there are cruel and fatal social constraints on denaturalization. As much as she crosses gender, sexuality, and race performatively, the hegemony that reinscribes the privileges of normative femininity and whiteness wields the final power to renaturalize Venus's body and cross out that prior crossing, an erasure that is her death (*Bodies That Matter*, 133).

Such a displacing renaturalization, however, one which moves Venus from unequal sexual partner to dead animal stuffed under a bed, cannot be performed by the constituted abjection of race and sexuality alone. Rather, its 'crossing-out of the crossing' must simultaneously cross, must pass through and cross out, the nonhuman animal.

Becoming-unrecognizable: challenging frames

Insofar as the various regulatory norms all deploy each other for the purpose of their own articulations, putting 'humanness' into question necesarily poses a challenge to the entire network of hegemonic oppression – a question which is nothing less than the question of *recognition*. However, in thus exposing one's being to the unintelligible outside in such a way as to interrupt the conservative machinery of recognition, in that very same moment the body necessarily undergoes the profound risk of becoming *un*recognizable. To affirm one's kinship with that which hegemonic norms habitually foreclose is, in other words, to risk the withdrawal not only of a viable subject status, but also the withdrawal of one's race or gender, one's class or sexuality, even one's membership of a species – a withdrawal that marks the effective neutralization of any such 'crossing' within and by a given state of affairs.

Regulatory practices, in that they are necessarily aimed both *at* everyone and *to* no one (there being no preexisting subject of will), are thus general, structural, and therefore recurrent, requiring endless reiteration in order to naturalize their power and efficacy. Yet that which guarantees the ongoing efficacy of such regulation – that is, the recontextualization that defines its *practice* – is also that which already undermines it, insofar as the very excess of this iterability ensures that the context of an utterance is never fully determined. Put simply, every reiteration of a norm, in being repeatedly forced to function in a different context, inevitably brings with it the risk of misinterpretation and revaluation resulting in an 'improper,' catechrestic inscription. This risk, moreover, is further compounded by its mutual deployment of other norms, which always presupposes the possibility of a radical interference. It is this *structural* excess which, as we know, thus opens up the possibility of challenging the normative framework insofar as its reproduction always runs the risk of a violent, unforeseeable transformation.

In being always *subject* to recognition, therefore, the singularity of any given interpellation necessarily retains the potential to put to work otherwise the machinery of materiality, violating the proper limit of identification and opening instead the ethical space called for by an encounter that challenges the frames of recognizability. Such then, is the site of the bodying of Venus Xtravaganza, a 'limit case' that allows us to recognize and thus move beyond the nomative framework insofar as she denaturalizes the founding-conserving network of regulatory norms. As such, however, the already existing state of affairs is for the same reason compelled to seek its neutralization – a neutralization that always involves the refusal or withdrawal of the rights and protections of personhood.

Hence, in placing oneself outside of a given state of affairs, one simultaneously places one's self at risk. As Butler says in her reading of Michel Foucault from *Giving an Account of Oneself*,

> To call into question a regime of truth, where that regime of truth governs subjectivation, is to call into question the truth of myself ... [It also] involves putting oneself at risk, imperiling the very possibility of being recognized by others, since to question the norms of recognition that govern what I might be, to ask what they leave out, what they might be compelled to accommodate, is, in relation to the present regime, to risk unrecognizability as a subject or at least to become an occasion for posing the questions of who one is (or can be) and whether or not one is recognizable (22-3).

This risk, moreover, not only concerns the refusal or withdrawal of recognition by society at large, but it is also to risk becoming unrecognizable to *oneself*. At its extreme, one finds oneself incapable of continuing to exist and thus risks falling prey to enforced cessation, be it suicidal or murderous. Being responsible, argues Butler, is to open oneself to this risk. Indeed, this is precisely what it means to *respond*.

Following Butler then, the ethical imperative concerns those unrecognizable others who already take place within our most intimate property and to whom we must respond no matter the risk to our selves. In *contrast* to Butler's position, however, such an imperative must remain excessively and vigilantly *non*human, as a brief consideration of the concluding paragraph of Butler's *Giving an Account of Oneself* makes clear. Here, Butler offers an important and succinct description of the ethical imperative. Ethics, she writes,

> requires us to risk ourselves precisely at moments of unknowingness ... To be undone by another is a primary necessity, an anguish, to be sure, but also a chance – to be addressed, claimed, bound to what is not me, but also to be moved, to be prompted to act, to address myself elsewhere, and so to vacate the self-sufficient 'I' as a kind of possession. If we speak and try to give an account from this place, we will not be irresponsible, or, if we are, we will surely be forgiven (136).

The problem, however, lies hidden behind that innocent-looking ellipsis in the first line, wherein Butler qualifies that such risky moments – moments 'when what forms us diverges from what lies before us' – are specifically those moments 'when our willingness to become undone in relation to others constitutes *our chance of becoming human*' (136, emphasis added). Such encounters, in short, are the proper and the property of human animals alone. However, if the human is simply a cumulative effect of intersecting praxes of power, as Butler contends, how then can ethics be restricted to the level of effect? Rather, I argue, 'the human' is precisely what the ethical encounter tears apart.

In fact, Butler here opens herself to the very same critique which, as mentioned above, she levels at Luce Irigaray in *Bodies That Matter*. Irigaray, we recall, idealizes and apropriates 'the "elsewhere" as the feminine,' and in so doing 'fails to follow through the metonymic link between women and these other Others' (*Bodies That Matter*, 49). Here then, the question Butler poses to Irigaray must in turn be posed to Butler herself: what or who is the 'elsewhere' of Butler's 'elsewhere'? What or who is excluded in the course of Butler analysis? Given her idealization and appropriation of the 'elsewhere' that are 'moments of unknowingness' as the uniquely human, the answer is all too obvious. But in what sense, it must be asked, can a properly human ethics authentically constitute an ethics of the unrecognisable other, that is, an address that risks forming and transforming an 'I' outside of all dominant structures of meaning?

If ethics is the becoming of the human, then the human is simply an animal + ethics, whereas 'other' animals are therefore pure or simple being without supplement – ontologically deprived of ethics and thus essentially outside of the ethical domain. In this, Butler simply repeats Emmanuel Levinas's very traditional claim that the 'ethical peculiarities' that determine the humanity of man constitute 'a rupture of being' – that is to say, that only the human animal can be ethical because only the human breaks with the pure animal being of instinctive self-preservation (Levinas, cit. Butler, *Precarious Life*, 132). Here, Butler is once again arguing that 'the human' comes to be only in dialectically overcoming and thus ceasing to be an animal, that is, in transcending its animal *pre*condition, in what is a variant of the all too familiar, all too human ascension from 'base nature' to 'higher culture.' As such, rather than positing a 'new basis' of humanism, she is in fact instaurating a very old one indeed.

In summary, Butler impels us to recognize ethics as risking 'our' selves in a moment of unknowingness and undoing that puts into question the norms of recognition. Simultaneously, however, she reproduces perhaps the most proper of recognizable norms: that of ethics, and thus the capacity to respond, as the limit and the proper of the human. Indeed, it is as an inevitable result of refusing to admit animals into one's self or one's philosophy that Butler remains helpless but to reinscribe the unrecognisable call and indecipherable demand of the other within the domain of the properly – similarly, familiarly – narcissistic.

Only once we break with the limitations that impose themselves on Butler's notion of a precarity and a grievability that is shared among the living in general can the norms that reproduce other lives as nonliving thenceforth be effectively challenged – only then might we recognize that killing an animal is murder, and only then might Venus Xtravaganza have survived her crossing. If, however, we instead continue to exclude the animal, then the only traces left by a seemingly infinite number of other animals – both human and nonhuman – will be the mark, unremarked and unmourned, of their erasure.

6. The Wild and the Tame

The Death of a Queer Centipede

They say only love can create, so who the fuck could love up a centipede?
William S. Burroughs, *Last Words*

In order to avoid unthinkingly falling back into the similar and the familiar, I extend a welcome in this chapter to the centipede against whom, according to the novelist William S. Burroughs, love – and thus the mirror – must shatter.

To do this, however, we must engage further with the notion of the domestic and, more specifically, with its function within various contemporary reiterations – both literary and philosophical – of the wild-tame and timeless-timebound dichotomies. Here, we find the 'walking ghost' realized in the dead zombie flesh of the instrumentalized animal, the inverse of the 'revolutionary spirit' of the living corpse that returns. Whereas the latter *stalls* the machinery of animalization, the former reproduces a symbolic logic of oppression which serves to constitute subjugated beings 'deserving' of their oppression. This will in turn allow us to distinguish a *third* machine of tropological displacement, one which works in concert with the two we already know: that which reconfigures 'other' humans *as* 'animal,' and that which withdraws a recognizable human status. Moreover, I will argue, this third machine, in orchestrating a displacement from living embodiment to inferior copy, serves to retroactively naturalize the other two.

The poor rejected Pede

Having published the semi-autobiographical *Junkie* in pulp imprint Ace Books in 1953, William S. Burroughs' first major novel, *Naked Lunch*, appeared in full for the first time in 1959 following the successful resolution of an obscenity trial. He followed this in the 1960s with several texts based on the 'cut-up' method (in which various heterogeneous texts are randomly sliced up and juxtaposed), before going on to publish a number of important novels including *The Wild Boys* and the Red Night Trilogy throughout the 1970s and 80s, continuing to write and publish until his death in 1997. In this chapter, I have chosen to focus on three of Burroughs' later texts: the novel *Ghost of Chance* (1991), the collection *The Cat Inside* (1986, 1992), and his final journals, which were published as *Last Words* in 2000. These texts not only explicitly explore the ethics of human-animal relations, but also, and more importantly for us here, they follow on chronologically from an encounter with cats which, according to Burroughs, saved him from a fatal ignorance, offering pure love in its place.

It is clear from this chapter's epigraph, however, that, despite this encounter, the centipede remains for Burroughs a creature beyond all possibility of love or creativity. The reason for this, he writes, is that 'the centipede was a step to a snake, a lizard, a furred lizard, an animal ... this is [the] basis for a centipede being rejected more than any rejection: looking down on the fall we might have taken, except for that repugnant, momentary ledge' (*Last Words*, 129-130). Here, Burroughs is clearly invoking Darwin's authority in order to posit a linear, teleological ladder (or, rather, staircase) of being, as opposed to a thinking of evolution as entanglement and reciprocity.[1] In this Christianized schema, evolutionary ascent reaches its apotheosis, its latest and greatest step, with 'Homo Sap,' meaning that centipedes – those unimaginably and almost unbearably ancient living beings – are inevitably relegated to the beginning and thus to the bottom, to the lowest of the low.

Such a reductive history of life, however, is complicated somewhat by Burroughs' refusal of both nonhuman history and nonhuman time. Consequently for Burroughs, centipedes have not evolved since their paradoxical appearing at the 'beginning' of nontime, and thus this 'once' is indeed an 'all at once.' Indeed, it follows that this must be the case for all those 'other'

---

[1] Interestingly, Plato also places the centipede at the foot of his hierarchy of living beings. In the *Phaedrus*, he orders animals into three groups – birds at the top, then quadrupeds, and finally those who crawl on or under the earth. In the *Timaeus*, moreover, it is the centipede who is specifically marked out (92a-b).

beings who, once having attained their respective and comparatively lowly steps along the *tēlos* of life, must remain there eternally hereafter. While we will come back to this shortly, and ignoring the fact that centipedes, this one and that one, have of course repeatedly both transformed themselves and being transformed, for the moment it is enough to note that, for Burroughs, the centipede is thus the rejected of the rejected, the abject being par excellence in a hierarchy of being: 'For the poor rejected Pede, the ledge was permanent' (130).

We can only understand the absolute abjection of this creature, however, by understanding his or her exclusion as an inhospitable refusal of a place that has nonetheless already been taken. An exclusion, in other words, of the absolutely foreign within the domestic. To do this, it is necessary first of all to track the dichotomy of the wild and the tame as it organizes and, indeed, fails to organize Burroughs' thinking of nonhuman animals. This distinction, while apparently affirming the ways of being of nonhuman animals, in fact serves only to reinscribe the exceptional humanist privilege it appears to disavow, thus remaining enchanted within a narcissistic privileging of the reflected human self. To further underscore the narcissistic functioning of the wild-tame dichotomy, it will be shown too how this same schema serves to 'ground' both the deep ecological perspective, and that which for Deleuze and Guattari provides the privileged access to becoming, namely 'becomings-animal [*devenirs-animaux*].'

The division into the wild and the tame, as we shall see, serves to constrain the entire Burroughsian bestiary within the absolute conditioning of an enchanted wilderness uncontaminated by the imposition of a properly human time, a temporality which in turn presupposes language as the proper of the human. It is here, moreover, that the differences and the similarities between Burroughs' posthuman becomings-animal and those of Deleuze and Guattari become visible. In similarly positing a potential human entry into the essentially timeless wild-animal nature from out of the tame and timebound culture of a given state of affairs, both Burroughs and Deleuze and Guattari end up condemning nonhuman being to the nonexistence of 'reality' without sense. A gesture, moreover, which marks becoming-*animal* as a uniquely *human* property.

Moving through these exclusive neighbourhoods of the wild and the tame as they are shared, in being *not* shared, by Deleuze and Guattari and Burroughs, I argue that such exclusivity both inhibits the beginning of ethics and naturalizes the interests of capitalism. Nevertheless, it is from here, from an ignorance and a saving that is the necessity of the *méconnaissable*, that the larger question of the ethical opening, and of its risk, can be more clearly addressed. In this, the centipede – this being of the step and the beginning, and of steps and repetition which for Burroughs stands beyond any possibility of love – will ascend to the stage of ethics and, once there, will stage an ethics of the unrecognisable other that has the potential to subversively rearticulate 'the human.'

Shattered Love

On the borders between fiction and documentary, between autobiography and political theory, and between philosophy and literature, the putting to work of language in Burroughs' texts serves to render explicit the impossibility of any such securely delimited domains. As with Lee's passage into the interzone of *Naked Lunch*, they leave in their wake only a convulsively negating Guard faced with the impossible task of reconstructing what was once imagined to be the unapproachable border of an unnameable frontier.

Despite this, it is *language*, the very structure of which determines the impossibility of closure, which for Burroughs, in his own convulsive negation, presents a final, non-negotiable and indivisible border. At once frontier and evolutionary ledge, language is that final step before which every nonhuman living being eternally remains, essentially innocent of 'contact' and thus of 'the pain and fear and the final death' by which such contact is defined (*Cat Inside*, 70). And yet, insists Burroughs, and in spite of this linguistic innocence, contact *with* animals nonetheless preserves the singular possibility of *human* knowledge and salvation: 'August 9, 1984, Thursday. My relationship with my cats has saved me from a deadly, pervasive ignorance' (46).

Such a contact, affirms Burroughs with the very last words of his *Last Words*, is the chance of a 'pure love' for nonhuman animals, one which moves humans beyond the contested spaces of conflict and pain: 'Only thing can resolve conflict is love, like I felt for Fletch and Ruski, Spooner and Calico. Pure love. What I feel for my cats present and past. Love? What is It? Most natural painkiller what there is' (253). This undetermined, indivisible purity of love has, however, already been corrupted, shattered by a testing animal which necessarily marks the limit of love. A limit, moreover, that it would seem is only reached by *Christian* love, by a love of one's *neighbour*, and which inscribes at its heart an ineffaceable contestation: 'A centipede can be seen as a test upon which Love, like St. Francis used to make, would shatter' (252).

Indeed, anyone familiar with Burrough's writings cannot fail to be aware of the fearful hatred repeatedly heaped upon the abject centipede. And yet, it is not only centipedes, and not only insects such as scorpions and spiders, in whom or with whom Burroughs refuses to rejoice: 'I don't care much for rabbits. They aren't cute at all, even the little ones. All they do is make stupid, galvanic attempts to get out of your hands, and big rabbits can give you a very nasty bite' (*Cat Inside*, 27). Perhaps then, the problem with centipedes is a combined lack of 'cuteness' and refusal to reciprocate human affection – except that this clearly cannot be the case in that the other nonhuman species most often subject to Burroughs' ire is none other than the *dog*. In this, and despite the repeated avowals of pure cat-Love, Burroughs squarely aligns himself, as we shall see, with Deleuze and Guattari and their infamous declaration that '*anyone who likes cats or dogs is a fool*' (*Thousand Plateaus*, 265). Dogs, it becomes clear, are contemptible for Burroughs because of their *domestication*, whereas cats retain their *wildness*:

> The red fox, the silver fox, the bat-eared fox of Africa … all beautiful beasts. Wolves and coyotes *in the wild condition are acceptable*. What went so hideously wrong with the domestic dog? Man molded the domestic dog in his own worst image … self-righteous as a lynch mob, servile and vicious, replete with the vilest coprophagic perversions … and what other animal tries to fuck your leg? Canine claims to our affection reek of contrived and fraudulent sentimentality. […] I am not a dog hater. I do hate what man has made of his best friend. The snarl of a panther is certainly more dangerous than the snarl of a dog, but it isn't ugly. A cat's rage is beautiful, burning with a pure cat flame […]. When you see [a dog] snarl you are looking at something that has no face of its own. A dog's rage is not his. It is dictated by his trainer. And lynch-mob rage is dictated by conditioning (*Cat Inside*, 62-3, emphasis added).

With the dog, we can now better understand the contempt reserved for the rabbit, as well as the hierarchy which underlies it: the dog is hated for his or her closeness – her proximity, familiarity and similarity – to the human. She is hated, in other words, precisely for having being dominated, for having been molded in the worst image of 'Homo Sap, the Ugly Animal' (*Ghost of Chance*, 48). The rabbit too, is disliked for the *stupidity* of her machine-like inability to escape her enforced 'petting' – uncared-for precisely because of her inability to resist oppression. Both big and small cats, meanwhile, are beautiful only insofar as they retain their danger and their rage – their 'wildness', in short.[2]

---

[2] Here, Burroughs thus places the various species of fox much closer to the cat rather than the dog. Positioning foxes, especially the red fox (*vulpes vulpes*), into a close proximity with dogs is in fact by far the more common strategy – for reasons which will become clear – both on the level of species (which has subsequently been chal-

Here then, the tamed are hated (by humans) for having being tamed (by humans), for not being free. They are thus hated, might it not already be suggested, for suffering under a form of colonialization subsequently reproduced as 'natural'? One thinks here of the colonized subject who must resemble the colonizer to a degree, but nevertheless not *too* well, as we have seen with Venus Xtravaganza.

Such contempt then, is the contempt of the bound by the free. And yet, according to Burroughs, it is only the *human* animal who comes into being already inextricably bound. As such, it thus becomes clear that this contempt is precisely a properly human derision reserved for all those other, *unbound-ed* beings who have nevertheless been *contaminated* by these bonds. It is contempt, in other words, for those nonhuman animals who have been contaminated by their proximity and similarity to the human. A corruption, as we will see, which comes in the sharing of the space, so to speak, of human *time* – of a temporalising and spatialising movement which has language as its condition of possibility. Put briefly, it is a contemptuous condescension for those other beings whom a properly human extension has overwritten.

Hence, Burroughs' scorn for 'pets' is a consequence of humans having, through the technicity of language, imposed time upon their 'naturally time-less' ways of being, a contamination rendering them unworthy of the purity of Love. It is here, then, that we discover the notion of a deadly human *touch* which is never that of 'contact'. This touch, a touch without touching, an excluding enclosing within the extension of human time-space, is, in other words, that which renders impossible a saving encounter with the finitude of the other. Human touching, in short, kills the chance of contact by dispossessing that which is touched of its naturally wild state: 'I have eulogized the fennec fox, a creature so delicate and timorous in the wild state that he dies of fright if touched by human hands' (*Cat Inside*, 63). Despite, or because of, the deadly effacement of finitude, this properly human touch is the contaminating touch of *time*.

---

lenged) and along the traditional wild-tame dichotomy. Thus, with Burroughs, the red fox would seem to share in a privilege more usually reserved only, and if at all, for the 'exotic' species. However, as we shall see, I do not believe that the red urban fox would be included by Burroughs in his list of 'beautiful beasts.'

Viruses, afflictions, contaminations

In the short novel *Ghost of Chance* (1991), Burroughs gives us the story of Libertatia, a revolutionary pirate settlement founded by Captain Mission in Madagascar. Learning of a threat to the settlement, Mission takes an overdose of a *yagé*-type hallucinogen named *indri* and enters into a vision through which is revealed the origin and prehistory of the land. One-hundred-and-sixty-million years before, Mission discovers, the 'long rift' of Madagascar had split from the African mainland, leaving 'a gaping wound in the earth's side' as it 'moved majestically out to sea' like 'a vast festive ship launched with fireworks' (16). Thereafter, Madagascar had 'lain moored in enchanted calm,' the home to a harmonious coexistence of species with no natural predators and providing 'a vast sanctuary for the lemurs and for the delicate spirits that breathe through them' (15-16). As a result, the autochthonous Lemur People think and feel differently to human animals, being both confused and repulsed by the concepts of time, sequence, and causality.[3]

This enchanted calm is shattered, however, with 'the appearance of man on earth,' an appearance synonymous with 'the beginning of time' (15). This 'appearing' that is an 'arriving' must be understood, however, in two different ways. Firstly, this arrival is the originary appearing of the human species, and thus the 'arrival' for the first time *of* time necessarily takes place *in* time, that is to say, along a temporal, evolutionary narrative. Secondly, the arriving of man is at once a colonization of extension: 'Man was born in time. He lives and dies in time. Wherever he goes, he takes time with him and imposes time' (17). Temporality is thus that *in* which Man appears and at once that which Man must take *with* his self – a human property but nonetheless not properly human. Humanity thus imposes time upon an originary nonhuman space at the same time as *time* marks the displacement of the human *outside* of this space. Outside, that is, of an impossible timeless and deathless spac*ing* that somehow remains undifferentiated, that is, remains without *space*. As a result, time for Burroughs is the mark *of* an inhuman violence which has always already alienated the human animal from nature. Hence, in coming to be, the way of being human is precisely to *mark time*, remarking an originary division which, in constituting the human, at once displaces and encloses it: 'Time is a human affliction; not a human invention but a prison' (16).

---

[3] The Lemur People, one must assume, are thus incapable of understanding this mythic narrative as it is telepathically transmitted *to* Mission and thus at once translated *for* Mission. See, for example, Mission's interpretative reading of the landscape, 15-16.

'Time,' in other words, which begins with the human and in which and with which the human arrives, is thus necessarily imposed by the human animal alone upon a 'previously' timeless environment. In this way its fairytale enchantment is contaminated by the arriving of human/time. It is, moreover, a coming to being which paradoxically imposes itself upon other beings as a dispossessing *lack* of time, insofar as it imposes the violence, conflict and pain which will ultimately render countless numbers of other animals extinct. Recalling here the 'all at once' of the Burroughsian hierarchy of being, we can now better understand why the world *before* the human (in both its spatial and temporal senses) – that timeless time before time – must exist therefore in an harmonious balance of permanent changlessness in which species neither evolve nor become extinct (and ignoring thus the great disappearance announcing the end of the Palaeozoic era, as well as the mass extinctions of the late Triassic, the Jurassic and, again, the late Eocence). Indeed, within 'The Museum of Lost Species' Mission recalls – always for the 'first time' in human time – the (non)memory of this perfect stasis, rediscovered 'first of all' in the museum's timeless memorials displaying 'all of the species … alive in dioramas of their natural habitats' (51).

Back outside in the heat of the pirate settlement, however, we discover that it is precisely its *u-topos* within the relation of the time-bound and the timeless which gives to Libertatia its revolutionary aspect. Appearing 'already timeless as houses in a fairyland' (3), Libertatia constitutes an inadequate point of contact between lemurs and humans that calls to this Edenic time before time. Thus refusing the quasi-Hegelian narrative of a prerecorded *human* future predicated upon conflict, sequence and causality, Libertatia's having taken place – a demonstration 'for all to see that three hundred souls can coexist in relative harmony with each other, with their neighbors, and with the ecosphere of flora and fauna' (8) – marks instead a rupture within the prediction of historical time which is nothing less than the definition of revolution.

As such, it is perhaps not by chance that the lemur is valued above all other animals, in that prosimians are thought to be the earliest primates, dating back some sixty million years and thus predating *Homo erectus* – and thus paradoxically 'predating' the appearing of *time* as such – by at least fifty-eight of those millions.[4] In the peculiarly Burroughsian sense of (pre)existing in an eternal stasis that has nevertheless somehow ended in becoming

---

[4] The visionary Captain Mission would presumably contest this dating, insofar as lemurs must have appeared 'at once' and at one with Madagascar's split from the mainland if The Lemur People are to remain suspended throughout its 'timeless' 158 million year period – an oxymoronic syntagm which to a degree encapsulates our problematic.

an evolutionary step on the way to the human, lemurs are thus 'proto-' and 'arche-typically' prehuman, insofar as they are at once the most similar and the most distant from man. A close family 'contact,' in other words, across the furthest reaches of time and thus beyond time itself – humans through the looking-glass, so to speak.

This inter-familial division, however, is for Burroughs in fact *prior* to the annihilating *arriving* of the human, an emergence into bondage which can never cease to inhabit and impose the inhuman violence of time, in that this bondage has as its condition the division of the (not yet) human by *language*. More precisely, 'the human' *is* the abyssal coming into being of language and *thus* time. Time, in other words, is not the taking place of the human, rather, being-human is being-temporal *insofar* as language is the *taking* place of the temporal-human's having *taken* place. What distinguishes humans from 'other animals,' writes Burroughs, is that only humans –

> can make information available through writing or oral tradition to other Sap humans outside his area of contact and to future generations. This distinction led Count Korzybski to call man 'a time-binding animal,' and it can be reduced to one word: *language* (48).

Clearly, 'language' for Burroughs is reducible to human verbal language, that is to say, to 'the word.' It thus becomes impossible for Burroughs, despite the Mugwumps who project pictograms and the Reptiles who communicate through the movements of green cartilage fans in *Naked Lunch*, to consider nonhuman languages even within his own, relatively broad definition of language as 'the representation of an object or process ... *by something it is not*' (48).

This is not, however, simply an unquestioned speciesism, and nor does this lack of the *as such* condemn 'the animal' to a comparative poverty, as it does for Heidegger. It is rather the case, as we shall see, that nonhuman animals cannot 'have' language because, for Burroughs, the revolutionary reversal and displacement that is the 'rubbing out of the word' is the possibility of a human *entry* (and, indeed, an impossible *re*entry) into the mythical 'wordless world' of the prehuman order of being (50). It is a distinction, in other words, which preserves for Burroughs and for humanity alone the possibility of *entering* a world with neither language nor time. The revolutionary possibility, that is to say, figured always inadequately (in that it takes place *in* and *of* language) by Libertatia, of accessing the wordless worldless world of and as the *post*human animal.

As we have seen in our previous discussions of Blanchot and Heidegger, however, just as there can be no time – and no finitude, sense, language, becoming, or historicity – without *a priori* iterability, equally importantly there can be no iterability without finitude, sense, time, becoming, and historicity. And thus, in positing a timeless – hence undying and undifferentiated – pre-originary domain of animality, Burroughs denies all of this to nonhuman animals. Within this economy, as we have seen time and again, the zootechnical genocide committed every day in the pursuit of profit is thus naturalized, insofar as the nonsubstitutable deaths of nonhuman animals continue to be rendered meaningless and thus unthinkable. Even more than this, however, is that, in going by way of an apparent affirmation of a 'wild' Nature from which 'Man' is excluded, Burroughs in fact further serves the death machines of capitalism in specifically devalorizing those particular nonhuman groups systematically oppressed by contemporary economic structures. This expression of 'pure animal Love,' in other words, this singular reiteration of the biblical and Promethean traditions, carries with it a further, absolutely devastating consequence: the expulsion from the sanctuary of 'Nature' of all those contaminated 'others' with whom we willingly or unwillingly share our space.

It is in fact this contested space of temporal contamination which for Burroughs organizes the distinction between the wild and the tame. In that time presupposes language, so the imposition of temporality constitutes the corruption of a certain 'domestic' group of essentially speechless (and thus undifferentiated) animals *by* language. The 'language virus,' which divides the human against itself and marks it as a temporal being, in this way contaminates those nonhuman animals that are 'touched' by the human hands of inhuman time. Hence, for Burroughs, dogs represent a particularly 'hideous' translation, having been 'remolded,' written over by man in and as man's 'own worst image,' they cease to be animals (*Cat Inside*, 63). Consumed, interiorized by the virus, the face and the rage of 'the domestic dog' are thus violently effaced, overwritten with a human metaphor.

Here, there are obvious parallels with Deleuze and Guattari's molarized 'pets,' those 'sentimental bow-wows' kept captive in the kennels of analysts, 'each with its own petty history … draw[ing] us into narcissistic contemplation … the better to discover a daddy, a mommy, a little brother behind them' (*Thousand Plateaus*, 32, 265). The Burroughsian dog too has been deprived of his or her natural state of wildness, made over into a material anthorpomorphism. Despite this, and again in common with Deleuze and Guattari, the Burroughsian 'domestic' dog perhaps retains a *virtual* wildness. Burroughs does not, he writes, hate *dogs*, that is, he does not hate the original, virile wild dogs that supposedly existed prior to their mutual entanglement with human animals. Rather he claims to hate only what has been made *of* them and what has been done *with* them, a hatred which implies there can be no possibility of mutual (ex)change. Cats, it thus becomes clear, are privileged by virtue of being the sole companion animals who, insofar as they retain their own face and rage and thus their originary being, have nonetheless resisted human subjugation.

In summary, the 'pet' can thus be defined as a nonhuman animal who submits to, or is subjugated to, the time of human extension, a submission and subjugation for which they are treated with scorn and contempt. Nevertheless, the 'sentimentality' attributed by Burroughs to humans by way of the mirror of 'contrived' canine *mimēsis* is a charge at least as likely to be leveled at those humans who value their *feline* companions. Deleuze and Guattari, for example, in equating the 'domesticated' with the 'foolish,' the 'petty' and the 'sentimental,' have nothing but scorn for the 'elderly woman who honors and cherishes' her 'little cat or dog' (*Thousand Plateaus*, 270).

Uninvited: the other racism

The scorn reserved by Burroughs for the domestic*ated* transforms into hate, however, into absolute rejection, when the foreigner, *un*invited, takes their place *in* the place of the domestic. Such is the imposition of 'other' beings *upon* human extension: those beings with whom one is *compelled* to share one's time and space but who are not 'us.' It is here, as we shall see, that the centipede, that test which shatters Love, thus finds – or rather *loses* – his or her place according to this schema of the wild and the tame.

Occupying the limit of the liminal space dividing tame from wild, the limit-other that is the centipede is at once the most distant and most close: the illegal, nondomesticated alien *within* the domestic, within the familiar and the familial. In this sense, the centipede is for Burroughs the polar opposite of the cat. Whereas cats retains their timeless wildness despite the 'touch' of death that is human extension, those unbearably ancient centipedes, arthropod kin to scorpions and cockroaches, remain always beyond such oppressive 'touch' whilst nevertheless placing themselves within the domestic domain – and thus *taking* our time – against all human attempts to the contrary. Hence centipedes (again, like cockroaches) can never be considered 'wild' according to the dominant, spectacular sense of the term.

In contrast therefore to the *exoticism* of the (impossibly) distant Other, the centipede marks the furthest limit of the foreign within the domestic, illegally occupying the 'home' of Man (a property albeit only recently acquired by the latter). Constituted thus as the worst of the worst – worse even than his colonized canine compatriot – this hatred of the centipede thus discloses as its condition a hatred of the illegal immigrant conjoined with a romantic, spectacular exoticism. Rather than the beginning of ethics, therefore, the affirmation of the 'wild,' depending as it does upon the exclusion of those 'others' who share our place but who are not 'us,' reiterates instead a conservative valorization of the self-same. It is founded, in other words, not upon the affirmation of the other, but upon hatred and narcissistic spectacularization. Nonplaced within the capitalist machinery of the wild-tame dichotomy, such insect ways of being on the threshold – insistent, illegal, and unassimilable – are thus included *as* excluded, as that which is beyond hospitality. And yet, returning to our central point, it is just such an absolute exclusion from closeness, an exclusion designated by hate and murder, which serves exactly to efface our originary relatedness.

Figured as that which 'contaminates' the purity of domestic property, be it the body, the home, or the nation, this group of beings placed-out-of-place – lice, cockroaches, rats, foxes, flies, fleas, slugs, snakes, even gnats, and so on – thus find themselves collected within categories marked out for extermination, excluded thus as 'feral,' 'vermin' or 'pests.' Never fully determined, however, such categories are rather always open to negotiation, a porosity which always betrays their limit "otherness" with the marking of historical contingency, and thus with the demands of capital. One thus understands the particular importance placed upon the maintainenance of such slippery categories as 'vermin' (generally a hindrance to commodification and a non-respecter of property boundaries), and 'feral' (generally useless to commodification but protected to some degree by proximity to either or, more usually, both, the categories of 'pet' and 'wild').

Furthermore, as we saw in the previous chapter, the reproduction of such internal 'outsides' cannot be dissociated from other regulatory ideals. One thinks here most obviously of blood-and-soil nationalisms, of the aggravated narcissism of the racist desire to 'purify' the 'body' of the nation of contaminants, of Jews reconfigured as both 'lice' and 'rats' in Nazi Germany, of the Hutus in Rwanda referring to the Tutsis as 'cockroaches,' of the Palestinians similarly considered 'cockroaches' by the Israeli army, and so on.[5] This too

---

[5] While the link between humanism and nationalism will be explored in more detail in chapter eight, a particularly interesting example can be found in Jean Rhys's 1966 novel

recalls us to the earlier discussion of Butler's *Bodies That Matter*, in which it was argued that women as well as (nonwhite) non-nationals are ultimately reproduced as foreign to the domain of the properly human. They are, moreover, foreign only to the degree that they are constituted *as* foreign within the Same by reference to the absolute outside of the animal. In this way, women too are 'domesticated', written over by a dominant patriarchal order which treats with contempt its 'feminine (out)side'. The nonwhite 'other', meanwhile, finds itself constituted as the fearsomely 'feral' – i.e. unassimilable – immigrant in contrast to the safe 'exoticism' of the impossibly distant cultural spectacle. This is not, however, to suggest an *analogical* relation between these constructions. Rather, they are all mutually supporting, thus reproducing the subject at and as the nexus of multiple vectors of power.

Moreover, it is not simply fortuitous that, amid this wild-tame dichotomy maintained by the liminal otherness of the foreign in the domestic, a further grouping of nonhuman animals *for all practical purposes* disappears. Neither sentimental 'pets' nor burning with the rage of the 'wild', so-called 'food', 'work', and 'laboratory' animals find themselves almost completely effaced, whilst nonetheless partaking of the construction of 'the woman' and 'the immigrant'. As we shall see, the reproduction of these other 'other' animals as senseless simulacra thus reserves the possibility of their value-free instrumentalization, even as the 'purity' of the wild-tame binary is reiterated. Silently situated somewhere between the domesticated and the unassimilable foreigner, the so-called 'common-sense' attitude towards instrumentalized animals thus shifts from contempt to despisal, whilst stopping short of hatred.

Hence, returning to Burroughs' *Ghost of Chance*, we discover that industrially commodified animal species, while dealt with occasionally and derisively in passing, for the most part remain silent and invisible, and this in spite of the novel's explicit concern with the negative impact of human instrumentalist thinking upon other species, and on lemurs in particular. The exploitation of nonhuman species, for example, is both marked and unremarked in a short passage describing a group of (presumably 'native' Madagascan) herdsmen who are busily engaged in providing for 'their worthless zebus, a small black hump-backed breed of ox' (32). Here, then, the native zebus *used* by the herdsmen are absolutely without value according to Bur-

---

Wide Sargasso Sea (London: Penguin, 1997). There, the white Creoles are named 'white cockroaches' by some of the native Dominicans and, immediately after the burning of Mr. Mason's colonial mansion, one Dominican insists that they kill Mason and his extended family of 'white niggers' because 'You mash centipede, mash it, leave one little piece and it grow again' (23).

roughs' schema. Small, black and deformed, and thus ugly, inferior copies of the 'original' ox, the only worth of these zebus is their use-value and, presumably, their exchange value solely among the men of the herd. Their instrumentalization, in short, has rendered them worthless as living beings, made over into mere metaphors of the life they have lost.

These same herdsmen, whilst foraging for fuel to maintain their worthless possessions, accidentally release the exhibits of the Museum of Lost Species. Containing examples of every species whose chance has been lost – presumably as a result of human extension – and therefore including viruses as well as animals, these various viral strains completely exhaust the abilities of the scientists hired to deal with them. 'As one viral strain burned itself out,' writes Burroughs, 'or in rare instances when the scientists finally perfected a vaccine or treatment, then another plague would take its place. Back to square one, Professor' (37). Precisely how scientists perfect such vaccines, however, is a question which for Burroughs, despite his 'pure Love' for the wildness of primates and felines, apparently does not arise.

We can now better understand why the division of nonhuman animals into either the 'wild' or the 'tame' is, above all, a question of familiarity, that is to say, of dogmatism: of *the disavowal of the opening of ethics* which slumbers within an apparent affirmation of 'other' others. Indeed, Barbara Noske is quite correct when she describes the prioritizing of wild animals over their 'domestic' kin as 'the other racism' (*Beyond Boundaries*, xii). To maintain such a division constitutes, in short, a 'pervasive ignorance' with absolutely devastating consequences. To further illustrate this, I turn in the next section to the somewhat more subtle wild-tame dichotomy which underwrites Deleuze and Guattari's key notion of 'becoming-animal,' only to find there the same 'grounding' exclusion of the foreign within the domestic. We will find too, the same categorical contempt reserved precisely for the victims of their own schema.

Treating animals

In recent years there has been a great deal of interest in the philosophy of Gilles Deleuze and Félix Guattari from within animal studies, particularly in the chapter of *A Thousand Plateaus* (1988) entitled '1730 – Becoming-Intense, Becoming-Animal, Becoming-Imperceptible …' This is not surprising perhaps – Alain Badiou, whose own philosophy is resolutely anthropocentric, has criticized Deleuze and Guattari for having produced what he considers to be an ignoble 'animal' philosophy.[6] One of the main reasons for this interest is that, famously or infamously, it appears that Deleuze and Guattari give to nonhuman animals an access to a 'becoming' that is equal—in power, in affect—to those valorized becomings open to the human animal: '[A]ffects and powers,' they write, 'grip every animal in a becoming just as [*non moins*] powerful as that of the human being with the animal' (*Thousand Plateaus*, 266). As I will demonstrate, however, upon closer reading it soon transpires that the equality marked by that "just as" is just as quickly refused. Indeed, in being "just as" or "no less" [*non moins*] powerful, an implicit division between a nonhuman animal-becoming and a human becoming-animal is already remarked. This will in turn enable a better understanding of the politics underlying the drawing of a rigorous division between the categories of the wild and the tame – a politics which ultimately derails the ethical and reiterates instead structures of oppression that are at once traditional and contemporary.

Before we can approach the discontinuity between human and animal, however, a discontinuity which in fact serves to *prohibit* nonhuman becoming despite its commensurate powerfulness, it is first of all necessary to consider Deleuze and Guattari's division of all nonhuman animals into three categories: Oedipal animals, State animals, and demonic animals. Oedipal animals are 'individuated animals, family pets, sentimental,' whereas State animals are those animals treated so as 'to extract from them series or structures, archetypes or models.' Finally, the valorized category of demonic animals consists of 'pack or affect animals that form a multiplicity, a becoming, a population, a tale [*à meutes et affects, et qui font multiplicité, devenir, population, conte*]' (265).

These three categories, however, Oedipal, State and pack, are far less secure and far more complex than is generally taken to be the case. To begin with, these divisions are divisions only of degree and of contingency:

> There is always the possibility that a given animal ... will be treated as a pet [*soit traité comme un animal familier*] ... it is also possible for any animal to be treated [*être traité*] in the mode of the pack ... Even the cat, even the dog. ... Yes, any animal is or can be a pack, but to varying degrees of vocation that make it easier

---

[6] For a great many of us, of course, such a charge would be wholly positive. It should be noted too that, according to Badiou's theory of the subject, nonhuman animals are necessarily condemned to an *eternal* oppression for which redress is neither possible nor sought. This follows from Badiou's claim that oppression is never to be fought against, but rather is always and only a consequence of the appearing of a human subject of truth. See *Logics of Worlds: Being and Event, 2*. Trans. Alberto Toscano. London & New York: Continuum, 2009. 60ff.

or harder to discover the multiplicity, or multiplicity-grade [*de teneur en multi-plicité*], an animal contains (actually or virtually according to the case) (265-6).

Moreover, we can see that what have been thus divided are *not* 'actual' non-human animals. The categories denote, that is to say, neither a zoological classification nor even what for Deleuze and Guattari constitutes the *reality* of nonhuman animals, as we shall see. Rather, the three categories represent the three possible ways in which nonhuman animals might be *treated* [*traité*], that is, in which they might be constituted *in relation to humans*: a dog can be treated *as* a pack, a panther can be treated as a 'pet' or *as* a model. In short, Oedipal, State and demonic are not three ways of being-animal, but rather three ways in which humans may produce other animals. We are thus contained within an (actual or virtual) *human* domain, constrained within the anthro-tropo-logical machine of human recognition and of the proper and improper ways of re-presenting a nonhuman being. Whether that is *as* a 'pet' or *as* a 'pack', this exceptional tropological function, this uniquely human capacity to constitute something *as* something, is itself symptomatic of what by now is an all too familiar human-animal discontinuity.

What then, do Deleuze and Guattari consider the 'reality' of nonhuman animals, outside of their categorization? Only in answering this question does it become possible to understand the privilege accorded to the category of the demonic, a category which, first of all, is not in fact that of a band or pack of *animals* (plural). Rather, for Deleuze and Guattari the animal – that is, *this* singular animal, this nonsubstitutable living being more commonly defined as a single, autonomous organism – *is* always already pack: 'We do not wish to say that certain animals live in packs [*vivent en meutes*] … What we are saying is that every animal is fundamentally [*d'abord*] a band, a pack' (264). 'The pack', they continue, is 'animal reality' (267). In other words, every individuated *non*human animal *is*, first of all, is *at first* [*d'abord*], a pack. This *is* 'its' mode, 'its' way of being rather than simply a quality or a distinguishing *mark*: 'it [*sic*] has pack modes, rather than characteristics, even if further distinctions interior to these modes are called for' (264, translation modified).

Every nonhuman animal thus 'is' in *a* mode of being-pack, rather than 'pack' being simply or only a *mark* – constituted by a human-animal relation – *of* and *as* 'animal reality'. Every animal *is* a pack then, but not every animal is treated *as* a pack. In being treated or constituted *as* an Oedipal or State animal, this being-pack that an animal contains is rendered merely 'virtual' in that her 'multiplicity-grade' is necessarily hard to discover. By contrast, those animals constituted *as* demonic pack-animals, insofar as the metaphorical vehicle that is such a relation properly signifies, or at least corresponds, to the essential 'reality' of nonhuman animals, therefore retain *in and as that relation* the 'actuality,' the sense, of their 'proper' way of being. It is just such a 'vocation' that keeps them at the greatest distance both from their domestication by way of 'petty' human 'sentimentality' and from the reduction to state characteristics. A proper vocation, in short, which ensures that they remain both 'wild' and 'real.'

The reason for this demonic propriety is that pack animals, in contrast to both the pet and the model, form a multiplicity that presupposes contagion rather than filiation, and involutions rather than hereditary production and sexual reproduction. 'Bands,' Deleuze and Guattari write, both 'human and animal, proliferate by contagion, epidemics, battlefields, and catastrophes' (266). However, it is in following this catastrophic contagion or contamination that we discover, in what is perhaps the central passage of the '1730' plateau, the positing of an absolute separation:

> These multiplicities with heterogeneous terms, cofunctioning by contagion, enter certain *assemblages* [*agencements*]; it is there that human beings effect their becomings-animal [*opère ses devenirs-animaux*]. ... The pack is simultaneously animal reality and the reality of the becoming-animal of the human being; contagion is simultaneously animal populating [*peuplement animal*], and propagation of the animal populating [or 'stocking'] of the human being [*et propagation du peuplement animal de l'homme*] (267, translation modified).

Being-pack therefore *is* the reality of the animal, the way of being of animals is the entering of assemblages by the contagion that is animal populating. At the same time, the pack *is* the reality of human *becoming*-animal, in contrast to *being*-human, insofar as the human being can *effect* [*opère*] a becoming-animal by *entering* the being-pack of a certain assemblage that is a contagion which propagates or passes over the animal populating of the human. The way of being-pack that is animal populating can, in other words, be passed on or over to human beings, enabling them to *enter* the assemblages which *effect* their becoming. Only in this way can the human being become animal. This is not to say, however, that the human enters the *reality* of the animal. Rather, as we shall see, this 'reality' of every other animal remains absolutely discontinuous with human being.

The human privilege of becoming-animal

Despite their scorn for 'ridiculous evolutionary classifications à la [Konrad] Lorenz, according to which there are inferior packs and superior societies'

(264), Deleuze and Guattari not only reduce *all* other animals to the general category of 'the animal' in opposition to 'the human' (albeit while calling for further 'internal' differentiation), they in fact place human culture over against 'the true Nature [*la vraie Nature*]' of every other living being. This 'true Nature' – the totality of '[u]nnatural participations' of nonhuman becoming – 'spans the kingdoms of nature' (266-7, translation modified). Becoming, in other words, the entering of assemblages by contagion, is the reality of *non*human being. 'Each multiplicity,' they write, 'is symbiotic; its becoming ties together animals, plants, microorganisms, mad particles, a whole galaxy' (275). Thus, whereas for Deleuze and Guattari 'the human' retains the potential to *enter* becomings-animal (which is not an animal becoming), the nonhuman animal 'exists' in a *permanent* becoming, 'in' this 'truly natural' mode of being-pack that 'is' the cosmological One-All of Life.

It thus follows that the human is always already outside of the 'true Nature' of permanent becoming. Consequently, as we shall see, humans are necessarily condemned to the 'stupidity [*bêtise*]' of language, and henceforth to relating to animals *as* animals, be that *as* Oedipal, *as* State, or *as* demonic. We are now better placed to understand the valorization – the higher degree – of the demonic *as* category, insofar as the determination of the categorical animal predicate relates only to *human entry*, or its refusal. Always already outside of 'Nature', the human being nevertheless comes to *approach* true Nature from which it is disposed through an anthropomorphic *positing* of the demonic. In other words, the metaphorical relation – the as such which at once remarks the displacement of the human from Nature – between the 'demonic' and the multiplicity-grade that 'is' the reality of animals performs and, in so doing *discloses*, its discontinuity from human being. A disclosure, moreover, which is at once the possibility of *entering* a properly *human* becoming.

This opposition between becoming and being, in a vertiginous oscillation between figure and figured, is represented on the one side by the 'demonic' wolf and on the other by the molarized Oedipal dog. Whereas even *within* the anthropomorphizing relation the wolf retains, in her distance from the molarized human, her essence as an 'actual' animal, the essential reality of the dog has, by contrast, become merely virtual, and has become so as a result of 'contamination' by a properly human iterability and thus temporality.

Moreover, it is this oscillation, this undecidability, which permits the making-virtual of the reality of an animal *in relation to the human*: dogs *can* be pack in that they *are* pack, but *as* (anthropomorphic molar*ized*) dogs this being-pack is effaced. An effacement which ensures the impossibility of disclosing a potential *human* becoming by way of an encounter with an Oedipal or State animal. A dog, however, *this* nonsubstitutable dog, *has* pack as his or her way of being, a reality which as such cannot be expropriated without her ceasing to be a dog. Without, in other words, this dog ceasing to be nonhuman and thus becoming human instead – an impossible expropriation within Deleuze and Guattari's human-animal division. For Deleuze and Guattari, therefore, the question of the animal is always and only a question of how 'animals' are *treated* [*traité*] within a discourse that remains essentially human.

Given the contempt displayed by Deleuze and Guattari for 'actual' so-called 'pets', however, it would nonetheless seem that the proximity to the human *does* somehow, albeit impossibly, impinge upon the way of being-animal. An anthropomorphism made literal, made *flesh*, so to speak, dogs and cats are thus somehow humanized *in spite of* their essential becoming. Within the reading being attempted here, however, *both* the 'tame' and the 'wild' are necessarily pure anthropomorphisms, a hierarchical ranking only in relation to the potential disclosure of human becoming. Nonetheless, this division of a putatively homogeneous 'animal reality' solely for human purposes – as the *means* of a theoretical disclosure of human *ends* – has devastating results for those nonsubstitutable living beings who fall outside of the valorized category. As we saw with Burroughs, such contempt for the 'pet' and, to an even greater extent, for those unmarked categories of 'instrumentalized' animals such as cows and sheep and of those undomesticable animals who inhabit the domestic such as foxes and rats, *thus amounts to a simple prejudice for the victim of its own posited schema.*

Insofar as it discloses – as a purely anthropocentric concern – becoming *as such*, with 'the Animal *is* pack' the entire economy of Deleuze and Guattari's becomings thus finds its centre. Becomings-animal, they write, 'are segments occupying a median region. On the near side, we encounter becomings-women, becomings-child ... On the far side, we find becoming-elementary, -cellular, -molecular, and even becomings-imperceptible' (274). *Between the betweens* in that it occupies the privileged place of entry, such a placing necessarily cannot be a horizontal measure of closeness or distance to the molarized human being. At the same time, however, insofar as the undifferentiated 'existence' of nonhuman animals 'is' permanent becoming, neither can it be positioned along a vertical hierarchy.[7] There can, in short,

---

[7] See *A Thousand Plateaus*: 'The error we must guard against is to believe that there is a kind of logical order to this string, these crossings or transformations. It is already going too far to postulate an order descending from the animal to the vegetable, then to molecules, to particles' (275).

be neither measure nor order because nonhuman being *is* becoming—a permanent becoming, moreover, which is at once the paradox of *timeless stasis* in that there can be no rupture, no revolutionary coming to be in its absolute dissolution. In other words, a nonhuman animal cannot come to be *other* because 'the animal' *is* becoming. Being human, therefore, is to reserve for itself alone the potential for becoming other, for which 'animal reality' provides the entry and the *vehicle*.

Becoming-animal is thus for Deleuze and Guattari an *essentially* human affair. Having nothing to do with animals, becoming is rather a uniquely human property: the *becoming* human of human *being*. Furthermore, for Deleuze and Guattari 'the Animal' – and indeed, 'the true Nature' that is the totality of nonhuman being, of the One-All of Life – is *a priori* excluded from this circular movement going from anthroprojection to point of entry that is access to the being of becoming from within the molarized everyday. Here then, we discover a similar structural disavowal, albeit substituting 'becoming' for 'knowing,' as that which for Heidegger, as we have seen, gives to the human Dasein alone both the '*possibility* of existence' and 'a positive possibility of the most primordial kind of knowing' (*Being and Time*, 62, 195). The 'demonic' animal in this sense provides for Deleuze and Guattari their own point of departure. And yet, it still remains to ask, how is a *permanent* becoming possible? How do such becomings *take* place, yet without *making* sense?

It is here that we find a certain hesitancy when, in their discussion of Lévi-Strauss, Deleuze and Guattari raise the question of what, or who, an animal comes to *be* in becoming: 'Lévi-Strauss is always encountering these rapid acts by which a human becomes animal at the same time as the animal becomes … (Becomes what? Human, or something else?)' (*Thousand Plateaus*, 262). Given the reality of permanent nonhuman becoming, the question necessarily remains unanswerable. 'Becoming,' they write, 'produces nothing other than itself' (262). However, in the pure potentiality that is permanent becoming, nothing can be produced (or, rather, *re*produced) in that it necessarily consists of the suspension and withholding of all actualized possibilities, and is thus precisely that which an 'I' – as actualized possibility – can never experience. And indeed, as will become clear, it is specifically this 'I' that is refused by Deleuze and Guattari to all but human being, thus dissolving nonhuman being within the *im*possibility of possibility that is Nietzsche's well of eternity.[8]

---

[8] In an often overlooked but nonetheless extremely important essay entitled 'The Animals: Territory and Metamorphoses,' philosopher Jean Baudrillard suggests that

In summary, as both entry and model for becoming, animals initially appear as valorized above the human animal, and yet, this is a would-be valorization which takes the very thing being valorized away from nonhuman animals and reserves it for the human alone. Animals remain suspended in the senseless undifferentiation of an ahistorical stasis, a permanent fluid (non) assemblage of eternal (non)becoming.

Animals, in other words, lack the becoming-space of time and the becoming-time of space. In contrast, it is only the time-bound human – time-bound in being disposed outside the 'true Nature' that is perpetual becoming – who can thus *enter into* an assemblage. 'The human' *becomes*, that is, only at the borderline between 'being-human' and 'true Nature.' Hence, the human comes into being at and as the limit of finite 'human being' and infinite being *as such*, on the border between the possible and the impossibility of possibility. In becoming, write Deleuze and Guattari, 'the demon[ic] functions as the borderline of an animal pack into which the human being passes or *on which* his or her becoming takes place, by contagion' (272, emphasis added). Here, Deleuze and Guattari are once again differentiating between the contagion that is 'animal populating' and the '*propagation*' of the 'animal populating *of* the human being' (267). Between, that is to say, the way of being of nonhuman animals and at once that *on which* human becoming takes place. Here then, there is an absolute discontinuity between Man and Nature, with the latter the eternal background *upon which*, at the border, human animals alone can affect their becomings-other by way of the demonic.

Deeply ecological Deleuze and Guattari

This distinction between humanity and true Nature thus places Deleuze and Guattari's project in proximity with the definitions of 'wild nature' as posited

---

Deleuze and Guattari's use of 'the animal' as a *model* of the absolute deterritorialization of desire is paradoxical, arguing instead that nonhuman animals are in fact territorial beings par excellence ('The Animals,' 137). In this paper, which is practically a primer for the constitution of Animal Studies, Baudrillard offers an alternative notion of alliance to that proposed by Deleuze and Guattari, one which depends first of all upon the destruction of the 'diabolic' symbolic division of species that necessarily constitutes humanism with '[a] logic parallel to racism' (133), and recognizing instead that every territory is a space of 'insurmountable reciprocity' (141 n3). For a more scathing – although somewhat unfocused – critique of Deleuze and Guattari's use of 'the animal,' see also Xavier Vitamvor's 'Unbecoming Animal Studies' in *The Minnesota Review*, 73/74 (2010), 183-187 (thanks to the anonymous reviewers at Humanimalia for drawing my attention to this article).

by deep ecologists such as Arne Naess, George Sessions, and Bill Devall.[9] Such deep ecological representations of nature have, however, increasingly come under attack for proposing what is seen by many to be a rather naïve and nonreflexive essentialism. Anthropologist and philosopher Barbara Noske, for example, argues that deep ecological ideas of nature –

> tend to be part of a wilderness ethic which totally overlooks sentient individuals in favor of species, collections of species and habitats of species. Deep ecologists give narrow and essentialist definitions of nature. The only nature worth talking about is wild. As a result, domesticated nature, feral nature, or anything which does not constitute 'the wild' - including humans themselves - tends to be disqualified as nature. *It is not the real thing*. ... For deep ecology the dichotomy between humanity and nature is final (*Beyond Boundaries*, xi, emphasis added).

While there is an argument to be made that Noske's representation of deep ecology is itself rather narrow and essentializing, it is nonetheless important to note that she is concerned here not with individual viewpoints, but rather with what she considers – quite correctly – to be a general *tendency* of deep ecological representations of nature. Indeed, it is this tendency which, insofar as it remains largely unexamined by the practitioners of deep ecology themselves, often results in a somewhat naive discourse insofar as it remains blind to its own presuppositions. In Devall and Sessions' foundation text *Deep Ecology: Living As If Nature Mattered* (1985), for instance, we find innumerable casual references to an apparent human/Nature dichotomy that is at other times explicitly refused (nor is it insignificant that 'Nature' is capitalized throughout). The essence of deep ecology, for example, is at one point defined as 'to keep asking more searching questions about human life, society, and Nature as in the Western philosophical tradition of Socrates' (65). In short, while not all deep ecologists would suggest that the dichotomy between humanity and nature is final or absolute, the simultaneous reliance on this binary as an organizational tool at the very least suggests a certain blindness as to fundamental presuppositions revealed by the use of language itself.

Similarly, Noske's critique of deep ecology as tending toward a deeply romanticized view of 'the wild' is difficult to refute. Turning to Devall and Sessions' *Deep Ecology* once again, we discover an admiring, large-print citation of an obscure text by Henry David Thoreau which reads: 'Life consists of wildness. The most alive is the wildest. Not yet subdued in man, its presence

---

[9] For a related critique, see Bruno Latour, *Politics of Nature: How to Bring the Sciences into Democracy*. Trans. Catherine Porter. Cambridge, MA & London: Harvard University Press, 2004. 26-29.

refreshes him ... There is the strength, the marrow, of Nature. In short, all good things are wild and free' (cit. 109). The wilderness, write Devall and Sessions, is for deep ecologists a 'sacred space' of 'free-flowing Nature' within which humans may seek 'communion with wild animals' (111-112). Indeed, the earth itself must be viewed as a 'resource that sustains our humanity' (111).

Remaining with our specific focus, however, one can already begin to understand why a reading of Deleuze, with or without Guattari, which aligns his project with that of deep ecology is not necessarily a misreading. Most telling, perhaps, is the familiar deep ecologist argument, put forward at various times by Baker Brownell, Paul Shepard, and others, which claims that 'humans need wild animals in their natural habitat to model themselves after and become fully human; domesticated pets and farm animals provide pathetically inadequate substitutes' (172). Robert Hurley, however, detects the connection even in Deleuze's early text *Spinoza: Practical Philosophy* (1970), claiming that Deleuze in fact offers a model thus far lacking in deep ecologist 'modalities of interaction' ("Introduction," ii).

With a clear reference to Deleuze's later work with Guattari, Hurley describes this model as 'the composition of affective relations between individuals, together with the "plane of consistency" *on which* they interact, that is, their "environment"' (ii, emphasis added). While this notion of 'individuals' (inter)acting *on* or *upon* their 'environment' already suggests a very traditional dichotomy, Hurley touches on the specific problematic being traced here when he affirms that this environment is 'not just a reservoir of information ... but also a field of forces whose actions await experiencing. In a *human* sense, it can be called the unconscious, or at least the ground *on which* the unconscious is constructed' (ii). Here then, the unconscious is the properly human, and is constructed *upon* the (natural) environment.

I will return to this notion of the Deleuzian unconscious in a moment, but first let us further consider some points of crossover between Deleuze and Guattari's process philosophy and the prescriptive discourse of deep ecology. As we have seen, for Deleuze and Guattari as for Hurley, 'true Nature' is relegated to a timeless background of permanent becoming from which only humans are excluded and that, in being *entered* in those exceptional encounters Deleuze and Guattari call becomings, can only ever be written *upon*. Compare this with Arne Naess's claim that the higher understanding characterizing the deep ecological perspective is a direct consequence of encounters between 'Nature' and individual human beings. During these exceptional encounters, the habitual sense of one's being an individual, windowless monad breaks down, giving way to an experience of the unlimited that Naess describes as *'oceanic,'* and which Deleuze and Guattari call absolute deterritorialization. By way of such encounters, the limitations of human being are overcome, the experience of the oceanic allowing the human, in Naess's well-known phrase, to 'think like a mountain.' Here, then, could we not also say that the deterritorialized oceanic opens the possibility of *'becomings-mountain'*?[10]

In the opposite direction, one can similarly detect something of deep ecology's 'macho ethic' in the structure of Deleuze and Guattari's becomings, insofar as nonhuman animals provide the site for an active human *entry* into becoming, effecting itself *upon* the receptacle that is true Nature in what is at once a masculine, phallicized penetration and (be)coming over of the exoticized timeless wild.[11] Man never exists-in-relation with other animals, but rather and necessarily *enters* a presumably feminine Nature *from* outside. Here, we find the same essentialist romantic *topos* that organizes both Aldo Leopold's liberalist 'land-ethic' (a touchstone discourse for deep ecology) and the deep ecological defense of hunting.[12]

Returning now to Robert Hurley's reading of the Deleuzian unconscious, we find that Hurley merely reaffirms without question the decentering of consciousness by the unconscious as a uniquely human property. Indeed, it is exactly this traditional exceptionalism which 'grounds' Deleuze's relegation of infinitely diverse nonhuman worlds to that of a homogeneous timeless background.[13] It is thus far from incidental that, in his reading of the place

---

[10] On this, see the interview with Arne Naess, reproduced in Devall and Sessions, *Deep Ecology*, 74-76.

[11] As regards the 'macho ethic' saturating this plateau, with obvious spleen Donna Haraway in *When Species Meet* wonders whether it would be possible to 'find in philosophy a clearer display of misogyny … It took some nerve for D&G to write about becoming-woman just a few pages later!' (30).

[12] Given the entangled vectors of power, it is not by chance that such a defense, in at least one of its major variants (what Marti Kheel calls the 'holy hunter' defense), depends upon the claim that the nonhuman animal chooses to end her life for the benefit of the (generally male) human hunter. A claim which 'has no more validity than the idea that a woman who is raped "asked for it" or "willingly" gave herself to the rapist' (Kheel, 'License to Kill,' 104). On the philosophical mysticism of 'holy hunters,' see the works of deep ecologists Holmes Rolston, Paul Shepard and, in particular, Gary Snyder. For Leopold's 'land ethic,' see *A Sand County Almanac: With Essays on Conservation from Round River*. Oxford: Oxford University Press, 1966, 237-64.

[13] Jean Baudrillard, in his remarkable essay 'The Animals' first published in 1981 (see note 8 above), already makes the point that, 'if formerly the privilege of Man was founded on the monopoly of consciousness, today it is founded on the monopoly of the unconscious' (138). Nonetheless, he continues, one can at least hope that this refusal of the unconscious, repression, and the symbolic to all other animals will, sooner or later,

of *bêtise* ['stupidity'] in Deleuze's *Difference and Repetition*, Jacques Derrida discloses the Deleuzian unconscious as being 'inconsistent'.[14] For Deleuze, as Derrida shows, *bêtise* is 'a problem of thinking' that is proper to man alone, indissociable from its relation to individuation as such which operates—as the groundless ground (*Ungrund*)—beneath all forms ('Transcendental "Stupidity," 49). Animals, by contrast, 'are in a sense forewarned [*en quelque sorte prémunis*] against this ground, protected by their explicit forms' (Deleuze, *Difference and Repetition*, 190, cit. Derrida, 'Transcendental "Stupidity"' 51). It is only the human, therefore, who 'remains nevertheless as an undetermined freedom in relation with this groundless ground, and that's where [a] properly human stability comes from' ('Transcendental "Stupidity," 56).

Proceeding to put this distinction into question from both sides, Derrida argues, first, for the necessity of a *non*human relation to this ground that is 'as abyssal as with man,' and second, as to the impossibility of an absolute distinction between explicit (animal) and implicit (human) forms. In so doing, he ultimately discloses the very traditional gesture underlying the Deleuzian human-animal distinction: that of the properly human capacity to constitute itself as an 'I,' and thus of the identity of *bêtise* and 'the thing of the I, of the ego' (58). Thus, writes Deleuze,

> Stupidity is neither the ground nor the individual, but rather this relation in which individuation brings the ground to the surface without being able to give it form (this ground rises by means of the I, penetrating deeply into the possibility of thought and constituting the unrecognized in every recognition) (*Difference and Repetition*, 190, cit. Derrida, 'Transcendental 'Stupidity,'" 57)

As we have seen, however, nonhuman animals cannot be excluded from this 'transcendental stupidity' which constitutes 'the unrecognized in every recognition,' in that such a *bêtise* is precisely that of the *trace*: the double movement of protention and retention that marks technicity at and as the origin of all living being and haunts every idealization through which a being makes sense.

---

cause us to 'put in question once again the validity of these concepts, just as they govern and distinguish us today' (138).

[14] In addition to the English language version entitled 'The Transcendental "Stupidity" ("*Bêtise*") of Man and the Becoming-Animal According to Deleuze' (2002) cited here, see the slightly different original version that makes up part of the fifth and sixth seminars collected in the first volume of *The Beast and the Sovereign*. As Derrida himself demonstrates throughout, the translation of *bêtise* by *stupidity* is far from satisfactory (as indeed is the point made, in different ways, by both Derrida and Deleuze), and hence in the following it will for the large part be left untranslated.

Burroughs with Deleuze, the fault

Central here is the structure of iterability, which can be equally described as the indissociability of the *taking* place and the having *taken* place that is this 'relation in which individuation brings the ground to the surface without being able to give it form' (Deleuze, *Difference and Repetition*, 190), and as the 'phenomenological fold … that separates being from appearing. The appearing of being, as such, as phenomenality of its phenomenon, is and is not the being that appears' (Derrida, *Specters of Marx*, 181-2). Refused to nonhuman animals by Deleuze in 1968, the very same refusal of the iterability of the trace remains to organize Deleuze and Guattari's human-animal distinction in *A Thousand Plateaus*. As with Burroughs, and by way of the wild-tame dichotomy, Deleuze and Guattari too reserve for humanity alone the possibility of encountering the timeless *im*mediacy of 'true Nature' at and as the limit of language. And again, as with Burroughs, they posit an undying and undifferentiated preoriginary domain of animality – an essential dissolution of Life that renders as senseless the singular deaths of nonhuman animals. And finally, Deleuze and Guattari too exclude from the 'truth' of 'Nature' all of the nonhuman beings improperly contaminated by the anthro-tropo-logical machine of human recognition.

Moreover, because for Deleuze and Guattari nonhuman animals exist in permanent becoming, we can now understand why they *must* leave open the question of who or what a nonhuman animal becomes in becoming. Insofar as an animal cannot *become* human, which is *the exception from, and the lack of*, the eternal becoming that is the reality of the animal, she or he can therefore never become any*thing* or any*one* at all. Indeed, for Deleuze and Guattari an animal – *this* dog or *that* wolf – is never an 'I,' never a 'who' or even a 'what,' never a 'he' or a 'she' or an 'it.' Furthermore, 'the human' may *enter* a (properly human) becoming only because he or she is excluded from the reality of the animal, an exceptionalism which presupposes the constitution of the human in originary lack. It is this 'lack' which, insofar as it constitutes the plane of transcendence, reserves the possibility of human becomings-animal or, better, of becoming-*other* than human *being* (cellular, molecular, etc.). In short, the human, and the human alone, is constituted in and as the lack that is *bêtise*, in and as the unrecognizable, the *méconaissance*, which exceeds all recognition.

In being refused entry into language and thus finitude, as we saw with the reading of Burroughs, nonhuman ways of being thus lack everything predicated upon this properly human lack: not only technics, language, time, and historicity, but also society, politics, ethics, law, and historiology.[15] This notion of an originary human lack is, of course, very familiar, belonging as it does to what Derrida calls 'the tried and true biblical and Promethean tradition' (*The Animal*, 122). That we should discover this tradition as supporting the valorization of the wild in writers who otherwise work with such originality and creativity to interrupt that very tradition is perhaps not that surprising however. Indeed, as Derrida writes, one finds 'the same dominant' throughout Western philosophical discourse, 'the same recurrence of a schema that is in truth invariable' (45). A schema, Derrida continues, in which –

> what is proper to man, his subjugating superiority over the animal, his very becoming-subject, his historicity, his emergence out of nature, his sociality, his access to knowledge and technics, all that, everything (in a nonfinite number of predicates) that is proper to man would derive from this originary fault, indeed, from this default in propriety—and from the imperative necessity that finds in it its development and resilience (45).

Positing an entry into becoming which effects itself upon the timelessness of the wild, whether that 'wild' is called 'prelapsarian innocence' or 'true Nature,' thus reproduces this dominant schema. A schema which dissolves the vast diversity of nonhuman animals in a becoming-Nature which necessarily lacks both responsibility and respond-ability. An absolute senselessness, in other words, from which a line of flight is ontologically impossible. Despite the positing of a 'pure animal Love' therefore, despite the potential for nonhuman animals to be gripped by a becoming 'just as powerful as that of the human being with the animal,' the subjugating superiority of Man's emergence from a feminized Nature and hence humanist exceptionalism is necessarily left unchallenged. Put simply, the apparent valorization of the (wild) animal remains essentially within the neighborhood of 'the human' with all that that implies for a consideration of ethics.

Shadow animals and zombie flesh: Naturalizing the colonialism of 'true Nature'

We can now understand how the drawing of a simple division between the wild and the tame reiterates contemporary structures of oppression, reinscribing the exceptional humanist privilege and thus remaining enchanted within a narcissistic privileging of the reflected human self. We can see too

---

[15] On Jacques Lacan and the notion of a nonhuman 'lack of lack,' see Derrida 'And Say the Animal Responded?' in *The Animal That Therefore I Am*, 119-140.

that the division of nonhuman animals into either the 'wild' or the 'tame' is, above all, a question of *familiarity*, that is, of the dogmatism that ensures a restricted ethics despite the apparent affirmation of 'other' others. Barbara Noske expresses this clearly when she describes the prioritizing of wild animals over their domestic kin as 'the other racism' (xii).

As a consequence of human 'contamination,' as we have seen, the proper ways of being-dog have been, for Burroughs, displaced by a narcissistic imaging, rendered merely virtual according to Deleuze and Guattari, and disqualified as 'unnatural' by deep ecologists. Dogs, therefore, are not, or are no longer, 'the real thing.' In this, as I will argue in this section, they in fact all reiterate a logic of colonialism that serves to constitute subjugated beings as *deserving* of oppression – an oppressive logic that tends to contaminate any number of animals, both human and nonhuman. This de-realizing contamination is, in short, a displacement of nonhuman animals by and within human language which renders their nonsubstitutable beings as mere simulacra.

In this, Burroughs' allusion to a supposedly 'non-hideous' canine prior to the timely human 'touch' perfectly exemplifies the 'common sense' of a dominant anthropocentrism. One which inscribes both domesticated and instrumentalized animals within an economy of *mimēsis* both Platonic and Biblical. It is, moreover, this economy of tropes that will return us once more to the 'vectors of power' and to their mutually articulating imbrication.

This reproduction of certain animals as 'not real,' that is, as 'pale imitations' of their idealized wild counterparts and/or forebears, is at once Christianized discourse and imperialist logic. Put simply, the Platonic economy of *mimēsis* with its devalorization of the simulacrum produces a symbolic economy and specious logic of oppression that ensures that colonized beings must, as a *result* of their oppression, become somehow dull and stupid and thus – albeit *ex post facto* – materially and economically deserving of being exploited and oppressed. It is according to this same tropology that the native zebus of Burroughs' Libertatia come to be derided as 'worthless' non-animals, shadowy ghosts unmarked but for their corruption by human proximity and by a putting to work which interrupts the timeless wild dioramas.

In this too we can understand the paradoxical semi-timelessness of Libertatia itself: responding to the timeless call of the wild, those revolutionary but necessarily time-bound settlers find only a coexistence of '*relative*' harmony not only with each other but also with 'the ecosphere of flora and fauna.' They can find, in other words, only an imitation, a simulacrum, of the timeless wild. Coexisting *only to a degree*, the nonhuman animals who share the time of the settlers are but inferior copies, the poor relations of those 'wild' beings suspended in the Edenic dioramas of true Nature which can be observed – always following the Fall into the distance of *time* – only within The Museum of *Lost* Species.

One of the best examples of the dominant, 'common sense' valorization of the wild, one which makes explicit its Biblical heritage as well as marking a nexus of the entangled hegemonies of oppression being tracked here, is the first 'chapter' of Julian Barnes' novel *A History of the World in 10½ Chapters* (1989). Rewriting the story of Noah's ark (Genesis 6-9) from the perspectives of the various animals, 'The Stowaway' is narrated by a woodworm who, by virtue of being both illegal and 'unclean' (and thus all too obviously among the abject category of the foreign within the domestic), is fully aware of the futility of applying for asylum from Noah. The futility, that is, of asking Noah for hospitality, or of attempting to justify why he or she is 'worth' saving - a request for hospitality from the human which thus crosses with the impossibility of salvation. While ostensibly seeking to refute the 'clean' and 'unclean' distinction imposed upon animals (Genesis 7:2), it soon becomes clear, however, that the narration nevertheless remains complicit both with Noah and with God, and thus against certain 'other' animals.

Initially, the woodworm-narrator, sexed being (his or her companions risk disclosure through their sexual activity) and illegal immigrant, seeks to reverse the traditional human-animal privilege. She or he does so, however, only on the condition, yet again, of every animal's timeless dissolution. Man, s/he writes, 'is a very unevolved species compared to the animals ... you are, as yet, at an early stage of your development. We, for instance, are *always ourselves*: that is what it means to be evolved' (28, emphasis added). Upon disembarkation, however, this absolute animal self-presence is contradicted in the reinscribing of another version of the clean-unclean distinction: that of the wild and the tame, of the effervescently exotic and the corrupt oppressed. Noah, the woodworm recalls, offered water and food during shortages to any animals willing to stay close to 'New Noah's Palace.' He offers them, that is to say, a place within the economic order: base reproduction of life in exchange for a plentiful supply of flesh. The offer, in short, of the capitalist and the colonial: mere day-to-day survival in exchange for the labor of their bodies, raising on their backs a profit for himself and his fellow colonials: his 'people.' Precisely at this point the collective nonhuman animal 'we' splits into an 'us' and a 'them.' To the astonishment of the woodworm,

> some of *them* – not the cleverest ones, it has to be said – stayed around .... The pigs, the cattle, the sheep, some of the stupider goats, the chickens ... *We* warned

them .... As I say, they weren't very bright, and were probably scared of going back into the wild; they'd grown dependent on their gaol, and their gaoler. What happened over the next few centuries was quite predictable: *they became shadows of their former selves* [and yet how can this be, given that such animals are '*always*' themselves, absolutely?]. The pigs and sheep you see walking around today are zombies compared to their effervescent [and yet 'stupid'] ancestors on the Ark (26-7, emphasis added).

In the space of a few paragraphs, so-called 'food' animals are thus transformed into ghosts, insubstantial shadows that are mere *copies* of their originary selves. In reiterating the Platonic logic of mimesis, these inferior, fallen copies thus lack the animating Idea, become dead bodies opposed to the living voice, and ultimately mutate into the pure animal remains of the 'zombie.' Without *anima*, in short, pigs, 'cattle,' sheep, goats, and chickens are reproduced as nothing but walking dead flesh.

In this way 'food' animals cease to be living, vibrant beings, cease to be 'the real thing.' Moreover, the spectral disembodiment through mimetic displacement thus paradoxically permits their transformation into 'pure' corporeality, bodily-shaped collections of dead zombie flesh ready to be disarticulated into 'meat.' In this way, the instrumentalized animal, the 'walking ghost,' is the inverse of the living corpse that returns, that 'revolutionary spirit' which, as we have seen in the discussion of Nietzsche and Marx, 'outlives' its actualization in being raised (again) within contexts where it had not previously belonged. Hence, whereas the latter interrupts the hegemonies of oppression, stalling the machinery of animalization, the Platonic devalorization of the simulacrum in the former thus reproduces a symbolic logic of oppression which serves to constitute subjugated beings who are 'in fact' *deserving* of oppression:[16]

The capitalist exploiter of the colored workers ... consigns them to employments and treatments that [are] humanly degrading. *In order to justify this treatment the exploiters must argue that the workers are innately degraded and degenerate, consequently they naturally merit their condition.* ... This, then, is the beginning of modern race relations. It was not an abstract, immemorial feeling of mutual antipathy between groups, but rather a practical exploitative relationship with its socio-attitudinal facilitation (Nibert, *Animal Rights / Human Rights*, 17, my emphasis).

---

[16] It has been convincingly argued that the domestication of nonhuman animals results in a decrease of brain size which both inhibits new characteristics and favors pathological conditions. This is not, however, a justification for exploitation, not a cause, but only its *effect*. A shameful effect, moreover, which in fact argues *against* the intensive imposition of non-mutual domestication.

We can thus more clearly understand Noske's contention that the devalorization of domestic and domesticated animals constitutes the 'other racism'. Just as there is nothing 'natural' about the capitalist exploitation of colored workers, in the same way the antipathy towards instrumentalized, and thus commodified, nonhuman animals is nothing natural. Rather, it comes to be 'natural-*ized*' as a result of practical exploitative relationships along with the co-constitutive reproduction of socio-attitudinal facilitation. This entanglement of vectors of power can perhaps be seen operating most clearly in the contemporary slaughter factory, with its interrelated 'devising and employing' of speciesism, race prejudice and sexual abuse for the pursuit of profit. For this reason, we shall return to these killing floors in the concluding chapters of this book.[17]

We are now, however, in a position to distinguish between three different, mutually articulating machines of tropological displacement. First, there is the reductive reconfiguration of 'other' humans *as* 'animal' (*active displacement to the status of animal*); and second, the withdrawal of recognized human status (*reactive displacement from the domain of reason*). Both of these depend upon what I have called the theatrics of animalization, that is, a displacing along an ontoteleological humanist dialectic. Finally, there is the displacement from living embodiment to inferior copy, which serves to retroactively naturalize both these processes of animalization.[18]

Moreover, we can now see how the 'clean' opposition of the wild and the tame serves to conceal its other others – the commodified and instrumentalized; the slave; the illegal, potentially terroristic immigrant; the asylum seeker; the woman naturally deserving of domestication – , all contained within a silent space of fear and exploitation.[19] Nor is it difficult to perceive in this

---

[17] The fate of the *culpeo* fox in Argentina serves as a good example of this production of antipathy for economic gain. For millenia, the culpeo had existed peaceably alongside humans, mainly because their fearlessness of humans meant they were of little interest to so-called 'sports' hunters. However, around 1915, as Martin Wallen writes, 'ranchers began to increase their flocks of sheep, at which time the *culpeo* ... suddenly came to be considered a pest. The Argentine situation exemplifies the way that commercial interests assign value – positive and negative – to animals' (*Fox*, 141-2).

[18] The same machinery of animalization thus reduces a particularly situated nonhuman animal, such as a fox, to the category of subanimal (the foreign in the domestic), and as such refused even the minimum protection generally accorded to other 'wild' animals. That a fox is categorized as 'vermin', yet remains close to the 'pet' category (as between a cat and a dog), is a major reason for its affective position.

[19] In another direction, upon this same dichotomy is constructed the contrary yet complimentary discourse which constitutes pets as more intelligent and responsive as a *result* of their domestication-interaction, that is, their anthropomorphic contamination, whereby their feral kin are once again configured in opposition to the valorized catego-

erasure the operation of economic interest.

This excluding entanglement of the animal, the woman and the slave circulates endlessly throughout the history of philosophy. Jean-Jacques Rousseau, one of the few writers to even consider nonhuman animals, insists for example in his *Discourse on the Origin of Inequality* that, in 'becoming domesticated, [man] … grows weak, timid, and servile; his *effeminate* way of life totally enervates his strength and courage.'[20] This linking together of the domesticated, the servile, and the feminine which, in their mutual articulation, constitutes a threat to manly virtues which must thus be constrained and excluded so as to avoid contamination, is far from incidental. Crossing too with this articulation of domesticity, women, and reproduction, the forced penetration and reproduction of female animals through which originary patriarchy reproduces only itself recalls us of course to the *khōra* of both Plato and Irigaray.

Here too, we further disclose the 'macho ethic' underlying Burroughs' land of timeless enchantment, as well as the discourses of Deleuze and Guattari and of deep ecology. The idealizing of the 'naturally' wild, unconstrained by time and uncontaminated by domestication, accords, as Karen Davis writes, 'with the "masculine" spirit of adventure and conquest' which in the West looks down on those beings constituted as 'unnatural, tame, and confined.' In this, Davis continues, the 'analogy between women and nonhuman animals overlooks perhaps a more specifically crucial comparison between women and farm animals' (193). One thinks most obviously here of reproductive rights, or the curtailing thereof by means of forced conception, be it by physical force – rape in whatever form or species – or by way of the prohibition of contraception and/or abortion.

On one side of the human-animal border therefore, the domesticated, the instrumentalized, and the foreign within the domestic, contaminated by *patriarchal* time, all cease to be nonsubstituable living beings, becoming instead *masculine artefacts*, the property of man who thus represents the power of reason. On the other side, contaminated by *human* time, the domesticated, the instrumentalized, and the foreign within the domestic all cease to be nonsubstituable living beings, becoming instead *human artefacts*, the property of man who thus holds the power of life *over* death. Constitited as artefactual, all such animals are thus already on the side of death, always living a

---

ry, that is, as *un*-tameable vermin, such dirty scavengers thus becoming "deserving" of extermination.

[20] '*The Social Contract' and 'Discourses*,' trans. Cole, Brumfitt, & Hall (London: Everyman's Library, 1973), 57; emphasis added.

death that is, in a double sense, a living death: both as living artefacts and as living beings whose existence has been stripped of everything but that which is useful to the profitable reproduction of death and of dead zombie flesh.

Indeed, it is impossible to understand the economy of speciesism that organizes the wild-tame dichotomy without also attending to its coextensivity with other vectors of power. Once again, Karen Davis is helpful here. 'Not only men,' she writes, 'but women and animal protectionists exhibit a culturally conditioned indifference toward, and prejudice against, creatures whose lives appear too slavishly, too boringly, too stupidly female, too "cow-like"' (196-7). It is this entanglement of difference and indifference that gives us one way of understanding that which Derrida has famously termed 'carnophallogocentrism.'[21] Within its network of inculcation, the gendering of singular nonhuman animals is thus of the greatest importance.

Returning to Burroughs, and in particular to those hated dogs and abject centipedes, we are now better placed to hear that which has been left unsaid. Referring to the 'ugly' and yet faceless snarl of the dog, it is not merely by chance that Burroughs describes it as 'a redneck lynch-mob Paki-basher snarl ... snarl of someone got a "Kill a Queer for Christ" sticker on his heap, a self-righteous occupied snarl' (Cat Inside, 63). The 'worst of the worst' is, for Burroughs, a murderous hate which excludes closeness, thus preventing an unconditional relation to another. Hatred is, in other words, that which prohibits the potential 'animal contact' which gives of itself a Love beyond all conflict and pain. Hatred prohibits, in short, the giving of one's self in unconditional hospitality. However, it is precisely this murderous hate which returns, devastating Burroughs' discourse from within, in the affirmation of only *some* nonhuman animals. In an echo of 'Kill a Queer for Christ,' in a late diary entry Burroughs writes:

> March 18, 19, 1997. Wednesday. They say only love can create, so who the fuck could love up a centipede? He's got more love in him than I got. Now, killing a centipede makes me feel safer—like, one less (Last Words, 126)

The spectres of speciesism, sexism, and racism, in being mutually articulated in the valorization of a timeless wild nature, here come to mark Burroughs' own 'lynch-mob rage' in its echo of the racist, mysogynistic and homophobic exclusion of closeness which manifests itself in hate speech such as 'kill a queer for Christ,' or 'killing a queer makes me feel safer, like one less.' While

---

[21] See '"Eating Well," or the Calculation of the Subject,' trans. Peter Connor & Avital Ronell, *Points... Interviews 1974-1994*. Stanford: Stanford University Press, 1995. 255-287.

for Burroughs those 'worst of the worst' – figured by a 'lynch-mob' of face-less dogs – are the queer killers, the neutralizers of those who denaturalize sexuality, who are foreign to heterosexual patriarchal domesticity, Burroughs himself nevertheless 'feels safer' killing those other 'others' who are foreign in and to the domestic, those queer centipedes who denaturalize the proper place of the human.[22]

To summarize, despite the apparent valorization of (wild) animals, both Burroughs' and Deleuze and Guattari's notions of becoming nevertheless re-main essentially enclosed within the narcissistic mirror of 'the human.' Such is the high-walled enclave patrolled by the convulsively negating Guardians with which this chapter opened, safeguarded by immigration police and so-called pest-controllers tasked with defending the indivisibility of the border, and of the impossibility and impassability of the Interzone of ethical space beyond. In this sense, 'immigration police' and 'pest-controllers,' in seeking to conserve an imaginary space of order by displacing others, can thus be considered metaphors of each other, mutually rearticulating an inviolable property and propriety constructed upon the refusal of hospitality.

Here then, for Burroughs and for Deleuze and Guattari, the 'proper' of the human is shown to depend upon a withholding of the offer of hospital-ity to all those who share our space and take our time but who are not 'us.' Instead of the placing of restrictions organized around the wild-tame dichot-omy, however, a *general* ethics (in itself a tautology) must by definition con-cern the giving of hospitality to *all* those other living beings who already find themselves excluded from it. Without this, the contemporary structures that oppress human as well as nonhuman animals will ultimately remain both intact and in force.

---

[22] Centipedes in fact offer a particular challenge both to the naturalization of hetero-sexuality and to the fixity of heterosexual reproduction. Arthropods (*phylum Arthrop-oda*), and thus kin to cockroaches and scorpions, there exist an estimated 8000 species of centipedes. Some species live up to six years, with periods of gestation and infancy varying widely from species to species. Most species lay eggs, but some give birth to liv-ing young, and some nurse both their eggs and the young centipedes to maturity. While usually the males produce a spermatophore for the female to take up, some centipede groups are, however, all female, with reproduction by parthenogenesis. Finally, some species of *Scolopendromorpha* are matriphagic (the offspring consume their mother). In this context, see also Rosi Braidotti's work on insect figurations within a feminist think-ing of sexual difference in *Metamorphoses: Towards a Materialist Theory of Becoming* (2002).

Conclusion: denaturalizing 'the human'

In 1990, a biography of William S. Burroughs by Ted Morgan was published, entitled *Literary Outlaw*. Burroughs, however, would later complain about the title, saying that he could not be inscribed within the opposition presupposed by 'outlaw' because of the fact that he had never been 'within' the law. What philosophers such as Michel Foucault, Jacques Derrida, and Judith Butler, among others, have made clear, however, is that this is simply not a choice. 'I,' insofar as I *am*, is constituted within or, rather, *before* the law. It is a law, moreover, which gives us to understand that animal encounters are not the privilege, the proper, of the human, but rather the *denaturalization* of 'human,' and this is precisely its *risk*—the risk of Venus Xtravaganza, and indeed, of William S. Burroughs.

There can be no timeless dioramas of nonhuman becoming, no utopian dreams of a harmonious pre- or posthuman wilderness. Rather, an animal encounter is always and only that which calls itself forth in dangerous conflict with the hegemonic identifications of a given social state of affairs of whatever species. As for 'the human,' such encounters are a 'becoming animal' or a 'becoming mad' only in the sense of coming to be unrecognisably (post)human, only in the risk of being excluded *as* 'animal' and/or *as* 'mad.' That which Burroughs names 'Love' is not the capitalized *end* of conflict but rather its beginning and its return, a beginning ever again. It is to hold one's 'self' exposed in and as the place without place: the space of invention.

7. Centipede Center Piece

Insects in Between

Introduction

It is now clear that the construction of speciesism – with 'species' (and here I am re-employing Judith Butler's formulation) understood in part as a production of the *history* of speciesism – is indissociable from that of racism, sexism, homophobia, and so forth. At the same time, however, it is important to note that this in no way reduces the irreducible differences between human and nonhuman animals. There is, in other words, no suggestion of biological continuism.

Perhaps the most obvious difference is that, in contrast to those human animals marginalized or 'animalized' by way of patriarchal and ethnocentric discourse, whether capitalist or fundamentalist (and if indeed these can be separated in practice), it is unlikely that many, or even any, of those billions of *other* living beings condemned to the abjected category of 'the animal' would seek to identify themselves with the phantasmatic ideals of *human* hegemonic norms. This is not to say, of course, that there exists no *non*human identification with *non*human phantasmatic norms within given social communities. However, as regards what I am calling the animal encounter at and as the limit of 'the human,' one question still remains: what's in it for nonhuman animals? What potential benefit, in other words, accrues to 'actual' other animals in terms of the strategy being outlined here? The answer is quite simple: insofar as the zoogenetic movement interrupts the devalorization of 'other humans,' its crossing *simultaneously* interrupts the devalorization of 'other' animals. The denaturalization of hegemonic human norms, in other words, at once denaturalizes the metaphysical human-animal discontinuity along with its attendant hierarchy.

As we have seen, the beginning of ethics demands, in some way, the giving of hospitality to all those beings who share our space and take our time, but who are not 'us.' One must, in other words, begin by being able to respond to those excluded within the domestic. Following from this, and by way of the promised return visit to the Museum of Lost Species, I argue in this chapter that the ethical beginning in fact resides within the detested figure of the Burroughsian centipede. *Ethics, in short, begins with being-with the being-there of such monstrosities* – a way of being which, as we shall see, moves Burroughs' posthuman beyond its masculinist, liberal-Aristotelian logic and toward a more generous notion of 'community.' Such is a community united not by an exclusive contract, but rather by the fact that *every* living being demands unconditional hospitality from every *other*, and yet is simultaneously incapable of giving it. Ultimately, it is only upon such a basis that the monstrously improper creature of Burroughs' dreams at last becomes possible, bringing with her the chance of being together beyond the human. Before this, however, we must return to Burroughs' earlier, cut-up novels.[1]

Stammering hospitality

The aim of Burroughs' infamous textual experiments, christened 'cut-ups,' was simple: to escape the domination of language, and thus to chance upon a *contact* that exceeds the constraints of sequence and causality or, more precisely, exceeds the historically contingent horizon of the possible. Premised upon a random chopping up and placing alongside of generically heterogeneous texts, Burroughs describes it is a process that cuts into the present in such a way as to allow the future to leak out. The cut-up method, in other words, is said to interrupt the mechanisms of control whose function is to ensure the apparent 'transparency' of language, and it does so through an inaugurating moment or movement which, in its taking place, at once escapes the present in opening itself to an unforeseeable other.

Burroughs' cut-ups, however, are not simple random compositions. Rather, insofar as they are composed through *the disjunctive repetition of random fragments and obsessive phrases*, they explicitly oppose any narrative

---

[1] While Burroughs continued to employ the cut-up method throughout his entire writing career, it is nonetheless possible to identify the three novels – *The Soft Machine*, *The Ticket That Exploded*, and *Nova Express*, all of which were composed between 1957 and 1963 – as the principal 'cut-up' texts.

closure of meaning, thus exposing traditional narrative to an unrelenting *stammer* that discloses the emptiness of all such attempts. Indeed, upon reading it soon becomes clear that Burroughs' entire oeuvre – from the 'cut-ups' through to the chance dislocations that mark his final diary entries – consists of an unceasing attempt to open a crack within the oppressive habituation of language.

This way of working language, of working it over, of doubling and redoubling it, is a way of working that Gilles Deleuze locates in the works of both Heidegger and playwright-prankster and author of *Père Ubu* Alfred Jarry. As such, both are 'unrecognized precursors' of Burroughs, while at the same time the 'wildness' of Burroughs' writing machine forms a strong rhizomatic connection with that of Deleuze, as Deleuze himself acknowledges in various places.[2] Heidegger and Jarry, writes Deleuze, 'work in principle with two languages, activating a dead language within a living language, in such a way that the living language is transformed and transmuted' ('An Unrecognized Precursor,' 98). Furthermore, continues Deleuze,

> The affect (A) produces in the current language (B) a kind of foot stomping, a stammering, an obsessional tom-tom, like a repetition that never ceases to create something new (C). Under the impulse of the affect, our language is set whirling, and in whirling it *forms a language of the future, as if it were a foreign language, an eternal reiteration*, but one that leaps and jumps (98, my emphasis).

While the contrast between 'dead' and 'living' languages in Burroughs is not the *literal* contrast that we find in Heidegger, it is nevertheless this interval between the living and the dead that marks the stammer of an inaugural citation as foreign to a given state of affairs.[3] Put in terms of the argument being proposed here, the *form* of the language of the future inheres in its posthumous reanimation of a dead phrasing within a 'living' context. Potentially disclosed by a stomping, stammering repetition, this monstrous form of the future must therefore outlive every determinable form and, thus, outlive the human. Only in this way, I argue, can we approach the notion of 'posthuman contact' as exemplified for Burroughs by a cat-human creature not seen for millions of years.

The problem here, however, is that, in the relentless stutter of his texts,

---

[2] In this, Heidegger and Jarry, in addition to Burroughs, are also (largely) unrecognized precursors of *Deleuze*. Indeed, I think an exploration of Deleuze's philosophy in the light of these three figures would undoubtedly provoke a fascinating reading.

[3] According to Heidegger writing in mid-1930s Germany, it is precisely the alleged correlation between ancient Greek and modern German that accords to Germany its privileged destiny.

Burroughs in fact *attempts to force, even to mime*, the chance and necessity of an animal encounter. Reiteration, as we know, necessarily carries a double risk: the risk of becoming unrecognizable on the one hand and, on the other, the risk of reiterating the very hegemonies of oppression such a miming seeks to disrupt. As Judith Butler writes,

> precisely because such terms have been produced and constrained within such regimes, they ought to be repeated in directions that reverse and displace their originating aims. One does not stand at an instrumental distance from the terms by which one experiences violation. Occupied by such terms and yet occupying them oneself risks a complicity, a repetition, a relapse into injury, but it is also the occasion to work the mobilising power of injury ... to acknowledge the force of repetition as the very condition of an affirmative response to violation (*Bodies that Matter*, 123-4).

In fact, as we have seen with Nietzsche, the moment of parody inheres in every repetition, making every affirmative posthumous phrasing *always already* a 'mime,' a walking ghost complicit with the hegemonies of oppression. Indeed, the chance of an encounter *is* the risk of becoming unrecognisable and at once of becoming complicit. More than this, however, in seeking the animal outliving of the human while at the same time placing conditions upon openness – that is, while refusing hospitality to certain beings – Burroughs enacts a sovereign gesture fully complitious with the injury of enslavement.

Sovereignty, as Derrida teaches us, if it is indeed sovereign, presupposes an indivisible power, and thus the violent exclusion of others. Hospitality, therefore, is incommensurable with sovereignty, that is, with the impassability sovereignty demands. Put simply, unconditional hospitality is the impossibility of the private and the autonomous, of the decision or law based on property. However, the *act* of hospitality nevertheless presupposes a sovereign decision, that is, an autonomy which authorizes the decision to open one's self or one's home. The host, in other words, must 'freely' choose to open herself to the other, a decision which therefore cannot be an obligation, neither convention nor duty. It cannot, in short, be *habitual*. Paradoxically then, there can be no hospitality, as Derrida says, 'without sovereignty of oneself over one's home, but since there is also no hospitality without finitude, sovereignty can only be exercised by filtering, choosing, and thus by excluding and doing violence' (*Of Hospitality*, 55). Hospitality therefore, if it is indeed hospitable, *must* be unconditional, it cannot impose conditions upon the 'who' or 'what' which comes, cannot impose limits upon the granting of asylum. Its opening, that is, cannot be determined by the 'already there,' cannot be predicted from within a given state of affairs. Hospitality is, in a word, *im*-possible. It can neither be expected nor prepared for, and hence the 'I' is constitutively – and always habitually – unprepared for the (be)coming of the other; structurally incapable therefore, of the sovereign decision hospitality otherwise demands of it. Hospitality as such is thus *posthumous*.

In this, hospitality is intimately related to what I am calling the animal encounter, as we can hear in Derrida's description of the 'taking place' of hospitality as that in which 'the impossible becomes possible but *as* impossible. The impossible, for me, for an "I," for what is "my own" or is properly my own in general' ('Hostipitality', 387). The example *par excellence*, according to Derrida, is the 'visitation' of Yahweh to Abraham that is simultaneously an 'announcement', an example which similarly exemplifies the animal encounter: 'This is indeed hospitality *par excellence* in which the visitor radically overwhelms the self of the "visited" and the *chez-soi* [the 'one's-home' or 'house' but also the 'with-self'] of the *hôte*' (372).

Moreover, given the originary technicity of all living being, the constitutive unpreparedness – the chance and necessity of being 'radically overwhelmed' by an other – is, as we have seen, a 'fault' necessarily shared across each and every living being. At the same time, it is this same shared 'fault', this originary division or *différance*, which ensures that every such being 'is' at once irreplaceably singular ('being-the-there') *and* always disposed outside of its self. '*We*' are all, in short, foreign to the properly 'at-home', dispossessed, exiled from the domestic by the already-there which already prohibits the sovereign decision. *Every living being therefore, is obliged by the machineries of being to forever seek asylum within the domestic, whilst always remaining, in her singularity, irredeemably foreign to the 'there' of being.*

In a single phrase then – at once echo and synonym of Rancière's 'We are all German Jews' – *We are all asylum seekers*. What this means, therefore, is that every living being demands hospitality and, insofar as hospitality demands a sovereign decision, every living being is constitutively incapable of offering it. Or rather, we are all able to do so always and only inadequately, always insufficiently. It is a capacity, in other words, *only insofar* as it is an *in*capacity.

This is, however, by no means to reduce the singular suffering of 'actual', historically contingent, asylum seekers. Rather, it discloses instead that the hatred of the foreign is precisely a hatred of *the other that I am* (and that I *follow*), a suicidal *self*-hatred of what is 'not itself'. This, as Nietzsche tells us, is 'of the essence of *ressentiment*' (*Genealogy*, I:10).[4] Furthermore, the

---

[4] It would be interesting here, if only time and space permitted, to explore Nietzsche's

liberal-Aristotelian contractual argument is revealed to be both unjust and unjustifiable. According to this argument, which philosopher Rosi Braidotti accurately describes as 'the trademark of liberal individualism and its idea of moral responsibility' (*Transpositions*, 111), nonhuman animals must be excluded from the ethical domain on the basis that, as they cannot offer hospitality, they are therefore not entitled to receive any in return. This, however, is clearly rendered null by the fact that *every* living being demands unconditional hospitality from every *other*, and yet is simultaneously incapable of giving it.[5]

Such is the reciprocity which paradoxically is the very condition of hospitality, and thus of ethics. Human animals can offer neither humans nor nonhumans hospitality, just as nonhuman animals can offer hospitality neither to nonhumans nor to humans – no one animal, in short, can offer hospitality to an other. This is, in other words, the condition of finitude, that of the doubled abyss – the repeatability of language and the singularity of being-there – which divides and shares each singular and nonsubstitutable living being from, and with, every other.

Returning to Burroughs, we can now see that, in his arthropodic *ressentiment*, he is attempting, in sovereign fashion, to exclude the utterly other, the illegal occupier, on the basis of a double evolutionary fault (and a doubly *teleological* fault, therefore, a lack of evolution that is, as the most unbearably ancient, at once an excess of time). He reinscribes, that is to say, the ontological division of the 'repugnant ledge' which serves to attribute a mute bestiality to the centipede. As we have seen, however, the constitutive technicity of the already-there demands the affirmation of encountering an other whose language we do *not* recognize while, in exactly the same movement, language ceases to be the privileged site from which one can, in just such a sovereign fashion, exclude the Other on the basis of lack.

In summary, sovereignty and hospitality are incommensurable yet indissociable, an aporia marked by the 'is' – the coming to being – of the 'I is other' that is never willed, never a choice. By contrast, the sovereign decision

---

thinking (in section 11 of the first essay of *On the Genealogy of Morals*) of the 'wildness' of the enslaved men of *ressentiment* who, 'once they go outside, where the strange, the stranger is found, they are not much better than uncaged beasts of prey.'

[5] This entire part could in fact be considered as a critique of Aristotle's position in the *Politics* in which he argues that 'it is the sharing of a common view in these matters [of morality] that makes a household [*oikia*] or a city [*polis*]' (*Politics*, I:2). Common-sense morality is thus, for Aristotle, the condition of community, its conservation of the Same being the very test which *a priori* excludes the foreigner. For a related critique, see also Cary Wolfe, *Animal Rites: American Culture, the Discourse of Species, and Posthumanist Theory* (Chicago: University of Chicago Press, 2003), 107-109.

presupposed by Burroughs' positing of the wild-tame dichotomy – its sovereignty displayed in the contempt expressed for the victims of the gesture – is in fact the denial of hospitality, and thus the closure of the ethical.

As yet unimaginable

If we accept that the notion of ethics centers upon the question of the foreigner, and thus of the foreign in the domestic (the 'foreign' being always foreign *to* somewhere), ethics can therefore be considered first of all a question of the *centipede*: a question of that which, since always, since before time, illegally occupies our space and thus makes demands on 'our' time. Unconditional hospitality demands that we do not impose conditions, that we do not risk indebting the other, nor indeed can we ask anything of the other, not even, or especially not, 'who?' or 'what?' of this other who is already there within our most private of properties. And yet, insofar as ethics is hospitality, the ethical is always inadequate, a demand *and* an incapacity from which the nonhuman animal *hôte* – guest, host and enemy – cannot be excluded.

This notion of being exposed at home to the hospitality of the centipede brings us in the end, in the beginning, to the porosity and infolding of Louise Bourgeois's well-known sculpture *Spider* (1997). In the late 1990s, Bourgeois – then in her eighties – produced a number of sculptures with spiders as the central theme. The largest, known as *Spider* or *Maman* and composed primarily of steel, was exhibited in the Turbine Hall of Tate Modern in London in 2000 where, at over nine meters tall, it towered above the gallery patrons. Further, encaged within the steel legs of the spider one discovers a single chair, a chair that is in its turn enclosed once again within a dense, tubular mesh cage that divides it from the spider who nonetheless all but engulfs it. Such is the seat, the space, of the human; a space that is thus sheltered and threatened twice over, at once protected and imprisoned by both the 'industrial' and the 'natural.' Here, then, the place of the human is striated by the fear, the power and the security of becoming-with the nonhuman – whether 'animal' or 'technological.' Interesting for us here, is that according to Bourgeois the artwork carries 'a set of maternal associations of a wholly positive kind, drawing on autobiographical references to connote shelter and protection' (Baker, *The Postmodern Animal*, 80). Indeed, she describes *Spider* as an ode to her mother who, as a weaver of tapestries, shares with spiders a common occupation. Nonetheless, as Steve Baker points out, it remains 'undeniably open to being read entirely differently' (80). Hospitality, then, is also a question of reading. Indeed, this is always the question of reading, and in particular of the undecidable interval between maternal shelter and the matriphagy of the other who already surrounds us, an unrecognisable other 'who,' as an unpassable frontier, imprisons us and is imprisoned within our own property and at once breaks downs the fences.

It is within this absolute proximity of the most distant that Anne Dufourmantelle, in dialogue with Derrida, locates the urgent demand of hospitality, describing it as an imperative –

> drawing the contours of an impossible, illicit geography of proximity. A proximity that would not be the opposite of an elsewhere come from outside and surrounding it, but 'close to the close,' that unbearable orb of intimacy that melts into hate. If we can say that murder and hate designate everything that excludes closeness, it is insofar as they ravage from within an original relationship to alterity ('Invitation,' 2-4).

Insofar as ethics begins where the familiar and the familial ends, we can now understand the urgency of an impossible hospitality, of a sharing of exile in which asylum is already offered to every other and which is always insufficient. In contrast to the self-hating hierarchy of the Same which organizes every properly human ethics according to distance and closeness, an ethics of the insectile, of the spider and of the unbearably ancient centipede, calls us instead to the apocalyptic untimely encounter. The other, foreign to the domestic, always comes first.

Never a test which shatters love, it is rather, as we saw with Nietzsche, the active forgetting of invention itself: an event the call of which shatters the mirror and at once the psyche. It is to step before and beyond one's self, a taking and a giving of place before any possibility of love and thus beyond the narcissism which limits love to one's fellow. Never a calculation, passing through the idiocy of bodyings demands only a response and a responsibility to its call – a demand which can, potentially fatally, always outstrip and be outstripped. The centipede, in short, sets the stage for an ethics of the unrecognisable other in which 'the human' comes to being subversively rearticulated.

Finally, we return, once again differently, to the hospitality offered to William S. Burroughs by his feline companions and, in particular, to that encounter which, on August 9th 1984, Burroughs claims saved him from a deadly, pervasive ignorance. Here, we discover that, insofar as it takes place across a zone of indecipherable and undecidable sense, such a life-affirming and enlightening contact is necessarily a relation without relation, one which marks instead only the abyssal distance of finitude:

Meeeowww. 'Hello, Bill.'
The distance from there to here is the measure of what I have learned from cats
(*Cat Inside*, 90).

This distance from there to here, from 'I' to other, 'is' (and is not) the caesura of pure potentiality. For Burroughs, moreover, it is the possibility of creating 'a creature that is part cat, part human, and part something as yet unimaginable, which might result from a union that has not taken place for millions of years' (*Cat Inside*, 3). This 'as yet unimaginable' is a *phrasing* holding the place of an unheard-of becoming, of an *animal encounter* in which being exposed comes to be other in being disposed together. The movement, in short, of *zoogenesis*. The coming of the unimagined and unimaginable other, however, demands an unconditional, centipedal hospitality, a hospitality that, contrasting explicitly with centripetal narcissism, Burroughs ultimately refuses. Only then, however, does the refusal of abjection become possible and, unhinging the teleology of humanism, with it comes the spacing of a community beyond the human.

Part Four. Community

Introduction to Part Four

In this part, I will explore in detail the notion of a 'community beyond the human,' alluded to at the end of the last chapter. To begin with, however, it will be necessary to consider the constitution of 'the human community' it purports to move beyond, which I will do through a reading of Carl Schmitt's *The Concept of the Political*. Such a community, it might be suggested, is simply the totality of common humanity, the kinship of the whole of the human species. However, as we have seen, the question of 'who,' 'what,' or 'which' counts as the properly human remains always open to negotiation, always again demanding the reproduction and thus the re-closure of its borders. As a result, the question must therefore turn to the *functioning* of this circumscription of a 'common' or 'universal' humanity – of its economy and its essential propriety which throughout history, on both the left and the right, is reiterated in the guise of a positive and privileged concept. It is this concept which will be taken up in the first half of this chapter. Not only will one recognize, it will be argued, in the founding-conserving of 'the nation,' and thus the nationalistic, the very same economy of dependence-exclusion by which 'the human,' and thus the humanist, constitutes itself over against the phantasm of 'the Animal,' but also that the 'fully realized' body of humanism is in fact the realization of the very pathic, undying animal against which it seeks to found its essential difference.

From there, I then shift my focus to the notion of 'community.' What, exactly, do we understand by this term? Is there always community, human or otherwise, whether as an empirical fact or a regulative Idea? Or, is there always only its impossibility? In an attempt to answer these questions, I consider how 'community' relates to both hospitality and sharing, concepts with which it seems inextricably bound. How might the concept of 'community' relate to common-sense and to common-law, to law and right, and to the state of law? What then of 'the nonhuman community' or of animal communities? Apartheid, writes Derrida in 'Racism's Last Word,' 'is the ultimate imposture of a so-called state of law that doesn't hesitate to base itself on a would-be original hierarchy – of natural right or divine right, the two are never mutually exclusive" (379). And yet, for the nonhuman animal such is *every* state of human law. If apartheid, the imposture of a law based upon a purportedly God-given, that is, *natural*(ized) hierarchy, is thus the denial by law of the common, might we not suggest, preliminarily at least, that the communal, the shared-in-common, can only take (its) place outside of racist, sexist, and speciesist states, a spacing or phrasing beyond both sovereignty *and* bestiality?

Beginning with an unorthodox reading (based upon conclusions drawn in the second chapter) of what Nietzsche describes as the right to make promises, in the second half of this part I aim to demonstrate that 'sharing' – as is the case with both 'hospitality' and 'community' – is *im*possible. That is, the infinite potentiality that 'is' being-shared-with *constitutes* being-togeth-er only insofar as it withdraws in and as every actualization. Community, I thus argue, is this shared passivity: the shared condition of not-being-able to share. Such an aporetic formulation echoes the inability and insufficiency which, as we saw in the previous chapters, marks the hospitable encounter. More specifically, we find that, as a result of *habit*, of habitat, of dwelling, of remaining, and of *ethos*, the actualization of sharing is always undone in be-ing already with others. It is, in other words, to always inhabit a community and thus to be excluded from that very community as a result.

Furthermore, I argue, every time we share, 'we' must betray 'our' com-munity or, rather, betray a shared community *affect*, and thus betray the very notion of 'we.' The question of community is thus transformed: in sharing – this notion which appears to be the very condition of community, this shar-ing and thus dividing or diluting of the One which is thus to share the very condition of community – is community therefore rendered impossible?

The answer, I suggest, is that betrayal is the very condition of community, and thus of vigilance, responsibility, and loyalty. In this sense, only betrayal calls forth a being with the *right to make promises*, that is, to rightfully mark improperly, to *revalue*, in contrast to those 'feeble windbags who promise without the right to so do' (Nietzsche, *Genealogy*, II:2). This betrayal, more-over, takes the paradoxical figure of the nomad, of the lone wanderer ever seeking community and commonality, recalling us as much to the lifelong undergoing of Kafka's Investigator as to Nietzsche's Zarathustra.

Finally, I will argue that, beyond humanity and thus beyond its domi-nation, community begins – albeit only ever posthumously – with 'giving' death, given time, to nonhuman beings: a giving of that which precisely cannot be given, and which in so doing always again betrays the 'human brotherhood.' To become animal is, as we shall see, the right to constitute the *future*, and with the Nietzschean animal in particular we find just such a futural being: a way of being with the strength to outlive the human.

8. Plus un 'Holocaust'

Speciesism, Nationalism, and Communities of Death

Introduction: The dignity of Man

To betray, to be traitors to humanity: what, exactly, might this mean? In *Eichmann in Jerusalem* (1965), Hannah Arendt follows the French prosecutor at Nuremberg in identifying the Shoah not as a crime against *humanity*, but rather as 'a crime against the human *status*' (257). This is a very important distinction, marking as it does the necessity of reckoning with the worst in any positing of a community beyond the human. Nevertheless, it will be argued, it is the vigilance of an unending and unlawful betrayal of the *notion* of 'humanity' which in fact remains to render such crimes against the human status *im*possible. And yet, in the promised betrayal of 'humanity,' what ways of being-in-common remain to be affirmed?

Humanism, as we have seen, depends upon an exclusion of 'the animal' in order to at once found and conserve what Claude Lévi-Strauss – perhaps but not necessarily referring to Kant's *Würdigkeit* – describes as 'the myth of a dignity exclusive to human nature' (cit. de Fontenay, *Le silence*, 47), and which Derrida describes as 'the infinite transcendence of that which is worth more than it' ('Faith and Knowledge,' 87).[1] Moreover, Lévi-Strauss continues,

---

[1] On the concept of 'dignity,' see Giorgio Agamben, *Remnants of Auschwitz: The Witness and the Archive* (1999). In section 2.15 – the importance of which will become increasingly clear – Agamben concludes as follows: 'When referring to the legal status of Jews after the racial laws, the Nazi's also used a term that implied a kind of dignity: *entwürdigen*, literally to 'deprive of dignity.' The Jew is a human being who has been deprived of all *Würde*, all dignity: he is merely human—and, for this reason, non-human' (68). Later, Agamben notes how 'the dignity offended in the camp is not that of life but rather of death' (70) and that, in Auschwitz, 'people did not die; rather, corpses were

it is this myth of a human value beyond 'merely' living which, in whatever historical guise, 'suffered [*a fait essuyer*] to nature itself its first mutilation from which all other mutilations must inevitably follow' (cit. de Fontenay, *Le silence*, 47). What then might such mutilations be which, insofar as they *inevitably* follow, are therefore structurally or genetically implicated in this ideology of a 'nature' which is exclusively, properly, human?

What *has* to follow, in other words, from the positing of an inalienable dignity of whatever stripe or mark which both constitutes, and consists in, a single animal species, an infinite transcendence which thus marks out one species, even before birth, as *not*-animal (rather than *non*-animal)? As we shall see, Carl Schmitt offers one answer when he asserts that the ideological construct that is this notion of the human's innate and universal humanity brings with it nothing less than the end of the political, its displacing and thus depoliticization of the site of politics providing instead only an 'especially useful' instrument of imperialism.

Purifying the political: Carl Schmitt

In *The Concept of the Political* (1932), Schmitt argues that the concept of 'humanity' is never political insofar as it 'excludes the concept of the enemy, because the enemy does not cease to be a human being – and hence there is no specific differentiation in that concept' (54). This follows necessarily from his claim that 'the political' inheres only in the discrimination of 'friend [*Freund*]' from 'enemy [*Fiend*],' the 'high points [*Die Höhepunkte*]' of which – and this will become important later – being 'simultaneously the moments [*Augenblicke*] in which the enemy is, in concrete clarity, recognized as the enemy' (67). The purest event or advent of the political, in other words, consists of, and is made manifest as, the instant in which 'the enemy' comes to be recognized as 'the enemy,' an instant in which 'the State [*Staat*]' delimits itself whilst thenceforth always reserving for itself the possibility of war [*pólemos*].

Hence, politics is never the revelation of an essential, 'natural' or even 'just' enmity, but rather only the moment in which the *production* of the enemy (who is as yet neither friend nor enemy) *as* 'the enemy' comes to make sense. Its material clarity, therefore, resides in its *performance* of the figure of the political, in the performing of its own figure. That is, in enacting the

---

produced. Corpses without death, non-humans whose decease is debased into a matter of serial production' (72). The intertwining of the economy of animalization and the logic of the slaughterhouse are in this way rendered explicit in the camps.

performative tautology "'the Enemy" is the enemy.' Its illumination, in other words, is the result of a *technical* political virtuosity which, in its inaugurating moment, produces the naturalizing transparency of a meaningful performative. At the instant of its founding 'high point,' however, such meaning must immediately succumb to a degree of obscurity, beginning its falling away from the summit [*Die Höhepunkte*] into the depoliticized darkness of its dissemination. Thus, lacking the specific friend-enemy differentiation which marks the opening of politics, 'humanity' for Schmitt cannot therefore 'wage war because it has no enemy, at least not on this planet' (54).

Even if, like Schmitt, we also (at least for the moment) all too obviously ignore the place of 'the animal' on 'this planet,' such a claim nonetheless finds itself immediately complicated by the introduction of the figure of 'the Jew' as reproduced in Germany under the Nazis and, further, by Schmitt's own role as self-appointed Nazi ideologue. The point here, of course, is that Jews under the Nazis were reconfigured as *non*human (as opposed to the 'primitive' humanity of the Slavs, for example), that is, precisely as a separate species, an *ahomo sapiens* and in this sense *as* an alien race.

Despite Schmitt's undeniably reductive logic and, indeed, the reactive defense of the nation-state which his concept of the political presupposes, a defence which needs to be read in the context of both its interwar production and Schmitt's own political committments, one cannot thereby simply exclude his discourse from consideration. Of particular importance is the part played by the production of the 'enemy' or, better, of the 'foreigner' or 'outsider,' in the constitution of boundaries not only geopolitical, but also ideological, which serve to differentiate the sovereign Self from absolute Other.

Indeed, it is Schmitt's 'purification' of the political, that is, his positing of the political as a domain apparently purified of any and all economic, aesthetic, moral or religious entanglements, which marks his reactionary discourse as dangerously right-wing. Such a 'purification' in fact constitutes its *own* depoliticization, insofar as it erases material and 'religious' interest (in the broadest sense) from the political realm. Instead, Schmitt claims that the whole of politics inheres in the constitution of an other *as* 'the Enemy,' an enemy which must remain abstract, a phantasm or specter, against and by which an equally phantasmatic 'homeland' *thence* constitutes itself. The production of fear, in other words, of the other and of war (whether potential or actual), serves both to unify a nation and to efface any thought of underlying economic and/or ideological interests. In this, one cannot fail to recognize the 'crypto-Schmittianism' of the Bush administration and beyond.[2]

---

[2] On this, see Simon Critchley, *Infinitely Demanding: Ethics of Commitment, Politics of*

Hence, and by way of the strange slave syllogism of Nietzsche's man of *ressentiment* [you are bad, therefore I am good],[3] it thus remains necessary to always again render an account of the mutual articulation of the putatively abstract 'political' (i.e. geopolitical) 'enemy' and the *doxa* (or *theodoxa*) of evil in the conservation of *both* the 'global' parliamentarian-capitalism of the West and the neo-liberal humanist subject. Only in this way does the value of the *symbolic* economy of the absolute other and of radical evil find itself interrupted by its articulation within a resolutely *material* economy. That is, by the uncanny reinscription of material suffering in place of an apparently iconic use, an economy of suffering within which all living beings are implicated.[4] Indeed, and as will be explored in more detail later, this is at least part of the reason for the hyperbolic reaction to the improper phrasing 'animal holocaust.' A phrasing which, insofar as it returns the thought of the Shoah to that of vulnerable bodies and to the intensity of suffering rather than invoking an empty notion of 'Evil,' thus recalls to cognition, from beyond its spectacular economy, the singular crime, ongoing, endlessly reiterated, that is the industrialized genocide of living beings.

Here, Schmitt's political commitments and extreme, lifelong anti-Semitism serve to focus ever more sharply the issue at hand. How is it that Schmitt, perhaps *the* theorist of the modern nation-state, became perhaps *the* supporter of the Nazi regime, given the absolute distinction between *hostis* and *inimicus* upon which he thus grounds his notion of the indivisible border? According to Schmitt, the external and abstract enemy [*hostis*] which, in being recognized *as* 'the Enemy' constitutes the unifying community effect of 'the Nation,' can and must never be that of a *particular* enemy [*inimicus*]. The enemy, in other words, can and must never be 'my' personal enemy, insofar as such subjective passions can never be political insofar as they can never be 'purified' of individual (economic, moral, aesthetic, religious, familial) interest. As a result, 'the Enemy,' which is rather always and only 'the Enemy *of* the State' ('of' thus understood in the double genitive) insofar as it functions both to determine and conserve the State's own borders by way of an abstract or *public* difference between enemy and friend, can and must never be this or that (or those) particular being(s) who dwell with 'us' within 'our' borders.

Resistance (London & New York: Verso, 2008), 133-148.

[3] See the first essay of *On the Genealogy of Morals*, as well as Deleuze, *Nietzsche and Philosophy*, 111-114.

[4] An intersection disclosed most explicitly by what might be termed 'animal capital,' as we will see in the final two chapters.

Indeed, this necessarily remains the case even if this or that particular enemy would nonetheless *seem* to belong to the abstract category of the 'public' enemy. Such a 'seeming' would for Schmitt thus constitute a misunderstanding or, rather, a mis*reading* of the political, in that such material specificity contaminates its 'pure' figure, breaching the traditional security of its borders. The Public Enemy reproduced 'in general' must therefore never evoke subjective passions, must never have the effect of inciting hatred or contempt for an enemy, whether publically or privately. The enemy *for* Schmitt (as 'subjected' to and by the State), rather than *of* Schmitt (as a would-be autonomous subject), may be 'Israel' or 'Judaism' or 'Islam', but must never, however, be *this* Jew or *this* Muslim who lives amongst 'us'.

The founding identification of the enemy, and thence the friend, is thus purely geographical, a geo-graphy determined by a fantastic border, its specter the nonplace through which both space and place come to be defined. Hence, we are returned to our question: how is it that Schmitt can support the elimination (in every sense, including its (in)digestive relation) of millions of German Jews under the Nazi regime and, indeed, remain a committed anti-Semite long after the collapse of the Reich?

This is a question which cannot be answered in any detail here, requiring as it does a far more extensive engagement with Schmitt's entire *oeuvre* than can be attempted here, but it nevertheless remains a question which needs to be pursued. Preliminarily, however, it is clear that the question concerns the possibility or otherwise of 'purifying' the concept of the Enemy of any 'subjective' enmity. It concerns, in other words, the separation of the public and the private.[5]

To recap, the summit of the political is attained only in the performance of its own figure, the instantaneous *coup* in which the not yet friend-or-enemy comes to be recognized *as* 'the Enemy'. At the same time, insofar as it is the figure of 'the Enemy' which thence *constitutes* the State, and thus the community affect which marks the differentiation of the public from the privately subjective, the fault-line between the 'public' and the 'private' too is necessarily drawn by this same instant of recognition. The instant of the political, in other words, divides 'the public' from 'the private', effacing an already existing complex of relations in the positing of a simple fantastical opposition which, founding and conserving the state, unifies the elements of both the friend-enemy and private-public dichotomies.

As we have seen, however, for such a re-cognition to take place it must, upon its 'first' appearance, always already be repeated. Hence, in its engen-

---

[5] On this, see Derrida, *The Politics of Friendship*, 83-137.

dering double movement of protention and retention, the 'high point' of the political, the indivisible instant of its *coup*, is therefore always already 'contaminated.' Inaugurated in the abrupt, naturalizing recognition of its sense,' its *meaning* has, in other words, already gone astray, destinerred. Hence, its falling away into the habitual obscurity of depoliticization. The friend-enemy and public-private divisions constituted in and as the 'purity' of the political perfomative are thus, as the condition of their founding, always impure, their borders already breached. In this, the pure concepts of both 'enemy' and 'public' are already corrupted by the 'friend' and the 'private' and vice versa, the particular within tainted by the abstract without. Viewed in another way, as Andrew Benjamin writes in his discussion of Pascal's *Pensées*, 'the Jew' (or 'the Muslim' or 'the Foreigner' or indeed, and with varying degrees of constraint, 'the Animal') is named and thus given an identity 'with which *actual* Jews [or Muslims or foreigners or nonhuman animals] would then have to live' (*Of Jews and Animals*, 186, my emphasis).

Making Enemies, Inhuman

Such problematising of the friend-enemy dichotomy thus inevitably returns us to the place or nonplace of the foreign in the Same, to the asylum seeker that 'is' every living being, and to the discursive production of both nationalism and racism. Furthermore, it re-turns the figure of 'the Animal' upon which every *human* community depends, an exclusive coming to be which, following Schmitt, opens in always opening itself to a future war [*pōlemos*] against actual nonhuman animals. What remains to be considered then, is what according to Schmitt is the absolute nonrelation between 'the concept of the political' and 'the concept of humanity.' It is here, I will argue in attempting to follow Lévi-Strauss, that 'the concept of humanity' – and, more precisely, its unavoidable opening onto a terrifying dehumanization by way of the abstract specter of 'the Animal' – in fact discloses, and in so doing deconstructs, the terrifying xenophobia which inheres in the Schmittian 'concept of the political.'

As we have seen, the impossible 'pure' abstraction that is 'the Enemy' – an abstraction which must remain as untouched by the economic, the juridical, and the religious as it is by any subjective passion – rather functions to efface complexity so as to *produce* a simple binary opposition. An opposition, moreover, which, insofar as the impermeability of its border cannot be maintained, must then be repeatedly *re*produced in what is a conservative re-founding of its foundation. 'The Enemy,' in other words, is a myth, a phantasm or a specter against which the *state* and *State* of *ressentiment* constitutes itself. In this, 'the Enemy' doubles and is doubled by, supports and is supported by, the myth or specter of 'the Animal' against which the properly human *status* constitutes itself. Necessarily mutually articulated, Schmitt's posited binaries collapse into each other in reinforcing each other. The result, as we will see, is that, insofar as private hatred passes through the animal, so too does the public enemy, contamination working in both directions: 'the Animal' corrupts 'the Enemy' just as this enemy contaminates this animal, the Enemy corrupts animals just as the Animal corrupts enemies, and so on. Speciesism and racism, in other words, cannot be dissociated in the (re)production both of the subject and of the subject's shared community affect.

To recap, the identification of the political enemy, the 'high point' of politics, is both purely abstract and geo-graphical, the recognized spacing in which the space and place of both the enemy and then the friend comes to be defined. It is, in other words, a distinction and delimitation thus rooted to the soil, the home-land. It is the soil therefore, which is the 'concrete' material in which is realized and which real-izes, that is, *makes* actual, the abstraction that is 'the political' (*Concept of the Political*, 30). Friends must belong to, and share in, the same soil. The community, the State, is bound, and bounded, by the soil, that of its proper ground.

What then, if the would-be 'friend' (in the abstract sense) is *not* bound by the same soil? What, for example, of the dispossessed, the diasporic, those without a *recognized* 'homeland' beneath their feet? The friend must share, and share in, the soil, but, as we know, this ground, this soil is already contaminated, invaded by parasites who have already rendered impure the political body in its very founding. The body politic, in short, will have been already corrupted by the rootless within, by the parasitical homeless who will have already breached the security of its borders. The exemplary figure of which is, of course, 'the wandering Jew,' condemned forever to seek a mythical promised land.

Here then, we discover yet again the specific bodies who inhabit the 'purely' *private* relation – those of the foreign in the Same – , and who are thus subject and subjected to the 'justifiable' hatred of the friend (*inimicus*) whilst at once serving to maintain the abstract, *public* Enemy (*hostis*). That is to say, all those actual beings who, having had an identity imposed upon them, then have to live it. The border delimiting the 'purely us,' in other words, insofar as it is *reproduced*, must thus be produced from *within* as from *without*. Such private hatred of the enemy-friend, moreover, must pass by way of the

Animal, without which the relation to the foreign in the Same would remain abstract, a simple, and above all passionless, question of territorial displacement. To understand this however, we must return to that danger which, as Schmitt writes, inheres in the concept of 'humanity.'

Schmitt, it should be recalled, claims that the concept of 'humanity' can never be political as it lacks the differentiation of friend and enemy, insofar as the enemy, that is, the *public* enemy, 'does not cease to be a human being' and therefore 'humanity' cannot 'wage war' (54). However, without the political – that is, the constitutive discrimination between enemy and friend – there can be no humanity, but only, for Schmitt, the extreme *in*humanity which is the world of purely *private* interest. The recognition of the enemy as 'the Enemy' is, therefore, the *properly human*. Humanity, in other words, is the condition of the shared yet agonistic community affect, and which for Schmitt is thus manifest 'properly' only in the *nation*-state. Being-human is, in short, *indissociable* from the recognition of the enemy. To be human is thus to maintain the real possibility or actuality of war (*pōlemos*). Such a war, therefore, is at once a war against the enemy, a war against inhumanity, and a war against the foreign in the Same. 'Life against life,' as Derrida, in an echo of Nietzsche, describes it in his reading of Schmitt.[6]

The constitution of 'the human' (against 'the animal') cannot be separated therefore from the constitution of 'the enemy' (against 'the inhumanity' of 'private interest'). A proper community of friends (the nation-state) is, in other words, constituted against the non-human or the not-properly-human which lacks access to the positing of a purely abstract externality and thus the sovereign decision. A decision which, moreover, remains undecidable: insofar as 'the friend' and at once 'the State' are constituted only subsequent to this founding decision which gives 'the enemy' to be recognized, 'who' or 'what' posits this originary exceptional decision prior to, and constitutive of, both the human and the common cannot be determined. Here then, we find yet another question of the nonplace of the Origin.

Returning to the claim as to the impossibility of a *political* concept of 'humanity,' this is not, as Schmitt makes clear, to say that wars cannot be, and are not, waged in the *name* of 'humanity.' In this latter, writes Schmitt in 'The Legal World Revolution,' instead of a political concept, 'humanity' becomes instead 'an asymmetrical counter-concept' (88, cit., *Concept*, xxii). This asymmetry – an asymmetry which, as I have argued throughout, is indissociable, on the structural level, from the concept of 'humanity' itself –

---

[6] See *The Politics of Friendship*, 112-137; especially 123-4 and 135-6n18. For Nietzsche's use of the phrase in relation to the ascetic ideal, see *On the Genealogy of Morals*, III:13.

inevitably manifests itself in its delineation, in the drawing of a line. A division or discrimination which, as Schmitt writes, 'thereby denies the quality of being human to a disturber or destroyer, ... the negatively valued person becomes an unperson, and his life is no longer of the highest value: it becomes worthless and must be destroyed' (xxii). We are of course very familiar with this process of displacement by now, this 'dehumanizing' or 'animalizing' reconfiguration by which the 'disturber' – this parasitical contaminant displaced and nonplaced within the State or community of 'friends' – ceases to be properly human.

Thus, as Schmitt writes in *The Concept of the Political*, '[t]hat wars are waged in the name of humanity is not a contradiction of this simple truth; quite the contrary, it has an especially intensive political meaning [*intensiven politischen Sinn*]' (54). However, insofar as the reproductive shift towards animality must for Schmitt remain unremarked in order to repress the founding-conserving recognition of the animal as 'the Animal' – the 'enemy', so to speak, against which 'humanity', the friendly community of humans *thence* constitutes itself in the positing of what Schmitt claims to be the purely *political* performative – Schmitt can thus only mark the *consequences* of its operation, but not the means:

> When a state fights its political enemy in the name of humanity [*Wenn ein Staat im Nammen der Menschheit seinen politischen Feind bekämpft*], it is not a war for the sake of humanity, but a war wherein a particular state [*Staat*] seeks to usurp a universal concept against its military opponent. At the expense of its opponent, it tries to identify itself with humanity in the same way as one can misuse peace, justice, progress, and civilization in order to claim these as one's own and to deny the same to the *enemy*. The 'concept of humanity' is an especially useful ideological instrument of imperialist expansion ['*Menschheit' ist ein besonders brauchbares ideologisches Instrument imperialistischer Expansionen*], and in its ethical-humanitarian form it is a specific vehicle of economic imperialism. ... To confiscate the word humanity, to invoke and monopolize such an exalted [*erhabenen*] term *can only be the sign of the terrifying demand* [*nur den schrecklichen Anspruch manifestieren*], such as *denying the enemy the quality of being human* and declaring him to be an outlaw of humanity; and a war can thereby be driven to the most extreme inhumanity [*zur äussersten Unmenschlichkeit*] (54, trans. modified and emphasis added).[7]

For Schmitt then, such a war waged against an enemy in the *name* [*Nammen*] of 'humanity' is, in common with civil war (*stāsis*), not a 'proper' war, but rather its 'misuse' which *destroys* rather than *conserves* the balance of states. Its monopolization of a universal concept for *private* gain – economic,

---

[7] Derrida discusses this passage in Seminar III of *The Beast and the Sovereign*. The modifications of the translation here are based largely on that reading.

ideological or territorial, or most likely all at once – corrupts the (impossible) passionless purity of a public enemy. As such, its impassioned demand is *terrifying*, inasmuch as it is driven by *non*political power, by subjective, economic, or even aesthetic desire, by moral or religious will, and is therefore necessarily without limit. Exceeding the concept and the limit of war [*pólemos*], its impropriety is no longer or not yet war, and as such threatens to push this so-called 'war' to the very extremes of destruction by way of the animalizing movement.

When the concept of 'humanity' is invoked, in other words, there can be no limit to the destruction which follows. Here then, we are given to understand what Lévi-Strauss calls the 'first mutilation' – that of the posited 'dignity' of humanity – *and* what inevitably follows: 'in the name of the human, of human rights and humanitarianism, other men are then treated like beasts, and consequently one becomes oneself inhuman' (Derrida, *Beast*, 73).

What is terrifying therefore, is the depoliticizing corruption of the political by the non-political, the contamination of the public by private interest. And yet, how is it that such a weakening or falling away from the 'high point' of the purely political can have 'an especially intensive political meaning'? Rather, such 'intensity' exceeds the limits of Schmitt's own discourse, breaching the purified domain of the political. In other words, the terrifying *political* maneuverings which reside within the would-be *de*-politicizing '*counter*-concept' of 'humanity' – i.e., a concept which is counter to the political, a-political or even anti-political and thus absolutely private – make explicit its imbrication with the political, that is, with the friend-enemy binary. Hence, Schmitt discloses within the political-nonpolitical dichotomy an *a priori* impropriety which is the condition for, and effaced in, the inauguration of their very differentiation. Indeed, this is already marked by the rhetoric of 'high points [*Höhepunkte*]' which thus gestures to differences of *degree*, and not of *kind* as Schmitt claims.

Part of the network of inculcation constituted along vectors of power, the friend-enemy and human-animal pairings thus, as we have already seen, 'require and deploy each other for the purpose of their own articulation' (Butler, *Bodies that Matter*, 18). Indeed, how could the positing of an external enemy by which a 'homeland' comes to be *not* in fact have an individual, 'private' affect, precisely in becoming a citizen of that homeland with all that that might entail, and never excluding – for Schmitt – the possibility of one's own sacrifice in a conserving war against the 'public' enemy?

The privately-public or publicly-private enemy, that of the rootless within, is thus always the subject of, and subject to, the 'real possibility' of 'physical killing [*physischen Tötung*]' which for Schmitt is indissociable from war (*pŏ-lemos*) and from the recognition of 'the Enemy' (*Concept of the Political*, 33). The real possibility of physical killing, in other words, falls back on the private as well as the public enemy. It is a possibility, however, which can only be 'founded' by way of the *animalization* of the foreign in the Same, rather than by the abstract, passionless conservation of the State. This privately-public enemy can never be 'the Enemy' in all its purity but, at the intersection of the domestic and the foreign, can thus only be a parasite, corrupting the purity of the homeland, an impure foreigner amidst the community of friends whose very presence contaminates the soil. Threatening the domestic, such foreigners carry with them the risk of civil war or revolution (*stăsis*), thus embodying in the specific the potential destruction of the State which in its turn then justifies a reactive politics of fear.

According to Schmitt's logic (and indeed, that of the crypto-Schmittian-ism of the US), a logic which values the integrity of the State above all else, such 'parasites' – improper beings – must therefore be eliminated, for which the reconfiguration of Jews as 'lice' under the Nazis constitutes the paradigmatic example. Moreover, the very phantasticity of 'the Enemy' means that its founding constitution does not require another 'actual' (constituted) nation-state, or even a determined geopolitical territory, in order to function. Indeed, the impossibility of determining and thus identifying the 'actual' enemy intensifies, in its indeterminacy, both the perception of the threat represented by the 'enemy' – who could now be anywhere and everywhere, the (almost) undetectable foreigner within the Same – and of course the reaction such fear subsequently justifies.

Insofar as this founding contamination is undeniable it can, as Derrida would say, therefore *only* be denied. Hence, in the moment of a phantasmatic founding disavowal, the body – here the Schmittian body politic but equally the properly humanist body, as we shall see in the next part – must remain pure, its borders inviolate. At the same time however, the phantasmatic nature of such borders always already requires their reproduction, and thus the conserving reiteration of its founding disavowal. Consequently, to maintain both the (spectral) purity of the State and the (spectral) purity of the human, and with each supporting the other, the foreign in the Same must ever again be excluded. An exclusion which is, as Arendt writes of the Shoah, 'a crime against the human *status*' rather than a 'crime against humanity' (*Eichmann in Jerusalem*, 257).[8]

---

[8] Interesting in this context is Schmitt's claim that not only is 'humanity' not a political concept, but furthermore that '*no status* [*Status*, rather than *Staat*] corresponds to it'

Hence, both animalized humans and nonhuman animals must suffer an endless, grossly asymmetrical war (*pōlemos* not *stāsis*) as a result of that 'ultimate imposture of a so-called state of law that doesn't hesitate to base itself on a would-be original hierarchy' (Derrida, "Racism's Last Word," 379). Such a war thereby delivers the relation of 'humanity' and 'the State,' the valorized terms of fabulous oppositions which serve to unify their elements in and as the effacement of the complex of already existing relations, over to the most extreme inhumanity. In this, one can hear too the Yiddish writer Isaac Bashevis Singer when he writes that scholars and philosophers –

> have convinced themselves that man, the worst transgressor of all the species, is the crown of creation. All other creatures were created merely to provide him with food, pelts, to be tormented, exterminated. In relation to them, all people are Nazis; for the animals it is an eternal Treblinka ('The Letter Writer,' epigraph to Patterson).

In summary then, in and with the name of 'humanity' we disclose only the figure of Western imperialist terror, a 'vehicle of economic imperialism' inflicting extreme inhumanity upon its enemies. It is also to begin to understand the need to move always beyond such delimitation – a move, as Jean-Luc Nancy writes, toward 'a world offered not to "humanity" but to its singular bodies' (*Corpus*, 41).

The inviolate body: poetics and politics of the organism

Considerations of 'common humanity' or of the 'human community' have occupied a privileged place throughout the history of philosophy. However, such a placing here of the notion of the 'human community' together with its common-sense synonym 'common humanity' is by no means fortuitous. Not only are these synonyms in fact antonyms – insofar as the latter refers to what is 'common' to every individual human being, rather than to a common relation *between* all human beings, and can thus be more helpfully termed 'universal humanity' – but also their everyday interchangeability in fact serves to disclose the limit, in every sense, of 'the human community.' This exchangeability of heterogeneous terms, that is to say, marks the imbrication of the organic body of ontotheological humanism with the biotic body of nationalism, with such compositions figured both by the phantasmatic boundaries of the human and the political organism, and by the mythic oneness both of the

(55, my emphasis).

common body and the individual bodies which compose it. The concepts of 'humanity' and of 'community' (which includes, but is not reducible to, 'the nation') thus come together in the positing of an immanent organism. As Jean-Luc Nancy writes in *The Inoperative Community* (1986), it is –

> precisely the immanence of man to man, or it is *man*, taken absolutely, considered as the immanent being par excellence, that constitutes the stumbling block to a thinking of community. A community presupposed as having to be one of human beings presupposes that it effect, or that it must effect, as such and integrally, its own essence, which is itself the accomplishment of the essence of humanness. ... Consequently, economic ties, technological operations, and political fusion (into a body or under a leader) represent or rather present, expose, and realize this essence necessarily in themselves. Essence is set to work in them; through them, it becomes its own work. This is what we have called 'totalitarianism,' but it might be better named 'immanentism,' as long as we do not restrict the term to designating certain types of societies or regimes but rather see in it the general horizon of our time (3).

The immanent or totalitarian body, insofar as it must work to accomplish its own essence 'as such and integrally,' demands first of all its circumscription. It depends for its existence, in other words, upon the exclusion of its other through the reproduction of its phantasmatic borders, coming into being as such only subsequent to the production of these borders and thus rendering it secondary to an originary complex of relations. A limit then, is the *a priori* condition of its positing of essence.

Moreover, for both the immanent human body and the immanent human community – and here one begins to understand how the one comes to stand in for the other – this constitutive limit works to fuse every human being who has ever lived or may ever live into a single body. This, it should be noted, is irrespective of whether the 'essence of humanness' being put to work is posited as internal to the individual human organism over against the non-human animal, or else as inhering within every relation between individuals over against the monad, that is, as either infra- or intersubjective. In the same way, the fascistic nation works to fuse into a single body every *citizen* who has ever lived or may ever live. One thinks here of those reclaimed 'national heroes' who come again to represent the 'essence' of the nation, to spectrally embody the spectral body, as well as the militaristic rhetoric concerning the 'threat' to its future integrity. The slave morality that is nationalism, in other words, demands the working of an immanent body, fused into the commonality of *ressentiment* by way of an outside against which it can then constitute itself. Nietzsche, we recall, defines 'slave morality' as that which 'from the outset says No to what is "outside," what is "different," what is "not itself"' ...

this *need* to direct one's view outward instead of back to oneself – is of the essence of *ressentiment*' (*Genealogy*, I:10).

That this essence must become the body's own work – an organic setting itself to work in order to accomplish itself, that is to say, a setting itself through its self the work of becoming *purely its self* – demands a specific concept of the border: that of the 'living membrane.' This is because, in a working towards the purity or immanence of a strictly delimited 'body,' the immanent body thus requires a 'natural' border. It requires, that is, a *hymen* through which impurities may be expelled, but which at the same time admits *only* what is assimilable within, or consumable by, the organic system in its work toward perfect autonomy and thus immortality that is the work of pure immanence. However, as Derrida points out, for such a 'living body' to achieve this immortality of autonomy 'it would have to die in advance, to let itself die or kill itself in advance, for fear of being *altered* by what comes from outside, by the other, period. Hence the theatre of death to which racisms, biologisms, organicisms, eugenics are so often given' ('Artifactualities,' 18-9). Here then, we can begin to discern the autodestructive *tēlos* – its structural 'suiciding' - of the totalitarian body, be it the human body, the delimited body politic, or the global body of 'humanity,' a suiciding intimately connected with that which Derrida elsewhere calls the 'autoimmunitary structure.'[9]

It is a *tēlos*, moreover, which renders *death* as the *truth* of undying, death as the truth of an ecstatic 'One-ness' beyond all division. Such, then, is the truth and the *tēlos* of the immanent, self-enclosed body: pathic and undying, its very lifeless perfection being nothing more nor less than the truth of 'the Animal' as traditionally conceived. We will return to this in a moment, but here it suffices to note that its work of oppression, of immanence, functions in the same way as the pathic, undying essence of 'the Animal' serves to stage the theatre of death that is the contemporary zoo-technical holocaust. Nancy puts it as follows:

> immanence, if it were to come about, would instantly suppress community, or communication, as such. Death is not only the example of this, it is its truth. In death ... there is no longer any community or communication: there is only the continuous identity of atoms. This is why political or collective enterprises dominated by a will to absolute immanence have as their truth the truth of death.

---

[9] 'The immunitary reaction protects the 'indemnity' of the body proper in producing antibodies against foreign antigens. As for the process of auto-immunization ... it consists for a living organism, as is well known and in short, of protecting itself against its self-protection by destroying its own immune system' ('Faith and Knowledge,' 80n27).

> Immanence, communal fusion, contains no other logic than that of the suicide of the community that is governed by it. … The fully realized person of individualistic or communistic humanism is the dead person (*Inoperative Community*, 12-13).

This suicidal logic, which Schmitt's conserving concept of the political inevitably gestures towards, can only produce a body of *ressentiment*, can only reproduce a private hatred for the improper, for the foreign body corrupting the purity of the Same, which henceforth comes to be seen in terms of a *destiny*. Such destiny must be understood in contrast to an abstract enmity justified by a publicly sanctioned 'enemy' which claims to render such intense – intensely produced and intensely productive – hatred as 'passionless', that is, *as* senseless. Rather, destiny, by definition, requires neither action nor passion, neither decision nor responsibility, and indeed, in the promised fulfillment of its auto-immanence, ultimately has as its goal the elimination of action and passion *as such* in the fusion of ecstatic One-ness.

It is not by chance that Derrida, in his discussion of the autoimmunitary structure, refers to what goes by the name of public *health* and military *security* as the 'two great forms of immunity' (*Rogues*, 155). 'The immune' here concerns nothing less than the immanent, self-determined and self-determining body which seeks, in its work and as its working toward perfect health, to expel in suicidal fashion that upon which it depends for its founding-conserving function: 'the autoimmunitary haunts the community and its system of immunitary survival like the hyperbole of its own possibility. Nothing in common, nothing immune, safe and sound, *heilig* and holy, nothing unscathed in the autonomous living present without a risk of autoimmunity' (Derrida, 'Faith and Knowledge', 82).

Setting itself through its self the work of becoming its self, death for the immanent body, continues Nancy,

> is not the unmasterable excess of finitude, but the infinite fulfillment of an immanent life …. Since [Gottfried Wilhelm] Leibniz there has been no death in our universe: in one way or another an absolute circulation of meaning (of values, of ends, of History) fills or reabsorbs all finite negativity, draws from each finite singular destiny a surplus value of humanity or an infinite superhumanity. But this presupposes, precisely, the death of each and all in the life of the infinite (*Inoperative Community*, 13).

The reference to Leibniz is instructive here, namely because the notion of the pathic, undying animal receives perhaps its most explicit formulation in Leibniz's 'Monadology' (1714). According to Leibniz, nonhuman animals, lacking reason, constitute a continuum of unfolding and enfolding, an unending reconfiguring with neither beginning nor end, neither birth nor death (a vitalism whose echo can still be found in Deleuze & Guattari and beyond[10]). Paradoxically then, the 'fully realized' body of individualistic or communistic humanism, constituted in its negation of 'the Animal,' turns full phantasmatic circle, *presupposing in its mythical perfection the very pathic, undying animal against which it sought to found its essential difference.* Thus, the dialectical teleology of humanism collapses in on itself, the fall of the Fall. The life of the fully-realized body is thus the perfection of the *non*living *beyond* finitude. It is in this sense that Derrida can write of 'absolute evil' as 'absolute life, fully present life, the one that does not know death and does not want to hear about it' (*Specters*, 220).

In summary, the impossibly immanent and immune body of both individualistic and communistic humanism is an originary absence of life, a nonliving body which must nevertheless be protected from contamination, which must thus turn against itself, extirpate itself of all finitude and thus of all life. Here again, it is necessary to recall, and to which we will return once again in the next chapter, Nietzsche's insistence that any way of being which excludes itself from all other ways of being necessarily degenerates, having excluded itself from that which reserves the possibility of its regeneration. As we have seen, however, Nietzsche is by no means attempting to restart the machinery of dialectical opposition and overcoming. Rather, he seeks to interrupt exactly that movement of Hegelian totality which must subsume or exclude all 'particularity' within its 'universality' – the former constituting for Hegel in *Philosophy of Nature* a danger analogous to a contagious disease within a body.

Throughout this chapter we have inevitably being thinking, with Arendt and with Schmitt, the placeless place of 'the Jew' as figured within Nazi ideology, but also of that placeless place which, so intensely produced and productive today, is marked both by the terms 'immigrant,' 'asylum seeker' and 'terrorist,' and by the rendering insensible and invisible rendering of nonhuman animals. The reference to Hegel, however, is vital to a further understanding of both the suicidal structure of the Nazi 'theatre of death' and of the organicism which ultimately serves as the justification for the Shoah.

First of all, it is only insofar as the living organism serves as the figure, the isomorphic model and the proper of the Nazi State, that it is therefore possible for its racist and patriarchal – at base, ethnico-religious – hierarchy to be naturalized by way of its conflation with the discourse of biology. This

---

[10] For a recent example, see Akira Mizuta Lippit's *Electric Animal: Toward a Rhetoric of Wildlife* (Minneapolis & London: University of Minnesota Press, 2000).

is evident, for example, in the words of Ernst Haeckel, who "often spoke of groups of people as cancerous growths or malignant viruses," and of the Nazi physician Fritz Klein, whose claim that '[t]he Jew is the gangrenous appendix in the body of mankind' was typical (Sax, *Animals in the Third Reich*, 105). For the Nazis as for Hegel, therefore, the 'natural(ized)' body of the state has to be protected from disease understood as an organic lesion that is both a hurt and an abnormality. One which, at least in the case of the former, results in 'the medicalization of virtually all ethical and social questions. ... The medical profession fighting disease became an image of absolute ruthlessness' (105). Moreover, this absolute privilege accorded to the notion of public health justifies that other 'great immunity' identified by Derrida, that of military security. As Boria Sax writes, the subordination of the individual organ[11] to the biotic community –

> served for an era of total war, of conflict that was waged through technologies of mass destruction. The idea complemented a militaristic nationalism, since it *fused the entire population together with the landscape into a single body.* Furthermore, it directed the aggression not only against enemy soldiers but also against civilians and entire environments (*Animals in the Third Reich*, 109, emphasis added).

Nazi Germany, however, was not, as Sax suggests (and by way of another animal trope), 'meant to be an enormous predator' (109). Rather, it is best figured by what Arendt terms 'the banality of evil': by the mundane directors of public 'health' programmes, of biopolitics in the most deadly sense – civil servants like Eichmann who manipulated people and corpses as if transporting freight. Under Hitler, 'the Aryan race' was constituted at once as both the proper and the proper future of 'humanity' – destined, if only its impurities could be eliminated, to approach perfection and thus immortality (as figured by the thousand-year Reich). In this sense then, given the impurity that was 'the Jew,' insofar as it figured that which must be eliminated in order for humanity to achieve its predestined perfection, this meant that the Jewish people were not, and could never be, 'human.'[12]

---

[11] Here, however, I argue that Sax is mistaken insofar as he writes of the subordination of the individual *organism* (109), when in fact there can be no 'individual organisms,' but rather only particular organs which, until holistically organized or incorporated within the body of the nation, remain lifeless and thus without value.

[12] This is by no means to overlook all those other 'foreign bodies' victimized by the Nazi regime – homosexuals, gypsies, communists, Slavic peoples –, all of whom need to be considered both independently and together, and which is necessarily beyond the scope of this book.

As that which humanity must overcome in order to become absolutely – integrally and immanently – human *as such*, the Jews thus find themselves reconfigured both *as* animals (*as* rats, *as* pigs, etc.) within a rigid zoological hierarchy and also, more specifically, as parasites (Jews were to be exterminated, Hitler announced, '*as* lice'). 'The Jew,' in other words, is reconfigured as ontologically distinct, a nonhuman species. Hence, in the official media the Jewish people are stripped of their generic human appearance, thus marking them out as excluded from the category 'humanity.' In this way, 'the Jew' (and always recalling that this is an identification in advance which actual Jews then have to live) within the body of Nazism comes to be reconstituted *as* inassimilable, rendered at once alien, threatening, insidious, corrupt and corrupting. Reproduced along with and alongside 'the animal' as *a priori* discontinuous, 'the Jew' is, in other words, beyond incorporation, a nonhuman contagion and a contagious inhumanity. As such, 'Jewish-ness' becomes a disease which cannot be overcome, and hence must be exterminated for the Reich to achieve its destiny and purity – irradiated like a cancer or cut away like a gangrenous limb. In this, the proper body of the human and the proper body of the human community thus require each other for their articulation, a relation marked by the nationalist privilege of blood *and* soil: the pure human body and the pure geophysical body.

What in Hegel ostensibly leads to a doctrine of tolerance, for the Nazis leads to the gas chambers. And yet, relying as they both do on the organic work of a body becoming purely its self, the two cannot be so easily separated. In the *Philosophy of Right*, as Andrew Benjamin demonstrates, Hegel has recourse to the will in positing the nonrelation of the 'person' and the 'animal,' insofar as '[t]he absence of a willed relation between the "I" and its life or body in the animals' means that for Hegel 'it [*sic*] does not have 'a right' [*Recht*] to that life' (*Of Jews and Animals*, 81). Furthermore, this 'entails that the continuity of animal life has a necessarily distinct form' (82). Here then, the absence of a willed relation between 'body and soul' serves to deny a *right* to life, which simultaneously justifies a putting to death.

At the same time, such a justification finds its echo in the figure of 'the Jew' as a distinct form of life which, once removed to the *Lagers*, is stripped of the willed relation which connects person and life – this is in one sense the 'logic' of the camps. In this way, the absence of the Jewish 'right' to life is retroactively 'proved,' thus providing the Nazis with the 'right' of putting to death. Again, what is disclosed is the operative machinery of animalization, the refusal of an abstract 'humanity' which opens the way to slaughter without murder: killing as animals. In other words, insofar as Hegel identifies animality as a disease to be overcome by the will to become human, his discourse always already *risks* the camps, a risk all too clearly marked by the figure of the 'inassimilable Jew' which haunts his philosophy of tolerance.[13] Nevertheless, and despite this complicity, the difference which *actualizes* the Lagers is, as Nancy and Lacoue-Labarthe write, that the Aryan 'Subject' transcends Hegel's speculative thinking 'in an immediate and absolutely 'natural' essence: that of blood and race. The Aryan race *is*, by this account, *the* Subject; within it, self-formation is realized and incarnated in 'the sacred collective egoism which is the "nation"' ('The Nazi Myth,' 310). The Nazi regime transcends Hegel's idealist philosophy, in other words, in the mythical fusion of 'human' and 'community' into a suicidal material body.

Shame, Guilt, and Analogizing the Holocaust

There is no direct *analogy*, it should be noted, being posited in the previous section between the intense pain and suffering undergone by those nonhuman animals, living and dead, within industrialized feedlots, slaughterhouses, and laboratories, and those human animals, living and dead, who were and are victims of the Shoah. Rather, what is being argued is their necessary *interrelation* or *reciprocity*, at once their absolute historical singularity and their indissociability. While not an analogy, therefore, there nonetheless remains a *relation* – the relation of humanism and nationalism –, one which I propose to mark here with the improper phrasing 'animal holocaust' (and without proper noun status).

It is this, I argue, which makes *permissible*, if not accurate, the holocaust analogy, insofar as the animalization of Jews in Nazi Germany has as its operative condition the machine which reproduces nonhuman animals as killable. Taking a cue once again from Derrida, this strategy could be figured as *plus un* 'Holocaust': more than one / no more one 'Holocaust,' insofar as the term recalls always more than one (and thus) no more one *community* (that is, no immanent or immune body), which is what *must* be learned if we are to ensure no more Holocaust(s). There remains, however, considerable controversy surrounding the use of the Holocaust analogy, which will be explored in this section. Entering into this debate, which will be sketched below, I argue that even if the relation remains implicit, the shock of its implied comparison is nevertheless strategically important (as too, as we shall see, is

---

[13] On this figure, see Benjamin, *Of Jews and Animals*, 151-177. See also Gayatri Spivak on the 'native informant' in *A Critique of Postcolonial Reason*, 37-67.

the comparison with slavery), insofar as it opens 'the question of the animal' to the related concerns of shame and guilt. We have already touched on the former in the discussion of Kafka's investigator, and here I will suggest, by way of Susan Buck-Morss's recent project, that the latter is precisely the guilt of humanism itself.

Proposed most notoriously by Martin Heidegger who, whilst remaining silent as to his own complicity, in 1949 compared the death camps to 'mechanized agriculture,' the Holocaust analogy is most often condemned on the basis that its equation, in reducing humans to animals, in fact repeats the movement of animalization which served to legitimize the genocide in the first place.[14] In response, however, philosopher David Wood acutely notes that, 'while the apparent comparison of the treatment of Jews with the fate of animals ... may be obscene, so too is the implication that these sort of practices would call for a quite different judgment if we were 'just' talking about nonhuman animals' (*The Step Back*, 49). He then recalls the strong argument that –

> the architecture and logistical organization of the death camps ... was stolen, or borrowed from the successful designs of the Chicago stockyards, also fed directly by the railway system. If the industrialization of killing was first perfected on cattle [*sic*], and then applied to humans, we have not an obscene analogy, but an obscene piece of history (49).

For her part, Donna Haraway describes the Holocaust analogy as 'a common, powerful, and in my view powerfully wrong approach' (*When Species Meet*, 336n23). This is *not* to say, however, and as Haraway makes clear, 'that the Nazi killings of the Jews and others and mass animal slaughter in the meat industry have no *relation* [emphasis mine],' but only that such an 'analogy culminating in equation can blunt our alertness to irreducible difference and multiplicity and their demands. Different atrocities deserve their own language' (336n23). Carol Adams too, in rare agreement with Haraway, refuses the analogy on similar grounds, claiming that it rips 'experience from its history' which thus 'does harm to Holocaust survivors. We must locate our ethic for animals so that it does not hurt people who are oppressed' (*Neither Man Nor Beast*, 83). Finally, Susan Coe in *Dead Meat* (1996) notes that –

---

[14] Heidegger's reference to the camps is quoted in the *Der Spiegel* interview 'Only a god can save us' (23 September 1966), pub. *Der Spiegel*, 31 May 1976. Reprinted in Gunther Neske & Emil Kettering (eds), *Martin Heidegger and National Socialism* (New York: Paragon House, 1996), 41-66.

My annoyance is exacerbated by the fact that the suffering I am witnessing now cannot exist on its own, it has to fall into the hierarchy of a 'lesser animal suffering.' In the made-for-TV reality of American culture, the only acceptable genocide is historical. It's comforting – it's over. Twenty million murdered humans deserve to be more than a reference point. I am annoyed that I don't have more power in communicating what I've seen apart from stuttering: 'It's like the Holocaust' (72)

The clear link between these critiques is not that the comparison is inaccurate or irrelevant, but rather that the positing of an *analogical* equation is inappropriate – on *both* sides – only insofar as it effaces the specific differences between them. However, *not* positing such an analogy can equally result in blindness. As Wood writes, '[i]f there is a worry that the distinctiveness of the human gets lost in such a comparison, there is an equal worry that the refusal of such analogies perpetuates our all-too-human blindness to the systematic violence we habitually inflict on other creatures' (*The Step Back*, 49).

In addition, such a critique of the trope of analogy in general (reasoning from parallel cases) fails to address the chance imperative of an improper *metonymy* holding open the place by which previously effaced singular differences actually come to make sense. It fails, that is to say, those forbidden, unheard-of phrasings explored throughout this book. It is just such a chance imperative which adds weight to Wood's warning that the 'expression may well provoke the very resistance it seeks to overcome, but the expression is not used unthinkingly, or irresponsibly' (49).

In *The Animal That Therefore I Am*, Derrida famously – and carefully – refers to 'animal genocides' (26), with the proviso that, 'concerning the figure of genocide, one should neither abuse nor acquit oneself [*ni abuser ni s'acquitter*] too quickly' (26, trans. modified). He then proceeds to compare the 'monstrous' suffering undergone by nonhuman animals with that of the Shoah, albeit ensuring, with all he has written on the subject of the prefatory 'as if,' that there can be no simple relation of identity or analogy:

As if, for example, instead of throwing a people into ovens and gas chambers [*dans des fours crématoires et dans des chambers à gaz*] (let's say Nazi) doctors and geneticists had decided to organize the overproduction and overgeneration of Jews, gypsies, and homosexuals by means of artificial insemination, so that, being continually more numerous and better fed, they could be destined in always increasing numbers for the same hell, that of the imposition of genetic experimentation, or extermination by gas or by fire. In the same abattoirs (26).

Here it is clear that Derrida is not proffering a simplistic, reductive analogy between the millions of Jews exterminated in the Nazi death camps and the billions of nonhuman animals slaughtered in the death camps of capitalism.

239

All this is, however, noted only by way of a contextualizing preface. In fact, I would argue that the necessarily blunted edge of any posited comparison is neither the sole, nor even the main, cause of controversy.

To begin with, it must be understood that the term 'Holocaust', referring to the extermination of the Jews during the Nazi period ('the Shoah', from *so-ah* meaning 'devastation' or 'catastrophe', is the Jewish term), is itself a trope. At once analogical metaphor and euphemism (in the strong sense of a palliative), it is one which moreover remains controversial to this day. Giorgio Agamben has traced this figure, and indeed, its 'essentially Christian' history, in a number of his texts, and offers a convincing argument as to the 'irresponsible historiographical blindness' of its positing, a blindness and blinding concerned precisely with the question of *analogy* (*Homo Sacer*, 114). Arguing that the term 'holocaust' (from the Greek *holocaustos*, signifying 'completely burned') is 'from its inception anti-Semitic' and thus 'intolerable' (*Remnants*, 31), Agamben notes how it marks an attempt 'to establish a connection, however distant, between Auschwitz and the Biblical olah and between death in the gas chamber and the "complete devotion to sacred and superior motives"' (31).[15]

It is here that the figure of analogy is identified as the origin of its intolerability: 'the term impl[ies] an unacceptable equation between crematoria and altars' (31). Indeed, with this 'wish to lend a sacrificial aura to the extermination of the Jews by means of the term "Holocaust"' (*Homo Sacer*, 114), it becomes clear that the term is if anything more appropriate as a figure for the extermination of animals for consumption, whether by gods or by men, than it is for the Shoah. And again, in terms of the meaning of the original Greek term, it is the industrialized genocide of nonhuman animals which most befits the adjective *holocaustos*, echoed by the industrial slaughterer's familiar boast (a boast already worn smooth with overuse in the Chicago stockyards of the late 19th century) that they 'use everything but the squeal.'

Returning to Agamben, the important and necessary desacralization of the Shoah serves, as is well known, as the zero point – marked by the camp *Muselmann* – for his notion of 'bare life.' Jews under Nazism, he writes, were constituted as 'a flagrant case of *homo sacer* in the sense of a life that may be killed but not sacrificed' (114). Bare life is, moreover, only *actualized* in its putting to death, which is "neither capital punishment nor a sacrifice, but simply the actualization of a mere 'capacity to be killed'" inherent in the condition of the Jew as such' (114). There was, in other words, no 'mad and giant holocaust' but rather only the actualization, enacted only through extermi-

---

[15] On this, see also Wood, *The Step Back*, 50.

nation, of 'mere' life, mere subsistence. That is, in being-killed 'the Jew' is reconfigured as pure animal remains ("'as lice," which is to say, as bare life' (114)), for which the mute *Muselmann* is the figure, the 'staggering corpse' (Jean Améry) or 'the living dead' (Wolfgang Sofsky) without the capacity to die, but only to be killed.

We can now begin to discern a more nuanced relation than a superficial equation marked by the phrasing 'animal holocaust.' Under the Nazis, Jews are thus reproduced as walking dead flesh, a *related*, but nonetheless singular, transformation into 'pure' corporeality, into bodily-shaped collections of dead zombie flesh ready to be disarticulated. Not into 'meat,' however, as we have seen with the so-called 'food' animals of the previous chapters, but into 'mere' animal remains. In other words, by way of a structurally interrelated spectral disembodiment through mimetic displacement, we find here too the instrumentalized 'walking ghosts' which reproduce a symbolic logic of oppression that ultimately serves to constitute subjugated beings who are precisely *deserving* of oppression. Not an analogy, therefore, but an inter- and intra-relation – a *founding reciprocity*.

Furthermore, the reciprocal relation of these singular historical genocides serves to highlight the specificity lacking in Agamben's conception of 'bare life.' As Andrew Benjamin clearly demonstrates, and in contrast to the 'undifferentiated ontology' which founds Agamben's 'bare life,' such a reconfiguration always involves –

> the violent imposition of identity. It is imposed in this way on Jews, thus under-scoring the vacuity of the claim that such a position involves 'bare life,' as though within such a life the particularity of being a Jew – that which prompted the figure's work in the first place – was not itself already marked out. In being there originally, that mark would always have been retained (*Of Jews and Animals*, 186-7).

It is this ineffaceable mark which calls to the guilt which, according to Primo Levi, must bear upon 'almost all' the Germans of the Nazi period, precisely because they failed to bear witness to what they could not *not* witness. The question – a related, even an analogous question – turns in a circle: Why do the majority choose not to see, to turn away and to refuse to hear, let alone to touch, taste or smell, the contemporary maltreatment of animals if not because of an unremarked sense of guilt and shame? *An experience, in other words, that is the murmur of the always restrained yet retained mark of constitutive exclusion.* This brings us to yet another important aspect of the holocaust analogy: in 'Thinking With Cats' (2004), David Wood argues that the posited relation is nonetheless –

wholly justified even if politically divisive. The reasons for this are deep, and *connected with the difficulty most of us have in coming to see that some social practices we take part in clear-headedly might be utterly contemptible.* This contrasts with our *shared* condemnation of all Nazi genocidal activity. The attempt to connect these events produces extreme reactions (215n37, emphasis added).

Here then, the impropriety of the metonymy 'animal holocaust' discloses the sharing of community based upon the guilt of exclusion, and marked by a failure to witness that which cannot not be witnessed (this latter despite its euphemistic effacement in the concept of 'meat', an effacing figured by the sterile, plastic-wrapped tropes of flesh on supermarket shelves). In this, another sense of the phrasing 'animal holocaust' is made manifest, its disconcealing power becoming evident when Primo Levi's absence is articulated together with a dialogue between Jacques Derrida and Elisabeth Roudinesco entitled 'Violence Against Animals.'

In the midst of this latter dialogue, Roudinesco professes an attachment to 'the idea of a certain division between the animal and the human' (72). This 'attachment' is, I believe, exactly what Derrida attempts to interrupt when, immediately prior to this statement of attachment (in response to a question about the apparent 'excess' of prohibitions against cruelty), he asks Roudinesco what she would do if she 'were actually placed every day before the spectacle of this industrial slaughter' (71). Roudinesco replies somewhat brusquely,

> I wouldn't eat meat anymore, or I would live somewhere else. But I prefer not to see it, even though I know that this intolerable thing exists. I don't think that the visibility of a situation allows one to know it better. Knowing is not the same as looking (71).

Derrida insists, however, that she consider the situation more deeply:

> But if, every day, there passed before your eyes, slowly, without giving you time to be distracted, a truck filled with calves leaving the stable on its way to the slaughterhouse, would you be unable to eat meat for a long time? (71)

To which Roudinesco responds:

> I would move away. But really, sometimes I believe that, in order to understand a situation better and to have the necessary distance, it is best not to be an eyewitness to it (72).

The point, of course, is that Roudinesco is *already* a witness, that it is not that she can choose *not* to witness, but rather that she can only choose not to be *a* witness to that which she cannot not witness – the sole form of guilt which, according to Levi, cannot be absolved. It is the guilt, in other words, of disavowal, of the refusal to bear witness to the trace which remains to interrupt every metaphysics, every oppressive structure of dependence-exclusion.

What Derrida's questioning in fact draws attention to is the refusal of a possible encounter through the conserving safety of a theoretical separation within the calculability of moral, economic, or religious discourse. One which serves to double the separation on the ontological level. In this way, contemptible socioeconomic practices becomes habitually – academically – denoted as 'intolerable', and which in so doing are thus rendered tolerable insofar as the unremarked guilt is neatly and conveniently assuaged. In other words, that which cannot not be witnessed is safely displaced onto the level of everyday facts. Indeed, there is nothing more factual and everyday than what for Roudinesco is the apparent '*necessity* for industrial organization in raising and slaughtering animals' (71).

By contrast, intolerability is precisely an injunction – never a choice – which displaces *this* bodying outside of the everyday and into the impossibility of continuing to be, and which is at once the affirmation of, and *attestation to*, the encounter. That which cannot be tolerated, that deafening blare of silent music from the furthest proximity, is never the tolerable-intolerable, but rather the most undeniable and the most material, that which can be no longer missed and not yet mis-taken.

Animal slavery and the guilt of humanism

Finally in this chapter, we explore via the 'unapologetic' humanism of Susan Buck-Morss's latest project, the relation – perhaps analogical – to that other improper metonymy or 'dreaded comparison': that of 'animal slavery.'

In *Hegel, Haiti, and Universal History* (2009), Buck-Morss asserts an 'undeniable political experience of guilt that we humans feel when witnessing something deeply wrong with the principles that govern our everyday world' (83). Here again, the question clearly concerns the relation of guilt and bearing witness, a witnessing which happens to a body before any possibility of choice and which, while it can indeed be spoken about, it cannot, however, 'be known' insofar as it contradicts the 'official order.' The 'truth,' writes Buck-Morss, while 'available to conscious perception, is at the same time "disavowed"' (83). As a result, this 'experience of guilt,' an experience which for

Buck-Morss presupposes the existence of universal moral truths, potentially places an individual in conflict with its community, and as such 'entails being a traitor to the collective that claims you (through nation or class, religion or race [and, I would add, through *species*])' (83).

More than this, however, Buck-Morss claims that such 'guilt has its source in the gap between reality and social fantasy, rather than between reality and individual fantasy. It can turn interpretative analysis into political critique by breaking the official silence that sanctions the wrong state of things' (83-4). Here, I argue, it is in fact the very espousal of an 'unapologetically humanist project' of universal history (xi) which prevents Buck-Morss from engaging with the encounter which renders such guilt *un*disavowable – the guilt of humanism itself.

It is all too easy, Buck-Morss suggests, to share in the 'moral outrage' over the way European Enlightenment philosophers responded to the ongoing systematic oppression that was slavery, and yet –

> we cannot deny that a comparable moral outrage is occurring at this moment, one that future generations will find just as deplorable (this is our moral hope), the fact that political collectives proclaim themselves champions of human rights and the rule of law and then deny these to a whole list of enemy exceptions, as if humanity itself were the monopoly of their own privileged members – their war a just war, their terrorist acts a moral duty, their death and destruction legitimated by reason, or progress, or the divine (149).

As we have seen, Schmitt argues that the claim to a universal humanity is always a particularly brutal ruse of war, passing off a specific interest as universal. Indeed, the evocation of a universal concept is in a certain sense always a usurpation, given the impossibility of a presuppositionless position. What, for example, might be the criteria for identifying 'humanity' without implying a whole determinate culture and, in this case, moving as it does via Hegel, an explicitly *Christian* culture? Irrespective of Buck-Morss's attempts to evade its implication in focusing upon 'the experience of historical rupture as a *moment* of clarity' (147), the claim to humanity is nonetheless always to proclaim *in*humanity, and thus repeat inversely the denied humanity which the claim claims to reclaim.

In other words, Buck-Morss misunderstands that humanism is only insofar as it sets up a limit between the human and the animal. Such is the demand for line-drawing which humanism can never avoid, and which ever again founds that animalization of the other which is the very condition for those political collectives she imagines her humanism will overcome, simply by its focus on the transitory. Without ever asking the question of the animal,

Buck-Morss never questions the very conditions of humanism. As a result, and while she would no doubt refuse any claim to a universal (essentialist) race or gender, in positing a 'new' humanism she in fact falls prey to that very thing for which she berates those Enlightenment philosophers. That is to say, to an absolute blindness to the slavery that literally exists all around her, and to the contradictions which remark our shared political guilt, a blindness which future, and indeed present, generations 'will find just as deplorable' (although it is not a hope I would define as *moral*). The irony of Buck-Morss's 'unapologetically humanist project' is, in other words, the absence of the 'contradictory guilt' of humanism itself.

9. Promise to Betray, Humanity

Introduction

Previously, we encountered Nietzsche's insistence that any way of being that is cut off from, or that cuts itself off from, all radically other ways of being can only ever *de*generate, insofar as it thus excludes itself from that which reserves the possibility of its own regeneration. Throughout this chapter, and in one form or another, I aim to read this claim again and again with the hope of gaining a deeper insight into what I am calling a 'community beyond the human'. With this in mind, I explore in the first sections the important notion of the *promise* as it is found in Nietzsche's *On the Genealogy of Morals* (1887). Here, I will argue that, for Nietzsche, to become animal – that is, to become an animal with the right to make promises, and with the right to constitute the *future* therefore – is to become a futural being beyond 'the human'. Furthermore, this possibility of *out*-living in and as an animal encounter is a possibility that humans always already share with other animals.

Recalling too the fundamental (albeit violently reductive) move of *giving death back* – in the sense of *finitude* and *nonsubstitutabilty* – to nonhuman animals, this will lead in the final section to a consideration of the centrality of death, and of finite negativity, to any thinking of a community beyond the human. Further engaging with texts by Jean-Luc Nancy and Maurice Blanchot, my aim here is to approach what Georges Bataille famously calls the 'community of those who have no community'. Only such an impossible community, I argue, has the potential to stage an ineffaceable rupture within our paranoid theatres of death whose sole hysterical demand is the *a priori* absence of life.

Before this, however, it will perhaps be helpful to briefly recap the conclusions drawn from the earlier reading of Nietzsche's 'On Truth and Lie'. As we have seen, in marking the originary porosity of being-with – this sharing of the proximal distance from the as such, and thus from each other and from the world –, a division is inscribed in and as language. Such is the division of finite beings imposed by a touch in which no limit, no separation, can be discerned, but rather only and habitually imposed. We saw too that the Nietzschean individual neither lives nor exists, but rather 'is' only that which exceeds every determinable form, that is, which *out-lives* [*über-leben*]. Such is the demand which, still to come, thus withdraws from all recognition in and as a silent announcing which necessarily out-lives any enclosure of the properly 'human.' As a result, responsible, affirmative (the two terms being synonymous) conduct is always a conducting-*toward* the other, an abyssal mark and remark of being-in-common which, in a *creative* forgetting of being, holds the place of the impossible encounter in which something comes to be that which it is as such.

In following Nietzsche therefore, *an originary being-with shared by all living beings prior to any making of sense is disclosed* (without, however, being able to draw a simple line between 'living' and 'non-living'). In short, being-with – the pure potentiality of being as such – bears its withdrawal *in* and *as* tropes marking a shared finitude. In this double movement of in and as – this double distancing that is at once the repeatability of language and the singularity of being-there – each is divided from, and shared with, every other.

Moreover, inasmuch as such ways of being in language – differential ways of being-with, of being-together as always already related in difference – can never be securely delimited, the spacing of ethical encounters which constitute unrecognisable phrasings is thus reserved. Such phrasings, we recall, only retain their inaugurating intensity insofar as they both *no longer and not yet* make sense, are *no longer and not yet* parodic. In opposition to the dominant legislation of value, and thus against the Law, such a phrasing manifests itself as a singular being, as an individual nonhuman monstrosity – as an *animal*. That is, as an (out)living being refusing to recognize the sense of the Law which functions to exclude the sense of its being and, who or which, in coming to being, thus betrays the map of its site of exclusion.

Along with Nietzsche, however, let us also recall that, according to Maurice Blanchot at least, 'community' is always and only human, inasmuch as becoming-human is the necessary condition of both community and communication (and if these terms are ever distinct). Finitude, writes Blanchot, is the distance that separates but which also prevents separation. Indeed. And yet, without death – undying and thus 'merely' existing – nonhuman animals can be neither separate nor can their separation be prevented. Put in this way, one begins to wonder if perhaps these ontologically opposed ways of being are not in fact indistinguishable. For Blanchot, as we know, this vertiginous proximal distancing serves to displace nonhuman animals, negatively defined as the excluded who cannot be excluded. By contrast, I would suggest that this uncanny reciprocity in fact describes a *community of those who share the incapacity to share*. In this way, we glimpse through Blanchot a being-in-common that is at once prior to, and interruptive of, any 'community service' and, indeed, of any *working* (in the sense given to the term by Nancy). This is, in short, the sharing of an impossible promise, which returns us once more to the Nietzschean *über*animal.

Prehistorical mnemotechnics and the community of animals

First of all, in the second essay of *The Genealogy of Morals*, Nietzsche does *not*, as is often taken to be the case, define 'Man' as the animal who promises. Being human, in other words, is not simply to be an animal with the additional ability to promise. Rather, writes Nietzsche, 'To breed an animal *with the right to make promises* – is not this the paradoxical *task* that nature has set itself *in the case of* man?' (II:1, latter emphases mine). Such a task – a task, moreover, which remains outstanding – is not paradoxical insofar as it juxtaposes animal + promise, but rather because it identifies promise with *right*. In other words, the entire history of humankind, of 'culture' traditionally conceived, is reducible to the preparation by 'nature' (and recalling here Nietzsche's ambivalent deconstruction of the nature-culture binary) for the coming of the animal, of the 'emancipated individual,' who not merely promises, but rather possesses the 'actual *right* to make promises.'

The ability to promise is thus not a property which marks out the human, but is rather that which marks 'the human' as a *prehistoric breeding project*. Such is a production and a labor which, even *if we imagine* ourselves placed 'at the end of this tremendous process' (and Nietzsche makes sure to mark that 'if'), by no means marks its completion, the being with this right still not yet having arrived in the present. 'Man' is the *pre*history of this *right*, and thus, so long as there is 'Man,' the task remains outstanding. How, then, is this task to be done with at last, lest 'we humans' be rendered eternal dyspeptics?

Perhaps 'to a large extent' complete, that is, *if* 'we' are at its end or are its end (and recalling too that the addressees of Nietzsche's texts were always 'the posthumous ones'), this tremendous prehistory is, writes Nietzsche, the development of an 'active desire' not to forget. In direct contrast to the strong force that is at once active forgetfulness and repression, this active desire *not* to forget permits a being 'to remain undisturbed by the noise and struggle of our underworld of utility organs' while simultaneously constituting the 'present' *and* 'making room' for the new. In short, the entire prehistory that is 'Man' is the opposing desire 'not to rid oneself, a desire for the continuance of something desired once, a real *memory of the will*' and thus, with the 'I shall,' the memory of the future (II:1).

Here, it should be noted, such a 'willing' is not a *real* willing – indeed, as Nietzsche writes in *The Will to Power*, there *is no will*, but rather only precision or oscillation (§46), only quanta of *force* (*Genealogy*, I:13) – , but rather a real *memory* of the will, a memory which, as with every memory, is habitually untrue, that is, a fiction or a fable. With this fiction of the will, we are thus recalled to Nietzsche's famous assertion that '"the doer" is merely a fiction added to the deed' (I:13). For Nietzsche, there is no subject, whether understood as 'substratum' or 'soul,' which is in fact simply a result of 'the misleading influence of language' (I:13). Consequently, it becomes necessary to rethink, and to revalue, what Nietzsche might mean when he writes of an 'emancipated' and 'sovereign' individual.

The opposing desire, the death-drive to remember, to repeat, is the *pre-condition* of history, of the emancipated individual with the right to make promises who, perhaps even now at the end of the process, is yet to come, yet to completely arrive in the present constituted by forgetting. Repetition, in short, is the precondition of the new, of the animal with the right to promise. The human is this precondition, moreover, only because the way of being-human is memory, is *mnemotechnics*. That is to say, the ability 'in general [to] be able to calculate and compute,' the development of which there is 'perhaps ... nothing more fearful and uncanny in the whole prehistory of man [i.e., in the prehistory that is man]' (II:3). Fearful and uncanny it may be, but the task of breeding an animal with the right to make promises, that is, of an animal whose way of being consists of the '*right to affirm oneself*' and thus the capacity to rightfully 'stand security for *his [sic] own future*,' nevertheless necessarily 'embraces and presupposes ... that one first *makes* men to a certain degree necessary, uniform, like among like, regular, and consequently calculable' (II:3). Hence, with the aid of morality and a 'social straitjacket,' 'Man' is thus *produced*.

Indeed, Nietzsche continues, all the solemnity and seriousness of 'man' is merely a holdover of 'the terror that formerly attended all promises, pledges, and vows,' merely the gloomy stain of a prehistory which, insofar as it is necessarily that which 'we humans' *as* humans can never move beyond, is therefore '*still effective*' (II:3).

This development of the memory is thus a prehistoric preface, an over-coming of forgetfulness in imposing the 'demands of social existence as *present realities*' (II:3) on the way to the emancipated individual. A mere preliminary to the coming of an out- or over-animal whose right to make promises is the liberation from custom and morality, and which, no longer prefatory, is thus free to *make* history. The *übermensch* then, as we saw in the reading of 'On Truth and Lie,' is this animal movement beyond 'the human.' An overcoming of habit and convention held, and held to, by the memory of the (imaginary) will, Nietzsche thus moves us beyond the Platonic virtues of immutability, beyond the 'vast overrating' of the 'virtue' of conviction (*Human, All Too Human*, §629).

One thinks here of Zarathustra's famous metaphor of 'Man' as the rope between 'animal' and 'overhuman' ('Prologue,' 4). The rope in this reading is thus the memory of the will, of a mnemotechnics which, forever linking the singular body to the possibility of invention, forgets to forget in the compulsive desire to repeat. This figure does not, however, mark a dialectical humanist *tēlos* resulting in a superhuman sublation, that is, in the negation of the negation of the animal. While Nietzsche is indeed concerned with the specific mnemotechnicity which marks the way of being-human, this is by no means to refuse to nonhuman animals other ways of being-mnemotechnical. Rather, as we have already seen with Nietzsche's gnat metaphysician, they too are similarly doubly-displaced in metaphor, and thus 'in' memory:

> The whole organic world is the weaving together of beings, each with their little imaginary world around themselves: their force, their lust, their habits are found in their experiences, projected as their *outside world*. The ability [*Fähigkeit*] for creation (formation, invention, imagination) is their fundamental capacity: of themselves, these beings have, of course, *likewise* [my emphasis] only an erroneous, imaginary, simplified representation. 'A being with the habit of ordering in dreaming' – that is a living being. Immense amounts of such habits have finally become so solid, that *species* live in accordance with these orders (Nietzsche, *Kritische Studienausgabe*, 11:34; cit. Lemm, 25).

The metaphor of 'the animal' must thus be understood as a figure of the impossible state of being prior to mnemotechnics, that is, of being prior to habit by which a being comes to be.[1] By contrast, 'the human' is the privileged

---

[1] With this, there emerges a very different way of reading Nietzsche's well-known claim in the second of the *Untimely Meditations* that 'the animal lives *unhistorically*' (UMII, 61), in which 'the animal' rather figures the constant (yet impossible) state of forgetfulness. The fact that this text was composed roughly contemporaneously with 'On Truth

figure of the anoriginal sedimentation of language, of the taking place which has always already *taken* place. Hence, neither 'Animal' nor 'Man' has the *right* to make promises. Moreover, in relation to the specific question under consideration here – that of the community beyond the human – what might be called 'the community of animals' is thus a network of pure singularities prior to any determination, and thus prior to any 'community' in the sense of the habitually imposed demands of social existence. 'The animal' refers not to living beings therefore, but is rather a *figure* of that which can precisely take no figure, the taking place which withdraws in always already having taken place, and which marks every living being 'with the habit of ordering in dreaming.'

Traitor to Humanity, Universally: Nietzsche

The outliving of 'the human,' that is, of habit, the inability not to forget, concerns, as we have seen, the right to promise on the one hand and, on the other, the '*one*' whose task of breeding this is. To begin with, the *right* to promise demands that the promise, insofar as it is a promise, *takes time*. Hence, it must not be given lightly, but rather 'reluctantly, rarely, slowly,' as its time to come requires the sufficient strength to maintain its coming into being come what may, that is, 'in the face of accidents, even "in the face of fate"' (II:2). The right to make promises, in short, demands an unwavering fidelity to that which remains to come, and which Nietzsche describes as 'the extraordinary privilege of *responsibility*' (II:2).[2]

Paradoxically, however, such a promise, such responsibility must, as we shall see, already be a *betrayal*, its nobility that of the traitor and its responsibility that of the capricious wanderer. The right to make promises, in other words, demands that the promise *must* be betrayed, and thus we must all be traitors to humanity, or rather, to its concept or, even better, to its *figure*. The Law of humanity then, *must* be broken – this is the law before the Law. And yet, how might this *über*human *right* to promise which is the betrayal of that promise be understood?

For this, the final chapter of philosopher Avital Ronell's *The Test Drive* (2005), in which she discusses the Nietzsche-Wagner break-up, proves inval-

---

and Lie' – in which Nietzsche argues that memory forms every living being, as we have seen – further supports such a figurative, even mythological, reading.

[2] Nietzschean mutability, as a result, thus contrasts with the *calculable* innovation of speculative capital, as we will see in the final part of this book.

uable. As Ronell makes clear, to promise is, like the positing of universals, to be blinded by, and blind to, an *excessive* obligation, that is, 'to an oppression that locks in the future: [thus] the promise portends madness' (312). In other words, and as Nietzsche suggests in section 629 of *Human, All Too Human*, the structural excess of the promise is thus the *madness* of fidelity which, insofar as it is blind to the tragedy of finitude – to 'the face of fate' – in fact serves to render every promise conditional. The non-sense of the promise, the *insensé* of unconditionality, is in this way withdrawn in its actualization: the excessive, gruesome night of its taking place always already effaced by the sober light of day of its having taken place.

In one sense then, as Ronell writes, 'Nietzsche sets up the promise in such a way as to let us escape its imperial purchase' (*The Test Drive*, 312). On the other hand, however, the *right* to make promises can, by contrast, only be the strength to face finitude, to face the face of fate – not as its master or in some Heideggerian sense of an authentic appropriation of being-towards-death, but in remaining faithful to the maddening displacement of its demand from the other. To face both the unconditional and the inadequacy of every response is, in other words, a responsibility to the infinite excess that is the unconditional, and which can thus only betray itself.[3]

However, in order to understand why the *right* to make promises must break with the *memory* of the (impossible) will, in that the prehistoricity of the latter is overcome by the former's inauguration of history, two things need to be noted. Firstly, that *every* utterance, that is, every making of sense, is *already* a promise, and thus always sundered by the excess of its demand. As Derrida writes,

> The performative of this promise is not one speech act among others. It is implied by any other performative, and this promise heralds the uniqueness of language to come. It is the 'there must be a language' …, 'I promise a language', 'a language is promised', which at once precedes all language, summons all speech and already belongs to each language as it does to all speech (*Monolingualism*, 67).

Here then, we see that the structural excess of the promise renders explicit the movement of *sense* already explored in the earlier reading of Nietzsche: the infinite promise is the *taking* place of language which has always already withdrawn in its finite having *taken* place. Secondly, this constitutive 'in difference with itself' ensures that "'the fatal precipitation of the promise must be dissociated from the values of the will, intention, or meaning-to-say that

---

[3] On this, see Keith Ansell Pearson's excellent *Viroid Life: Perspectives on Nietzsche and the Transhuman Condition* (London & New York: Routledge, 1997), 27-8.

are reasonably attached to it' (67). In fact, the ubiquity of the promise and its dissociation from the will are indissociable, insofar as the taking place of the mark necessarily exceeds every semantic intention. This is not to say that every such mark, as Werner Hamacher makes clear, is 'thereby disburdened of its semantic gravitation' ('Lectio,' 196). Rather, '[n]o text has the power to exclude the possibility that it says the truth, or at least something true; but no text can guarantee this truth because every attempt to secure it must proliferate the indeterminacy of its meaning' (196). In other words, every promise – as an act of will – inevitably exceeds its own performance, making of it necessarily a mis-promise.

We can now better understand Ronell's assertion that for Nietzsche the promise necessarily 'entails the act of *versprechen*, which means both mis-speaking and promising' (*Test Drive*, 312). More than this, however, it follows that the emancipated individual, the animal with the right to make promises, is thus a being with *the right to mis-mark*, that is, to rightfully mark improperly, to *revalue*, in contrast to the simple mis-speaking of those 'feeble windbags who promise without the right to so do' (Nietzsche, *Genealogy*, II:2).

Moreover, the Nietzschean 'individual' – that which, as we have seen, outlives itself in improperly remarking the unheard-of and yet already forbidden – is 'emancipated' only in relation to the limit imposed upon what counts, what *makes* sense, within a given state of affairs. The sovereignty of the individual is, in short, always *posthumous*, insofar as it out-lives all recognized sense and thus value. The *right* to make promises therefore demands a response and a responsibility to betray every custom and every moral, to be a traitor to every firmly held belief.

Such a right, moreover, entails the strength to remain faithful to this no-madism, to the vigilance of this wandering, which is to remain loyal and response-able to the being-in-common. That is, to the community of others which we share and which shares us in the not-being-able to share, in not-being-able to fuse the more-than-one in One. In and as the memory of the 'I shall,' which already congeals into habit and thus refuses forgetting, and which constitutes our being-shared in and across language, the willing subject shatters in its being already exposed in-common. *Such is a community, in other words, of traitors who affirm and betray in common.* As we have seen, hospitality is exactly this: an affirmation which interrupts every social convention and every duty to the *socius*, an unrecognizable, incalculable decision without sovereignty whose every actualization betrays hospitality as such.

This has profound consequences for a reading of Nietzsche's 'animal with the right to make promises' as the completion of prehistory in the coming to be of the *human*, or even of the superhuman. If the right to make promises promises at the same time to make history, then the strength to hold faithfully to an unending betrayal of the dominant rule becomes the rule: this is the individual's promise and right to break every promise, every contract, every calculation.

> No – there is no law, no obligation of that kind; we must becomes traitors, act unfaithfully, forsake our ideals again and again. We do not pass from one period of life to another without causing these pains of betrayal, and without suffering from them in turn (*Human, All Too Human*, §261).

If the right to make promises overcomes or outlives the prehistory that is at one and the same time 'the human' and the development of a phantasmatic memory of the will, then this promise that is humanity must in its turn be overcome, must be broken. As animals, we must overcome the memory which prepares for, without arriving, the appearance of universal 'humanity.' Such is the demand and a promise which calls forth a common betrayal of 'humanity' or, rather, of its *concept*.

The law of humanity, of its memory of the will which produces the uniform calculable subject is that which, in other words, *must* be broken in a being-common and a being-in-common of singularities. As Ronell writes, if we are to pass to another stage of life, "our relation to the promise needs to be a broken one. The promise can be counted on only to enforce its breakability" (*The Test Drive*, 313). Moreover, she continues, referring to the above citation from *Human, All Too Human*, the diacritical mark following the initial negation 'can be read as an absence of a link, operating simultaneously as severance and connector: No, dash, there is no law. In a place where no law is asserted to stand, he posits law' (313). To outlive the human, for Nietzsche, is thus to betray humanity, to cease to *be* human in becoming otherwise. Only here do we at last approach the completion, the ends, of 'the human.' Only in this way will the community beyond the human, a community shared by all living beings (which is not to say 'living' *organisms*), have arrived: a community of the impossible *perhaps* which only comes to be *with* every other animal, a community whose chance of becoming inheres in its being exposed and disposed with others.

The extended consideration of the 'human community' in this part sheds further light upon what Derrida describes as 'democracy to-come [*a-venir*].' In deconstructing 'the essential link of a certain concept of democracy to autochthony and to eugenics' (*Politics of Friendship*, 110n25), such a thinking, Derrida writes, thus excludes it from the phantasm or fiction of a genealogical tie which is always only ever 'posed, constructed, induced, [which] always implies a symbolic effect of discourse' (93). In so doing, it 'confide[s] it to or open[s] it to another memory, another immemoriality, another history, another future' (111n25). To exclude community from the fiction of immanence and immunity, from the appeal to birth, to nature, to nation, and to universal humanity, is thus to move beyond the human, and thus beyond the bad dream of 'a *determined politics*' (93).

In contrast to an all too common *ressentiment* which says No to what is 'outside,' to what is 'different,' the opening to another memory and another immemorality calls to a community that can only ever be posthumous, the mark of which 'is' to suffer the agonies of outliving. Thus, writes Nietzsche, 'the more a present-day individual determines the future, the more he will suffer' (*Will to Power*, §686). To outlive our walking ghosts, to live on in the tragedy of our shared finitude and thus to refuse the living death of zombie slaves, 'I' must therefore 'die several times while still alive' (*Ecce Homo*, §5 on *Zarathustra*). Loyalty and responsibility demands that, as living beings, we must always again turn against the self-congratulatory 'purity' of *ressentiment*. Must always again turn against the suicidal machines of immanent-immunity which, having *cut itself off from itself* in cutting itself off from all radically other ways of being, can thus only ever turn against itself, can only extirpate itself. This latter, as we have seen, necessarily degenerates, having excluded itself from that which reserves the possibility of its regeneration: such is the compulsive suiciding of gated, bounded communities.

In the end then, it is no surprise that, in a no longer extant preface to *The Twilight of the Idols*, Nietzsche affirms that 'the individual' – this being with the right to promise – is recognized, marked out, by a creative relation to nonhuman others: '*His love of animals* – men have always recognized the solitary by means of this trait' (cit. in Heidegger, *Nietzsche*, II:45).

Meeting Our Solitude: Making Friends

In contrast to the bad dream of a *determined* politics then, such a *posthumous community is, in common with the human being, a singular bodying which is neither nameable nor substantial. It is, in short, undetermined.* To name a community, for example, is necessarily to determine a community in opposition to another, and it is for this reason that Alain Badiou calls the community and the collective 'the unnameables of political truth,' insofar as 'every attempt "politically" to name a community induces a disastrous Evil … to force the naming of the unnameable. Such, exactly, is the principle of disaster' (*Ethics*, 86). Hence, an infinite community – that is, being *as such* – can neither *be*, nor *be named*, but rather, inasmuch as it is beyond completion and incompletion, can only and always have already withdrawn. A withdrawal which is, moreover, its *demand*. As Maurice Blanchot writes,

> There it is: something had taken place which, for a few moments and due to the misunderstandings peculiar to singular existences, gave permission to recognize the possibility of a community established previously though at the same time already posthumous: nothing of it would remain, which saddened the heart while also exalting it, like the very ordeal of effacement writing demands (*The Unavowable Community*, 21).

While it is indeed the case that nothing of this *community* would remain, at the same time, however, the *trace* of this community remains. It is its *demand*, in other words, which remains, that of 'the very ordeal of effacement' imposed by writing by the taking place of spacing having always already taken place. Demanding a response, demanding responsibility, its withdrawal is nothing less than an injunction of existence: the imperative to give place to, and to be given place by, that which is refused sense within a given 'community affect.' Such is the place out of place of a shared *commonality*, understood as *sharing in the politicization of the individual ethical demand*.

> Sharing comes down to this: what community reveals to me … is my existence outside myself. Which does not mean my existence reinvested in or by community, as if community were another subject that would sublate me, in a dialectical or communal mode. *Community does not sublate the finitude it exposes. Community itself, in sum, is nothing but this exposition.* It is the community of finite beings, and as such it is itself a *finite* community. In other words, not a limited community as opposed to an infinite or absolute community, but a community *of* finitude, because finitude 'is' communitarian, and because finitude alone is communitarian (Nancy, *The Inoperative Community*, 26-7).

Given death, a giving finitude, nonhuman animals must thus take part, eksist, only in exposing themselves in and as this community of finitude. Community 'is' the sharing that is being as such, without memory and without forgetting, beyond completion and incompletion. As we learned in chapter four, its ethical injunction interpellates other beings who come to be in sharing the disorientating call of its encounter which, only insofar as it remains unnameable, that is, only insofar as it *no longer and not yet makes sense*, resonates in the clothes of an improper phrasing. Thus, through the movement of *zoogenesis* is constituted a nonreactive affirmative micropolitics which, tracing a community to come, opens a potential emergent trajectory of escape that is the redoubled space of *respond-ability*: the excessive recursivity between concept and singular experience, between the deafness of a given state of affairs and the inaudible clamor of *infinite* community.

In summary then, 'community' – infinite ethos, unconditional hospitality – is that which must withdraw in the opening of the finite space of politics. In withdrawing, its trace of displacement composes the senseless ethical demand, calling forth the placeholding phrasing that is *political nomination*, a nomination which presupposes neither identity, nor substance, nor proper meaning.[4]

Here, we at last approach the sense of 'community beyond the human,' of a community of finite beings already beyond 'the human.' Such a community affirms itself only in its withdrawal in and as the political, and in so doing it interrupts the phantasmatic effect of every genealogical tie and silences the everyday mis-speaking of those 'feeble windbags who promise without the right to so do' (Nietzsche, *Genealogy*, II:2). It is *community* which, in *withdrawing*, 'is' the distance that separates, or rather *spaces* – i.e. finitude, or the shared incapacity to share – but which also *prevents* separation in the trace of its withdrawal, marking the irreducible porosity that is exposition. It is this which gives us to understand the Nietzschean community of solitary friends as an announcing of those who, as Derrida writes,

> love in separation. The invitation comes to you from those who can *love only at a distance, in separation* [*qui n'aiment qu'à se séparer au loin*]. This is not all they love, but they love; they love lovence, they love to love – in love or in friendship – providing there is this withdrawal. Those who love only in cutting ties are the uncompromising friends of solitary singularity. They invite you to enter into this community of social disaggregation [*déliaison*] (*Politics of Friendship*, 35-6).

We are now in a position to define this 'community without limit' as an infinite commonality of singularities which shares and in which is shared all finite living beings. Hence, to affirm the community of separation, of withdrawal, is to love without limit in the greatest possible proximity: that is, in sharing the inability to share, in sharing an unbridgeable displacement from immanence, in sharing the withdrawal of community, in sharing the demand of an impossible hospitality, and in sharing the ethical demand which opens the space of the political.

---

[4] The *political*, writes Nancy, designates 'the disposition of community as such' (*The Inoperative Community*, 40). In this, we can understand why the political is always *communist*, but not necessarily communist *politics*.

Such a community of separation thus stands in direct contrast to the exclusion by which the man of *ressentiment* figures the other as 'evil' and thence himself as 'good,' a division which, insofar as it depends upon exclusion, necessarily de-generates. Rather, it is only in the withdrawal of community that can be found, in Blanchot's words, 'the friendship that discovers the unknown we ourselves are, and the meeting of our own solitude which, precisely, we cannot be alone to experience ("incapable, by myself alone, of going to the limits of the extreme")' (*The Unavowable Community*, 25). Only in this way might 'crimes against the human *status*' become impossible, having rendered inoperative, *unworking*, the greasy workings of the brutalizing machineries of animalization which serve to render 'brutes' on both sides of the imaginary division.

Betrayal then, is the very condition of community, and thus paradoxically of vigilance, responsibility, and loyalty. A betrayal which, exemplified by Kafka's Investigator, takes the figure of a nomadic animal, of a lone wanderer ever seeking community and commonality. Such is the futural being who or which bears the strength to outlive 'the human.' Such fidelity, I propose, must hold itself to a giving finitude which, in bearing witness, responds to the nonsubstitutable deaths of living beings in re-marking the shared proximal distance that is being-with.

So it is that here too we find the disjunctive space of the phrasing 'animal holocaust': for friends of a community beyond the human, there can be neither death camp nor slaughterhouse. Despite this, however, it is to the slaughterhouse, that degenerate basement of capitalism, which we turn in the final part. There, I will further explore the notion of the promise and mutability, revisiting along the way various arguments from earlier chapters, in considering the increasing centrality of biotechnology to so-called 'post-Fordist' capitalism.

Zoogenesis, a fable

By way of yet another reading of 'animal holocaust,' let us conclude this part, however, by briefly recalling the memory of Bobby, recapitulated here in the short form of a fable. Bobby was the name given to the dog who recognized, despite the enforced degradation which marked so-called 'life' in the camps, the 'humanness' of a group of Jewish POWs in Nazi Germany, a group which included philosopher Emmanuel Levinas among their number. The 'free' men who gave the orders, as well as the children and women who passed by and sometimes raised their eyes, recalls Levinas, 'stripped us of our human skin,' that is to say, stripped them of their recognizable human status, thus rendering them 'subhuman, a gang of apes' ('Name of a Dog,' 48). Bobby – the 'last Kantian in Nazi Germany' who, 'unable to universalize maxims and drives' and thus no Kantian at all – was not fooled however: 'For him, there was no doubt that we were men' (49).

In the holocaust of animalization, therefore, in which the skin is stripped both metaphorically and literally from the bodies of Jews, only this singular way of being-dog amid the determined territory and determining theatre of war, only this nonsubstitutable dog to whom these men give the proper name 'Bobby,' could, in the mutual recognition of their ways of being, in turn return to these bodyings their human skin. Such, *inter alia*, is our fable: the promise of zoogenesis.

Part Five. Bio/Capital

The reinvention of capitalism: a discontinuous dependence

In *The Jungle* (1906), a novelistic exposé of exploitative working practices in the Chicago stockyards at the beginning of the twentieth century, Upton Sinclair describes the industrialization of 'meat' as 'the spirit of Capitalism made flesh' (376-7). A century later, however, it would be more accurate to say that the spirit of Capitalism promises to *transcend* all flesh, even as animal bodies are exploited and consumed ever more intensely. Indeed, this shift within agribusiness is, as we shall see in this part, in fact symptomatic of the much broader transformation undergone by capitalism in recent decades. A shift that is, paradoxically, both discontinuous with, and yet dependent upon, the industrial capitalism it nonetheless claims to leave behind.

Here, this reinvention of capitalism will be explored through the example of the slaughterhouse, as its shifting site offers a particularly compelling display of the *dis*continuity of 'postindustrial' capitalism, while simultaneously demonstrating the latter's continuing dependence upon an increasingly marginalized industrial underbelly. (Here, I am using the word 'slaughterhouse' as a general term to refer to large disassembly factories in which living nonhuman animals are killed, disarticulated, and transformed into 'meat', be that as 'cuts', offal, pastes, etc., and other component parts such as skin, eyes, teeth, hair, and bone, as well as into 'by-products' such as glue, gelatin, fertilizer, and so on.) One immediate way to perceive this is through the changing ways the slaughterhouse in the West is framed for, and consumed by, the public gaze. In Sinclair's day, slaughterhouses offered popular tours in which a 'visceral, affective response ... [was] arguably integral to the spectacle of slaughter' (Shukin, *Animal Capital*, 95). Should an American 'socialist whistleblower' publish such a book today, however, she might well, as a result of the USA PATRIOT ACT (2001) and its successors, end up in court charged with being a terrorist. While this will be explored in detail in due course, here, I just want to make clear my initial point that 'new' postindustrial capital intersects with the 'old' industrial capital *most explicitly in the penetration of animal bodies* – human as well as nonhuman.

Prophetically defined by Karl Marx as 'the abolition of the capitalist mode of production within the capitalist mode of production itself' (*Capital* III:569), the contemporary transformation of capitalism has been categorized in a variety of ways since then: as the movement from Fordism to post-Fordism; from disciplinary societies to societies of control; from national industries to trans- and multinational corporations; from commodity capital to 'fictitious' or speculative capital; from geophysical colonialism to economic neo-colonialism; and from petrochemical to biospheric modes of accumulation. To this list I would also add the movement from stockyards and packingtowns to 'Concentrated Animal Feeding Operations' (CAFOs) and so-called 'pharm' animals, of which a transgenic sheep named Polly, albeit less famous than her kin Dolly, is still the best-known example. Ultimately, as we will see, this historical shift is also a shift in the conception of *time* itself.

In addition, we will follow too the less immediate, but perhaps more significant way of tracing this movement through the transformed notion of reproduction itself. It is, of course, by no means incidental that control over the reproduction of bodies – of nonhuman animals, of human and nonhuman workers, and of capital itself – finds one of its most contentious sites in the female gendered body of the nonhuman animal. It is here that we find the figure of Dolly, the first cloned sheep who, born in June 1996, was scientifically 'fathered' by human males by way of her 'parent' company PPL therapeutics.

As we shall discover in more detail in chapter ten, Dolly's emergence too marks *both* the transformation of capitalist relations *and* their continuing dependence upon the industrial mode of production. We get a clear sense of this double orientation – the simultaneously straight and queer, so to speak – through the fact that, while it was essential that the Dolly "experiment" show that her 'natural' (i.e., germinal) ability to reproduce could be bypassed in favor of a more efficient (i.e., patriarchal) means of reproduction, it was *also* essential that Dolly should continue to produce spring lambs who are perceived as 'natural' in every sense, thus serving, *inter alia*, to ensure that cloning would not thereby deny postindustrial capitalism of its slaughterhouses. It is somewhat ironic, therefore, that the ideologues of cloning insist upon the absolute 'naturalness' of its reproduction at the very same moment that cloning crosses most clearly with slavery insofar, as Sarah Franklin notes, they share 'this recognition of the shame and disempowerment that occasions the loss of reproductive power' ('Dolly's Body,' 355). Furthermore, I will argue that it is here, inscribed in consumable flesh of Dolly's offspring, that the danger of an incomplete or, rather, of a *stalled* deconstruction of the nature-culture dichotomy can be most clearly perceived – a deconstruction traced throughout this book as quite literally the 'grounding' question of 'the animal.'

While the 'post' of *post*-industrialism or *post*-Fordism is thus in a strict sense a misnomer, it nonetheless remains a highly productive one, as we shall see, insofar as it functions to further marginalize contemporaneous industrial modes of production as being 'primitive' or 'backward.' This, I suggest, is experienced most clearly by those who find themselves ground under the wheels of agribusiness 'wet work.' Indeed, the biotechnological revolution, the veritable flagship of postindustrial capitalism, both demands and effaces an ever increasing exploitation, alienation, and consumption of both factory workers and factory animals. Moreover, in the process, the distinction between the two becomes increasingly blurred.

At the same time, however, the transformation marked by the 'post' is in another sense absolutely discontinuous with industrial production, a sense which must be understood *as a shift from the conditioned to the unconditioned*. A shift, that is to say, from a determined linear temporality (exemplified somewhat ironically by the slaughterhouse *dis*assembly line) to an undetermined, *pharmacological* movement of reversibility and 'recapacitation.' By 'pharmacological,' I am here following both Derrida and Bernard Stiegler to denote that which structurally reserves for itself the function of both remedy and poison at once. The pharmacological, therefore, is always already both promise and threat. Here, it will be shown, this rupturing of linear determinism not only interrupts traditional notions of patriarchy and genealogical descent with the promise of a material 'transhuman' immortality, but also interrupts any possible recourse to the all too familiar response-reaction dichotomy so often employed to exclude nonhuman animals.

This is not to say, however, that postindustrial 'biocapitalism' is therefore more responsive as far as actual, nonsubstitutable nonhuman animals are concerned. Rather, we will find instead that 'the animal' is yet again represented – albeit in a transformed and, indeed, *patentable* sense – as both pathic and undying, and thus excluded from the shared concerns of finitude. This, I will argue, results from the fact that the promise of biotechnology remains dependent upon a rhetoric of genetic determinism, both for its moral justification and in order to efface the threat of its necessary indeterminism. Nevertheless, what Dolly demonstrates is precisely the impossibility of biological determinism insofar as, at both the cellular and the organismic level, she interrupts, and even reverses, the arrow of time in what is *a writing of and on the body*.

At this point, I turn in the final chapter to philosopher Bernard Stiegler's ongoing attempt to reinstall a secure human-animal distinction through an exploration of the notion of 'life always already freed from life.' Here, I will argue that, insofar as human 'psychotechnics' cannot in fact be separated from what Stiegler calls 'animal vigilance,' this necessarily renders inoperative the very human-animal distinction that serves to ground Stiegler's promise of a technical remedy to the poison of technology.

Despite this, however, and by way of a reworking of Stiegler's core concept of *epiphylogenesis*, I will argue that the 'new' science of biotechnology nonetheless produces new possibilities for interrupting both the sadistic reduction of nonhuman animals to reactive machinery, and the very rhetoric of genetic determinism required for their biotechnological capitalization in the first place. Finally, by way of the dispersed temporality of promissory capital, I will conclude this book by exploring the notion of biotechnology as a redoubled pharmakon of *excessive mutability*, allowing me at the same time to draw together the various threads of my argument.

10. Promises, Promises, Promises …

Capital After Life and Life After Capital

Sadism is about the structure of scientific vision, in which the body becomes a rhetoric,
a 'persuasive' language linked to social practice.
Donna J. Haraway, *Primate Visions*

Marginalization and the industrial underbelly

In 'Postscript on the Societies of Control' (1990), Gilles Deleuze, in a concise addendum to the work of Michel Foucault, offers a broad sketch of the key markers of the shift from 'disciplinary societies' to 'societies of control.' Whereas disciplinary societies, evidenced by the standardization imposed by large-scale industry, institute a 'capitalism of concentration, for production and for property,' societies of control rather constitute "essentially dispersive" circuits which are "continuous and without limit" (6). Thus, writes Deleuze, in the disciplinary period, the enclosing of space and the Taylorist disciplining of time and motion finds its exemplary figures in the factory and the prison, whereas control societies by contrast are characterized by an open-ended rhizomatic network populated by "undulatory" orbiting subjects always in debt and dominated by corporations (6).[1]

In the earlier book *Foucault* (1986), however, Deleuze rightly emphasizes the fact that, in his profound and inspiring analyses of the disciplinary societies which constitute the industrializing period of the eighteenth, nineteenth, and early twentieth-centuries, Foucault insists throughout on the *uneven and gradual transition* from one order to another with each new formation emerging 'with gaps, traces and reactivations of former elements' (19).

---

[1] In this context, see also Michael Hardt & Antonio Negri's *Empire* (2000) on the shift from the hegemony of material labour to that of immaterial labour, exemplified by the reproduction of affect common to both the entertainment and service industries.

The emergence of disciplinary societies, in other words, constitutes but one historical epoch, both subsequent to, and overlapping with, earlier 'societies of sovereignty,' and prior to, and overlapping with, the 'societies of control' instituted following World War II. There is, therefore, no abrupt discontinuity of such epochs, but rather an always uneven topography of change that shares uncertain borders with both past and future, and sheltering within itself shadows, outlines, and pockets of other times.

It produces something of a jarring note, therefore, when Deleuze then claims in his 'Postscript' that, even while Foucault was writing, 'a disciplinary society was what we already no longer were' (3). In his recently published lectures, however, Foucault makes it clear that, while the disciplinary order had indeed already seceded its primacy to the generalized mechanisms of what he calls 'security' (synonymous with Deleuze's 'control'), the fragmentary orderings of both disciplinarity *and* sovereignty not only remain, but are vital to our understanding both of history and of practices of resistance. For example, in locating the invocation of right as 'taking place on the front where the heterogeneous layers of discipline and sovereignty meet,' it becomes all too clear that not only can the contemporary reactivation of bourgeois right in no way limit the effects of disciplinary power, but also that an entirely new resistance politics is required once we begin to attend to the generalized order of security or control.[2] Today, however, it is the multiply-penetrated bodies of nonhuman animals that most explicitly demonstrate both the continuing overlap, and the mutual dependence of, the two later orders or modalities – an overlap that tends broadly to coalesce along the global North/South divide.

Industrial capitalism is itself characterized by two distinct yet continuous stages. Firstly, there is the large-scale division of labor that institutes *manufacture* and which, in the process, 'mutilates the worker, turning him [*sic*] into a fragment of himself' (Marx, *Capital I*, 482). In the place of specialized knowledge, in other words, all that is required of the worker is the endless automatic repetition of a single simple task. Secondly, *industrial* capitalism comes into being when, in addition to the division of labor, the application of machines for producing surplus value further reduce workers to mere 'organs' in the service of 'a productive mechanism' (457). In manufacture, labor was thus for the first time concentrated or assembled in one place *at the same*

---

[2] Foucault '*Society Must Be Defended*,' 39. At the same time, the reactivation of bourgeois sovereign right – with, for example, the application of rights to nonhuman animals – becomes increasingly untenable as a challenge to disciplinary power. Indeed, Foucault was making this important point long before the publication of Tom Regan's *The Case for Animal Rights*.

time as the workers themselves were disassembled or, better, *disarticulated* in every sense. Thereafter, with the introduction of industrial machinery, workers were increasingly reduced to simple organic – yet infinitely reproducible and substitutable – parts of the great machinery, both literal and symbolic, of capitalist reproduction. To this we can further add the institution of the assembly line in the Ford automobile factories of the early twentieth-century, an institution which must be considered as an *intensification* – in the sense of both increased productivity and increased fragmentation and evisceration – of both of these processes, the product as well as the worker being rationalized and standardized.

The fact that it was the slaughterhouse which, with its literal as well as figural fragmentation and evisceration, so fittingly provided the model for Fordism helps us to understand the *co-constitutive* reduction of human *and* nonhuman animals to 'mere' organs. A co-constitution, that is to say, formed by their interpenetration as fragments of 'merely' living flesh, and by their consumption for profit. This can be seen, for example, in the largely overlapping discourses supporting economic neocolonialism (as described below) on the one hand, and the exclusion of the foreign in the Same on the other (as explored in part four). Moreover, it is not by chance that it is within the windowless walls of Western slaughterhouses and 'meat'-packing factories that, more than anywhere else today (or at least more explicitly, if that term can be used to refer to something systematically hidden), the apparently outmoded forms of a capitalism of enclosure are maintained right alongside, and meshing with, the most futural informatic and control networks, exemplified by both the transnational giants of agribusiness and by the genetically engineered animals of biotechnology, be they oversized blind hens or so-called 'pharm' animals biologically modified so as to produce helpful pharmaceuticals along with their more usual bodily fluids. In this way, while all the excesses of the industrial period are retained within the slaughterhouse, agribusiness *production* is nonetheless thoroughly postindustrial, depending as it does upon venture capital and stock market investment, rather than vice versa. To understand the combined discipline and security of slaughter, however, requires that we follow Foucault and analyze how infinitesimal mechanisms of disciplinary power come to be invested, transformed, displaced, and re-used by the increasingly general mechanism of security in such a way as to disclose how, at this given moment and in this specific formation, such technologies of power become once again economically profitable and politically useful.[3]

---

[3] On this, see Foucault *'Society Must Be Defended,'* 30-33.

This apparent contradiction of transition is perhaps most clearly evident in the neocolonialism underwriting so much of the so-called 'Green Revolution.' Beginning in the 1960s, wealthy countries of the North used economic and legislative power to force farmers in poorer countries such as India, Argentina, Paraguay and Brazil to maximize acreage productivity by planting monoculture cash crops such as soybeans and corn for export (the former almost entirely used to feed 'livestock' in the EU, China, and the US). This in turn required the importing of high-priced pesticides, herbicides, and chemical-based and petroleum-driven fertilizers from the North at the cost of a spiraling debt and dependency. Similarly, throughout the 1970s and beyond, the US and the World Bank only offered loans to countries such as Mexico, Nicaragua and Costa Rica on the condition that huge areas of rainforest were to be cleared to provide grazing for 'cattle.'

Since the 1980s, however, as the Western markets for meat consumption began to decline as a result of increasing health concerns, agribusiness behemoths such as Smithfield and Tyson have sought instead to open up new markets in developing countries, again with the help of the World Bank. This shift has been achieved in part by framing notions of 'development,' 'progress,' and 'modernity' – and by way of such terms as 'nutrition,' 'health,' 'status,' 'virility,' 'need,' 'demand,' and so forth – in terms of an increased consumption of animal protein.[4] Along with exporting this 'lifestyle,' the same giants of agribusiness began the targeted construction of enormous institutions of disciplined death and disarticulation in the West which, masked and yet releasing the unmistakable odors of industrial pollutants, are invariably constructed on the outskirts of towns already devastated by poverty and racial tensions. In this way, the slaughterhouses and packing-houses of the ghettoized North continue to render explicit the contemporary wound of the West's colonial past, highlighting its structural racism and – implicit or explicit – discourses of eugenics, as we shall see in the discussion concerning the apocalyptic rhetoric of a cross-species pandemic in the final chapter. Indeed, part of the reason for the movement from the spectacular guided tours of the slaughterhouses of Upton Sinclair's day to the blank walls, the accusatory rhetoric of sentimentality, and the guards whose explicit function is to block the public gaze, is in fact in order to conceal this remnant of something supposedly long past. Such a degree of concentration, enclosure and exploitation, in other words, is no longer considered acceptable in the

---

[4] On this see, for example, Richard Twine, *Animals as Biotechnology*, 127-135; Juliet Gellatley & Tony Wardle, *The Silent Ark* (London & SF: Thorsons, 1996), 145-184; and David Nibert, *Human Rights Animal Rights*, 102-113. On the inextricability of 'meat,' patriarchy, and 'virility,' see Derrida '"Eating Well," or the Calculation of the Subject.'

'clean' disembodied information age of postindustrial society – at least, that is to say, for the 'civilized' citizens of the North.

Another way to say this would be that, insofar as the marks of the colonial-imperial order are necessarily retained by the disciplinary apparatuses despite their reutilization, they must therefore be hidden. As Foucault insists, the new technology of power does not *exclude* disciplinary technologies, but rather dovetails into them, transforming their uses as it embeds itself within them.[5] Thus, within our contemporary control societies, disciplinary techniques are put to work solely in order to maximize those elements which provide the best possible circulation whilst minimizing the chances of blockage – blockages which include not only theft and illness, but also worker solidarity, empathy, unionizing, capitalist-worker polarization, and so on.[6] In Foucault's words, the essential function of security is to 'respond to a reality in such a way that this response cancels out the reality to which it responds,' a function which makes use of instruments of discipline where necessary (*Security, Territory, Population*, 47). Central to this process is that of ensuring that everything is constantly moving around, continually going from one point to another – a circulation which paradoxically cancels the very dangers of circulation (65). In this way, certain types of 'risky' communities and shared knowledges are blocked, while other empty forms, such as those employed by agribusinesses based upon native-foreigner, legal-illegal, and men's work-women's work binaries, with all their concomitant animalization, are naturalized through this constant movement, thus guaranteeing that nothing blocks the smooth functioning of the economic mechanism and ensuring therefore the control of processes intrinsic to production.[7]

Taking the hidden enclosure of the slaughterhouse as our specific example, we find that the fragmentation inherent in the concentrated division of labor common to manufacture is clearly evident in the devalorization of the slaughterer's labor, coinciding with the replacement of individuals possessing specialist knowledge as to the killing, bleeding, and 'butchering' of nonhuman animals by a labor process divided into a number of single, endlessly repeated tasks. This remains today the modality of slaughter, for the simple reason that large and, for the most part, healthy nonhuman animals are unpredictable: they resist, they bolt and revolt, they fight for their lives. Not yet rendered sufficiently docile by selective breeding, the labor of slaughter thus requires that these still-living beings be physically dominated by other, tech-

---

[5] On this, see Foucault, '*Society Must Be Defended*,' 242.

[6] See Foucault, *Security, Territory, Population*, 19.

[7] Ibid., 353.

nologically-assisted living beings. Thus, one worker fires a retractable bolt into the brain of one cow after another. A second worker attaches a chain to one hind leg after another. A third, the 'sticker,' cuts one throat after another, and so on. Within the same windowless enclosure, the unstoppable disassembly line further transforms hundreds of other, 'less skilled' workers into animate organs of its machine, compelled by its relentless speed to cut out a set number of kidneys every hour, to slice off so many feet and to empty out so many stomachs.

The disassembly line remains today identical in all but scale to those of the Chicago slaughterhouses which, in his 1922 autobiography *My Life and Work*, Henry Ford describes as the inspiration for his factory assembly line. The general idea, he writes, came from the mechanized chain by which the suspended corpses of nonhuman animals were moved from worker to worker, each of whom repeatedly performed one step in the process of 'dressing beef.' It was, claimed Ford, 'the first moving line ever installed' (cit. Patterson, *Eternal Treblinka*, 72). This process, at once technological and disciplined and disciplinary, introduced something new, as Charles Patterson notes, into the ongoing industrialized exploitation of labor: that of 'the neutralization of killing and a new level of detachment' (72), further reducing workers to mere adjuncts of the machinery of capitalism.[8]

Nevertheless, the 'less-skilled' operations – the labor performed upon corpses, in short – are increasingly coming to be carried out today by machines utilizing the same knives as the 'less efficient' workers once did. Hence, a single machine now carries millions of chickens, suspended upside-down from hooks, through an electrocution bath. A second machine then automatically chops off their heads. Meanwhile, a third machine scrapes clean the skins of a million pigs, and another immerses them in a tank of boiling water, and so on, each of these machines being for the most part overseen by a single worker. Along the length of the contemporary disassembly line, therefore, the disciplinary modalities of manufacture, large-scale industry and Fordism all continue to coexist.

It is not by chance, however, that, in addition to the countless numbers of domesticated animals, the *human* animals who find themselves exploited by these 'older' yet contemporary modalities of capitalist production in particu-

---

[8] In keeping with our discussions of the previous chapters, and particularly with regard to the improper phrasing 'animal holocaust,' it should be noted that Henry Ford was also a fanatical anti-Semite who throughout the 1920s used his own newspaper to promulgate a vicious anti-Semitic campaign. These publications were hugely popular in Germany and with Hitler himself, who came to regard Ford as 'a comrade-in-arms.' On this, see Patterson, *Eternal Treblinka*, 71-79.

lar are almost exclusively those figured as 'less than (properly) human': illegal immigrants, asylum seekers, people of color, women, the dispossessed and the globally disenfranchised. Excluded as the foreign in the Same, the various devalorized groupings are then pitted against each other (and the Other) in a brutal and brutally cynical displacing exercise of corporate capitalism. As Michael Hardt and Antonio Negri explain in *Empire*:

> Multiple ethnic divisions among the workers function as an element of control in the labor process. The transnational corporation *addresses with different methods and degrees of exploitation and repression each of the ethnic groups of workers ...* and divisions among the workers along the various lines of ethnicity and identification prove to enhance profit and facilitate control (200, italics added).[9]

Here, we begin to perceive that, while the archetypal Taylorist and Fordist techniques of disciplinary control remain clearly visible within the slaughter-factory, a new order of power has nonetheless embedded itself within them. While the same unstoppable disassembly lines continue to neutralize the violence of killing and to transform tens of thousands of workers into animate organs of its machine, a major and widespread mechanism of contemporary security is nonetheless explicitly revealed, one which displaces, extends, and works over the figures and spaces of colonialism by organizing multiple so-called 'natural' ethnic divisions among the workers as an element of control in the labor process. Hence the second reason for the institutionalized blinding of the slaughter-factory.

In being reactivated by control mechanisms in this way, as Foucault explains, instruments of discipline no longer serve to ensure the artificial standardization of the worker, but rather only the naturalization of the freedom of production. Such mechanisms, in short, are not strictly economic, but rather ensure the functioning of economic exchange.[10] Thus, Foucault continues, security technologies operate instead upon legislation, upon structures and institutions of society, facilitating in this way population transfers and migration while organizing enmities and privileges by placing restrictions on training, instigating national hatreds by modifying certain laws while conspicuously ignoring others, by articulating advantageous oppositions between the legal and the illegal, by imposing routine conditions on aid packages enabling a greater exploitation of foreign grazing lands, and so on and so on.

---

[9] On this, see also *Fast Food Nation*, dir. Richard Linklater (Tartan Video, 2007).

[10] See Foucault, *The Birth of Biopolitics*, 140-141.

Furthermore, Foucault's analysis of neoliberalism as both associative and dissociative enables a move beyond the simplistic notion of liberal individualism which even Deleuze occasionally falls back on, such as when he claims in his 'Postscript on the Societies of Control' that transnationals protect themselves from mass resistance by 'presenting the brashest rivalry as an excellent motivational force that opposes individuals against one another and runs through each, dividing each within' (5). Against this two-dimensional myth of a capitalist 'state of nature,' of a war of each against all, which serves to naturalize neoliberal individualism, Foucault instead opens the space for a potentially far more radical critique of neoliberal societies of control by insisting that we shift our focus to the gap between the 'non-local' bond between economic subjects, and the localized bonds of sympathy and benevolence and of contempt and malice between some individuals in so-called 'civil' society. It is this gap, Foucault argues, which enables the economic manipulation of social differences, and yet it is these differences which formally serve as the 'medium' of its manipulation. In this way, however, economic manipulation inevitably destroys the very medium of community it requires in order to function. As such, this points instead to the necessity of resistance networks that function outside of both the oppositions constituting local 'civil' society *and* the empty formalism of a global economic structure.[11]

Postindustrial factories: bioreactive bodies and manimals

Along with the reactivation of disciplinary technologies, postindustrial capitalism, with its new technologies of dispersion, seeks to contemporaneously construct entirely new types of factories, factories which instantiate not only a new reproductivity and a corresponding new paternity, but also a 'new' *temporality*. Whereas the disciplinary order discretized time into minutes and seconds and disarticulated bodies into elemental gestures in the quest for a perfectly efficient worker-tool, the aim of our new postindustrial factories is to both employ and embody 'life itself' by displacing the linear irreversibility of 'natural' chronological time and instituting an undetermined network in its place. Among these 'new' postindustrial factories are the so-called *transgenic* animals themselves – also known as 'bioreactors' or 'pharm' animals – whose bodyings contain man-made genetic modifications (and which Sarah Franklin very deliberately calls 'manimals' rather than the more neutral 'humanimals'). For example, a transgenic 'dairy' animal may be con-

---

[11] Ibid., 301-2.

structed so as to carry and express a human gene in order to produce certain proteins in her milk or blood which can then be used to make pharmaceutical commodities for rare genetic diseases as well as for common metabolic disorders such as diabetes.

Transgenic animals are, in other words, material givens worked over by mechanisms of control in the hope of opening them up to an undetermined circulation by the facilitation of apparently 'natural' processes. Indeed, it is no coincidence that the term 'bioreactor' also names the machines which both culture cells and subject them to physical stimuli in order to incite non-specific 'protoforms' to *self-assemble* into specified morphologies. The aim, in short, is not to discipline, but only to facilitate an apparently natural economy of exchange. At the same time, as Sarah Franklin has shown, such facilitation requires that the scientific labourers voluntarily impose upon themselves various regimes of disciplinary technologies in order to protect the articifically enclosed space of their labs from natural processes of contamination.[12]

While Polly the sheep was one such 'manimal,' her much more famous queer kin Dolly was not, insofar as she was not 'fashioned' into becoming a pharm animal. Rather, the 'purpose' of Dolly is to validate through her being the very experimental technology which promises to produce 'manimals' in the future. Nevertheless, Dolly too, as Franklin says, can be 'thought of as a nuclear breeder reactor in that she, too, is a model of a specific kind of manufacture – not through her milk, but in her embodiment of the viability of [somatic cell] nuclear transfer using differentiated adult cells from culture' (*Dolly Mixtures*, 210-211n3). *In this, Dolly in fact exemplifies the functioning of the 'promise' not only within the biotechnological domain, but in the neoliberal financialization of the globe in general.*

More than even this, however, Dolly embodies the ability to *reverse time* and thus, as we will see, promises nothing less than a potential *immortality* – a claim in no way contradicted by her untimely death in 2003 as a result of lung disease common to animals kept in close confinement. For the moment, however, it is sufficient to note that, in the context of the transformation from disciplinary societies to societies of control, the shift to postgenomics –

> has been occasioned by changes in how the gene is imaged and imagined, whereby the language of genetic codes, messages, and information has yielded to discourses of genetic pathways, switches, or constructs to be downloaded.... It is these transformations – at once conceptual and technological, as well as commercial and political, and nationally specific – that the making of Dolly the sheep both demonstrates and performs (Franklin, *Dolly Mixtures*, 34).

---

[12] See Franklin, 'The Cyborg Embryo: Our Path to Transbiology' (2006), 174.

It is this postgenomic shift – that is to say, a movement subsequent to, and dependent upon, the mapping of the human genome – away from an understanding of the gene as determined and determining which permits, among other things, an ever more intimate experimentation speculating upon the conversion of nonhuman bodies into innovative forms of capital. As such, biotechnology right away finds itself – by way of available funding opportunities, changes in patent law, and so forth – inseparably enmeshed with both the pharmaceutical and agribusiness industries in the quest to capitalize on farmed animals in ever more novel ways.

However, as a number of theorists have pointed out, in addition to favourable regulation and a promissory rhetoric, this speculative venture depends upon a reductive view of 'the animal' as genetic knowledge. The reasons for this are quite simple: in order to justify the instrumentalization of other animals, those animals must first be objectified as instruments. Such animals, that is, must first be reduced to 'mere' mechanisms entirely determined by cause and effect, and in stark contrast to the 'free will' attributed only to the human animal. Such a view, in other words, reduces nonsubstitutable living beings to Cartesian *factories* of reproduction. Moreover, biotechnology, as sociologist Richard Twine writes, not only perpetuates the factory metaphor, but in fact *realizes* it:

> Under biopower, the factory metaphor is unsurprising – the emphasis is on the controlled productivity of the body, be that in the form of meat, labour, fitness or new offspring. ... In a reductionist sense, animal bodies are factories for the production of protein for human consumption, for the conversion of plant material into animal commodities. The commercialization of animal bodies for the production of biopharmaceuticals serves to bring this literal 'body as factory' explicitly into relief. ... Whereas the conversion of the animal body into information takes the organic into an inorganic media, the body as factory and laboratory reverses this, but similarly blurs the boundaries between organic and inorganic, and between body and technology (93-4).

This reworked notion of the genetically-engineered animal-as-factory is symptomatic of the more general shift from life conceived *metaphorically* as information, to life understood practically as its *literal* actualization which can be patented and thus commodified. Constituted as an accumulation of determined genetic knowledge, such a body is thus re-constituted as a mediated and distributed materiality entirely suited to the highly mobile, geographically dispersed networks of postindustrial capital.

In contrast to the industrial model of selective breeding therefore, Dolly as a standardized *product* is no longer what matters. Rather, it is only as a promise, as a venture of capital, that she counts. Her value, in other words, resides only in her potential to generate innumerable and unpredictable future life forms, and thus infinite surplus value. It is in this way that the promise of biotechnology is promoted as the answer to apparent limits of capitalist growth, a claim which parallels, and depends upon, the shift beyond the biological barrier formerly considered as a 'natural' boundary beyond which only God could trespass. In this context, the promissory value of both bioremediation and 'extremophiles', for example, is obvious. By way of the former, new microbes can be designed which will 'clean up' industrial – even radioactive – waste, whilst at the same time reproducing surplus value for their 'owners'. Extremophiles, meanwhile, are microorganisms who thrive in environments previously thought impossible to support any life – environments without oxygen and light, for example.[13]

Reproducible at the genetic level, manufactured and manufacturing cyborg bodyings – neither wholly living nor wholly organic, and forever working towards their own consumption – are thus by definition infinitely replaceable. Thus, while no longer constituted as a mass pathic body at the level of the species, individual nonhuman animals nonetheless remain resolutely undying, eminently 'lose-able' and thus killable. Indeed, somewhat ironically, actual nonsubstitutable animals such as Dolly and Polly are now considered *so* individual as to be *patentable*, but only insofar as they are *identically reproducible*, a process which thus both presupposes and extends the naturalization of 'the animal' as *property*.

Such bodies, never entirely alive, have no value in *being*. Their value resides entirely in the informatic promise articulating their fleshly materiality, a value which can only be actualized in their *dis*articulation, be that into 'cuts' or into cells. The nonhuman animal thus becomes at once informatic network and speculative capital, already calculated as fragments for consumption before being born and already commodified for future consumption in as yet unknown forms.

At the same time, legislation, structures, and institutions play their part in securing for corporate capitalism control, and indeed ownership, over the transnational flows of a new form of *techno-bio-logical* reproduction, facilitating for example both the outsourcing of clinical trials from North to South and the unregulated global trade in unfertilized human eggs from South to North. Typically, in both of these instances it is women who must bear the

---

[13] It is in the context of the promissory value of extremophiles that one could do well to consider the way an antienvironmentalist neoliberalism has appropriated complexity theory. See, for example, James E. Lovelock, *Gaia: A New Look at Life on Earth* (1987). On the affinities between such a position and neoliberal economics, see Cooper, *Life as Surplus*, 41-50.

brunt of this implicit notion of a lesser value placed upon the lives and bodies of the nonWestern 'other.' Meanwhile, in the suburban ghettos of the North, the old disciplinary-model slaughterhouse remains, only it is has been de-regulated and displaced into the margins by way of an increasing *immigran-tization* of 'meat,' further faciliating the transfer of things and the migration of bodies by way of a continuous noxious counter-circulation from North to South and back again.

Moreover, the promise of industrial slaughterhouses and ever-larger feedlots (or CAFOs: 'Concentrated Animal Feeding Operations') remains dependent in many ways upon the postindustrial promise of biotechnology. This is not just in order to produce more cost-effective 'food' animals such as genetically-engineered blind hens who would apparently 'benefit' from not having to witness their own conditions, but also to justify the contin-uing slaughter on environmental grounds. If bioremediated microbes, for example, can be built not only to clean the enormous and enormously toxic lagoons of fecal matter that are the inevitable by-product of mass slaughter, but moreover to flourish in doing so, then a major 'natural' limit on the in-dustrialization of 'meat' will have been overcome. Indeed, like the capitalist appropriation of 'green' concerns like recycling, the massive overproduction of cowshit promises to become a profitable venture in itself.

The promise of new times: serpents and sheep

Finally then, by analyzing the displacement and re-investment of discipli-nary technologies within the order of control, it therefore becomes possible to disclose the two contradictory temporalities underpinning their interar-ticulation. On the one side, the North exports to the South an evolutionary narrative of 'progress' and 'modernity' as a rationale for market and geophys-ical coercion while, on the other, we find a second narrative in operation within the North itself, that of post-modernist reversibility, recapacitation, and immortality. This in turn serves to push the South ever further into the margins of 'base' industrial production figured by a myth of redemptive tem-porality: the promise of a 'modern' future for which the poor must sacrifice themselves today. At the same time, the poor and marginalized of the North are reduced to desolation on the basis of the capitalist promise of an incal-culable future which nonetheless remains dependent upon the historical yet naturalized limits of capitalism, limits which 'unfortunately' but inevitably impoverish – and excuse – the present. Whereas Deleuze writes that societies of control have as their emblematic animal the 'undulatory' serpent ('Post-script,' 5), I would argue that it is rather a certain postgenomic sheep who, as we shall see, best embodies the postindustrial narrative. This is because Dolly, at both cellular and organismic levels, not so much undulates or or-bits but rather *interrupts*, and even *reverses*, the arrow of time itself, and it is around this promised reversal that the imaginary of a certain neoliberal transhumanism coheres.[14]

'Developed' by Ian Wilmut, Dolly was not fashioned with the specific intention of producing a clone, but was rather part of a large, heavily-fund-ed corporate project to build more efficient transgenic animals capable of expressing pharmaceutical products for human commodification and con-sumption (Dolly herself was not transgenic). In fact, her status as a clone is largely irrelevant to her promise (indeed, she is arguably not a clone anyway, insofar as she was generated from the merger of *two* cells from *two* female parents, a Finn Dorset ewe and a Scottish Blackface). Rather, Dolly's value is as a *technique*, that of somatic cell nuclear transfer (SCNT) – a technique which transforms the very notion of the biological.

Recalling here that the promise of biotechnology depends upon a reduc-tion of 'the animal' to determined genetic knowledge for its moral justifica-tion, what the 'viability' of Dolly teaches us, however, is that it is precisely such a notion of genetic determinism that can no longer be maintained. For so long considered self-evident – at least as far as nonhuman beings are con-cerned – prior to Dolly the genetic was 'defined by its one-way instructional, coding or determining capacity' (Franklin, *Dolly Mixtures*, 33).[15] According to such an understanding of genetic function, however, Dolly constitutes a biological impossibility. This is because deterministic gene function presup-poses that in its development each cell must irretrievably 'commit' itself to becoming a specific type, be it a heart cell or a skin cell or whatever and, in thus committing itself, it loses the capacity to become any other type of cell.

According to this linear schema, therefore, cells must 'decide' once and for all at each stage of their teleological differentiation, with each decision be-ing irreversible and irrevocable. Coincident with its differentiation, these de-cisive steps lead immutably to the aging and death of the mortal cell. Hence, the determinist view of the gene insists, by virtue of an irrevocable unidi-

---

[14] There are of course many different ways of understanding or applying the notion of the 'transhuman.' For a good example of a radical interpretation that opposes the reac-tionary neoliberal version outlined here, see Ansell Pearson's *Viroid Life: Perspectives on Nietzsche and the Transhuman Condition.*

[15] In the following discussion of the science behind Dolly's emergence, I am greatly indebted to the work of Sarah Franklin.

rectionality, on an uninterrupted progress towards a specificity of function. Any given cell can therefore become nothing other than what it already is, that is, it can neither reverse time to become newly totipotent (i.e., an undifferentiated cell with the potential to become any form of tissue, of which the embryonic stem cell is the most celebrated, and controversial, example), nor can it reverse direction in order to embark upon a specific new trajectory of development.

What Wilmut, Keith Campbell and the team at the Roslin Institute established, however, is that biological development *can* in fact be reversed, even in fully differentiated adult cells. Indeed, this is the main reason why Dolly herself is seen as breaching an apparently 'natural' boundary. 'Produced' from a mortal adult mammary cell, the very bodying of Dolly demonstrates that such cells can indeed re-function as *im*mortal reproductive germline cells. Dolly the sheep, in short, embodies this pluridirectional movement at the most elemental level. Initially described by Wilmut as a process of 'de-differentiation,' Franklin more accurately describes it as a *'recapacitation'* of cell functionality (*Dolly Mixtures*, 41). In this, a capacity thought to be decisively lost in the temporalizing of specialization either turns out never to have been lost, or else such 'decisions' never in fact take place. Thus, Franklin points out, 'another way to describe what the Dolly technique enables is a retemporalization of biology. In other words, through biotechniques, the temporality of the biological is being rescaled, or even recreated' (41).

Cell recapacitation, in other words, promises cell immortality. While various implications of this, specifically in the domain of tissue engineering, will be considered in detail later insofar as it informs the utopian discourse of 'transhuman' enhancement, for the moment I want to consider how this impacts specifically upon the ways of being – and their removal – of nonhuman animals. Most importantly, recapacitation promises to transform the lived temporality of domesticated animals – so-called 'livestock' – insofar as breeding stock in the form of actual nonhuman animals, or even just the eggs and the sperm (which still require actual animals, however distanced in space and time), are no longer required for viable reproduction. Rather, a single animal, living or dead, in whole or in part, can now be transformed into a gene bank from which an entire herd of cloned animals can be produced in the space of a few months, rather than over several years. This compression of genealogical time is taken to be an advance over the unpredictability of sexual reproduction in that, as Franklin explains, it 'offers total nuclear genetic purity, in perpetuity, and under patent' ('Dolly's Body,' 353). Hence, whereas Fordist breeding techniques reproduce genealogy (i.e., pedigree) as a source of individual value and thus surplus value, somatic cell nuclear transfer instead deranges this temporality and spatiality entirely. In short, no *actual* animals are required to achieve a perpetual germline repository and thus a certain form of immortality – what Franklin terms 'life stock.'

While no actual animals are required to *produce* a genetically pure herd, however, the actual, supposedly identical nonhuman animals *of* that herd must nonetheless continue to produce *viable* offspring of their own – with 'viable' here referring to 'natural' sexual reproduction as well as to the process of commodification itself. Bioengineered animals, in short, must *also* be able to reproduce 'naturally', if only to reassure potential consumers concerned by the apparent 'unnaturalness' of bioengineered commodities. In this way, the viability – in the sense of their literal consumability – of the herd's 'natural' offspring serves to retroactively naturalize the bioengineered herd at the same time as ensuring that all the 'old' industrial disassembly lines concealed behind blank slaughterhouse walls continue to run at breakneck speed.

We can now further understand the viability – that is, the *promise* – performed so conspicuously by Dolly herself. As a singular, nonsubstitutable materiality that is both patentable and infinitely reproducible, she brings together in and as one body the promise of both the industrial and the postindustrial, of both discipline and control. As such, Dolly enacts a double promise: the promise of a mutual articulation of informatics, biotechnology and immortality, and the promise of a global agribusiness dealing in bio-technologically-accelerated death. At the multiple intersections of her body, she enacts the biopolitical pharmacology of health: a privileged site whereby life-enhancing pharmaceuticals are crossed with death-accelerating antibiotics and growth hormones. At one extreme there is a perpetually-extended human lifespan for the few, and at the other there is the accelerated death of the slaughterhouse for the many, the two extremes moving ever further apart. Further, just as 'meat' serves to efface the more difficult human-nonhuman interactions behind an unidentifiable, plastic-wrapped trope, so too biotechnology continues to efface its most problematic human-nonhuman interactions by way of a determinist rhetoric of 'data banks' and 'sequencing.'

Owning emergence, determining the undetermined

To reiterate, Dolly's value lies *not* in her actual, nonsubstitutable being, but rather in the *technique* of which she provides the proof of viability. In this,

Dolly *herself* is without value. Unlike in the case of the stud animal, as Franklin makes clear,

> *neither* her own genes *nor* her own generative capacity are valuable. ... In this sense, cloning by nuclear transfer enables genetic capital *to be removed from the animal herself* – and doubly so. ... Dolly's own ability to produce lambs is merely a subordinated sign of her individual viability as a natural-technical product of corporate bioscience. ... The aim of producing Dolly was to demonstrate the viability of a technique that *bypasses* her own reproductive capacity, which is too inexact ('Dolly's Body,' 352-3).

It is exactly here, by way of these new temporalities, that biocapitalism indeed seeks to, *once again*, bypass its own apparently 'natural' biological and temporal limits.[16] The vertical linearity of genealogy is thus rewritten as a postindustrial rhizomatic network at the level of both genes and bodies. Moreover, these two 'levels' – as we shall see in the critique of Bernard Stiegler's philosophical anthropology in the final chapter – in fact coexist on the same plane, reciprocally articulating one another in a transductive relationship.

Furthermore, Dolly here embodies, as both engineered technique and organism, the promise of regenerative medicine at the level of tissue engineering. This is because it is only the (patentable) generative *process*, not its actualizations, which counts: an informatic and material *speculation*, the biological promise is the future which remains to be ventured into and, with at least an equal importance, ventured *upon*. A promise, moreover, of future *property* rights regulated by an ever-looser patent law, and of a newly-instituted *paternity* beyond all limits – what Melinda Cooper terms 'a not yet realized surplus of life' (*Life as Surplus*, 140). It is the promise, in other words, of the transformation of life into a patentable property of origin and infinite potential, in which one holds the rights to all possible future forms. It is, in short, the promised ownership of 'the moment of emergence' itself (127).

That this premise depends upon the deconstruction of biological time understood as a determined linearity has an enormous array of consequences, not least for the presupposition – that nonhuman animals are reducible to genetic information – which serves to 'ground' the promissory discourse of biotechnology in the first place. *The promise of an infinite surplus of life, in other words, contradicts the very reduction of life which functions to justify its*

---

[16] It is this apparently natural autolimitation of capitalist accumulation that Karl Marx identifies as the law of the tendential fall in the rate of profit; an unbreakable law which, he argues, results in the inevitable self-destruction of capitalism. On this, see Part Three of *Capital: Volume III*, 317-375. Tragically, of course, this inevitable suiciding of Capital has not yet taken place.

use *as property*. As we have seen, *a rhetoric of genetic determinism is employed so as to morally enable the ongoing experimental practice of genetic indetermination*. This, however, is not its only purpose. In addition, the discursive reduction of nonhuman life to an instinctive, unidirectional mechanism, to the transmission of a simple code, serves at once to *efface the threat of excessive mutability inherent in the post-Dolly practices of biotechnology*.

In short, the rhetoric of genetic determinism is a convention and a fetish that serves to simultaneously ground the promise of biocapital in moral terms *and* efface the very real danger attending its excessive *in*determinism. Lastly, one must not forget the supporting role such as that played by the 'old' patriarchal and Platonic economy of genetic determinism – wherein the male imprints its DNA upon the passive female egg – in the constitution of Dolly's 'new' scientific 'paternity.' While the Dolly *technique*, insofar as it is the egg cytoplasm which serves as the 'instructor,' in practice overturns this original patriarchal determinism, Dolly *herself* is nonetheless rapidly reappropriated to a discourse of scientific paternity founded upon a male-human mastery of the female-animal body.

Lastly, and most important, however, is the fact that *Dolly bodies an explicit* refusal *of genetic determinism, that is, a repudiation of behaviorist biological conditioning, and performs instead a biological* plasticity.[17] Moreover, insofar as pathways of genetic development can be reversed and reinstructed by external stimulus, this means that, *in addition to their newfound flexibility, genes have thus become thoroughly 'situational and contextual'* (Franklin, *Dolly Mixtures*, 44). In other words, as a result of the singular bodyings of Dolly and Polly, and of their various queer kin, the undetermined process of life in general must henceforth be understood as *the mutual articulation of genetic and epigenetic effects within positive feedback loops*. It is this process – nothing less than the way of being-alive – to which we must turn in the final chapter, and which Bernard Stiegler terms *epiphylogenesis*. Here, we hope to find dreams and desires common to all living beings, here the ever-renewing promise of emancipation.

---

[17] For nearly twenty years, French philosopher Catherine Malabou has been evolving the important concept of *plasticity* (*plasticité*) understood as the *hermeneutic motor scheme* of our age. By this, she means that plasticity is a singular scheme that opens the door to the current epoch by enabling the interpretation of phenomena and major events as they arise. See, for example, *The Future of Hegel: Plasticity, Temporality and Dialectic* (1996); *Plasticity at the Dusk of Writing: Dialectic, Destruction, Deconstruction* (2005); and *Ontology of the Accident: An Essay on Destructive Plasticity* (2009).

11. The Pharmacology of Betrayal

The Threat of the Transhuman, the Promise of Posthumanism

The appropriation of Bernard Stiegler

The capitalization of nonhuman animals, as we have seen, increasingly unsettles the boundary between the organic and the inorganic, between body and technology, from both directions, that is, animal-as-information on the one hand, animal-as-factory on the other. In what, following both Derrida and Bernard Stiegler, I am calling *the pharmacology of the promise*, I will argue here that such biocapitalization in fact constitutes both the dark side and dystopian material support of the transhuman utopia. The reference to Stiegler is not merely fortuitous moreover. The unsettling of the limit between the organic and the inorganic is, as we shall see, central to Stiegler's recent – and hugely influential – attempt to install a new and apparently secure metaphysical boundary separating humans from all other animals.

For Stiegler, this boundary is re-drawn through the concept of *epiphylogenesis*, which denotes the transmission down the generations of *both* inherited information (genetic) *and* newly-learned knowledge in the form of artefactual memory aids such as books (epigenetic). Only the human, argues Stiegler, passes along knowledge genetically *and* epigenetically, whereas all other animals are capable of passing on their genes, but nothing more. Moreover, writes Stiegler, insofar as these artefactual memory supports or *hypomnemata* are an *exteriorization*, the technical and the human are *co-constituting*. This, he continues, is because exteriorization and interiorization (i.e., consciousness) necessarily originate in a *transductive* relation, that is, a relation in which the elements do not pre-exist their relating. In this sense, the appearing in evolutionary time of 'the human' as consciousness (interiorization) only emerges in its relation to a technics, just as the technological (exteriorization) only comes into being in its relation to the human.

Hence, according to Stiegler, *animals can never be technical bodies*. Moreover, not only do nonhuman animals *not* exteriorize, and thus not conserve epigeneses, nor can they therefore possess any form of 'internal' consciousness whatsoever. As a result, nonhuman beings, insofar as they possess neither collective heritage nor the capacity to teach others, can *never* respond, but only and always *react*.[1] A nonhuman living being, writes Stiegler – albeit with the prefatory proviso that this is the case only 'If molecular biology is correct' – 'is defined by the somatic memory of the *epigenetic* and the germinal memory of the *genetic, which in principle do not communicate with each other*' (*Technics and Time*, II:4, final emphasis added). In other words, nonhuman animals are determined solely on the level of species and entirely by their genetic – as opposed to technical or symbolic – characteristics which precede any actual appearing of an individual nonhuman being. Such an 'individual' thus exists in a state of something akin to the non-consciousness of perpetual forgetting (in the blackest darkness, Stiegler will say).[2]

Such determinism, it should be noted straight away, inscribes nonhuman beings as entirely substitutable and reproducible: every newborn is indistinguishable from any other of the same species at the same stage of evolutionary development, the only possible differentiation being in the species as a whole across the aeons of evolutionary time. By contrast, for Stiegler the technical-body that is the human constitutes an absolute rupture with this 'pure life' of animals. The problem, however, is that Stiegler nonetheless maintains his agreement with Jacques Derrida as to the *différance* which constitutes 'life' itself – here understood by Stiegler as the 'pure life' devoid of technicity – and which thus inscribes every living being as *already* ruptured by the trace. While Stiegler, in drawing his human-animal distinction, then goes on to argue that the emergence of 'the human' as a technical-body con-

---

[1] In *Bioethics in the Age of New Media* (2009), Joanna Zylinska also engages with Stiegler in order to argue for a new ethics founded upon a prior relationality of the human and the nonhuman. She does not, however, question the founding exceptionalism organising Stiegler's discourse.

[2] Stiegler can here be read as reiterating Nietzsche's famous contention in the second of the *Untimely Meditations* that 'the animal' is a being who 'at once forgets and for whom every moment really dies, sinks back into night and fog and is extinguished forever. Thus the animal lives *unhistorically*' ('On the Uses and Disadvantages of History for Life,' 61). However, as I have argued in the previous chapter, Nietzsche's notion of 'the animal' – in contrast to Stiegler's – refers not to living beings, but functions rather as a *figure* of the impossible state of being prior to mnemotechnics.

stitutes a second, utterly discontinuous rupture, what must be noted here is that the differantial trace in fact *already* inscribes the bodying of 'pure life' as a co-constitutive (transductive) technical-body.

Indeed, this last is further supported by the very practice of molecular biology upon whose authority Stiegler would otherwise like to found his claim. As Sunder Rajan explains, while 'a central source of authority for genomics' stems from genetic determinism, the relationship of genes to traits is rather 'a set of complex, multifactorial interactions (*which are multifactorial both at the genetic level and in the interactions of "genetic" and "environmental"* [i.e., epigenetic] *factors*)' (*Biocapital*, 145, emphasis added). Paradoxically, Stiegler thus reduces nonhuman animals to non-conscious causal mechanisms while at once affirming that such 'pure biology' or 'pure life' is nonetheless *différant* from nonliving automata.

We have, by way of Nietzsche's notion of an auto-ordering and mutually forming memory, to a large degree already engaged with this latest charge by Stiegler, a charge which denies all consciousness, and thus all *sense*, to non-human animals. We have briefly noted too the historicity and historiology of the aggressive, oddly nocturnal Addo elephants, who have transmitted down through the generations of their specific sociocultural group a learned hatred for human animals. We might also recall the famous troop of Japanese macaques studied by Itani Junichiro and Kawamura Syunzo. One of the troop, a young female, began washing her sweet potatoes clean of grit and sand before consuming them in order to protect her teeth. This habit, which is undoubtedly a *technique* as well as a gestural writing, was quickly transmitted to other youngsters and females via female-lineage hierarchies, with the sub-adult males being the last to learn. In this way, as Donna Haraway notes, 'social and technical innovation emerged from the practices of youngsters and their mothers' (*Primate Visions*, 253-4). It of course follows that, if such new habits can be learned by contemporaries in the group, they can therefore also be passed on down the generations insofar as one's contemporary may also be one's child.

However, the bodying of Dolly, both as Dolly herself and as 'the Dolly technique,' has direct consequences *at the genetic level* for Stiegler's re-founding of the human-animal distinction. Stiegler, we recall, proposes the origin of the human in and as its exteriorization as retentional technologies, of which writing is his privileged example. What Dolly shows us, however, is that recapacitation is *already* a writing, a retentional technology of and on the body. It is a writing, that is, which, in contrast to the one-way signaling presupposed by genetic determinism, is transmissible both intergenerationally and, indirectly by way of epigenetic recapacitation in situ, to one's contemporaries.

There is, in other words, already iterability at the genetic level, and thus sedimentation, habit, and encounter. In fact, this reiterates in one short sentence the complex notion of 'life already outside of itself' traced throughout this book. This is further supported by recent developments within molecular biology as a discipline, which is witnessing a dramatic shift towards the study of epigenetic effects. The molecular focus, in other words, is moving away from the study of species as an abstract category comprised of identical, and thus infinitely replaceable, genetic mechanisms, and towards the study of context, interaction and relation among singularly situated, and thus irreplaceable and nonreplicable, way(s) of being. Similarly, this shift is increasingly coming to inform laboratory as well as ethological studies of nonhuman animal behaviors, with the focus being newly placed upon the reciprocal relations that co-constitute in part the *experience* of both individual nonhuman animals *and* individual human animals, who thus both study and respond to each other.[3]

Despite calling upon the authority of microbiology, however, Stiegler nonetheless refuses just such an 'experience' to all other animals. Furthermore, his hugely problematic human-animal distinction, which at first glance may appear somewhat peripheral, is in fact absolutely central to his philosophical project as a whole, insofar as it serves as the foundation of Stiegler's critique of *human* audiovisual and informatic 'psychotechnologies' which, he claims, break up the 'long circuits' of *generational time* at the behest of speculative capital. This is because, as we shall see, it is 'the animal' – or else an 'aspect' of animality – to whom or to which such psychotechnologies end up reducing 'the human.' In other words, in order to ground this devolutionary movement of postindustrial capital, Stiegler must reduce – at least for the most part, as we will see – the infinite variety of nonhuman ways of being to the level of 'mere' instinctive (i.e., genetically determined) anticipation. He names this way of being, which is the permanent forgetting of non-consciousness, 'vigilance.' Against this impossible abstraction, what the singular bodying of Dolly renders explicit is precisely the fact that the postindustrial breaking up of generational time, both symbolically and literally, characterizes societies of control *in general*, rather than being something which, as

---

[3] On this, see for example the recent work of Donna J. Haraway and Élisabeth de Fontenay, as well as the influential (albeit as yet largely untranslated) work of Vinciane Despret, including *Quand le loup habitera avec l'agneau* (2002), *Hans, le cheval qui savait compter* (2004), *Penser comme un rat* (2009) and, in particular, *Être Bête* with Jocelyne Porcher (2007).

Stiegler contends, can only happen to human animals by way of mass media psychotechnologies.[4]

Whereas Stiegler bases his account on the paleontology of André Leroi-Gourhan, here, I have decided to put aside the considerable amount of recent ethological findings that, in their various ways, all refute Stiegler's claims for a human exceptionalism. Instead, I have chosen to focus on the challenges that Dolly's way of being poses for Stiegler's notion of exteriorization understood as a break with 'pure life.' This is because, not only will this open up the possibility of further rethinking the notion of 'life' as always already freed from life, but also, and more importantly, it will provide a way to understand what I am calling the pharmacology of the promise from the position of actual animals.

Brought together with the dispersed temporality of promissory capital, I will argue that we find here a redoubling of the *pharmakon*. In other words, despite the difference in the remedies promised by the transhuman and the posthumanist, they must both contend with the threat of a poisonous mutability, albeit a poison that is figured very differently in each case. Hence, whereas the promised immortality of the transhuman assemblage fears the poison of a potential zoonotic (i.e. inter-species) pandemic, the zoogenetic promise of the Nietzschean posthuman instead risks itself against a self-interested nihilism that inevitably finds its place within a rigorously deconstructed Nature-Culture binary.

A darkness as black as one will

While not as widespread as it once was, it nonetheless remains a common misapprehension that cloned beings (irrespective of species) will not only be *genetically* identical, not only *physically* identical, but also will be somehow condemned to lead identical *lives* – a misunderstanding which, knowingly or otherwise, presupposes that every being is therefore entirely reproducible and thus substitutable. This in part accounts for the anxiety cloning inspires, insofar as it explicitly puts into question both the uniqueness of the individual human subject and the exceptional status of the human being. The basis of both the misapprehension and the anxiety is thus the presupposition that

---

[4] This is not to suggest there was no manipulation of generational time within Fordist agribusiness – one thinks of artificial insemination and the chemical synchronization of menstrual cycles. I am rather referring here to the institution of a new, post-Fordist temporality no longer defined by the modernist paradigm of linear progress.

living beings are entirely determined by their DNA, and are thus entirely predictable – that is, *machinic*. In this schema, all epigenetic variation, even before any question of transmissibility, is rendered *a priori* impossible insofar as behavior is rather programmed in advance at the genetic level, and is thus independent of the being-there of existence. According to such a schema, evolution therefore progresses not by adaptation, but only by accidental genomic mutation. At the same time, and against overwhelming empirical evidence, this presupposes that no actual animal, including a human, can respond in any way to significant unprecedented and relatively sudden environmental change, but can do so only as the passive recipients of chance 'aberrations' over the immense evolutionary time of speciation.

While this is patently not the case – cloning, precisely because of genetic plasticity, will rather result in a proliferation of individual mutations[5] – one nonetheless wonders how Stiegler's reduction of nonhuman animals to a non-conscious 'vigilance' differs from such an absolute privileging of 'nature' at the cost of 'nurture.' On the one hand, Stiegler indeed affirms that 'the tracing of any simple boundary [*frontière*] between humanity and animality must be called into question' (*Technics and Time*, I:151) and yet, on the other, insists upon 'the simple automatic or programmatic-genetic behavior of a fabricating animal [*animal fabricateur*]' (151).

How might these contradictory statements be resolved? For Stiegler, I would argue, the 'simple boundary' necessarily refers to a peculiar kind of 'creationist' humanism, in which 'a forthrightly recognizable human' appears fully-formed amid an otherwise genetically programmed animal landscape. In this way, he indeed refuses the essential and timeless human subject, but only so as to reinscribe the division *within time*, insofar as the human both evolves *from* the animal, and yet, in a single technical blow (*coup*), becomes absolutely other. This is the moment in which the human appears in and as its transductive relation with technicity, whose uniqueness consists in its potential to free itself from 'socioethnic' constraints, in contrast to the animal who rather 'has no possibility [*n'a pas de possibilité*] of freeing herself from genetic constraints [*de s'affranchir des contraintes génétiques*]' (171, trans. modified).

This blow dealt to life, this difference (or *différance*) is, writes Stiegler, the 'modality of programming of, and by, memory, the consequence of the passage from liberation to exteriorization, [which] concretizes its new possibilities at the individual level, reinserting them, when they are totally re-

---

[5] On this, see Luciana Parisi, *Abstract Sex: Philosophy, Bio-technology and the Mutations of Desire* (London & New York: Continuum, 2004).

alized, into the socioethnic level' (171-2). This 'idiomatic differentiation,' in other words, is not only the ability both to learn and to transmit possibilities beyond the *individual* lifespan, but it is also the condition of the 'new' itself. This constitutes –

> an essential shift [*déplacement essentiel*] from the level of the species to that of the individual, who is undetermined in its behavioral possibilities, if not in its zoological limits and in the already-there of the world in which it lives, from which it inherits, to which it must answer [*enchaîner*], and which it appropriates by altering it (172).

The human, in other words, is *relatively undetermined*, as a result of cultural (symbolic, technological) inheritance, in contrast to the animal who is *instinctively determined* as a result of genetic (natural, material) inheritance. This is of course a very traditional gesture: the positing of an originary 'liberation' of the human as (relative) free-will from the programmed machinery of animality.

Indeed, at times Stiegler himself seems to draw back from this absolute position when, in what is a very Heideggerian gesture, he suggests that there is nonetheless 'certainly a kind of "privative" form of anticipation' available to nonhuman animals (163). Anticipation, it should be noted, is for Stiegler the futural way of being which defines the human alone insofar as it possesses a 'unique and incontestable relation to death' (164) – a claim which is itself, as we have already seen, eminently contestable. Stiegler is not, however, so much as offering some kind of limited consciousness to nonhuman animals as he is rather organizing a necessary precondition so as to ensure the consistency of his exceptionalist argument. In fact, this hesitant 'privative' anticipation is necessary for Stiegler so as to *maintain* the division it appears to put back into question. The positing of a 'privative,' instinctive form of anticipation for base survival is, in other words, that which preserves, by way of a simultaneous evolutionary continuity and discontinuity, the possibility of the human itself. It is a possibility, as Stiegler writes, 'that is opened however minutely, *in a darkness as black as one will* [*une pénombre aussi opaque que l'on voudra*], but that is already the possibility of a divergence and therefore *something of a projection* [*une sorte quelconque de projection*] of a "symbolic" type rather than of a type of "survival behavior"' (163, emphases added).

Absolute genetic determinism, as we have seen, not only denies all possibility of epiphylogenesis, but also of *epigenesis* as well, in contrast to both empirical evidence and scientific argument. This 'minute opening,' however, permits a nonhuman animal 'some sort of' or 'something like' a symbolic projection, something which seems to exceed determinism, but which is none-theless only a 'privative' version of what remains uniquely human. Much the same as Heidegger's 'worldly poor' animals, Stiegler's animals might *appear* to have access to the symbolic, might *appear* to 'have' the 'as,' but in reality they remain dissolved within the 'pure life' of the darkest non-consciousness. As a result, Stiegler's attribution of privation concedes that while one may encounter a 'clever' nonhuman animal (albeit this in fact only appears to be the case), the *species* is nonetheless condemned to perpetual dumbness, nev-er able, whether as a whole or within specific social groupings, to learn either from their individual mistakes or their triumphs. 'Privative' anticipation is, in short, simply the possibility of a human rupture in an otherwise absolutely determined biosphere.

As we will see, however, there is more at stake here than a simple, un-thinking reiteration of a traditional culture-nature dichotomy. The exclusion of 'the animal' in fact serves an essential function in the construction of the postindustrial posthuman dystopia which Stiegler's critical philosophy seeks to combat. As such, nonhuman animals become rather a mere tool with-in Stiegler's anthropocentrism. Here, let us recall how the 'fetishist' rhetoric of genetic determinism permits an instrumentalising of nonhuman animals which in turn justifies the promise of biocapital in moral terms, whilst at the same time effacing the threat of genetic flexibility which organizes the promissory discourse of biotechnology. We can now see how Stiegler's reduc-tive notion of animal 'vigilance' parallels that of biotechnology itself. Just as genetic determinism serves both to secure and efface a transductive relation of interior and exterior within the discourse of biotechnology, so too genetic determinism serves both to secure and efface epiphylogenetic variation with-in Stiegler's philosophical anthropocentrism. Indeed, this might well help explain the recurrent references to agribusiness, embryology, and biotech-nology that populate Stiegler's texts. To understand its importance, however, one must understand how the exclusivity of human epiphylogenesis permits Stiegler's own promissory rhetoric of psycho*technics*, in which the potenti-ality of an inventive breaking with 'socioethnic constraints' is constructed in opposition to an (impossible) regressive becoming-animal at the behest of postindustrial psycho*technologies*.

Nonhuman animals are genetically determined, human animals are rel-atively undetermined. This is Stiegler's argument. Culture is defined by a transductive organic-technological relation, in contrast to a state of Nature defined as an 'absence of all relation' (128). The question, then, is who or what, or who *and* what, are transgenic animals according to this founding exclusion which underpins Stiegler's philosophy? Given that they are both human and animal at the genetic level, itself a writing of and in the body, do they *become* human artefacts, or do they *produce* human, or animal, artefacts? Are they technological beings, or simply 'pure life'? Dolly, Polly, and the others all promise, in short, to highlight the ungrounded assumptions underlying Stiegler's anthropocentrism.

Stepping into, and falling from, the light: being human becoming animal

In considering the structural undecidability of such ways of being, it is first of all necessary to recall once again the humanist paralogism. In the first form, as we know, the human depends upon the death or the ceasing to exist of the animal and, in the second, the human is required to repeatedly overcome the animal in a constant struggle both to become and to remain human. Stiegler, it is clear, founds his thinking of the co-constitution of the human and the technical upon an evolutionary dialectic of the first type. In other words, the coming into being-exteriorized of the human is a *coup* in which the human is always already not animal, insofar as the human *is* only in ceasing to be an animal. Such a blow or coup thus takes place once and for all.

Indeed, Stiegler locates the precise moment of anthropogenesis in the technics of the Zinjanthropian period. Responding, for example, to Leroi-Gourhan's suggestion that the Zinjanthropian is still in fact a 'quasi-zoology', Stiegler states with absolute certainty that 'it is already no longer anything of the kind, otherwise one could not speak of exteriorization' (142). It is rather the case, he says, that it is in the intermediary period between 'the Zinjanthropian who is *already a man*, and the Neanthropian opening onto the human that we are' (142), that the human 'free[s] itself [*se dégageant*] slowly from the shadows like a statue out of a block of marble' (141). Here, I am assuming that this notion of the shadow [*ombre*] refers to the darkness [*pénombre*] that marks the animal's absence of relation from which the human, *already a man* by virtue of technicity, emerges into the full light of humanity.

The obvious question, at this stage, concerns the numerous technological forms employed by nonhuman animals, ranging as they do from carefully prepared (and subsequently retained) wooden levers and sharpened stones (the use of flint tools, claims Stiegler, constitutes the origin of the human) to the construction of complex dwellings and the sharing of meanings by way of otherwise arbitrary signifiers. What too of the gestural language of chimpanzees, of the ritualized enactments of social status combined with the imparting of site-specific knowledge, that is, information localized in both space and time? Are all of these not also material artefacts, repositories of knowledge and conventional languages, and thus also exteriorizations? To my knowledge, Stiegler offers nothing on this question, despite its relevance to his own claims and to the ongoing debates in related fields.

The second point is that, despite this insistence on the absolute exceptionalism of the human by way a co-constitutive technicity, in *Taking Care of Youth and the Generations* (2008), Stiegler nonetheless seems to suggest that the human can be somehow reduced to, or even returned to, an animal way of being. It is a reduction, or perhaps devolution, moreover, which is a *consequence* of exteriorization in general, and of those biotechnologies in particular which Stiegler calls 'psychotechnologies.' This, then, would suggest a supplemental – and mutually exclusive – reiteration of the humanist paralogism based upon an evolutionary dialectic of the *second* type.

How then, can exteriorization – the defining property of the human – effect an (ontologically impossible) reduction of 'the human' to 'the animal'? Stiegler in fact attempts to evade this contradiction by suggesting that this post-human animal is rather only one '*aspect*' or '*side*' [pan] of animal vigilance. Vigilance, it should be recalled, is the reactive will to survival lived instinctively from within the utter darkness of non-consciousness, the latter consisting in the absence of both *un*consciousness and *pre*consciousness. Here, after again acknowledging only that his argument is founded upon the *assumption* that 'human attention is defined as *separate* from nervous system vigilance' (*Taking Care*, 96), Stiegler then suggests that the *capture* of human attention by postindustrial marketing systems results in 'a regression to instincts' (97). A regression, that is to say, to *animality*.

Attention capture, he argues, results specifically from the *abandoning* exteriorization of the human psychic realm onto psychotechnological or computational devices. The human, in other words, in delegating both memory and decision to artefactual computers (in the broadest sense), no longer exists in a transductive relation with technicity, but rather abandons that very interiorization which marks the human out from the animal. Whereas properly human transductive relations with exteriorized (inherited) knowledge constitute what Stiegler calls 'long circuits' or circuits of 'transindividuation,' the contemporary marketing system, he argues, thus 'short circuits' this relation in the abandonment of the interior to the exterior. Together, these constitute for Stiegler the *pharmakon* of human-technical becoming.

Hence, Stiegler names the curative transindividuation psycho*technics*, in order to distinguish it from the poisonous psycho*technological* short-circuit. The question, however, remains: how can 'the human' *regress* to that being which he or she never was?

For Stiegler, it is the combination of marketing systems, speculative capital, and psychotechnologies which constitutes societies of control in contrast to the disciplinary societies of 'modernity' (103). As a result, the capture of attention requires –

> the biological model of a human central nervous system technologically produced by technologies of control; this kind of nervous system is an attribute of a gregarious, disindividuated mass whose brains have been stripped [*énucléés*] of consciousness ... a nervous system forever enclosed within strict neurological limits, significantly constraining both training and consciousness (97-8).

The difficulty here concerns the contrast between the human 'aspect' of animality and animality as such, as well as the animal him- or herself, whom Stiegler deems genetically incapable of taking on any aspect of humanity whatsoever. With this notion of a no longer conscious human mass reduced to the biological, to the *animal*, by way of disindividuating psychotechnologies, Stiegler in fact suggests a symbolic *animalization* that is actually a literal *becoming-animal* in its reduction to non-conscious vigilance. In other words, how can these two 'aspects' of biological short-circuit be differentiated, except perhaps by reference to pre-existing classification systems?

However, it would seem that, despite being thus reduced to the darkness of an animal enclosed within 'strict neurological limits,' Stiegler's non-conscious post-human nonetheless somehow retains a specific – albeit significantly constrained – capacity for both epiphylogenesis (training) and consciousness, which Stiegler will later call 'the most minimal human "subject"' (100). How can this be? Without that consciousness that Stiegler, by way of an explicit misreading of Derrida's *Of Grammatology* in the first volume of *Technics and Time*, claims is the appearing of the grammē *as such*, the human must thus necessarily become 'pure life' in an originary *transformation* that can never be a *regression* to instincts.[6]

---

[6] Stiegler cites Derrida in support of his claim that the 'emergence of the grammē as such' is at once the emergence of a uniquely human consciousness – it marks, in other words, the second *coup*, the 'the *différance* of *différance*' (*Technics and Time*, I:137). However, there is no suggestion whatsoever of this in Derrida's text. In fact, the opposite is the case. Derrida rather makes clear in the passage cited by Stiegler that the *originary* movement of *différance* – 'the trace as the unity of the double movement of protention and retention' – always 'goes far beyond the possibilities of "intentional consciousness"' (*Of Grammatology*, 84). It is, he makes clear, already this 'first' *coup*, this

Again, Stiegler must attempt to separate the two 'aspects,' that is, if he is to continue to assume a 'separation' between attention and vigilance. Psychotechnologies, he suggests at this point, do indeed eliminate consciousness, 'but through the *elimination* of attention, not its capture [*captation*]' (102, my emphasis). But again, how can these 'aspects' be differentiated, insofar as the human, defined futurally, must have attention and thus anticipation *eliminated* in order to *become* a *captured* animal. The difference, in short, concerns only the process by which 'the human' becomes what 'the animal' always already is. Moreover, it is this question of *how* such a reduction takes place which will return us to the question of pure life, of the trace, and of the recapacitation of the cell.

Automatic biology

Firstly, writes Stiegler, the human is made 'minimal' insofar as attention is delegated to 'automata that then become its captors, meters, gauges, warning signals, alarms, and so on. Attention in this sense is precisely folded back [*rabattue*] on its automatizable behaviors of vigilance, the psychic having been reduced to a pure function of the biological' (*Taking Care*, 101; trans. modified). Here then, 'pure biology' is the equivalent, or at least a variant, 'another side or aspect of [*tout un pan de*],' of an alarm clock telling you to brush your teeth or, better, of a pop-up telling you consume some 'meat,' this latter irrespective of whether it takes place within limits imposed by agribusiness or by the availability of prey.[7]

In Stiegler's terms, both the 'minimal' (post)human and the vigilant animal are determined, and condemned, to retention without protention; the *différance* of *grammatization* limited absolutely by a fully-automated archive retrieval which offers no possibility of individuation. In other words, both nonhuman animals and posthuman animals can only react, but never respond, insofar as they lack the necessary lack. This, insists Stiegler, is the poisonous aspect of the *pharmakon* which is technological becoming, the danger *indissociable* from its promised remedy. And yet, this is also the very *negation* of technical becoming (as transindividuation), which Stiegler posits as the very essence of the human. The human is, in short, at once indis-

---

'new structure of nonpresence,' which 'makes the *grammē* appear *as such*' (84).

[7] One can thus better understand why Stiegler's primary example of this animalizing process is the way the marketing systems of agribusiness exclude, a priori, 'the possibility of any choice of foodstuffs outside of the intelligence associated with agriculture and of food itself' (*Taking Care*, 213n8).

sociable *and* dissociable from technical becoming. Moreover, I will argue, insofar as human psycho*technics* cannot be separated from both animal and posthuman vigilance, the latter effected by psycho*technologies*, this necessarily undoes Stiegler's founding human-animal distinction which promises a technical remedy to technological poison.

To understand this contradiction at the heart of technical becoming, it is necessary to explore in more detail exactly how it is that psychotechnologies produce the posthuman. In abandoning the psychic realm to artefactual computers, claims Stiegler, the unconscious and preconscious (i.e., habitual) interiorization of 'the structure of inheritance and transmission' is interrupted (*Technics and Time*, I:140). In this way sociocultural inheritance is replaced by 'tertiary retentions', that is to say, by exteriorized memory aids which have been standardized so as to be 'formalizable, calculable, and finally controllable' (*Taking Care*, 99). In other words, both nonhuman animals and their posthuman aspect are reduced to a calculable uniformity. However, whereas for the former this takes place at the level of speciation through the 'natural' biotechnologies of their genes, the latter are rather transformed into a 'disindividuated mass' through the psychotechnologies that are computational devices, and which are thus also *bio*technologies. Here then, this notion of the human as that which is made calculable through memory returns us yet again to Nietzsche, and it is from there, finally, that we can approach Dolly once more.

As we have seen, Stiegler agrees with Derrida's understanding of *différance* as 'the history of life in general' (*Technics and Time*, I:137), only then to shift the terms of Derrida's argument so as to posit a second, supplemental 'stage of différance' from which the possibility of human consciousness emerges. Derrida, however, explicitly refuses any such 'second coup.' Rather, he affirms that the 'double movement of protention and retention' is precisely the mark, or the trace, of *living* being (which is not necessarily to say *organic* being) and at once 'the becoming-time of space and the becoming-space of time' ('Différance', 8). This trace of being-futural we located too in Nietzsche's philosophy, through the notion of *translation* that is at once a *re-cognition of sense*. It is this recognition which, irreducible to cogitating activity, inscribes both finitude and memory – understood as the sedimented, habitual 'already-there' – in and as every living being. It is precisely this notion of finitude and memory, however, which Stiegler seeks to reserve for the human alone.

Despite this, there remain interesting parallels between Nietzsche and Stiegler. Both, for example, insist on the importance of memory aids –

whether these are called *mnemotechnics* or tertiary retentions. For both, they make possible a calculation and computation which is necessarily pharma-cological: at once poisonous threat and curative gift. For Stiegler, tertiary retentions reserve the possibility of inventive transindividuation as well as posthuman disindividuation. For Nietzsche, they represent the precondition for breeding an animal with the right to make promises as well as that most fearful development whereby 'ghostly schemata' efface the appearing of rad-ical particularity. The major difference, however, concerns *calculability*. For Nietzsche, 'the human' – in common with all living beings – must *first be produced* as uniformly calculable as the immanent condition for the taking place of posthuman invention *beyond* calculability and uniformity. By con-trast, this production of the calculable human is, for Stiegler, the reduction *to* a nonhuman animal, and thus the elimination of all possibility of invention. *Stiegler's animal, in other words, is Nietzsche's human, and vice versa.*

Whereas for Stiegler technology is pharmacological insofar as, in addi-tion to its curative action, it simultaneously threatens to *poison* the excep-tional status of the human, for Nietzsche, by contrast, the threat *concerns* the exceptional *transhuman*. Furthermore, it is here that the pharmacology of the Nietzschean promise, explored in its creative aspect in the chapter nine, intersects with Stiegler's by way of the notion of 'infidelity.'

A further major difference between them, however, concerns the fact that Nietzsche does not require a reinstalled human-animal, culture-nature di-chotomy in order to articulate the threat within the promise of technicity, the inseparable poison-remedy of its *pharmakon*. Insofar as for Stiegler 'compu-tational psychotechnology always aims at substituting for attention, theoriz-ing and modeling attention and its institutions, destroying them by seeming not even to imagine an attention beyond vigilance' (*Taking Care*, 102), what I am suggesting here is that together Nietzsche and Derrida allow us to see that it is Stiegler himself who seems unable to imagine an attention beyond 'mere' vigilance.[8] By way of a prefatory gesture, let us recall that everything which Stiegler reserves for the human, both Nietzsche and Derrida extend to every living being – that which, in Stiegler's words,

> comes from an originary forgetting, *ēpimētheia* as delay, the fault of Epimetheus. This becomes meaningful only in the melancholy of Prometheus, as anticipa-tion of death, where the facticity of the already-there that equipment is for the

---

[8] It is therefore something of an irony that Stiegler collapses the 'cybernetic reduction-ism' of psychotechnologies – a reductionism identical to that through which he figures nonhuman animals – into 'a field of applications within agribusiness, in its pejorative sense' (*Taking Care*, 103).

person born into the world signifies the end: this is a Promethean structure of being-for-death, a structure in which concern [*pré-occupation*] is not the simple covering-over [*occultation*] of *Eigenlichkeit*. This is the question of time (*Technics and Time*. I:142).

Rather than requiring an instauration of human exceptionalism, it is the very deconstruction of the human-animal and nature-culture binaries which installs the curative *promise* of invention. Such a promise, moreover, retains within itself not the threat of a poisonous animality, but rather *the threat of an excessive mutability*. Furthermore, as the 'Dolly technique' demonstrates, this *pharmakon* of technical becoming is found at the genetic as well as at the sensory level: a writing, a *technicity*, of and on the body. It is already there, in other words, in the iterability that is recapacitation.

Taking care with the generations

Let us recall that, for Stiegler – and only insofar as one can assume molecular biology is correct – 'the somatic memory of the *epigenetic* and the germinal memory of the *genetic* … in principle do not communicate with each other' (*Technics and Time*, II:4). Even at the time of Stiegler's writing, however, this claim was already becoming increasingly untenable within the praxis of molecular biology, as we have seen in our discussion of the Dolly technique.

Basically, Stiegler here subscribes, at least as far as *non*human animals are concerned, to August Weismann's theory of generation. Hugely influential during the 'industrializing' period of disciplinary society, generational inheritance is here conceived of as vertical movement only through the germ line, with germ line cells understood as distinct from somatic cells insofar as, while they reproduce themselves in the finite bodies of living beings by way of linear differentiation, they themselves remain undifferentiated and thus immortal. Indeed, it is far from surprising that the legacy of Weismannian theory functioned most explicitly in the notion of industrial selective-breeding programmes. In our brave new postindustrial era of complex multifactorial interactions, however, it is instead 'becoming plausible,' as Melinda Cooper writes, 'that "life itself" might be more comprehensively defined by the proliferative, self-regenerative powers of the ES [embryonic stem] cell rather than the Weismannian theory of the germ line' (*Life as Surplus*, 139).

As we have seen, the discovery of an inherent potentiality of cellular recapacitation interrupts the notion of a linear temporality moving irrevocably towards a specificity of function. It interrupts, that is to say, a causally determined genetic movement, replacing it with a biological plasticity. Hence, it is only insofar as genes are situational and contextual that there can be at once a reversal, a transversal, and re-becoming of genetic initiation as the result of 'external' or 'environmental' factors. In short, the genetic (*germen*) and the epigenetic (*sōma*) are *co-constituted in a transductive relation* – the elements of which do not precede their relating – which can be *transmitted both genetically and epigenetically.* Put as simply as possible, what this notion of 'situated biological communication' implies is that what is 'learned' has an affect at the cellular level, and vice versa, in positive feedback loops. The epigenetic can be transmitted genetically, and the genetic epigenetically, albeit with the necessary translations which result from the 'overleaping' of discontinuous, yet reciprocally determining, domains.

This is, of course, worded in such a way as to recall Nietzsche's notion of translation as discussed in chapter two. However, instead of 'beginning with a nerve stimulus,' as Nietzsche does in 'On Truth and Lie,' there is rather already before and beyond that singular touch an overleaping both from the *cell* to the epigenetic-*as*-metaphor, and from recognition (the iterative making of sense) to the genetic-*as*-metaphor, in a complete disorientation of linear temporality. Every differentiated cell, in other words, constitutes a stammering 'material' translation or *exteriorization* of the habitual 'already-there' of an (epigenetic) experienced context. Every 'experience,' every apprehension, constitutes a stammering 'sensible' translation or *exteriorization* of the habitual 'already-there' of a genetic context. Both genesis and epigenesis are thus reciprocally articulated, each acting as tenor to the other's stimulus, that is, *each losing itself and each other in a movement of errant transmission, of dissemination.* Such is 'life' that 'has freed itself from life' (Derrida, *Demeure*, 89) or, in an *extension and transformation* of Stiegler's definition of epiphylogenesis, it is *'living by other means than life* [*vivant par d'autres moyens que la vie*] – which is what the history of technics consists in' (*Technics and Time*, I:135).

Writing – Stiegler's privileged example of exteriorization – is here already *a writing of and on the body.* The dislocating movement of *différance*, the trace as the unity of the double movement of protention and retention, is thus indeed that 'new structure of nonpresence' which Derrida describes as the emergence *of the living* from the amoeba to *homo sapiens* and beyond. Such is the movement which both 'makes the grammē appear *as such*' and at once 'makes possible the emergence of the systems of writing in the narrow sense' (*Of Grammatology*, 84). There is, in short, at every level – and, indeed, more precisely when and where such levels can in fact no longer be distinguished

– the denaturalizing movement *of* life that is *the originary technic*ity *of living being*. Why should exteriorization be restricted to 'organized albeit inorganic matter,' as Stiegler repeatedly claims? Is language organic, or inorganic? Is the organized matter of the cell 'interior' to living being or 'exterior,' exteriorized or interiorized, or are they rather co-constituted feedback effects?

What then, is Dolly for Stiegler? *Who* then, is she for Nietzsche? *Who* and *what*, such is Dolly insofar as she *is*. As a result, it is no longer necessary to evade the question of nonhuman tool use, or to get bogged down in the interminable 'nature versus nurture' debate. Recalling the historicity *and* historiology of the Addo elephants, we can now perhaps better understand how their memory of the murderousness of humans comes to transmitted through the generations at both the genetic and epigenetic (and thus epiphylogenetic) levels, the elephants having become both 'instinctively' nocturnal as a result *of* their relations with human animals, and 'socially' aggressive *in* their relations with human animals. Barbara Noske highlights this undecidability in her description of the third- and fourth-generation post-event elephants as 'the cultural heirs of the fear and hatred among their ancestors for our species' (*Beyond Boundaries*, 155). Interesting here, is that fear is traditionally conceived as 'instinctive,' whereas hatred is generally considered to be a 'cultural' manifestation. And yet, can such fear be considered instinctive to the species? As genetically determined? Or is it rather a *learned* fear? And what of hatred? Is it taught and learned, passed along, over and over again in the elephant equivalent of an oral tradition? Or has this hatred in actuality pervaded these nonsubstitutable living beings at the cellular level of their very way(s) of being?

Indeed, I completely agree with Stiegler's description of epiphylogenesis as that which 'bestows [*accorde*] its identity' upon an individual: 'the accents of his [or her] speech, the style of his [or her] approach, the force of his [or her] gesture, the unity of his [or her] world' (*Technics and Time*, I:140). I would, however, insist upon a single – but by no means minor – coda: such an individual is never 'the human,' but 'is' rather the way of being as such and, as such, being is always already being-with. One result of this is that Stiegler's founding human-animal distinction, in its attempt to distinguish the psychotechnics of transindividuation from the reductive vigilance effected by psychotechnologies, promises a technical remedy to the poison of technology which can no longer be maintained. In its place, however, the originary technicity of living being – the iterative writing of and on the body – founds both the pharmacological *promise* of postgenomics and the promissory discourse known as transhumanism. In the next section, we will see how just such a doubling of the promise helps us to understand the dangers of a prematurely stalled deconstruction of the nature-culture and human-animal dichotomies.

The transhuman promise

Transhumanism, such as espoused by philosopher Nick Bostrom and referred to briefly in the introduction to this book, can be schematically described as both the desire and the promise of *enhancing* the human by way of technological, informatic, and bioengineering developments.[9] In the main, however, transhumanist discourse is equally characterized by a dogmatic refusal to put into question the supreme value it attributes to 'the human' as well as its belief in a sovereign human agency. Moreover, I agree with Richard Twine when he claims a close relation between the transhumanist imaginary as organico-technical *assemblage* and 'the capitalist desire to reinvent itself ... through the biotechnological trumping of ecological and material limits' (*Animals as Biotechnology*, 14). This relation is, I would argue, that of a spatiotemporal *mapping*: mutually articulating both a topography and a temporality. Indeed, it is with the notion of cell recapacitation and especially, as suggested above, in its relation to the heavily speculated and highly speculative field of tissue engineering (TE), that the *promise* sustaining the utopian transhumanist imaginary comes most clearly to the fore. As Melinda Cooper writes, TE is, in principle at least,

> capable of perpetuating embryogenesis, of reliving the emergence of the body over and over again, independently of all progression. Here it is not only spaces, forms, and bodies that become continuously transformable, but also the divisible instants of a chronological lifetime, so that any one body can be returned to or catapulted into any point in its past or future, and into any past or future it *could have* and *could still* materialize. In other words TE not only seeks to 'return' the body to nonmetric *space* but also to nonmetric *time* – and to recapitulate the various chronologies of morphogenesis from here. In principle, then, the adult body will be able to relive its embryogenesis again and again – including those it has never experienced before (*Life as Surplus*, 121).

---

[9] See, for example, Bostrom's 'A History of Transhumanist Thought' in *Journal of Evolution and Technology*, 14:1 (2005), 1-25; Ray Kurzweil, *The Singularity is Near: When Humans Transcend Biology* (London: Gerald Duckworth & Co., 2005); and *H+/-: Transhumanism and Its Critics*, ed. Gregory R. Hansell and William Grassie (Philadelphia, PA: Metanexus Institute, 2011).

Here then, is the dream – and the promise, itself necessarily temporal, that capital is being ventured on – of the transhuman: not only would the human form be continuously updatable and editable, but death itself would cease to impose its limit. Temporality thus promises its own overcoming, and hence the overcoming of finitude, the humanness of being having become immortal and without limit, able to relive its own life eternally as well as the infinite number of lives otherwise denied to it by the fleshly finite necessity of choice and chance. The transhuman utopia is, in other words, Nietzsche's reactive *ascetic ideal* (*Genealogy*, III:28). Seeking to overcome the constraints of life itself, the transhuman is rather the *absolute irresponsibility of an unconditional infidelity*, with being itself having become endlessly reversible, reproducible, revisable, and transmutable.

It is not by chance that this description can, mutatis mutandis, be applied to the constant innovation of speculative, 'fictitious' capital, which Stiegler describes as the 'systemic organization of *infidelity*' (*New Critique*, 83). No longer materially dependent upon commodity production, and thus upon constant and variable capital, for speculative capital the stake is rather *time itself*, that is to say, the risk inherent in the undetermination of the temporal. Its promise is thus a promise *because* it is without material reality. The future, in other words, determines the present.

At the same time, however, speculative capital seeks to *overcome time* – and thus finitude – by its constant innovation, exemplified above all by the promise of speculative biocapital and of supply-siding (the economic theology so beloved of neoliberals which states that supply will create demand, if we only have faith), and thus melds with the promise of the transhuman. Indeed, the transhuman consumer promises, and is promised by, biocapital to modify itself precisely so as to enable itself to consume that undemanded supply.

For example, an individualized therapeutics deploys a rhetoric of genetic determinism in order to justify its promised utility by way of a promised threat (of future disease), and as such *performs* genetic determinism so as to constitute fetishized individuals as 'consumers-in-waiting.'[10] In increasingly constructing such therapeutics as preventative, that is, as *speculative*, the potential market for drugs is thus massively enlarged from the 'sick' to the 'potentially sick' – that is, to every single living being with sufficient purchasing power – in a further fragmentation of sociopolitical groupings into pharmaceutically mediated individuals. At the same time, this speculation upon future health and future illness also serves to 'prove' the determinist rhetoric as scientific 'fact,' but only insofar as no material consequences of 'effective'

---

[10] On this, see chapter four of Sunder Rajan's *Biocapital*.

preventative medicine – which itself is based entirely on probability – can be recorded.

The individual, in other words, in remaining healthy, at once both justifies the founding rhetoric of genetic determinism while at the same time must put into question the notion of just how determined such determinism can therefore actually be. Personalized therapeutics thus feeds into the transhumanist promise of technological enhancement or even immortality, a (primarily financial) sacrifice for salvation which at the same time ties in with the promissory, messianic discourse of the 'old' industrial notion of 'modernity.' Such a rhetoric, as we have seen, employs a teleological determinism in order to demand that the imperfect countries of the South sacrifice themselves today for the promise of a perfect First-World Tomorrow.

All of this, perhaps, is promised by Dolly – both as a technique and as a rewritten body, a supply to be literally consumed and a supply for the consumerist need for constant innovation. And as too with Dolly, within the transhumanist dream-promise of a technologically mediated immortality, the future constitutes at once the threat and the promise of the present thoroughly overdetermined by economic interest.

The pharmakon is double: immortality and mutability

Initially, I suggested that the pharmacology of the promise consisted of the remedy of betrayal and the poison of the transhuman. This, however, is not sufficient. Rather schematically, we can now say that the pharmacology of the promise is itself double: on one hand, there is the promised remedy and poisonous threat of biocapital and, on the other, there is the promised remedy and poisonous threat of a Nietzschean betrayal. More precisely, the promise of a transhuman utopia necessarily brings with it the threat of a catastrophic and cancerous zoonosis, just as the promise of the right to make promises must at once threaten to collapse differences in the cynical nihilism of an absolute relativism. This latter, as we shall see, will return us, by way of a conclusion, to the question of the revolutionary animal encounter and of its congealing into an interested parody of itself.

For both, then, the promised cure concerns a deconstruction of human-animal, nature-culture and organic-inorganic binaries, a cure which at the same time threatens to release the poison of *excessive mutability*. The difference, however, is between a neoliberal appropriation which seeks to stall, and thus *master*, that very deconstructive movement, and the vigilance of a deconstruction which seeks always again to respond.

In this, it comes as no suprise that the economically-invested rhetoric deployed to justify the promise of biotechnology depends upon a reductive notion of the nonhuman animal as genetically determined, even as the promise of biotechnology resides in the potential capitalization of genetic *in*determination. This is because, insofar as the transhuman promise seeks to gift to itself – albeit at a price yet to be determined – an ever greater *mastery* of so-called 'nature', it must therefore at the same time install a 'humanism beyond humanism'. It must maintain, in short, an absolute culture-nature dichotomy in order to justify the promise of its ongoing deconstruction.

Such an incomplete, or stalled, deconstruction of the human-animal and nature-culture binaries, such as one finds too in the genetic determinism brought in to 'ground' Stiegler's philosophy, thus permits a naturalizing discourse which effaces flexibility so as to pre-empt (or short-circuit) any possibility of unconditional hospitality. In this way, both discourses reproduce an exclusive hierarchy which, in refusing the nonsubstituability and thus the value of other beings, renders them mere instruments in the production and reproduction of commodification. It serves, in other words, to close down the ethical opening (as discussed in part three) in order to justify an ongoing mastery – a determined mastery of life operating with the authority of *facts*. At the same time, it underwrites the transhumanist promise in effacing the threat of excessive mutability – of the *non-mastery* of life – figured by the incalculable emergence of zoonotic (inter-species) disease and by the media spectacle of ever more catastrophic killings of nonhuman animals. It is, in this sense, the *master* which only ever reacts, and who never responds.

To better understand this, let us return, with the help of Melinda Cooper, to the Weismannian theory of generation. Charles Minot, who helped to secure the influence of the theory, did so by contrasting the 'normal' linear and irreversible differentiation of cells by reference to the pathological exception that is, in Cooper's phrase, the 'indifferent divisibility' of cancer. For Minot, 'abnormal growth' such as tumors and cancers constitute the 'familiar' phenomenon 'of things escaping from inhibitory control and overgrowing' (Minot; cit. Cooper, *Life as Surplus*, 137). Such growth power, he maintains, results from cells remaining in the undifferentiated 'immortal' state insofar as they have somehow 'got beyond the control of the inhibitory [i.e. differentiating] force, the regulatory power which ordinarily keeps them in' (cit. Cooper 137). The cancerous cell is thus pathological as a result of 'its indifference to the normal limits to differentiation and division' (138).

Recalling here how tissue engineering (TE) can be considered as sustaining the promise of the utopian transhumanist imaginary, Cooper points out that with TE there is 'the distinct possibility, in particular, that the extremely plastic, mutable cells of the early embryo may end up proliferating too well, giving rise to cancerous growths rather than restoring health' (125). Genes, in other words, insofar as they cannot be determined, always reserve the risk of an incalculably errant dissemination.

Hugely important to the discussion here, Cooper then goes on to write that it is here, with the promise and threat of excessive mutability, that one can locate once again the move from Fordism to post-Fordism, and from disciplinary societies to societies of control. 'Where the machine body of the industrial era,' she writes, 'was plagued by the problems of fatigue, depletion, or entropy ..., the postindustrial body is more likely to be overcome by a *surplus productivity that is indistinguishable from a surplus of life* – that is, crises of overproduction or the dangerous, excessive vitality of cancer' (125). One thinks here again of those 'extremophiles' who, potentially developed to consume industrial waste such as the gigantic cowshit lagoons generated by agribusiness feedlots, in fact constitute a 'surplus of life' engineered to survive on the crises of overproductivity, but whose very vitality, or liveliness, may well result in ever more dangerous metastasizing diseases.

The pathological, therefore, is also that which refuses differentiation, refuses finitude, that which 'refuses to submit to the limits of generational time and death' (139). It is thus no surprise that during the industrial, disciplinary period cancerous cells were considered unproductive and 'inherently sterile,' whereas today the 'quasi-cancerous properties of the ES [embryonic stem] cell line are in fact enormously productive' (139).[11] (And it is here, of course, that one must mention the patented, cancer-bearing OncoMouse.) With such postindustrial crises of capitalist overproduction, however, what Marx describes in the third volume of *Capital* as the tendential fall in the rate of profit must henceforth be resituated at the level of the biosphere itself.

The *promise* of excessive mutability – and thus of the organic-technological assemblage of transhuman immortality – that is located in the recapacitation of stem cells, and located too in Dolly and Polly's bodyings, is thus at once the *threat* of excessive mutability, of the cancerous overabundance of life which ends up consuming all life in its relentless pursuit of its own accumulation. One can only think here of its parallels, both *topographical* and *temporal*, with the current financialization of the globe: of the relentless

---

[11] As Cooper notes, the term 'embryonic stem cell' was in fact initially interchangeable with that of 'embryonal carcinoma cell' (*Life as Surplus*, 140).

accumulation of speculative capital concealed behind an apparently 'neutral' rhetoric of the market as merely instrumental, and of an incalculable future which both determines and impoverishes the present. As Sunder Rajan writes,

> Excess, expenditure, exuberance, risk, and gambling can be generative because they can create that which is unanticipated, perhaps even unimagined. But this can only be so if the temporal order of production is inverted, away from the present building toward the future and instead toward the future always been called in to account for the present (*Biocapital*, 116).

Here then, I have argued that the *promise* of a transhumanist organic-technological assemblage is explicitly disclosed in the promise of tissue engineering – a promise of excessive mutability and mobility equally valorized in neoliberal discourses of telecommunications and postindustrial capital. Turning in the next section to focus on the *threat* of excessive mutability, and of the future being called in to account for the present, I aim to show that the latter is just as clearly disclosed in the contemporary discourse of zoonotic pandemics.

Making sense beyond species: zoonoses

Diseases such as HIV/AIDS, foot-and-mouth disease (FMD), bovine spongiform encephalopathy (BSE) and its human variant Creutzfeldt-Jakob disease (CJD), severe acute respiratory syndrome (SARS), avian flu, and swine flu are all termed *zoonoses*, meaning that they fracture the imaginary boundaries between species for so long held to be impregnable. They mark then, sites of excessive mutability that are also in a sense 'transgenic.' While it may transpire that zoonoses are in fact far from uncommon, they are at present the 'natural' equivalents of rogue states, in the sense that both serve to interrupt the 'smooth' Western discourse of free market globalization constituted as the transcendence of neoliberalism over the barbarism of primitive nature.

Zoonoses are, in other words, diseases of mutability and mobility at the levels of biology, class, and geography, exceeding the imaginary limits of both the homogeneous species and the homogeneous nation-state and just as likely to infect the affluent as the poor (which is by no means to suggest a parity of *treatment*, in every sense). Paradoxically, one result of this rupturing of the human-animal division is that, while the rhetoric of genetic determinism preserves nonhuman animals as automata and thus instrumentalizable, the accompanying rhetoric of imminent zoonotic pandemic functions to support and further reinforce that very division. There emerge, in other words, 'new discourses and technologies seeking to secure human health through the segregation of human and animal life and finding in the specter of pandemic a universal rationale for institutionalizing speciesism on a hitherto unprecedented scale' (Shukin, *Animal Capital*, 184).

Most obvious here are the holocausts of nonhuman animals which accompanied the recent announcements of the apparent threat posed to human health by foot-and-mouth disease, avian flu, and swine flu. Interestingly, FMD in particular makes explicit the economic interests which underwrite such announcements. Once one realizes that foot-and-mouth is a disease that is dangerous neither to human nor to nonhuman animals, but only to *productivity*, it becomes all too clear that the mounds of corpses were simply nodes in a network of political and economic strategies concerned with protecting export revenue.

Indeed, this renders explicit the performative dimension of the fear produced by the promised threat of zoonotic irruption. Alongside the constitution of a global humanity united by the threat of pandemic, what *also* gets constituted, as Shukin notes, 'are those populations, both human and animal, perceived as compromising its survival and therefore at risk of being socially ghettoized or materially sacrificed' (*Animal Capital*, 183). There are any number of examples, but two will here suffice: that of the unfounded narratives of HIV originating in 'unhygienic' and 'primitive' Africa, and of BSE-CJD originating in 'backward' India, both figured as a result of overly intimate relationships between human and nonhuman animals (rather than being, as in the case of BSE at least, a result of the Western industrial practice of feeding herbivorous farmed animals the 'waste' – that is, previously non-commodifiable – body parts of their own kin).[12]

In this, one can see how the promised threat of excessive mutability can both justify a racist pre-emptive interventionist national strategy, such as that recently implemented by US neoconservatives, as well as further increasing the value of, and thus the financial speculation upon, an individualized therapeutics and the promise of biotechnology in general. In short, the promise of excessive mutability is, in a further pharmacological twist, both a poison and its *own* remedy. This then constitutes the threat and promise of neoliberal capitalism as it seeks, yet again, to reproduce itself beyond its own limit:

---

[12] Similar 'ghettoising' discourses of origin can be seen accompanying the mediatization of the SARS outbreak (China), as well as avian flu (China, in particular the Guangdong province) and swine flu (South America).

the technological promise of a material human transcendence and the threat of an unending imperialist war against a newly hostile 'nature.'

Here, we have located a number of mutually articulating discourses that together help to mark the shift from industrial disciplinary societies to postindustrial societies of biopolitical control. It is a shift, however, which nonetheless retains within its borders an (albeit marginalized) industrial commodity production, which carries the mark both of 'backwardness' and of a (mythic) promise of modernity to be further exploited. Together, the transhumanist biotechnological promise and the threat of biological mutability thus authorize an ever greater institutionalization of 'life as such,' a self-authorization exceeding every nation-state boundary and extending beyond an imagined 'universal humanity' and on through all levels of the biosphere. In this way, 'life itself' is figured as that which must be controlled at all costs.

In summary, the *pharmakon* of mutability supplies the rationale for an ever more intensive capture of the contingencies of biological life within the calculus of power: the promise demands control at the microbiological level, the threat demands control at the globalizing level – all of which is intimately bound up with financial speculation and the promise of astronomical returns. Further, the very incalculability of the promise-threat is precisely that which authorizes both an imperial violence in the name of the 'humanitarian' and a pre-emptive violence in the name of the future.

The pharmacology of betrayal: the over-animal and collapsed animality

Contrast this, however, with the *post*humanist promise demanded by Nietzsche, and with the animal encounter as a process and a fidelity which demands a promise of excessive responsibility. On the one hand, as we have seen, the pharmacology of the promise is at once the transhuman and the posthumanist, with each being the remedy and the poison of the other. On the other hand, however, the posthumanist promise too, as I have argued, is *the promise of excessive mutability*, and as such it must also, whilst promising a cure, simultaneously threaten to poison. The difference, I would suggest, is that this latter demands an unwavering fidelity to that which remains to come, while the neoliberal promise requires an unwavering *in*fidelity to that which already is.

Nietzschean mutability – otherwise known as *will to power* – contrasts, in other words, with the constant and *calculable* innovation of speculative capital. The *difference*, rather than the *opposition*, is, in short, between responsibility and irresponsibility. While the latter seeks to master time and finitude by way of a calculation which can thus never be inventive, the former must, in opening itself to the new, both *give* and *take* time insofar as it remains vigilant to an already shared finitude.

Similarly, while the excessive mutability underpinning the transhuman promise of immortality – the mastery of 'nature' itself – seeks both to efface and to pre-emptively remedy the threat of a poisonous cancerous mutability, so too the promise of the zoogenetic animal encounter in which the new comes into being, insofar as it depends upon the mutability of sense, must at once contend with the poison of nihilistic parody. In other words, it is, as we have seen, the simultaneous mutability of *recognized* sense into habit and dogma – bringing at once the possibility of a cynical, self-interested play which seeks to reinstall mastery – which haunts every inventive phrasing. Indeed, we should recall in this context Werner Hamacher's reference to the 'still undrained, still unexhausted decay' which must always live on ('Disgregation,' 160). Hence, the *pharmakon* of mutability demands, if we are to be responsible, the vigilance of an eternally returning demand which must 'take leave of all faith and every wish for certainty' (Nietzsche, *The Gay Science*, §347). This is the chance, the threat and the promise, to interrupt the nihilism of economic interest and the sedimented investiture of power.

Another way to understand this *pharmakon* of mutability is by way of *iterability*, synonymous throughout this book with both *recapacitation* and being *as such*. In this sense, the threat of an ever vigilant deconstruction is also that of excessive mutability: that of *collapsing* difference(s), rather than encountering singular ways of being. To collapse the singularities of difference amid a generalized indifference of equality is to render everything equally without value, and thus to fall into the nihilism of absolute relativism. A fall, in other words, into *infidelity* – a negation of the world in advocating the parodic play of cynical self-interest.

Conclusion. Giving death to other animals: an ethics of vigilance

The poison of mastery demands the remedy of vigilance: a *pharmakon* which must ever again be renegotiated. It demands too, as we have seen, the strength to face finitude in remaining faithful to the maddening displacement of its demand from the other. Such is the animal encounter which calls forth those tropes which function in the opposite direction to the reactive ordering of animalization, marking instead with the borrowed costume of a forbidden metonymy the coming into being of a monstrous, unheard-of relation, thus staging the creation of an indecipherable and unmasterable materiality. While excessive mutability interrupts the *phantasmatic* effect of every genealogical tie – its promise and its threat, its poison and its remedy – it demands too the strength to outlive 'the human' in attesting to the precarity of a shared finitude, and thus to the nonsubstitutable deaths of all living beings. Only in this way might it become *un*thinkable that other animals, whether human or nonhuman, can be put to death with impunity.

The dead zombie flesh of the instrumentalized animal is, I have argued, the inverse of the 'revolutionary spirit' of the living corpse that returns. Whereas the latter dismantles the machinery of animalization, the former serves only to reproduce a symbolic logic of oppression which ultimately constitutes subjugated beings 'deserving' of their oppression. While a giving finitude does *not* necessarily prohibit the production of cloned or 'pharm' animals, it does however *displace the relation*, demanding as it does an ethical encounter in place of that sadistic mastery defined so well by Donna Haraway in the epigraph to the previous chapter. At the same time, such vigilance inevitably demands that we engage in the wider question of whether nonhuman animals should indeed be farmed at all. This is not mastery, but fidelity to being together: a post-humanism rather than a transhuman-ism. For actual animals, human and nonhuman, the transhuman promises only an ever increasing exploitation and control, whereas a vigilant posthumanism promises to open itself to the zoogenetic encounter, and thus to the incalculability of the future.

In this, one must, as Nietzsche insists, take leave of all certainty in order to dance even at the edges of abysses (*The Gay Science*, §347). Only then will the genocidal economy be interrupted, and only in this way might there come an unbounded community of those who love, of those who share their inability to share and who must ever again risk everything in search of asylum. Such is the ever-renewing *promise* of zoogenesis which resides in the responsibility of a vigilant betrayal, called into being in and as a thinking encounter with animals which interrupts the instrumentality of the transhuman, replacing its reductive calculation with an ethics of emergence.

Bibliography

Abraham, Nicolas and Maria Torok, *The Shell and the Kernel*, Volume I, ed. & trans. Nicholas T. Rand (Chicago & London: The University of Chicago Press, 1994).

_____ , *The Wolf Man's Magic Word: A Cryptonomy*, trans. Nicholas Rand (Minneapolis, University of Minnesota Press, 1986).

Acampora, Ralph, *Corporeal Compassion: Animal Ethics and Philosophy of Body* (Pittsburgh, PA: University of Pittsburg Press, 2006).

Acampora, Christa D. and Ralph Acampora (eds), *A Nietzschean Bestiary: Becoming Animal Beyond Docile and Brutal* (Lanham & New York: Rowman & Littlefield, 2004).

Adams, Carol J., T*he Sexual Politics of Meat: A Feminist-Vegetarian Critical Theory*, Twentieth Anniversary Edition (New York & London: Continuum, 2010).

_____ , *Neither Man nor Beast: Feminism and the Defense of Animals* (New York: Continuum, 1995).

_____ , 'An Animal Manifesto: Gender, Identity, and Vegan-Feminism in the Twenty-First Century' in *parallax*, 12:1 (2006), 120-128.

Adams, Carol J. and Josephine Donovan (eds), *Animals and Women: Feminist Theoretical Explorations* (Durham & London: Duke University Press, 1995).

Adorno, Theodor W. and Max Horkheimer, *Dialectic of Enlightenment*, trans. John Cumming (London & New York: Verso, 1997).

Agamben, Giorgio, *Infancy and History: On the Destruction of Experience*, trans. Liz Heron (London & New York: Verso, 2007).

_____ , *Language and Death: The Place of Negativity*, trans. Karen E. Pinkus (Minneapolis: University of Minnesota Press, 1991).

_____ , *The Coming Community*, trans. Michael Hardt (Minneapolis & London: University of Minnesota Press, 1993).

_____ , *Homo Sacer: Sovereign Power and Bare Life*, trans. Daniel Heller-Roazen (Stanford: Stanford University Press, 1998).

_____ , *Remnants of Auschwitz: The Witness and the Archive*, trans. Daniel Heller-Roazen (New York: Zone Books, 2002).

_____ , *The Open: Man and Animal*, trans. Kevin Attell (Stanford: Stanford University Press, 2004).

Agha-Jaffar, Tamara, *Demeter and Persephone: Lessons from a Myth* (Jefferson, NC: McFarland & Co., 2002).

Al-Kassim, Dina, 'The Face of Foreclosure' in *Interventions* 4:2 (2002), 168-174.

Althusser, Louis, *Lenin and Philosophy and other essays*, trans. Ben Brewster (New York: Monthly Review Press, 2001).

Althusser, Louis and Etienne Balibar, *Reading Capital*, trans. Ben Brewster (London: Verso, 1979).

Ansell Pearson, Keith, *Viroid Life: Perspectives on Nietzsche and the Transhuman Condition* (London & New York: Routledge, 1997).

_____ , *Germinal Life: The Difference and Repetition of Deleuze* (London & New York: Routledge, 1999).

Arendt, Hannah, *Eichmann in Jerusalem: A Report on the Banality of Evil*, revised & enlarged ed. (Harmondsworth: Penguin Books, 1977).

Aristotle, *Politics* in *The Basic Works of Aristotle*, ed. Richard McKeon (New York: The Modern Library, 2001), 1127-1324.

Armstrong, Susan J. and Richard G. Botzler, *The Animal Ethics Reader*, 2nd ed. (London & New York: Routledge, 2008).

Atterton, Peter and Matthew Calarco (eds), *Animal Philosophy: Essential Readings of Continental Thought* (London & New York: Continuum, 2004).

Auerbach, Erich, *Mimesis: The Representation of Reality in Western Literature*, trans. Willard R. Trask (Princeton, NJ: Princeton University Press, 1953).

Austin, J. L., *How to Do Things with Words*, eds J. O. Urmson & Marina Sbisá (Oxford: Oxford University Press, 1976).

Badiou, Alain, *Ethics: An Essay on the Understanding of Evil*, trans. Peter Hallward (London & New York: Verso, 2001).

_____ , *Polemics* ,trans. Steve Corcoran (London & New York: Verso, 2006).

_____ , *Metapolitics*, trans. Jason Barker (London & New York: Verso, 2006).

_____ , *Logics of Worlds: Being and Event*, 2 trans. Alberto Toscano (London & New York: Continuum, 2009).

_____ , *The Communist Hypothesis*, trans. David Macey & Steve Corcoran (London & New York: Verso, 2010).

Bajorek, Jennifer, 'Animadversions: *Tekhne* after Capital / Life after Work' in *diacritics* 33:1 (2003), 42-59.

Baker, Steve, *The Postmodern Animal* (London: Reaktion Books, 2000).

Balibar, Etienne, *Masses, Classes and Ideas: Studies on Politics and Philosophy Before and After Marx*, trans. James Swenson (New York: Routledge, 1994).

_____ , *We, the People of Europe? Reflections on Transnational Citizenship*, trans. James Swenson (Princeton: Princeton University Press, 2004).

_____ , 'Subjection and Subjectivation' in Copjec, Joan (ed.), *Supposing the Subject* (London & New York: Verso, 1994), 1-15.

Baring, Anne and Jules Cashford, *The Myth of the Goddess: Evolution of an Image* (London & New York: Penguin, 1993).

Barnes, Julian, *The History of the World in 10½ Chapters* (New York: Picador, 2005).

Bataille, Georges, *Literature and Evil*, trans. Alastair Hamilton (New York & London: Marion Boyars, 1985).

_____ , *Visions of Excess: Selected Writings, 1927-1939*, ed. & trans. Allan Stoekl with Carl R. Lovitt & Donald M. Leslie Jr. (Minneapolis: University of Minnesota Press, 1985).

_____ , *On Nietzsche*, trans. Bruce Boone (London & New York: Continuum, 2004).

_____ , *The Accursed Share Volume I: Consumption*, trans. Robert Hurley (New York: Zone Books, 1988).

Bateson, Gregory, *Steps to an Ecology of Mind* (Chicago & London: The University of Chicago Press, 2000).

Baudrillard, Jean, *For a Critique of the Political Economy of the Sign*, trans. Charles Levin (New York: Telos Press, 1981).

_____ , 'The Animals: Territory and Metamorphosis' in *Simulacra and Simulation*, trans. Sheila Faria Glaser (Ann Arbor: University of Michigan Press, 1994), 129-43.

Bekoff, Marc and Dale Jamieson (eds), *Interpretation and Explanation in the Study of Animal Behaviour, Volume I: Interpretation, Intentionality, and Communication* (Boulder, SF & Oxford: Westview Press, 1990).

_____ , *Interpretation and Explanation in the Study of Animal Behaviour, Volume II: Explanation, Evolution, and Adaptation* (Boulder, SF & Oxford: Westview Press, 1990).

Benjamin, Andrew, 'What if the Other were an Animal? Hegel on Jews, Animals and Disease' in *Critical Horizons: A Journal of Philosophy and Social Theory* 8:1 (2007), 61-77.

_____ , 'Particularity and Exceptions: On Jews and Animals' in *South Atlantic Quarterly* 107:1 (2008), 71-87.

_____ , 'Another Naming, a Living Animal: Blanchot's Community' in *SubStance* #117, 37:3 (2008), 207-227.

_____ , 'On Tolerance: Working Through Kant' in *Contretemps* 2 (May 2001), 25-38.

_____ , 'Raving Sibyls, Signifying Gods: Noise and Sense in Heraclitus Fragments 92 and 93' in *Culture, Theory & Critique* 46:1 (2005), 75-90.

_____ , 'Having to Exist' in *Angelaki* 5:3 (2000), 51-6.

_____ , 'Indefinite Play and "The Name of Man"' in *Derrida Today* 1:1 (2008) 1-18.

_____ , *Of Jews and Animals* (Edinburgh: Edinburgh University Press, 2010).

Benjamin, Walter, *Illuminations*, trans. H. Zohn (London: Fontana Press, 1992).

Bennett, Jane, *Vibrant Matter: A Political Ecology of Things* (Durham & London: Duke University Press, 2010).

Bergson, Henri, *Creative Evolution*, trans. Arthur Mitchell (Mineola, NY: Dover Publications, 1998).

Best, Steven & Anthony J. Nocella II (eds), *Terrorists or Freedom Fighters? Reflections on the Liberation of Animals* (New York: Lantern Books, 2004).

Blanchot, Maurice, *The Space of Literature*, trans. Ann Smock (Lincoln: University of Nebraska Press, 1989).

_____ , *The Unavowable Community*, trans. Pierre Joris (New York: Station Hill Press, 1988).

_____ , *The Infinite Conversation*, trans. Susan Hanson (Minneapolis: University of Minnesota Press, 1993).

_____ , *The Writing of the Disaster,* trans. Ann Smock (Lincoln: University of Nebraska Press, 1995).

_____ , 'Literature and the Right to Death' in *The Work of Fire*, trans. Charlotte Mandell (Stanford: Stanford University Press, 1995).

Blum, Deborah, *The Monkey Wars* (New York & Oxford: Oxford University Press, 1994).

Bois, Yve-Alain and Rosalind E. Krauss, *Formless: A User's Guide* (New York: Zone Books, 1997).

Bostrom, Nick, 'A History of Transhumanist Thought' in *Journal of Evolution and Technology* 14:1 (2005), 1-25.

Braidotti, Rosi, *Metamorphoses: Towards a Materialist Theory of Becoming* (Cambridge and Malden, MA: Polity Press, 2002).

_____ , *Transpositions: On Nomadic Ethics* (Cambridge and Malden, MA: Polity Press, 2006).

Brooke-Rose, Christine, *A Rhetoric of the Unreal: Studies in Narrative and Structure, Especially of the Fantastic* (Cambridge: Cambridge University Press, 1983).

Buck-Morss, Susan, *Hegel, Haiti, and Universal History* (Pittsburgh, PA: University of Pittsburgh Press, 2009).

Burroughs, William S., *Naked Lunch* (London: Flamingo, 1993).

_____ , *The Wild Boys: A Book of the Dead* (New York: Grove Press / Atlantic Monthly Press, 1994).

_____ , *The Cat Inside* (London: Penguin Classics, 2009).

_____ , *Ghost of Chance* (New York & London: Serpent's Tail, 1995).

_____ , *Last Words: The Final Journals of William S. Burroughs*, ed. James Grauerholz (New York: Grove Press, 2000).

Butler, Judith, *Gender Trouble: Feminism and the Subversion of Identity* (New York & London: Routledge, 1999).

_____ , *Bodies That Matter: On the Discursive Limits of 'Sex'* (New York & London: Routledge, 1993).

_____ , *Excitable Speech: A Politics of the Performative* (New York & London: Routledge, 1997).

_____ , *The Psychic Life of Power: Theories in Subjection* (Stanford: Stanford University Press, 1997).

_____ , *Precarious Life: The Powers of Mourning and Violence* (London & New York: Verso, 2006).

_____ , *Giving an Account of Oneself* (New York: Fordham University Press, 2005).

_____ , *Frames of War: When Is Life Grievable?* (London & New York: Verso, 2010).

Butler, Judith & Gayatri Chakravorty Spivak, *Who Sings the Nation-State? Language, Politics, Belonging* (Calcutta, London & NY: Seagull Books, 2007).

Caillois, Roger, *The Edge of Surrealism: A Roger Caillois Reader*, ed. & trans. Claudine Frank & Camille Nash (Durham & London: Duke University Press, 2003).

Calarco, Matthew, *Zoographies: The Question of the Animal from Heidegger to Derrida* (NY: Columbia University Press, 2008).

Choat, Simon, 'Deleuze, Marx and the Politicization of Philosophy' in *Deleuze Studies* 3 (2009), 8-27.

Cixous, Hélène, *Insister of Jacques Derrida*, trans. Peggy Kamuf (Stanford: Stanford University Press, 2007).

_____ , 'The Cat's Arrival' in *parallax*, 12:1 (2006), 21-42.

Coe, Susan, *Dead Meat* (New York & London: Four Walls Eight Windows, 1996).

Coetzee, J. M., *The Lives of Animals*, ed. Amy Gutman (Princeton, NJ: Princeton University Press, 2001).

Cooper, Melinda, *Life as Surplus: Biotechnology and Capitalism in the Neoliberal Era* (Seattle & London: University of Washington Press, 2008).

Copeland, Marion, *Cockroach (Animal)* (London: Reaktion Books, 2003).

Critchley, Simon, *Infinitely Demanding: Ethics of Commitment, Politics of Resistance* (London & New York: Verso, 2008).

Davis, Karen, 'Thinking Like a Chicken: Farm Animals and the Feminine Connection' in Carol J. Adams & Josephine Donovan (eds), *Animals and Women: Feminist Theoretical Explorations* (Durham & London: Duke University Press, 1995), 192-212.

de Fontenay, Elisabeth, *Le silence des bêtes: La philosophie à l'épreuve de l'animalité* (Paris: Fayard, 1998).

DeLanda, Manuel, *Philosophy and Simulation: The Emergence of Synthetic Reason* (London & New York: Continuum, 2011).

Deleuze, Gilles, *Proust and Signs*, trans. Richard Howard (New York: Braziller, 1972).

Deleuze, Gilles, *Nietzsche and Philosophy*, trans. Hugh Tomlinson (London & New York: Continuum, 2006).

_____ , *Kant's Critical Philosophy: The Doctrine of the Faculties*, trans. Hugh Tomlinson & Barbara Habberjam (London & New York: Continuum, 2008).

_____ , *Difference and Repetition*, trans. Paul Patton (London & New York: Continuum, 2004).

_____ , *Spinoza: Practical Philosophy*, trans. Robert Hurley (San Francisco: City Lights Books, 1988).

_____ , *Foucault*, trans. Seán Hand (London & New York: Continuum, 2006).

_____ , 'An Unrecognized Precursor to Heidegger: Alfred Jarry' in *Essays Critical and Clinical*, trans. Daniel W. Smith & Michael A. Greco (Minneapolis: University of Minnesota Press, 1997), 91-98.

_____ , 'To Have Done With Judgment' in *Essays Critical and Clinical*, trans. Daniel W. Smith & Michael A. Greco (Minneapolis: University of Minnesota Press, 1997), 126-135.

_____ , 'Postscript on the Societies of Control' in *October* 59 (1992), 3-7.

_____ , 'Literature and Life,' trans. Daniel W. Smith & Michael A. Greco in *Critical Enquiry* 23 (1997), 225-230.

Deleuze, Gilles and Félix Guattari, *Anti-Oedipus: Capitalism and Schizophrenia I*, trans. Robert Hurley, Mark Seem, Helen R. Lane (London & New York: Continuum, 2003).

_____ , *Kafka: Towards a Minor Literature*, trans. Dana Polan (Minneapolis: University of Minnesota Press, 1986).

_____ , *A Thousand Plateaus: Capitalism and Schizophrenia II*, trans. Brian Massumi (London & New York: Continuum, 2004).

_____ , *What is Philosophy?*, trans. Graham Birchill & Hugh Tomlinson (London: Verso, 1994).

de Man, Paul, *Allegories of Reading: Figural Language in Rousseau, Nietzsche, Rilke, and Proust* (New Haven & London: Yale University Press, 1979).

_____ , *Blindness and Insight: Essays in the Rhetoric of Contemporary Criticism* (Minneapolis: University of Minnesota Press, 1983).

_____ , *The Resistance of Theory* (Minneapolis: University of Minnesota Press, 1986).

_____ , *The Rhetoric of Romanticism* (New York: Columbia University Press, 1986).

_____ , *Aesthetic Ideology* (Minneapolis & London: University of Minnesota Press, 1996).

_____ , 'Autobiography as De-facement' in *MLN* 94 (1979), 919-930.

Derrida, Jacques, *Of Grammatology*, trans. Gayatri Chakravorty Spivak (Baltimore & London: The Johns Hopkins University Press, 1974, 1997).

_____ , 'Structure, Sign, and Play in the Discourse of the Human Sciences' in *Writing and Difference*, trans. Alan Bass (London & New York: Routledge, 2001), 351-370.

_____ , 'Tympan' in *Margins of Philosophy*, trans. Alan Bass (Chicago & London: The University of Chicago Press, 1984), ix-xxix.

_____ , 'Différance,' in *Margins of Philosophy*, trans. Alan Bass (Chicago: University of Chicago Press, 1984), 1-28.

_____ , 'The Ends of Man' in *Margins of Philosophy*, trans. Alan Bass (Chicago & London: The University of Chicago Press, 1984), 109-136.

_____ , 'White Mythology' in *Margins of Philosophy*, trans. Alan Bass (Chicago: University of Chicago Press, 1984), 207-271.

_____ , 'Signature Event Context' in *Margins of Philosophy*, trans. Alan Bass (Chicago: University of Chicago Press, 1984), 307-330.

_____ , 'Outwork' in *Dissemination*, trans. Barbara Johnson (London & New York: Continuum, 2004), 1-66.

_____ , 'Plato's Pharmacy' in *Dissemination*, trans. Barbara Johnson (London & New York: Continuum, 2004), 67-186.

_____ , 'Fors: The Anglish Words of Nicolas Abraham and Maria Torok,' trans. Barbara Johnson in Abraham, Nicolas & Maria Torok, *The Wolf Man's Magic Word: A Cryptonomy* (Minneapolis, University of Minnesota Press, 1986), xi-xlviii.

_____ , *Spurs: Nietzsche's Styles / Éperons: Les Styles de Nietzsche*, trans. Barbara Harlow (Chicago & London: The University of Chicago Press, 1979).

_____ , 'Geschlecht II: Heidegger's Hand' in Sallis, John (ed.), *Deconstruction and Philosophy: The Texts of Jacques Derrida* (Chicago & London: The University of Chicago Press, 1987), 161-196.

_____ , *The Postcard: From Socrates to Freud and Beyond*, trans. Alan Bass (Chicago & London: The University of Chicago Press, 1987).

_____ , 'No Apocalypse, Not Now (full speed ahead, seven missiles, seven missives),' trans. Catherine Porter & Philip Lewis in *diacritics* 14:2 Nuclear Criticism (1984), 20-31.

_____ , 'Otobiographies: The Teaching of Nietzsche and the Politics of the Proper Name,' trans. Avital Ronell in *The Ear of the Other: Otobiography, Transference, Translation; Texts and Discussions with Jacques Derrida*, ed. Christie V. McDonald (New York: Schocken Books, 1985), 1-38.

_____ , 'Living On – Border Lines' in Harold Bloom et al., *Deconstruction and Criticism* (New York: Continuum, 1979), 75-176.

_____ , *Of Spirit: Heidegger and the Question*, trans. Geoffrey Bennington & Rachel Bowlby (Chicago & London: The University of Chicago Press, 1989).

_____ , *Psyche: Inventions of the Other*, Volume 1, trans. Peggy Kamuf (Stanford: Stanford University Press, 2007).

_____ , 'Racism's Last Word,' trans. Peggy Kamuf in *Psyché: Inventions of the Other*, Volume 1 (Stanford: Stanford University Press, 2007), 377-386.

_____ , *Limited Inc.*, trans. Samuel Weber & Jeffrey Mehlman (Evanston, Ill.: Northwestern University Press, 1988).

_____ , 'Che cos'è la poesia?,' trans. Peggy Kamuf in *Points... Interviews 1974-1994* (Stanford: Stanford University Press, 1995), 288-299.

_____ , '"This Strange Institution Called Literature" An Interview with Jacques Derrida,' trans. Geoffrey Bennington & Rachel Bowlby in *Acts of Literature*, ed. Derek Attridge (New York & London: Routledge, 1992), 33-75.

_____ , '"Eating Well," or the Calculation of the Subject,' trans. Peter Connor & Avital Ronell in *Points... Interviews 1974-1994* (Stanford: Stanford University Press, 1995), 255-287.

_____ , *On The Name*, trans. David Wood & Ian McLeod (Stanford: Stanford University Press, 2005).

_____ , *Specters of Marx: The State of the Debt, the Work of Mourning and the New International*, trans. Peggy Kamuf (New York: Routledge, 2006).

_____ , 'Force of Law: The "Mystical Foundation of Authority"' in *Deconstruction and the Possibility of Justice*, eds. Drucilla Cornell, Michel Rosenfeld & David Gray Carlson (New York: Routledge, 1992), 3-67.

_____ , *The Politics of Friendship*, trans. George Collins (London & New York: Verso, 1997).

_____ , *The Gift of Death*, trans. David Wills (Chicago & London: The University of Chicago Press, 1995).

Derrida, Jacques, *Aporias: awaiting (one another at) the 'limits of truth,'* trans. Thomas Dutoit (Stanford: Stanford University Press, 1993).

_____ , 'Artifactualities' in Derrida, Jacques & Bernard Stiegler, *Echographies of Television*, trans. Jennifer Bajorek (Cambridge: Polity Press, 2002), 1-28.

_____ , *Monolingualism of the Other; or, the Prothesis of Origin*, trans. Patrick Mensah (Stanford: Stanford University Press, 1998).

_____ , 'Faith and Knowledge: The Two Sources of 'Religion' at the Limits of Reason Alone,' trans. Samuel Weber in *Acts of Religion*, ed. Gil Anidjar (New York & London: Routledge, 2002), 40-101.

_____ , 'Hostipitality' in *Acts of Religion*, ed. Gil Anidjar (New York & London: Routledge, 2002), 356-419.

_____ , 'A Silkworm of One's Own' in *Acts of Religion*, ed. Gil Anidjar (New York & London: Routledge, 2002), 309-355.

_____ , *Demeure: Fiction and Testimony* with Maurice Blanchot *The Instant of My Death*, trans. Elizabeth Rottenberg (Stanford: Stanford University Press, 2000).

_____ , *On Cosmopolitanism and Forgiveness* (London & New York: Routledge, 2001).

_____ , 'Typewriter Ribbon: Limited Ink (2)' in *Without Alibi*, ed. & trans. Peggy Kamuf (Stanford: Stanford University Press, 2002), 71-160.

_____ , 'The University Without Condition' in *Without Alibi*, ed. & trans. Peggy Kamuf (Stanford: Stanford University Press, 2002), 202-237.

_____ , 'Nietzsche and the Machine' in *Negotiations: Interventions and Interviews, 1971-2001*, ed. & trans. Elizabeth Rottenberg (Stanford: Stanford University Press, 2002).

_____ , *On Touching—Jean-Luc Nancy*, trans. Christine Irizarry (Stanford: Stanford University Press, 2005).

_____ , *Paper Machine*, trans. Rachel Bowlby (Stanford: Stanford University Press, 2005).

_____ , *Rogues: Two Essays on Reason*, trans. Pascale-Anne Brault & Michael Naas (Stanford: Stanford University Press, 2005).

_____ , *L'animal que donc je suis* (Paris: Galilée, 2006).

_____ , *The Animal That Therefore I Am*, trans. David Wills (New York: Fordham University Press, 2008).

_____ , 'The Transcendental "Stupidity" ("Bêtise") of Man and the Becoming-Animal According to Deleuze' (ed. Erin Ferris) in *Derrida, Deleuze, Psychoanalysis*, ed. Gabriele Schwab (New York: Columbia University Press, 2007), 35-60.

_____ , *The Beast and the Sovereign*, Volume One, trans. Geoffrey Bennington (Chicago & London: The University of Chicago Press, 2009).

Derrida, Jacques et al., *Ghostly Demarcations: A Symposium on Jacques Derrida's Spectres of Marx* (London & New York: Verso, 2008).

Derrida, Jacques and Anne Dufourmantelle, *Of Hospitality: Anne Dufourmantelle invites Jacques Derrida to respond*, trans. Rachel Bowlby (Stanford: Stanford University Press, 2000).

Derrida, Jacques and Elisabeth Roudinesco, 'Violence Against Animals' in *For What Tomorrow ... A Dialogue*, trans. Jeff Fort (Stanford: Stanford University Press, 2004), 62-76.

Descartes, René, *Meditations on First Philosophy With Selections from the Objections and Replies*, ed. & trans. John Cottingham (Cambridge: Cambridge University Press, 1996).

Despret, Vinciane, 'The Body We Care For: Figures of Anthropo-zoo-genesis' in *Body and Society* 10:2 (2004), 111-134.

_____ , *Quand le loup habitera avec l'agneau* (Paris: Les Empêcheurs de penser en rond, 2002).

_____ , *Hans, le cheval qui savait compter* (Paris: Les Empêcheurs de penser en rond, 2004).

_____ , *Penser comme un rat* (Versailles: Éditions Quæ, 2009).

Despret, Vinciane and Jocelyne Porcher, *Être bête* (Arles: Actes Sud, 2007).

Devall, Bill, and George Sessions, *Deep Ecology: Living As If Nature Mattered* (Layton, Utah: Gibbs Smith, 1985).

de Waal, Frans, *Chimpanzee Politics: Power and Sex Among Apes* (25th Anniversary Edition) (Baltimore, MA: The Johns Hopkins University Press, 2007)

Diamond, Cora, 'The Difficulty of Reality and the Difficulty of Philosophy' in Cavell, Stanley et al., *Philosophy and Animal Life* (New York: Columbia University Press, 2008), 43-90.

Dufourmantelle, Anne, 'Invitation' in Derrida, Jacques and Anne Dufourmantelle, *Of Hospitality: Anne Dufourmantelle invites Jacques Derrida to respond*, trans. Rachel Bowlby (Stanford: Stanford University Press, 2000).

Fanon, Frantz, *The Wretched of the Earth*, trans. Constance Farrington (London: Penguin Books, 2001).

Fisher, Mark, *Capitalist Realism: Is There No Alternative?* (Winchester, UK & Washingotn, USA: O Books, 2009).

Foucault, Michel, *Madness and Civilisation: A History of Insanity in the Age of Reason*, trans. Richard Howard (New York: Vintage Books, 1988).

_____ , *The Order of Things: An Archaeology of the Human Sciences*, trans. Anon (London & New York: Routledge, 2002).

_____ , *Discipline and Punish: The Birth of the Prison*, trans. Alan Sheridan (Harmondsworth: Penguin Books, 1991).

_____ , *Language, Counter-Memory, Practice: Selected Essays and Interviews*, trans. Donald F. Bouchard & Sherry Simon (Ithaca, NY: Cornell University Press, 1980).

_____ , *The Will to Knowledge: History of Sexuality Volume I*, trans. Robert Hurley (Harmondsworth: Penguin Books, 1998).

_____ , *Essential Works 1954-1984: Volume One: Ethics, Subjectivity and Truth*, trans. Robert Hurley (London & New York: Penguin Books, 2000).

_____ , *Essential Works of Foucault 1954-1984, Volume Two: Aesthetics*, trans. Robert Hurley & others (London & New York: Penguin, 2000).

_____ , *Abnormal: Lectures at the Collège de France, 1974-75*, trans. Graham Burchell (New York: Picador, 2003).

_____ , *'Society Must be Defended': Lectures at the Collège de France, 1975-76*, trans. David Macey (London & New York: Penguin Books, 2004).

_____ , *Security, Territory, Population: Lectures at the Collège de France, 1977-78*, trans. Graham Burchell (New York: Palgrave Macmillan, 2009).

_____ , *The Birth of Biopolitics: Lectures at the Collège de France, 1978-79*, trans. Graham Burchell (New York: Palgrave Macmillan, 2010).

_____ , *Fearless Speech*, ed. Joseph Pearson (Los Angeles: Semiotext(e), 2001).

Franklin, Sarah, *Dolly Mixtures: The Remaking of Genealogy* (Durham & London: Duke University Press, 2007).

_____ , 'Dolly's Body: Gender, Genetics and the New Genetic Capital' in *The Animals Reader: The Essential Classic and Contemporary Writings*, eds Linda Kalof & Amy Fitzgerald (Oxford & New York: Berg, 2007), 349-361.

_____ , 'The Cyborg Embryo: Our Path to Transbiology' in *Theory, Culture & Society*, 23:7-8 (2006), 167-187.

Freud, Sigmund, *The Freud Reader*, ed. Peter Gay (London: Vintage, 1995).

Fukayama, Francis, *Our Posthuman Future: Consequences of the Biotechnology Revolution* (London: Profile Books, 2002).

Fynsk, Christopher, *Heidegger: Thought and Historicity expanded*, ed. (Ithaca & London: Cornell University Press, 1993).

Fynsk, Christopher, *Language and Relation ... that there is language* (Stanford: Stanford University Press, 1996).

Gaard, Greta (ed.), *Ecofeminism: Women, Animals, Nature* (Philadelphia, PA: Temple University Press, 1993).

Gellatley, Juliet (with Tony Wardle), *The Silent Ark: A Chilling Exposé of Meat— the Global Killer* (London: Thorsons, 1996).

Gilman, Sander L., *Franz Kafka: Critical Lives* (London: Reaktion Books, 2005).

Gould, Stephen. J., *The Mismeasure of Man* (New York: Norton, 1981).

Grebowicz, Magret, 'When Species Meat: Confronting Bestiality Pornography' in *Humanimalia* 1:2 (2010), 1-17.

Guattari, Félix, *The Three Ecologies*, trans. Ian Pindar & Paul Sutton (London & New Brunswick, NJ: The Athlone Press, 2000).

Guyer, Sara, 'Albeit Eating: Towards an Ethics of Cannibalism' in *Angelaki* 2:1 (1997), 63-80.

_____ , 'The Girl with the Open Mouth: through the Looking Glass' in *Angelaki* 9:1 (2004), 159-163.

_____ , 'Buccality' in Gabriele Schwab (ed.), *Derrida, Deleuze, Psychoanalysis* (New York: Columbia University Press, 2007), 77-104.

Hansell, Gregory R. And William Grassie (eds), *H± Transhumanisn and its Critics* (Philidelphia, PA: Metanexus Institute, 2011).

Hamacher, Werner, '"Disgregation of the Will": Nietzsche on the Individual and Individuality' in *Premises: Essays on Philosophy and Literature from Kant to Celan*, trans. Peter Fenves (Stanford: Stanford University Press, 1999), 143-180.

_____ , '"Lectio": de Man's Imperative' in *Premises: Essays on Philosophy and Literature from Kant to Celan*, trans. Peter Fenves (Stanford: Stanford University Press, 1999), 181-221.

_____ , 'The Gesture in the Name: On Benjamin and Kafka' in *Premises: Essays on Philosophy and Literature from Kant to Celan*, trans. Peter Fenves (Stanford: Stanford University Press, 1999), 294-336.

Haraway, Donna J., 'A Manifesto for Cyborgs: Science, Technology, and Socialist Feminism in the 1980s' in *The Haraway Reader* (New York & London: Routledge, 2004), 7-45.

_____ , *Primate Visions: Gender, Race, and Nature in the World of Modern Science* (New York & London: Routledge, 1989).

_____ , *Modest_Witness@Second_Millennium.FemaleMan©_Meets_ OncoMouse™: Feminism and Technoscience* (London & New York: Routledge, 1997).

_____ , *The Companion Species Manifesto: Dogs, People, and Significant Otherness* (Chicago: Prickly Paradigm Press, 2003).

_____ , *When Species Meet* (Minneapolis: University of Minnesota Press, 2008).

Hardt, Michael and Antonio Negri, *Empire* (Cambridge, MA & London: Harvard University Press, 2001).

_____ , *Multitude: War and Democracy in the Age of Empire* (London & New York: Penguin, 2005).

Harman, Graham, *Guerilla Metaphysics: Phenomenology and the Carpentry of Things* (Chicago, Ill: Open Court Publishing Co., 2005).

_____ , *Circus Philosophicus* (Winchester, UK & Washington, USA: O Books, 2010).

Hayes, Elizabeth T. (ed.), *Images of Persephone: Feminist Readings in Western Literature* (Florida: University of Florida Press, 1994).

Hayles, N. Katherine, *How We Became Posthuman: Virtual Bodies in Cybernetics, Literature, and Informatics* (Chicago & London: The University of Chicago Press, 1999).

_____ , *Writing Machines* (Cambridge, MA & London: The MIT Press, 2002).

Hegel, Georg Wilhelm Friedrich, *Encyclopedia of the Philosophical Sciences in Outline and Critical Writings (1817)*, ed. Ernst Behler, trans. Steven A. Taubeneck (London: Continuum, 1990).

_____ , *Lectures on the Philosophy of History*, trans. John Sibree (Charleston: BiblioBazaar, 2010).

_____ , *Jenenser Realphilosophie I, Die Vorlesungen von 1803-1804*, ed. J. Hoffmeister, Leipzig, 1932).

_____ , *Phenomenology of Spirit*, trans. A. V. Miller (Oxford: Oxford University Press, 1979).

Heidegger, Martin, *Being and Time*, trans. John Macquarrie & Edward Robinson (Malden, MA & Oxford: Blackwell Publishing, 1962).

_____ , *Being and Time: A Translation of Sein und Zeit*, trans. Joan Stambaugh (Albany, New York: State University of New York, 1996).

_____ , *Kant and the Problem of Metaphysics*, 5th ed., trans. Richard Taft (Bloomington, IN: Indiana University Press, 1997).

_____ , *The Fundamental Concepts of Metaphysics: World, Finitude, Solitude*, trans. W. McNeil & N. Walker (Bloomington, IN: Indiana University Press, 1995).

_____ , *Die Grundbegriffe der Metaphysik. Gesamtausgabe* Ln, BD. 29/30 (Vittorio Klostermann, 1992).

_____ , *Introduction to Metaphysics*, trans. Gregory Fried & Richard Polt (New Haven & London: Yale University Press, 2000).

_____ , *Nietzsche Volumes One and Two*, trans. David Farrell Krell (New York: HarperCollins, 1991).

_____ , *Nietzsche Volumes Three and Four*, trans. Joan Stambaugh, David Farrell Krell, & Frank A. Capuzzi (New York: HarperCollins, 1991).

_____ , *What is Called Thinking?*, trans. J. Glenn Gray (New York: Perennial, 2004).

_____ , *On Time and Being*, trans. Joan Stambaugh (New York: Harper & Row, 1972).

_____ , *On the Way to Language*, trans. Peter D. Hertz (New York: Harper-Collins, 1982).

_____ , *The Question Concerning Technology and Other Essays*, trans. William Lovitt (New York: Perennial, 1977).

_____ , 'Letter on Humanism' in *Basic Writings*, ed. David Farrell Krell, revised edition (London: Routledge, 1993), 217-265.

_____ , 'The Origin of the Work of Art' from *Basic Writings*, ed. David Farrell Krell, revised edition (London: Routledge, 1993), 140-211.

_____ , 'Only a god can save us,' *Der Spiegel* Interview (23/09/66) pub. *Der Spiegel* 31/5/76. From Gunther Neske & Emil Kettering (eds), *Martin Heidegger and National Socialism* (New York: Paragon House, 1996), 41-66.

Heller-Roazen, Daniel, *The Inner Touch: Archaeology of a Sensation* (Cambridge, MA & London: The MIT Press, 2007).

Herrnstein Smith, Barbara, 'Animal Relatives, Difficult Relations' in *differences: A Journal of Feminist Cultural Studies* 15:1 (2004), 2-23.

Hodge, Joanna, *Derrida on Time* (London & New York: Routledge, 2007).

hooks, bell, 'Is Paris Burning?' Z, Sisters of the Yam (June 1991).

Hubert, Henri and Marcel Mauss, *Sacrifice: Its Nature and Functions*, trans. W.D. Halls (Chicago & London: The University of Chicago Press, 1964).

Hurley, Robert, 'Introduction' in Gilles Deleuze, *Spinoza: Practical Philosophy*, trans. Robert Hurley (San Francisco: City Lights Books, 1988).

Hutnyk, John, *Bad Marxism: Capitalism and Cultural Studies* (London & Ann Arbor, MI: Pluto Press, 2004).

_____ , 'Proletarianization or Cretinization' in New Formations 77 (2012), 127-149.

Ihde, Don, *Postphenomenology and Technoscience: The Peking University Lectures* (Albany, NY: State University of New York Press, 2009).

Imhoff, Daniel (ed.), *CAFO (Concentrated Animal Feeding Operations): The Tragedy of Industrial Animal Factories* (San Rafael, CA: Earth Aware, 2010).

Invisible Committee, The, *The Coming Insurrection*, trans. Anon (Los Angeles, CA: Semiotext(e), 2009).

Irigaray, Luce, *Speculum of the Other Woman*, trans. Gillian C. Gill (Ithaca, NY: Cornell University Press, 1985).

Iveson, Richard, 'Animals Living Death: Closing the Book of Derrida' in *Parallax* 18:2 (2012), 102-106.

—————— , 'Rewiring the Brain or, Why our Children are not Human' in *Parallax* 18:4 (2012), 121-125.

—————— , 'Swarms of Technology, Melodies of Life' in *Body and Society* 19:1 (2013), 108-122.

Jackson, Rosemary, *Fantasy: The Literature of Subversion* (London & NY: Methuen, 1981).

Jakobson, Roman, *Language in Literature*, ed. Krystyna Pomorska & Stephen Rudy (Cambridge, MA & London: The Belknap Press of Harvard University Press, 1987).

Jameson, Fredric, *Archaeologies of the Future: The Desire Called Utopia and Other Science Fictions* (London & New York: Verso, 2005).

Kafka, Franz, 'Investigations of a Dog' in *The Complete Short Stories*, trans. Willa & Edwin Muir (London: Vintage, 2005), 278-316.

—————— , '*Forschungen eines Hundes*' Projekt Gutenberg-DE, Spiegel Online. Accessed 18 Dec. 2009.

—————— , 'In the Penal Colony,' in *The Complete Short Stories*, trans. Willa & Edwin Muir (London: Vintage, 2005), 140-167.

—————— , *The Complete Novels*, trans. Willa & Edwin Muir (London: Minerva, 1992).

Kalof, Linda and Amy Fitzgerald (eds), *The Animals Reader: The Essential Classic and Contemporary Writings* (Oxford & New York: Berg, 2007).

Kant, Immanuel, *Critique of Pure Reason*, trans. Werner S. Pluhar (Indianapolis & Cambridge: Hackett, 1996).

—————— , *Political Writings*, 2nd ed., trans. H. B. Nisbet (Cambridge: Cambridge University Press, 1991).

Karatani, Kojin, *Transcritique: On Kant and Marx*, trans. Sabu Kohso (Cambridge, MA: The MIT Press, 2005).

Kaufmann, Walter, *Nietzsche: Philosopher, Psychologist, Antichrist*, Fourth Ed. (Princeton, NJ: Princeton University Press, 1974).

Keenan, Thomas, *Fables of Responsibility: Aberrations and Predicaments in Ethics and Politics* (Stanford: Stanford University Press, 1997).

—————— , 'Mobilizing Shame' in *The South Atlantic Quarterly* 103: 2/3 (2004), 435-449.

—————— , 'Drift: Politics and the Simulation of Real Life,' *Grey Room* 21 (2005), 94-111.

_____ , '"Where are Human Rights ...": Reading a Communiqué from Iraq' in *PMLA* 121: 5 (2006), 1597-1607.

Kerenyi, Carl, *Eleusis: Archetypal Image of Mother and Daughter*, trans. Ralph Manheim (New Jersey: Princeton University Press, 1991).

Kheel, Marti, 'License to Kill: An Ecofeminist Critique of Hunters' Discourse' in Carol J. Adams & Josephine Donovan (eds), *Animals and Women: Feminist Theoretical Explorations* (Durham & London: Duke University Press, 1995), 85-125.

Kofman, Sarah, *Nietzsche and Metaphor*, trans. Duncan Large (London: The Athlone Press, 1993).

Kurzweil, Ray, *The Singularity is Near: When Humans Transcend Biology* (London: Duckworth, 2005).

Lacan, Jacques, *Écrits: A Selection*, trans. Alan Sheridan (London: Routledge, 1995).

Laclau, Ernesto and Chantal Mouffe, *Hegemony and Socialist Strategy: Towards a Radical Democratic Politics*, 2nd ed. (London & New York: Verso, 2001).

Lacoue-Labarthe, Philippe, *The Subject of Philosophy*, trans. Thomas Trezise, Hugh J. Silverman, Gary M. Cole, Timothy D. Bent, Karen McPherson, & Claudette Sartiliot (Minneapolis & London: University of Minnesota Press, 1993).

Latour, Bruno, *Politics of Nature: How to Bring the Sciences into Democracy*, trans. Catherine Porter (Cambridge, MA & London: Harvard University Press, 2004).

_____ , *Reassembling the Social: An Introduction to Actor-Network Theory* (Oxford: Oxford Univerity Press, 2007).

Lawlor, Leonard, *This Is Not Sufficient: An Essay on Animality and Human Nature in Derrida* (New York: Columbia University Press, 2007).

Lee, Kyoo, 'The Other of Dialogue: Opening Silences of the Dumb Foreigner' in *Social Identities* 12:1 (2006), 59-77.

Lemm, Vanessa, *Nietzsche's Animal Philosophy: Culture, Politics, and the Animality of the Human Being* (New York: Fordham University Press, 2009).

Lemming, David and Jake Page, *Goddess: Myth of the Female Divine* (New York: Oxford University Press USA, 1996).

Leopold, Aldo, *A Sand County Almanac: With Essays on Conservation from Round River* (Oxford: Oxford University Press, 1966).

Levinas, Emmanuel, *Otherwise than Being, Or, Beyond Essence*, trans. Alphonso Lingis (Pittsburgh, PA: Duquesne University Press,1999).

_____ , 'The Name of a Dog, or Natural Rights' in *Animal Philosophy: Essential Readings of Continental Thought*, eds Peter Atterton and Matthew Calarco (London & New York: Continuum, 2004), 47-50.

Lippit, Akira Mizuta, *Electric Animal: Toward a Rhetoric of Wildlife* (Minneapolis & London: University of Minnesota Press, 2000).

Lorraine, Tamsin, *Irigaray and Deleuze: Experiments in Visceral Philosophy* (Ithaca, NY & London: Cornell University Press, 1999).

Lovelock, James E., *Gaia: A New Look at Life on Earth* (Oxford: Oxford University Press, 2000).

Lukács, Georg, *The Meaning of Contemporary Realism*, trans. John & Necke Mander (London: Merlin Press, 1963).

Lyotard, Jean-Francois, *The Inhuman: Reflections on Time*, trans. Geoffrey Bennington & Rachel Bowlby (Cambridge: Polity Press, 1993).

Malabou, Catherine and Jacques Derrida, *Counterpath: Traveling with Jacques Derrida*, trans. David Wills (Stanford: Stanford University Press, 2004).

Marazzi, Christian, *Capital and Language: From the New Economy to the War Economy*, trans. Gregory Conti (Los Angeles, CA.: Semiotext(e), 2008).

Marchesini, Roberto, 'Alterity and the Non-human' in *Humanimalia* 1:2 (2010), 92-96.

Marx, Karl, *The Eighteenth Brumaire of Louis Bonaparte*, trans. Ben Fowkes in *Surveys from Exile: Political Writings*, Volume 2 ed. David Fernbach (Harmondsworth: Penguin Books, 1973), 143-249.

_____ , *Grundrisse: Foundations of the Critique of Political Economy*, trans. Martin Nicolaus (London: Penguin Books, 1993).

_____ , *Capital: A Critique of Political Economy*, Volume I, trans. Ben Fowkes (London: Penguin Books, 1990).

_____ , *Capital: A Critique of Political Economy*, Volume III, trans. David Fernbach (London: Penguin Books, 1991).

Marx, Karl and Friedrich Engels, *The Communist Manifesto*, trans. Samuel Moore (London: Penguin Books, 2002).

Mason, Jim, *An Unnatural Order: Why We Are Destroying the Planet and Each Other* (New York: Continuum, 1997).

Mauss, Marcel, *The Gift: The Form and Reason for Exchange in Archaic Societies*, trans. W.D. Halls (London & New York: Routledge, 2002).

Mengue, Philippe, 'The Absent People and the Void of Democracy' in *Contemporary Political Theory* 4:4 (2005), 386-397.

Miller, Donald F., *The Reason of Metaphor: A Study in Politics* (New Delhi: Sage Publications, 1992).

Miller, J. Hillis, 'Promises, Promises: Speech Act Theory, Literary Theory, and Politico-Economic Theory in Marx and de Man' in *New Literary History* 33 (2002), 1-20.

Montag, Warren, *Bodies, Masses, Power: Spinoza and His Contemporaries* (London & New York: Verso, 1999).

Montaigne, Michel de, *An Apology for Raymond Sebond*, trans. M. A. Screech (London: Penguin Books, 1987).

Mylonas, George E., *Eleusis and the Eleusinian Mysteries* (New Jersey: Princeton University Press, 1961).

Nagel, Thomas, 'What is it like to be a bat?' in *Mortal Questions* (Cambridge: Cambridge University Press, 1991), 165-180.

Nancy, Jean-Luc, *L'oubli de la philosophie* (Paris: Galilée, 1986).

_____ , '"Our Probity" On Truth in the Moral Sense in Nietzsche' in *Looking After Nietzsche*, ed. Laurence A. Rickels (Albany: State University of New York Press, 1990), 67-89.

_____ , *The Inoperative Community*, trans. Peter Connor, Lisa Garbus, Michael Holland, Simona Sawhney (Minneapolis & London: University of Minnesota Press, 1991).

_____ , *The Birth to Presence*, trans. Brian Holmes et al (Stanford: Stanford University Press, 1993).

_____ , *Being Singular Plural*, trans. Robert D. Richardson & Anne E. O'Byrne (Stanford: Stanford University Press, 2000).

_____ , *The Creation of the World or Globalization*, trans. François Raffoul & David Pettigrew (Albany, NY: State University of New York Press, 2007).

_____ , *Corpus*, trans. Richard A. Rand (New York: Fordham University Press, 2008).

Nancy, Jean-Luc and Philippe Lacoue-Labarthe, 'The Nazi Myth,' trans. Brian Holmes in *Critical Inquiry* 16 (1990), 291-312.

Nibert, David, *Animal Rights Human Rights: Entanglements of Oppression and Liberation* (Lanham, Maryland: Rowman and Littlefield, 2002).

Nietzsche, Friedrich, *Kritische Studienausgabe in 15 Bänden*, ed. Giorgio Colli & Mazzino Montinari (Berlin: De Gruyter, 1988).

_____ , 'The Philosopher: Reflections on the Struggle between Art and Knowledge' in *Philosophy and Truth: Selections from Nietzsche's Notebooks of the Early 1870s*, trans. & ed. Daniel Breazeale (New Jersey: Humanities Press International Inc., 1993), 3-58.

_____ , 'On Truth and Lies in a Nonmoral Sense' in *Philosophy and Truth: Selections from Nietzsche's Notebooks of the Early 1870s*, trans. & ed. Daniel Breazeale (New Jersey: Humanities Press International Inc., 1993), 79-97.

_____ , *The Birth of Tragedy in Basic Writings of Nietzsche*, trans. W. Kaufmann (New York: The Modern Library, 2000), 1-144.

_____ , 'On the Uses and Disadvantages of History for Life' in *Untimely Meditations*, trans. R. J. Hollingdale (Cambridge: Cambridge University Press, 1997), 57-123.

_____ , *Human, All Too Human: A Book for Free Spirits*, trans. Marion Faber with Stephen Lehmann (Lincoln: University of Nebraska Press, 1984).

_____ , *The Gay Science*, trans. Walter Kaufmann (New York: Vintage Books, 1974).

_____ , *Thus Spoke Zarathustra: A Book for Everyone and No One*, trans. R. J. Hollingdale (London: Penguin Books, 2003).

_____ , *Beyond Good and Evil in Basic Writings of Nietzsche*, trans. W. Kaufmann (New York: The Modern Library, 2000), 179-435.

_____ , *On the Genealogy of Morals in Basic Writings of Nietzsche*, trans. Walter Kaufmann (New York: The Modern Library, 2000), 449-599.

_____ , *Ecce Homo in Basic Writings of Nietzsche*, trans. W. Kaufmann (New York: The Modern Library, 2000), 655-800.

_____ , *The Will to Power*, trans. Walter Kaufmann & R. J. Hollingdale (New York: Vintage, 1968).

Norris, Margot, *Beasts of the Modern Imagination: Darwin, Nietzsche, Kafka, Ernst, and Lawrence* (Baltimore, MA: The Johns Hopkins University Press, 1985).

Noske, Barbara, *Beyond Boundaries: Humans and Animals* (Montreal, New York and London: Black Rose Books, 1997).

Oliver, Kelly, *Animal Lessons: How They Teach Us to Be Human* (New York: Columbia University Press, 2009).

Parikka, Jussi, *Insect Media: An Archaeology of Insects and Technology* (Minneapolis: University of Minnesota Press, 2010).

Parisi, Luciana, *Abstract Sex: Philosophy, Bio-technology and the Mutations of Desire* (London & New York: Continuum, 2004).

Patterson, Charles, *Eternal Treblinka: Our Treatment of Animals and the Holocaust* (New York: Lantern Books, 2002).

Paulhan, Jean, *The Flowers of Tarbes or, Terror in Literature*, trans. Michael Syrotinski (Urbana & Chicago: University of Illinois Press, 2006).

Peacock, Doug and Andrea Peacock, *In the Presence of Grizzlies: The Ancient Bond Between Men and Bears* (Guilford, Connecticut: The Lyons Press, 2009).

Plato, *Protagoras and Meno*, trans. W. K. C. Guthrie (Harmondsworth: Penguin Books, 1956).

_____ , *Phaedrus and Letters VII and VII*, trans. Walter Hamilton (Harmondsworth: Penguin Books, 1973).

_____ , *Phaedo in The Last Days of Socrates*, trans Hugh Tredennick (London: Penguin Books, 2003), 97-199.

_____ , *Cratylus*, trans. C. D. C. Reeve in *Complete Works*, ed. John M. Cooper (Indianapolis & Cambridge: Hackett, 1997), 101-156.

_____ , *Theaetetus*, trans. M. J. Levett & rev. Myles Burnyeat in *Complete Works*, ed. John M. Cooper (Indianapolis & Cambridge: Hackett, 1997), 157-234.

_____ , *Sophist*, trans. Nicholas P. White in *Complete Works*, ed. John M. Cooper (Indianapolis & Cambridge: Hackett, 1997), 235-293.

_____ , *Republic*, trans. G. M. A. Grube & rev. C. D. C. Reeve in *Complete Works*, ed. John M. Cooper (Indianapolis & Cambridge: Hackett, 1997), 971-1223.

_____ , *Timaeus*, trans. Donald J. Zeyl in *Complete Works*, ed. John M. Cooper (Indianapolis & Cambridge: Hackett, 1997), 1224-1291.

Porphyry, *Select Works*, trans. Thomas Taylor (London: Thomas Rodd, 1823).

Rabkin, Eric S., *The Fantastic in Literature* (Princeton, NJ: Princeton University Press, 1976).

Rajan, Kaushik Sunder, *Biocapital: The Constitution of Postgenomic Life* (Durham & London: Duke University Press, 2006).

Rancière, Jacques, *On the Shores of Politics*, trans. Liz Heron (London & New York: Verso, 2007).

_____ , 'Politics, Identification, and Subjectivization' in *October* 61 (1992) The Identity in Question, 58-64.

_____ , *Disagreement: Politics and Philosophy*, trans. Julie Rose (Minneapolis: University of Minnesota Press, 1999).

_____ , 'Dissenting Words: A Conversation with Jacques Rancière,' conducted & trans. David Panagia in *diacritics* 30:2 (2000), 113-26.

_____ , 'The Politics of Literature' in *SubStance* 33.1 (2004), 10-24.

_____ , *The Politics of Aesthetics: The Distribution of the Sensible*, trans. Gabriel Rockhill (London & New York: Continuum, 2004).

_____ , *The Flesh of Words: The Politics of Writing*, trans. Charlotte Mandell (Stanford: Stanford University Press, 2004)

_____ , *The Future of the Image*, trans. Gregory Elliott (London & New York: Verso, 2007).

_____ , *Dissensus: On Politics and Aesthetics*, ed. & trans. Steven Corcoran (London & New York: Continuum, 2010).

Regan, Tom, *The Case for Animal Rights*, rev. ed. (Berkeley, CA: University of California Press, 2004).

Rhys, Jean, *Wide Sargasso Sea* (London: Penguin Books, 1997).

Roberts, Mark S., *The Mark of the Beast: Animality and Human Oppression* (West Lafayette, IN: Purdue University Press, 2008).

Ronell, Avital, *The Telephone Book: Technology, Schizophrenia, Electric Speech* (Lincoln & London: University of Nebraska Press, 1989).

_____, *Stupidity* (Urbana & Chicago: University of Illinois Press, 2003).

_____, *The Test Drive* (Urbana & Chicago: University of Illinois Press, 2005).

Roof, Judith, *The Poetics of DNA* (Minneapolis & London: University of Minnesota Press, 2007).

Rousseau, Jean-Jacques, 'The Social Contract' and 'Discourses' trans. Cole, Brumfitt & Hall (London: Everyman's Library, 1973).

_____, *Animals in the Third Reich: Pets, Scapegoats, and the Holocaust* (New York & London: Continuum, 2000).

_____, 'The Posthumanism of Roberto Marchesini' in *Humanimalia* 1:2 (2010), 87-90.

Schlosser, Eric, *Fast Food Nation: What the All-American Meal is Doing to the World* (London & New York: Penguin Books, 2002).

Schmitt, Carl, *The Concept of the Political*, trans. George Schwab (Chicago & London: The University of Chicago Press, 1996).

Serres, Michel, *The Five Senses: A Philosophy of Mingled Bodies (I)*, trans. Margaret Sankey & Peter Cowley (London & New York: Continuum, 2008).

Shapiro, Gary, *Alcyone: Nietzsche on Gift, Noise and Women* (Albany, NY: State University of New York Press, 1991).

Shukin, Nicole, *Animal Capital: Rendering Life in Biopolitical Times* (Minneapolis & London: University of Minnesota Press, 2009).

Simondon, Gilbert, *On the Mode of Existence of Technical Objects*, trans. Ninian Mellamphy (Ontario, Canada: University of Western Ontario, 1980).

_____, *Deux leçons sur l'animal et l'homme* (Paris: Ellipses, 2004).

Sinclair, Upton, *The Jungle* (London & New York: Penguin Classics, 1986).

_____, *Animal Liberation*, 2nd ed. (London: Pimlico, 1995).

_____, 'Heavy Petting' in *Nerve* (2001) http://www.utilitarian.net/singer/by/2001----.htm. Accessed 16 May. 2010.

Sontag, Susan, *Illness as Metaphor and AIDS and its Metaphors* (London: Penguin Books, 2009).

Sorabji, Richard, *Animal Minds and Human Morals: The Origins of the Western Debate* (London: Duckworth, 2001).

Spiegel, Marjorie, *The Dreaded Comparison: Human and Animal Slavery* (Mirror Books/I D E a, 1989).

Spinoza, Benedict de, *Ethics*, ed. & trans. Edwin Curley (London: Penguin Books, 1996).

Spivak, Gayatri Chakravorty, *A Critique of Postcolonial Reason: Toward a History of the Vanishing Present* (Cambridge, MA & London: Harvard University Press, 1999).

_____ , 'Revolutions That As Yet Have No Model: Derrida's Limited Inc' in *diacritics* 10 (1980), 29-49.

_____ , 'Ghostwriting' in *diacritics* 25.2 (1995), 65-84.

Stewart, Susan, *Nonsense: Aspects of Intertextuality in Folklore and Literature* (Baltimore, MA & London: The Johns Hopkins University Press, 1979).

Stiegler, Bernard, *Technics and Time, 1: The Fault of Epimetheus*, trans. Richard Beardsworth & George Collins (Stanford: Stanford University Press, 1998).

_____ , *Technics and Time, 2: Disorientation*, trans. Stephen Barker (Stanford: Stanford University Press, 2009).

_____ , *Technics and Time, 3: Cinematic Time and the Question of Malaise*, trans. Stephen Barker (Stanford: Stanford University Press, 2011).

_____ , *Taking Care of Youth and the Generations*, trans. Stephen Barker (Stanford: Stanford University Press, 2010).

_____ , *For a New Critique of Political Economy*, trans. Daniel Ross (Cambridge: Polity Press, 2010).

Streeves, H. P. (ed.), *Animal Others: Ethics, Ontology, and Animal Life* (Albany, NY: State University of New York Press, 1999).

Suleiman, Susan Rubin, *Subversive Intent: Gender, Politics, and the Avant-Garde* (Cambridge, MA: Harvard University Press, 1990).

Taylor, Chloe, 'The Precarious Lives of Animals: Butler, Coetzee, and Animal Ethics' in *Philosophy Today* 52 (2008), 60-72.

Thacker, Eugene, *After Life* (Chicago & London: The University of Chicago Press, 2010).

_____ , *The Global Genome: Biotechnology, Politics, and Culture* (Cambridge, MA: The MIT Press, 2005).

Todorov, Tzvetan, *The Fantastic: A Structural Approach to a Literary Genre*, trans. Richard Howard (Ithaca, NY: Cornell University Press, 1975).

Torres, Bob, *Making a Killing: The Political Economy of Animal Rights* (Oakland, Edinburgh & West Virginia: AK Press, 2007).

Turner, Lynn, 'Seeks-Zoos—some recent correspondance between animals' in *The Issues in Contemporary Culture and Aesthetics University of Greenwich* (2009), 10-21.

Twine, Richard, *Animals as Biotechnology: Ethics, Sustainability and Critical Animal Studies* (London & Washington DC: Earthscan, 2010).

Various, *The First Philosophers: The Presocratics and the Sophists*, trans. Robin Waterfield (Oxford: Oxford University Press, 2000).

Vitamvor, Xavier, 'Unbecoming Animal Studies,' *The Minnesota Review* 73/74 (2010): 183-187.

von Uexküll, Jakob, *A Foray into the Worlds of Animals and Humans with A Theory of Meaning*, trans. Joseph D. O'Neil (Minneapolis & London: University of Minnesota Press, 2010).

Wallen, Martin, *Fox (Animal)* (London: Reaktion Books, 2006).

Warminski, Andrzej, *Readings and Interpretation: Holderlin, Hegel, Heidegger* (Minneapolis: University of Minnesota Press, 1987) .

Warminski, Andrzej, 'Towards a Fabulous Reading: Nietzsche's "On Truth and Lie in the Extra-Moral Sense"' in *Graduate Faculty Philosophy Journal* 15:2 (1991), 93-120.

Warminski, Andrzej, 'Reading for Example: "Sense-Certainty" in Hegel's Phenomenology of Spirit' in *diacritics* 11 (1981), 83-96.

Weber, Samuel, *Mass Mediauras: Form, Technics, Media* (Stanford: Stanford University Press, 1996).

Wills, David, *Dorsality: Thinking Back through Technology and Politics* (Minneapolis: University of Minnesota Press, 2008).

Wise, Steven M., *Rattling the Cage: Towards Legal Rights for Animals* (London: Profile Books, 2000).

Wittgenstein, Ludwig, *Philosophical Investigations*, 2nd ed., trans. G. E. M. Anscombe (Oxford: Blackwell Publishers, 1997).

Wolfe, Cary, 'Old Orders for New: Ecology, Animal Rights, and the Poverty of Humanism' in *diacritics* 28.2 (1998), 21-40.

_____ , *Animal Rites: American Culture, the Discourse of Species, and Posthumanist Theory* (Chicago & London: The University of Chicago Press, 2003).

_____ , (ed.) *Zoontologies: The Question of the Animal* (Minneapolis & London: University of Minnesota Press, 2003).

_____ , 'From Dead Meat to Glow in the Dark Bunnies: Seeing "the Animal Question" in Contemporary Art" in *parallax* 12:1 (2006), 95-109.

_____ , 'Bring the Noise: The Parasite and the Multiple Genealogies of Posthumanism' in *Michel Serres The Parasite* (Minneapolis: University of Minnesota Press, 2007), xi-xxviii.

_____ , 'Flesh and Finitude: Thinking Animals in (Post)Humanist Philosophy' in *SubStance* #117, 37:3 (2008), 8-36.

_____ , *What is Posthumanism?* (Minneapolis & London: University of Minnesota Press, 2010).

Wood, David, *Thinking After Heidegger* (Cambridge: Polity Press, 2002).

_____ , 'Thinking with Cats' in *Animal Philosophy: Essential Readings of Continental Thought*, eds Peter Atterton & Matthew Calarco (London & New York: Continuum, 2004), 129-144.

_____ , *The Step Back: Ethics and Politics After Deconstruction* (Albany, NY: State University of New York Press, 2005).

_____ , *Time After Time* (Bloomington & Indianapolis: Indiana University Press, 2007).

Zylinska, Joanna, *Bioethics in the Age of New Media* (Cambridge, MA & London: The MIT Press, 2009).

Journals

PMLA 'Animal Studies' 124:2 (2009), 472-575.

Filmography

Paris is Burning, prod. & dir. Jennie Livingstone (Off White Productions / Academy Entertainment, 1990). DVD.

The Animals' Film, dirs Myriam Alaux & Victor Schonfeld, (BFI, 2008). DVD.

Fast Food Nation, dir. Richard Linklater (Tartan Video, 2007). DVD.

Index

Index

Index

Shoah (Holocaust) 72n10, 219, 222,
229, 234, 237-243
Shukin, Nicole 263, 308
Simondon, Gilbert 4n2
Sinclair, Upton 263, 270
Singer, Isaac Bashevis 230
Singer, Peter 5-6
Slaughterhouse (see also Capitalism,
Agribusiness) 219-220n1, 242, 259,
263, 265, 269-274, 278, 281
Slavery analogy 243-245
Socrates, see Plato
Sofsky, Wolfgang 241
Sophistry and the 'trick argument' (see
also Plato) 33-34
Species 8, 13-15, 17, 19, 23, 82, 87,
100, 106, 114n11, 138, 162, 171n2,
179, 188, 220-221, 220n22, 230, 236,
244, 251, 270, 277, 286-288, 289,
291-292, 307
Speciesism, economy of 3, 7n5, 149,
151, 154, 175, 197, 199, 203, 225,
308
Species difference 149, 151, 155-156,
162, 203
Specter, Spectrality 54, 55, 69, 71, 90,
106, 111, 112, 130, 152, 156, 196,
221, 223-225, 229-231, 241, 308
Spider 209-210
Spivak, Gayatri Chakravorty 54n15,
133n5, 237n13
Stiegler, Bernard (see also Epiphylogenesis) 26, 28, 33n3, 91n31, 265-
266, 283, 285-302 passim, 303
psychotechnologies and psychotechnics 288, 292-293, 294-297, 301
Structuralism 16-17
Sunder Rajan, Kaushik 287, 303n10,
307
Swine flu (see also Zoonosis) 307, 308
Taylor, Chloe 148n2
Temporality, linear, and interruption
of 118
Tissue Engineering (TE) (see also
Biotechnology, Gene) 280, 282, 302-
303, 305-307

Transductive relation 26, 116-117,
125, 136, 282, 285, 287, 290, 292-
294, 300
Transhuman, Transhumanism 10-11,
12, 253n3, 265, 279n14, 285, 289,
298-311 passim
and neoliberalism 10-11, 28, 279-
280, 302-311 passim
Treblinka 230
Tropology of sense (see also Originary
technicity) 74, 76-82 passim, 83, 86,
90, 110, 131
Twine, Richard 270n4, 276, 302
Uexkull, Jakob von 57, 61, 74n13
Uncanny, Uncanniness 17, 51-52, 54,
56, 70, 79, 87, 91, 103, 106-107, 113,
115, 118, 120, 222, 249-250
Universal humanity, see Schmitt
Untimely 113, 120, 123, 129, 141, 210
Utilitarianism 6, 8
Venus (of the House of) Xtravaganza
144, 147-148, 149, 151, 152, 159-
165, 172, 201
Virtue 38, 42n7, 251
Vitalism 18, 76, 100, 234
Walking ghost (see also Nietzsche,
Marx, Parody) 27, 103, 129, 130-
134, 167, 196, 206, 241, 256
Warminski, Andrzej 75n15, 78n17
Weismann, August 299, 305
Wheeler, Wendy 83n22
Wild, Wildness 37, 144, 161, 205, 207-
208n4
wild-tame dichotomy144, 167-200
passim, 208-209
Wilmut, Ian 279, 280
Wolfe, Cary 94n34, 113n9, 208n5
Wood, David 238, 239, 241-242
Zombie 167, 193, 196, 199, 241, 256,
311
Zoogenocide (see also Animalization)
25, 26
Zoogenesis (see also Animal Encoun-
ter, Phrasing, Prosthesis, Emer-
gence) 5, 18, 22, 25-26, 27-28, 54,
79, 81, 91, 100, 103, 120, 126, 131,

345

Lightning Source UK Ltd.
Milton Keynes UK
UKOW04f2200160914

238651UK00010B/120/P